AIRBORNE OPERATIONS

AIRBORNE OPERATIONS

An Illustrated Encyclopedia of the Great Battles of Airborne Forces

a Salamander book

Published by Salamander Books Limited
LONDON

A Salamander Book

Published 1978 by
Salamander Books Ltd.,
27 Old Gloucester Street,
London, WC1N 3AF
Great Britain
ⒸSalamander Books Ltd. 1978

ISBN 0 86101 014 0

Credits

Editor: Philip de Ste. Croix

Designer: Chris Steer

Colour drawings of uniforms:
Jeff Burn Ⓒ Salamander Books Ltd.

Colour technical section:
Peter North Ⓒ Salamander Books Ltd.

Colour drawings of aircraft:
ⒸPilot Press Ltd. and Terry Hadler,
ⒸSalamander Books Ltd.

Three-views of aircraft:
ⒸPilot Press Ltd.

Colour photography of weapons:
Bruce Scott, courtesy Q.A.D. (W)
Pattern Room, Enfield
ⒸSalamander Books Ltd.

Maps: Ⓒ Richard Natkiel

Diagrams of Entebbe and Mogadishu:
Alan Hollingbery
ⒸSalamander Books Ltd.

Picture research: Jonathan Moore

Filmset by SX Composing Ltd., England

Colour reproduction by Culver Graphics Ltd.,
Silverscan Ltd., and
Tenreck Ltd., England

Printed by Henri Proost et Cie.,
Turnhout, Belgium

The publisher is grateful to W. H. Allen
and Co Ltd. for permission to reproduce
passages from Christopher Hogg's
The Unquiet Peace, and to Les Editions
de Minuit, William Heinemann Ltd. and
Georges Borchardt Inc. for permission
to reproduce passages from Pierre
Leulliette's *Saint-Michel et le Diagon*
in chapter 18.

Contents

Technical
Section

BALING OUT

As if to belie the old adage, the parachute was invented before it was necessary, indeed before man learnt to fly. Early balloonists used them to enhance the spectacle. The seeds of growth from these shaky beginnings into a new weapon in the military armoury, capable of dropping whole armies and equipment into battle from the air, were sown in the rapid expansion in flying during World War I. Then the the advantages gained by lifting an observer into the sky to increase his range of vision became so obvious that each side gave high priority to shooting down each others' balloons and aircraft. The first reliable parachute, introduced to save the lives of balloon observers (it being thought that pilots would avoid combat if they had means to save themselves), contained many of the qualities required of the true paratroopers' parachute used in Crete in 1941, Normandy in 1944, Korea in 1953 and subsequent airborne operations worldwide.

THE GUARDIAN ANGEL

E. R. Calthrop designed the Guardian Angel parachute specifically to save the lives of balloon observers, although after they were introduced in 1916, the average life of an observer was only fifteen days. When attacked, he would leap from his basket as his fear of remaining overcame his fear of jumping.

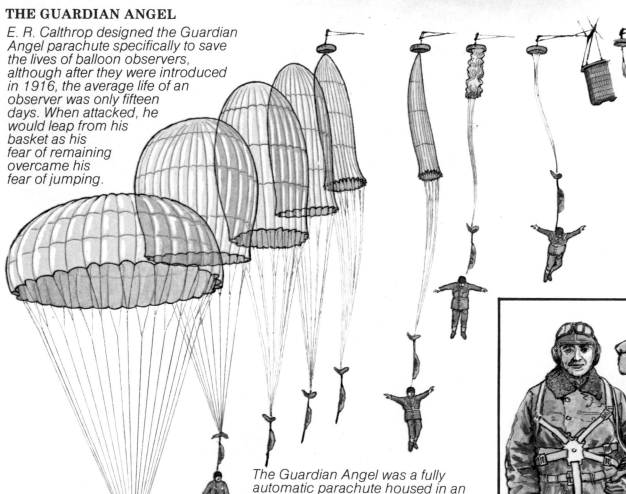

The Guardian Angel was a fully automatic parachute housed in an aluminium or canvas container fixed to the balloon. When the observer jumped, a single line attached to the back of his harness broke the pack open and pulled out first the rigging lines, then the canopy. When both had streamed, the apex tie parted and the canopy opened. Had the container been attached to the jumper's harness and the line to the balloon, it would have gone a long way to being a static line parachute.

Because the canopy opened last, after the 'chute had streamed, the shock was reduced, and only a simple harness was required. This 1918 version is far more sophisticated.

THE IRVIN PARACHUTE

Jumping from an aircraft with a Guardian Angel could be more dangerous than staying. The Irvin parachute overcame this by being self-contained, with the pack clipped to the harness, and opened by a 'rip-cord' when the jumper cleared his machine. a small 'pilot-'chute' pulled the canopy out of the pack, then dragged out the rigging lines. A seat belt to absorb 'opening shock' is still part of a modern harness.

Right: A jumper has just pulled the 'rip-cord' of his Irvin 'chute and the 'pilot-'chute' is pulling the canopy from the back-pack.

BLIND ALLEYS

Italy ignored Irvin and adapted the Guardian Angel into a manually opened back-pack 'chute, with a single lift web and a primitive harness—further adapting it to static line after paratrooping experiments in 1927. The Russians adopted the Irvin, complete with 'rip-cord', but developed a square canopy. Both systems had faults, but Italian parachutes and Russian mass drops deeply influenced German theory.

THE GERMAN RZ SERIES

Realizing that paratroops were a natural extension of the blitzkrieg concept, Germany studied other nation's efforts. The RZ series improved the Italian static line and adopted the Irvin type harness, but kept the Italian single lift web. This left a jumper hanging face forward and violently swinging his limbs. It was to cost many injuries during training and operations.

THE BRITISH 'X' TYPE

As work on the GQ 'X' type was not begun until spurred by 1940 German successes, its design could include lessons learned in the light of experience. A static line opened a 28-ft round canopy. The Irvin type harness incorporated a new quick-release box, and the canopy-first opening caused little shock. Also, by manipulating the four lift webs, a parachutist could control his flight.

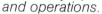

Above: An RZ 20 parachute swinging wildly, showing the single web attachment and the face-down attitude of the jumper.

9

THE PARACHUTE

On the right is a cutaway drawing of the current British PX1 Mk. 5 para-troop parachute. Save in refinement, the principles have changed little since the 1916 Guardian Angel. 'Canopy-first' opened by static line, the 28ft circular canopy is divided radially into 32 gores, and annularly by four seats of seams. Eight rigging lines run from one lift web 'D' ring through the canopy to the opposite lift web. The harness, with the main 'chute bag on its back, has quick release levers to free the lift webs if the canopy drags the jumper on landing, a seat strap, quick release leg and chest strap clips and fit adjustment buckles. A reserve 'chute clips on the front. By pulling one or more lift webs, the jumper can turn and control the drift of his parachute. The paratrooper below is turning in a drill called 'all round observation' in order to check that he has unobstructed space to descend.

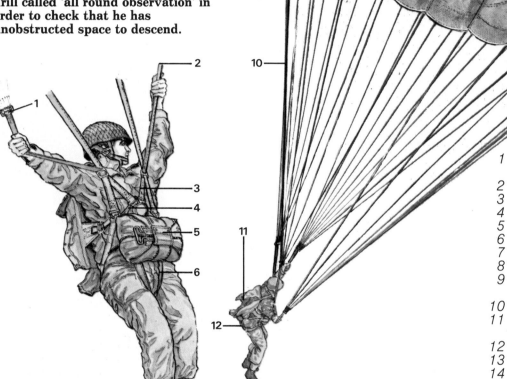

1 Rigging lines fixed to lift web 'D' ring
2 One of 4 lift webs
3 Shoulder straps
4 Chest straps
5 Reserve parachute
6 Leg straps
7 Apex hole
8 Ribbon to hold 'skirt' in shape
9 Gauze peripheral strip helps canopy develop and aids airflow
10 One of 16 rigging lines
11 Main 'chute pack outer bag open
12 Seat strap
13 One of 32 canopy gores
14 Seams dividing inner (porous) fabric from outer panels
15 Gore seam containing tunnel to hold rigging lines over canopy

This 1941 paratrooper dons his 'X' type 'chute by (A) pulling shoulder straps on; (B) clipping chest strap into release box; (C) pulling leg straps through legs, passing them round the seat strap and clipping them to release box and finally (D) adjusting and checking straps and giving release box a bang. If not locked, it will all come apart.

If laid out flat, a parachute canopy forms a circle. The fabric becomes more airtight from the centre outwards.

Experiments continue to improve types of parachutes and dropping techniques. Rudimentary control has been improved to the point that parachutes can be flown like gliders, and though this complicates training, the advantage in reducing dropping zone scatter is obvious. Once a cargo parachute is in the air, however, there is no way to control it. It must thus be quick to open for low drops, and should be extremely stable to avoid swinging goods into the ground. Many canopy shapes have been designed purely for dropping cargo, some under the influence of the space programme.

Above left are a number of sporting developments which point the way to future operations. The Para-Commando is a vented parachute which can be 'flown' to spot landings at an angle of about 45°. The Rogolo, above, an unframed hang glider, is hard to fly. The Para-Wing can glide at more than 4 in 1 and reach air speeds of 30mph.

The 'Baseball' (top), a hemispherical canopy 'chute, was developed in the US during WWII for mines and small bombs requiring a stable drop. The Goodyear 'sombrero' canopy (left) recovers US re-entry vehicles, and the cluster of four 64ft cargo canopies will disconnect from the 2,300kg load as it hits the ground to avoid it being dragged.

High Altitude, Low Opening (HALO), in which troops with oxygen would fall freely from 20,000ft and open their 'chutes at 3,000 to evade enemy radar, has been found unsuccessful as men lost touch during night drops.

'Stand-Off' is the newest technique. Paratroops dropped at 12,000ft can 'fly' 10 miles, each with a 60lb load and can land within yards of each other at a pre-selected target.

On exit, the stick opens its para-wings, tucks in behind the leader and follows him, silent, and invisible to man's eyes or radar.

PACK DRILL

No man will sufficiently overcome his natural fear of falling to jump 500ft into space unless he has complete confidence in his parachute. Perhaps the motto of No. 1 Parachute Training School 'Knowledge Dispels Fear', may not be entirely true, but if a man is sure that if his parachute is packed correctly it must open, he will gain that confidence. As a measure of the care taken, out of over 400,000 parachutes packed by the WAAF at RAF Ringway during the war, only one accident was traced to faulty packing. This is not to say that nothing can go wrong. A tumbling exit can tangle or twist the rigging lines, a canopy might not open symmetrically, all of which will increase the rate of sink. Rarely, the canopy does not open at all, the dreaded 'roman candle' or 'streamer', but usually all goes well, and the parachutist will find himself falling at about 20ft/s which, from 500ft, gives him 25 seconds to carry out his drills, lower his kitbag and land at a speed equivalent to jumping from a 12ft high wall. No injury will occur so long as the correct landing procedure is followed.

To pack a PX parachute, lay it on the packing table. Peg apex. Check and straighten. Sort canopy, gore over gore, into 32 wedge-shaped 'flakes'. Divide in half and lay flat. A: tie (1) canopy apex to top of inner bag. Fold 'flakes' down length into three. B: concertina fold into bag. Gather rigging lines into 'rope'. Tie (2) mouth of bag round rigging lines. C: pass rigging lines under anti-chafe flap to back of bag, then hook them through loops to front. Finish with lift webs at correct corners. D: Tie (3) down cover. E: turn bag and place in outer bag. F: arrange and tie static line (4) and lift webs (5) to length. G: bring up outer bag flaps and tie (6)

round static line. Lightly tie (7) static line to top of pack. Check pack correctly fixed to harness. Pack and harness now ready to wear as illustrated below.

Shown right is the opening sequence of a typical 'canopy-first' parachute. As the jumper falls, his weight pulls through the static line to the aircraft, breaking each tie in order of strength. The numbers refer to the ties in the packing sequence above.

A: jumper waits 'Go' with static line hooked on. B: 'Go'! Steps out. (7) Tie breaks and static line pulls out of pack. C: static line tightens, breaks tie (6) to open pack. Tie (5) breaks and inner bag pulls up to length of lift webs. D: cover ties (3) break and rigging lines pull out. E: rigging lines break inner bag mouth tie (2) when streamed. F: canopy pulls out of bag. G: canopy streams. H: apex (1) breaks. Canopy flies back. Static line with bag towed in slipstream to be pulled in later. J, K and L: canopy fills. M: canopy 'breathes'; flattens to spill air as it slows and deploys.

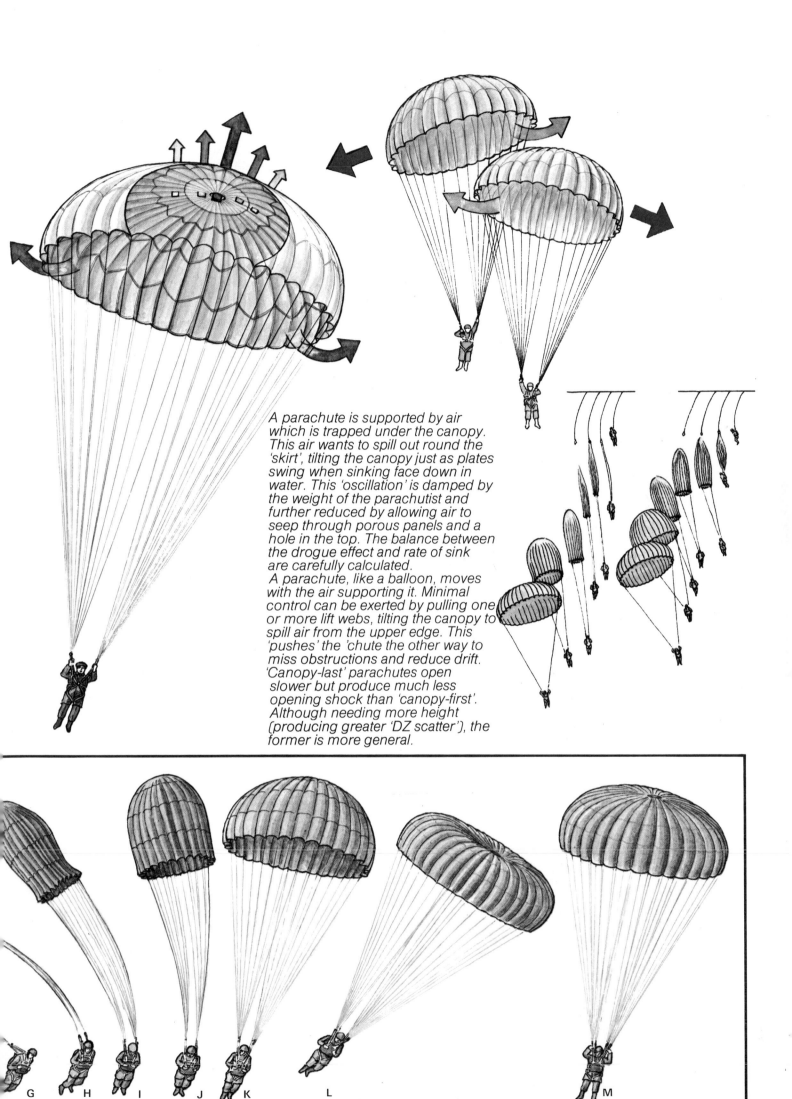

A parachute is supported by air which is trapped under the canopy. This air wants to spill out round the 'skirt', tilting the canopy just as plates swing when sinking face down in water. This 'oscillation' is damped by the weight of the parachutist and further reduced by allowing air to seep through porous panels and a hole in the top. The balance between the drogue effect and rate of sink are carefully calculated.

A parachute, like a balloon, moves with the air supporting it. Minimal control can be exerted by pulling one or more lift webs, tilting the canopy to spill air from the upper edge. This 'pushes' the 'chute the other way to miss obstructions and reduce drift. 'Canopy-last' parachutes open slower but produce much less opening shock than 'canopy-first'. Although needing more height (producing greater 'DZ scatter'), the former is more general.

G H I J K L M

TRAINING

The name 'Paras' engenders respect, sometimes fear, throughout the world. The elitist reputation is fostered to attract the fittest men with that extra dash and initiative: training designed to weed out the weak links. Parachute training is only part of the course, the aim being to produce tough, resourceful soldiers able to fight and hold against the fiercest odds, but also to drop into battle from the air, and that part of the training is as hard as the rest. It reproduces, with increasing degrees of reality, everything a man might meet when he first jumps operation-

ally. Each country's training is geared to suit the particular equipment used by that nation. Parachutes open and behave differently, each aircraft has special exit techniques. Parachute training familiarizes each trainee with every aspect of a descent: the exit, correcting twists, lowering a kitbag, landing and releasing the 'chute to be ready to fight as soon as he lands. Refusal to jump means dismissal. Discipline is so ingrained that when the 'green' lights up, it is almost impossible to stop a stick once the first man has left the aircraft.

Learning to land is a basic and early skill. Training starts off at ground level. German wartime training included forward rolls over crouching men, British recruits had to jump backwards from platforms. Post-war American paratroops (below) are going through the same routine.

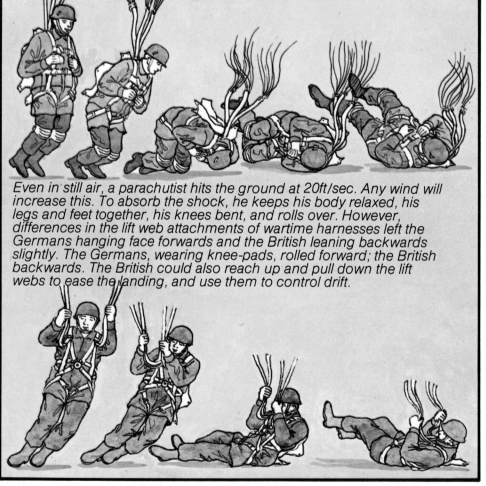

Even in still air, a parachutist hits the ground at 20ft/sec. Any wind will increase this. To absorb the shock, he keeps his body relaxed, his legs and feet together, his knees bent, and rolls over. However, differences in the lift web attachments of wartime harnesses left the Germans hanging face forwards and the British leaning backwards slightly. The Germans, wearing knee-pads, rolled forward; the British backwards. The British could also reach up and pull down the lift webs to ease the landing, and use them to control drift.

Represented below are the 'fans', a useful British invention designed to simulate an exit, the fall and the landing. The jumping platform can be as high as 25ft. A wire attached to the jumper's harness unwinds from a drum which is slowed by a pair of paddles turning in wire mesh cages.

Recruits practise jumping from a C-47 and landing in a wind by riding under pulley blocks on wires past the 34ft tower at Fort Benning, the US Parachute School.

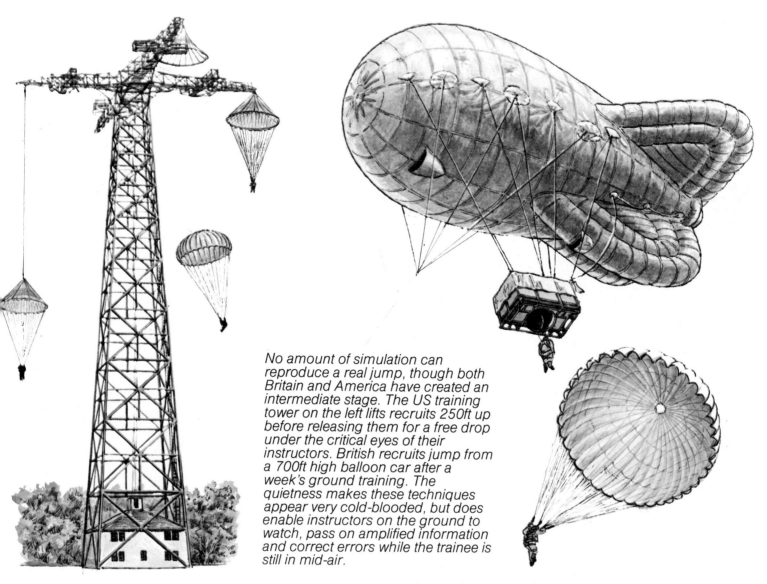

No amount of simulation can reproduce a real jump, though both Britain and America have created an intermediate stage. The US training tower on the left lifts recruits 250ft up before releasing them for a free drop under the critical eyes of their instructors. British recruits jump from a 700ft high balloon car after a week's ground training. The quietness makes these techniques appear very cold-blooded, but does enable instructors on the ground to watch, pass on amplified information and correct errors while the trainee is still in mid-air.

Below: two recruits make their first jump from a Fairchild C-119 aircraft, wearing a T.7 main 'chute and a reserve. Note the static line clipped on to the strong-point cable, and the slack held in loops on the pack.

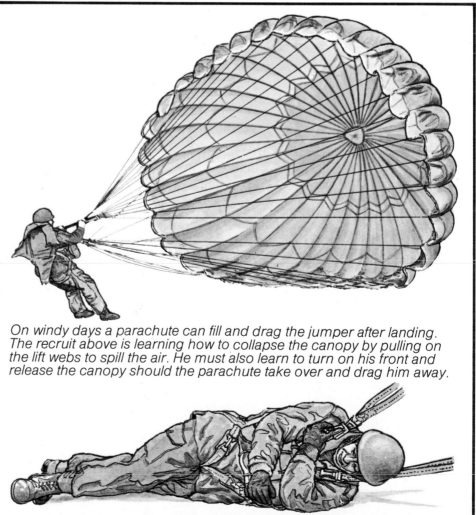

On windy days a parachute can fill and drag the jumper after landing. The recruit above is learning how to collapse the canopy by pulling on the lift webs to spill the air. He must also learn to turn on his front and release the canopy should the parachute take over and drag him away.

THE CARRIERS

Germany, long before it started training paratroops, built up a fleet of dropping aircraft by ensuring that civil airliners could be quickly converted into military transports. The Ju 52/3m was a three-engined, low wing monoplane which could carry 13 paratroops a distance of 700 miles. Britain was caught completely unprepared. She converted a motley group of bombers and patrol aircraft into paratroop carriers by cutting holes in the floor. The Whitley, an ageing bomber, was used on two early raids. Each aircraft could carry ten men a distance of 1,000 miles in cramped and cold discomfort, and the exit down a modified gun turret was difficult. Not until 1942 did the Allies receive a suitable carrier aircraft. The C-47 Skytrain (called Dakota by the RAF), based on the civil Douglas DC3, could fly 20 paratroops 1,500 miles at 180mph. Over 10,000 were built in the USA and 2,000 more in Russia to replace their ageing ANT-6 transports. Postwar developments led, via the Fairchild C-82 and later C-119 (the whole of whose rear fuselage removed), to the Lockheed C-130 which can carry up to 70 paratroops, and the Russian Antonov An-12 carrying 100. They are both pressurised, but can open large rear doors to drop heavy loads. In the C-130 (right) they sit in four rows, facing each other. They need only form two sticks, hook up and jump.

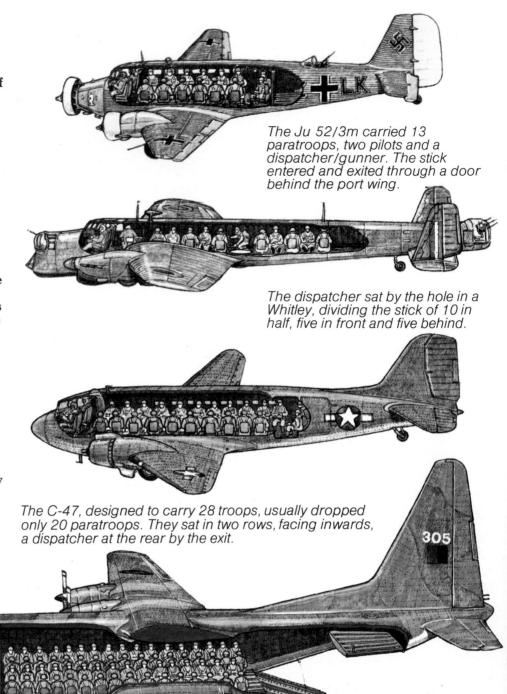

The Ju 52/3m carried 13 paratroops, two pilots and a dispatcher/gunner. The stick entered and exited through a door behind the port wing.

The dispatcher sat by the hole in a Whitley, dividing the stick of 10 in half, five in front and five behind.

The C-47, designed to carry 28 troops, usually dropped only 20 paratroops. They sat in two rows, facing inwards, a dispatcher at the rear by the exit.

The impossibly perfect paratroop drop would have everyone landing side by side, but this could never happen. The faster an aircraft flies, the wider spaced the stick. The higher the drop, or the stronger the wind, the wider the drift. The slower the men are to jump, the further apart they land. The latter is a matter of training, but the rest are matters of compromise between type of aircraft, conditions, opposition and determination.

The nature of the exit, and the tendency for Whitleys to drop paratroops from 700ft meant that even if all went well, the stick length would be more than 500yds.

The Ju 52 dropped 13 men to the Whitley's 10 in 260yds, by flying at 400ft. It also had a much better exit, enabling the whole stick to leave in 9 seconds.

The small door of a Ju-52 necessitated the admired and stylish exit leap of a German paratrooper, which started with a crouch and ended with the swallow dive.

100 paratroopers can exit from the rear door of an An-12 in under one minute but in still air this represents a distance on the ground of 1000yds.

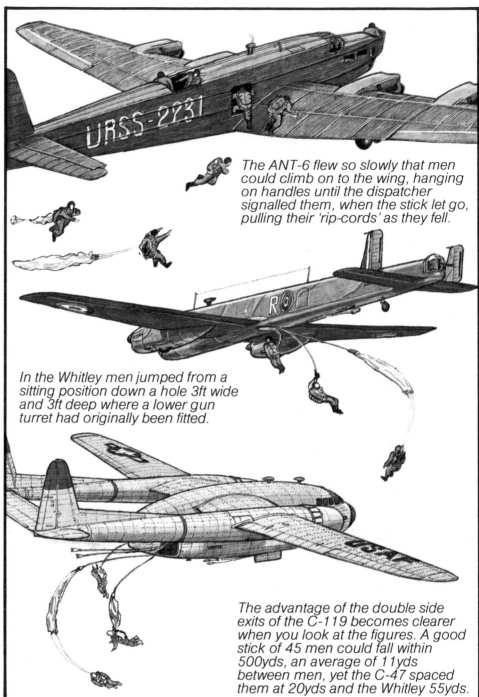

The ANT-6 flew so slowly that men could climb on to the wing, hanging on handles until the dispatcher signalled them, when the stick let go, pulling their 'rip-cords' as they fell.

In the Whitley men jumped from a sitting position down a hole 3ft wide and 3ft deep where a lower gun turret had originally been fitted.

The advantage of the double side exits of the C-119 becomes clearer when you look at the figures. A good stick of 45 men could fall within 500yds, an average of 11yds between men, yet the C-47 spaced them at 20yds and the Whitley 55yds.

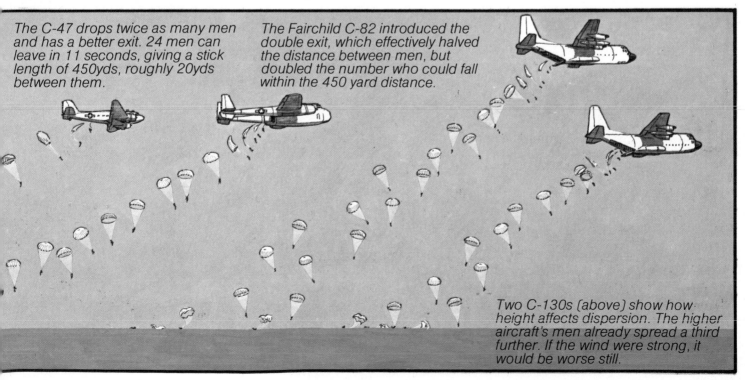

The C-47 drops twice as many men and has a better exit. 24 men can leave in 11 seconds, giving a stick length of 450yds, roughly 20yds between them.

The Fairchild C-82 introduced the double exit, which effectively halved the distance between men, but doubled the number who could fall within the 450 yard distance.

Two C-130s (above) show how height affects dispersion. The higher aircraft's men already spread a third further. If the wind were strong, it would be worse still.

BACK-UP

A parachute force relies on surprise and speed for its success. If faced by a prepared defence with armour and artillery, the parachutists are usually quickly scattered and mopped up. The difficulty is to get heavier equipment on to the DZ. A man can carry a bare 50lb of extra weight without injuring himself on landing, and other methods have had to be devised. Kitbags and weapon valises weighing up to 130lb can be dropped below a man on a 20ft rope, or large containers dropped from under the wings. Jeeps and guns had to be flown in by glider until after 1945 when they were parachuted from bombers. Nowadays transport aircraft with rear doors can drop loads of up to 30 tons on special platforms.

In order to increase mobility, German containers (or 'waffenhalter') were fitted with wheels and a handle. Above, two paratroopers slowly haul one from the Dropping Zone.

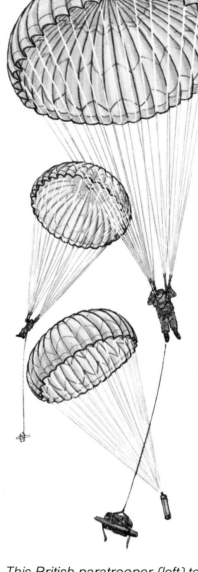

This British paratrooper (left) tops 285lbs with kit. He drops the kitbag and valise on a line after jumping (above), and when they hit the ground he will slow down for a safe landing.

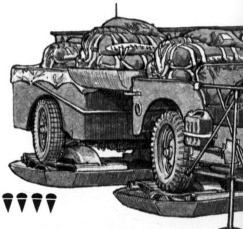

The Jeep and trailer (above) are fixed to a 'beam' which could be winched into the bomb-bay of a converted bomber. When they drop, the 'beam' stays in the aircraft. The guns below were dropped in pieces. The components had to be found and assembled for use, no easy task in the midst of battle. Parachutes could be colour coded to help the gunners collect all the parts.

The German LG 40 75mm recoilless Light Gun weighed 300lbs, fired a 13lb HE shell 7,500 yds and was dropped in 3 parts.

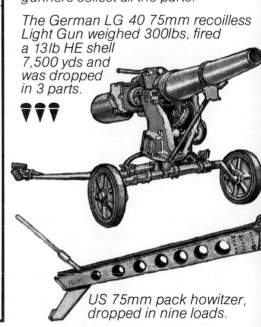

A bomber may have a load capacity well over the weight of the stick of paratroops it drops. Containers with extra supplies could be carried and dropped to use up the surplus.

The metal containers had a 'crash-pan' to avoid impact damage and used a static line-opened standard 'chute. Their major problem was that they were lost easily, specially at night.

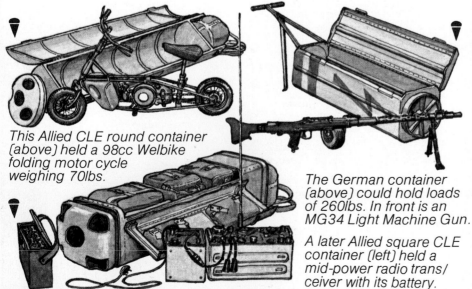

This Allied CLE round container (above) held a 98cc Welbike folding motor cycle weighing 70lbs.

The German container (above) could hold loads of 260lbs. In front is an MG34 Light Machine Gun.

A later Allied square CLE container (left) held a mid-power radio trans/ceiver with its battery.

US 75mm pack howitzer, dropped in nine loads.

(Note: the parachute symbols ▼ next to the drawings indicate how many canopies are required to drop a load.)

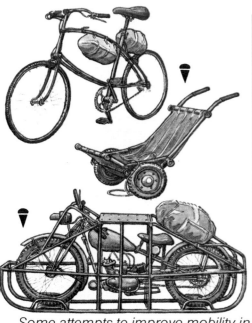

Some attempts to improve mobility in the field: the folding bicycle and barrow (top) could be pushed out of the door after the stick. The 125cc motor cycle was dropped from under the wing.

The British 3-inch mortar (left) threw a 10lb bomb 1,600 yards. Weight 124lbs dropped in container

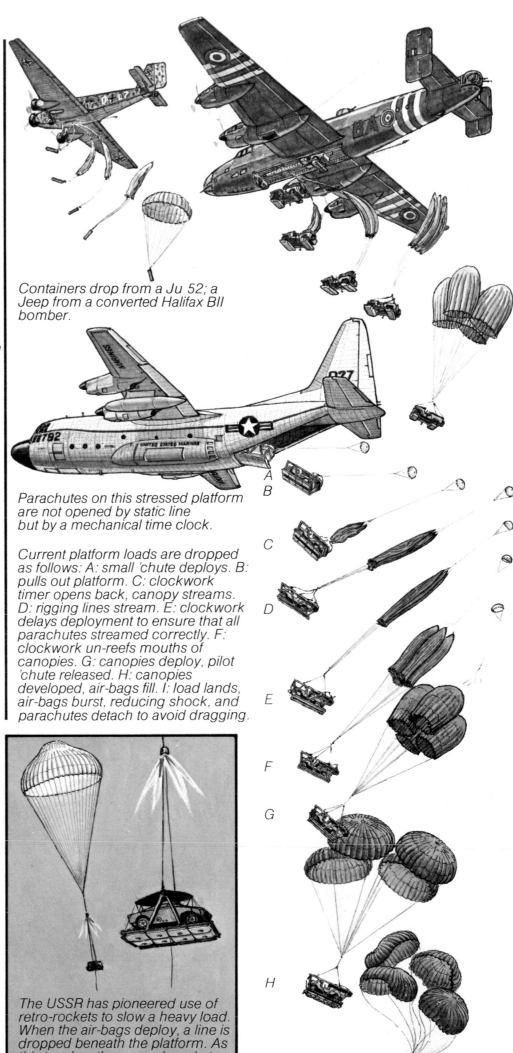

Containers drop from a Ju 52; a Jeep from a converted Halifax BII bomber.

Parachutes on this stressed platform are not opened by static line but by a mechanical time clock.

Current platform loads are dropped as follows: A: small 'chute deploys. B: pulls out platform. C: clockwork timer opens back, canopy streams. D: rigging lines stream. E: clockwork delays deployment to ensure that all parachutes streamed correctly. F: clockwork un-reefs mouths of canopies. G: canopies deploy, pilot 'chute released. H: canopies developed, air-bags fill. I: load lands, air-bags burst, reducing shock, and parachutes detach to avoid dragging.

A
B
C
D
E
F
G
H
I

The USSR has pioneered use of retro-rockets to slow a heavy load. When the air-bags deploy, a line is dropped beneath the platform. As this touches the ground, rockets fire for one second, enough to reduce speed and landing shock.

THE WEIGHTLIFTERS

A fighting force delivered by air must live from the air until relieved on the ground. Furthermore, no attack can succeed if the besieged can be supplied by air-drops. The German airborne army had to rely on air delivery to get its support weapons and ammunition on the battlefield. This forced them to drop their parachute force onto airfields in the opening stages of the assault in order to seize the landing strips for the transports. Modern airborne armies need to use the same tactics. The ideal military supply aircraft must be a series of opposites: fast yet capable of operating from small, rough fields; comfortable for troops, yet able to open up to allow air-drop loads or paratroops; capable of lifting heavy freight, carry it long distances, yet load and unload it quickly and easily in primitive conditions. As technology advanced, so did the design of transports. The C-119 was a big improvement on the Ju 52, C-47 and C-54, but not until the introduction of the C-130, An-12 and later types were all the criteria for a multi-role freighter fulfilled.

The Blackburn Beverley (right) was used by the RAF from 1958. Based on a 1944 design, it could carry a load of 45,000lbs 1,300 miles at a cruising speed of 173mph. It could air-drop 2 medium platforms, 70 paratroops and carry 98 troops, and could land in 350yds and take off in 810yds loaded.

The Ju 52/3m carried a 4,914lbs load, 18 troops or 13 paratroops in a 560 cu ft cabin. Range 610 miles at 155mph; 800 miles with extra fuel. Designed in 1932 as an airliner, it had to land to deliver freight, whose bulk was restricted by the small door.

Douglas DC3 (above), US name C-47 Skytrain, RAF name, 'Dakota'. Could fly a 7,500lbs load 1,500 miles at 185mph. Its size (95ft span, 64ft 5in length), was almost identical to the Ju-52 yet it was able to carry up to 2 Jeeps or 28 troops.

The Fairchild C-82 Packet and later improved C-119 (above) were twin-boom transports. The rear fuselage opened for loading and air-drops. It carried 20,000lbs of freight; 62 paratroops. Range 900 to 1,900 miles. Top speed 245mph. Hold capacious enought to fly ¾-ton truck or 105mm howitzer.

The Antonov An-12, introduced in 1960 as the Russian counterpart to the Lockheed C-130, carries more than 44,100lbs to the latter's 45,000lbs and flies 100mph faster at 482mph. Pressurized, its rear doors can open in flight to drop 100 paratroopers in a minute, or it can land on rough fields to deliver the ASU-85 SU-Gun, APCs, ZSU-23-4 AA Gun or SAM Carrier.

The Lockheed C-5A Galaxy can carry 220,967lb (98 tons) 3,749 miles, and has a top speed of 571mph. The interior is 19ft wide, 13ft 6in high and can hold 2 M60 battle tanks or 3 crated CH-47 Chinook helicopters in its fuselage.

A 28-wheel high flotation undercarriage allows it to operate at 343 tons from short, unpaved airstrips.

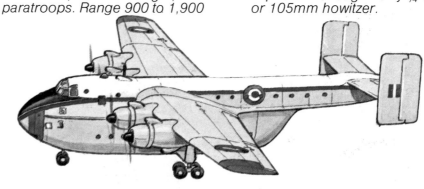

A converted Halifax II bomber (above) drops a Jeep and trailer from the 'beam' in the bomb-bay on a cluster of four parachutes. The vehicle has crash-pans and bracing to absorb the landing shock and minimize damage. In 1944 such improvisations were experimented with but the technique was a difficult one to perfect.

A heavy load (below) descends on a cluster of sixteen 64ft cargo 'chutes. Clusters are more stable than single large canopies, and have the safety factor of numbers should one fail.

The long-wheelbase Land-Rover (above) in its stressed platform prior to dropping in 1962. The parachutes are attached to the framework, and the platform absorbs landing shock.

The lashings can be quickly dismantled to free the load, and the platform retrieved (if not damaged) for re-use. In war it is left on the DZ.

Ultra Low Level Aerial Delivery, ULLAD, is a technique developed with rear door aircraft such as the C-130 below, when platforms or bales are pulled out of the aircraft by parachute as it flies low and slow over the dropping zone. Skilful piloting is needed to counteract the changes in trim.

The Me 323 (above) is an Me 321 glider with six engines fitted. It could carry 100 troops or a 40,146lbs load in and out of relatively rough fields, but its top speed of only 140mph made it dangerous vulnerable to Allied fighter attack and anti-aircraft fire.

Despite the technical difficulties, ULLAD ensures that the load does not drift off the dropping zone to be lost in awkward terrain, one of the hazards of aerial delivery. Another system is to rope together a number of bales or boxes so that they stay together in the air. However, these particular techniques are only used when the DZ is small. When space allows, the time-honoured method of pushing goods out of rear or side doors (left) on static line 'chutes is still the standard system.

A WING AND A PRAYER

Gliders seem, at first sight, a wasteful way to deliver men and equipment, but they had their advantages. They set a body of regular soldiers or heavy equipment down in one place, instead of scattering them at the whim of the wind. Although the first generation, the DFS 230, GA Hotspur and Antonov A-7 were too small, the second wave, the Airspeed Horsa, Gotha 242 and Waco CG-4 'Hadrian' could deliver Jeeps, trailers, anti-tank and AA guns, complete with ammunition and crews, into restricted spaces, while big gliders such as the GA Hamilcar and Me 321 Gigant could carry light tanks, medium artillery, bulldozers and crews. In World War II gliders were the only way of delivering such large loads.

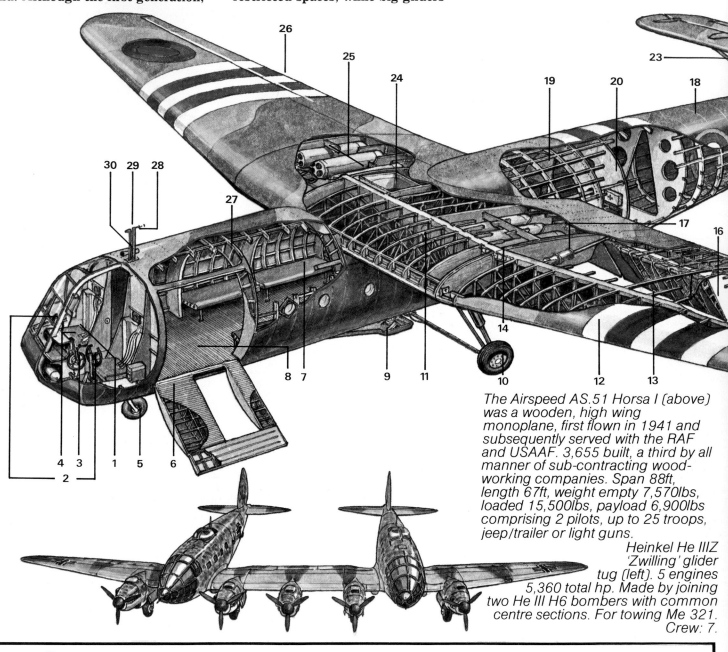

The Airspeed AS.51 Horsa I (above) was a wooden, high wing monoplane, first flown in 1941 and subsequently served with the RAF and USAAF. 3,655 built, a third by all manner of sub-contracting wood-working companies. Span 88ft, length 67ft, weight empty 7,570lbs, loaded 15,500lbs, payload 6,900lbs comprising 2 pilots, up to 25 troops, jeep/trailer or light guns.

Heinkel He IIIZ 'Zwilling' glider tug (left). 5 engines 5,360 total hp. Made by joining two He III H6 bombers with common centre sections. For towing Me 321. Crew: 7.

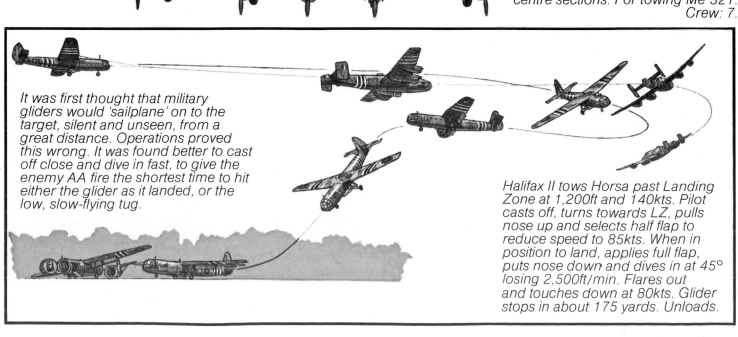

It was first thought that military gliders would 'sailplane' on to the target, silent and unseen, from a great distance. Operations proved this wrong. It was found better to cast off close and dive in fast, to give the enemy AA fire the shortest time to hit either the glider as it landed, or the low, slow-flying tug.

Halifax II tows Horsa past Landing Zone at 1,200ft and 140kts. Pilot casts off, turns towards LZ, pulls nose up and selects half flap to reduce speed to 85kts. When in position to land, applies full flap, puts nose down and dives in at 45° losing 2,500ft/min. Flares out and touches down at 80kts. Glider stops in about 175 yards. Unloads.

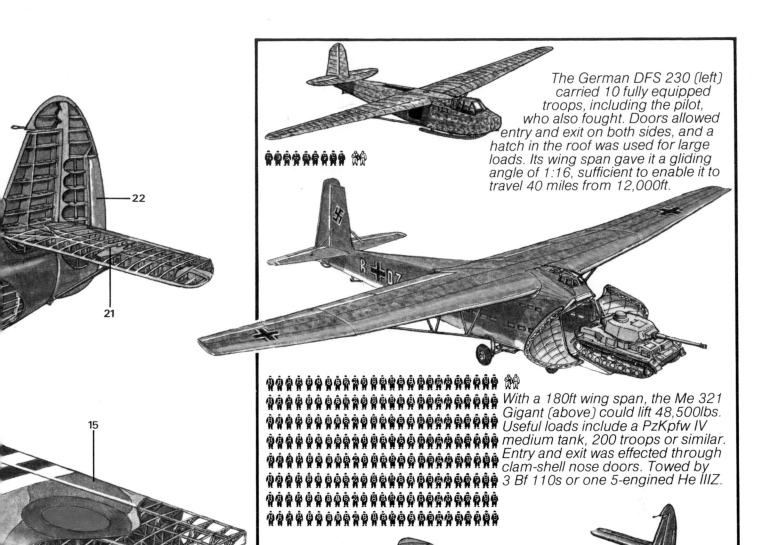

The German DFS 230 (left) carried 10 fully equipped troops, including the pilot, who also fought. Doors allowed entry and exit on both sides, and a hatch in the roof was used for large loads. Its wing span gave it a gliding angle of 1:16, sufficient to enable it to travel 40 miles from 12,000ft.

With a 180ft wing span, the Me 321 Gigant (above) could lift 48,500lbs. Useful loads include a PzKpfw IV medium tank, 200 troops or similar. Entry and exit were effected through clam-shell nose doors. Towed by 3 Bf 110s or one 5-engined He IIIZ.

KEY

1: seats for pilot (left) and co-pilot. 2: control column. 3: elevator trim wheel. 4: tow release lever. 5: fixed nosewheel. 6: loading hatch/ramp with door in it. 7: bench seats for 20 troops. 8: reinforced ply floor. 9: landing skid. 10: main undercarriage (may be jettisoned from cockpit). 11: wing centre section. 12: outer wing. 13: main spar. 14: outer wing main spar attachment. 15: fabric covered port aileron. 16: flap. 17: flap actuating reservoir. 18: plywood skin. 19: seat on rear bulkhead. 20: detachable fuselage joint. 21: elevator hinge brackets. 22: rudder trim tab. 23: tail struts. 24: roof hatch. 25: 3 CLE containers in starboard wing. 26: starboard aileron. 27: front fuselage joint. 28: aerial mast. 29: pitot head tube. 30: venturi (waisted tube).

In 1934, Hitler and some senior staff chanced to see the OBS research glider. A seed was sown, which resulted in the design and successful use of the DFS 230 assault glider in Belgium and the Netherlands in 1940. The implications set off a wave of development work in Britain, Japan and Russia, and later the USA. All were quick to shift from the small 10-seat troop glider to larger aircraft capable of lifting 20 to 30 men or an equivalent weight of ordnance. In the case of Britain and Germany, this was followed by gliders capable of carrying light tanks and heavy guns. Despite a worldwide shortage of towing aircraft (Britain and Germany relied on converted bombers), more than 21,000 gliders were built: 12,493 in USA, 5,104 in UK, 3,333 in Germany and a combined total of 300 in Russia and Japan.

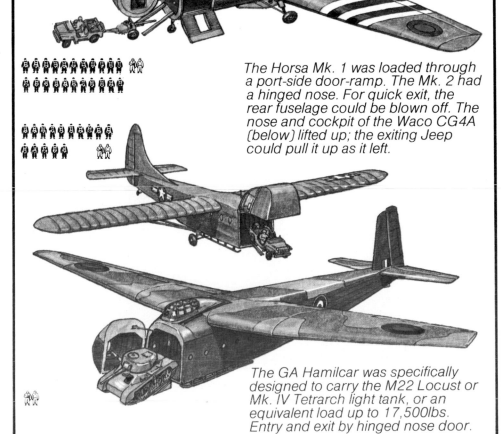

The Horsa Mk. 1 was loaded through a port-side door-ramp. The Mk. 2 had a hinged nose. For quick exit, the rear fuselage could be blown off. The nose and cockpit of the Waco CG4A (below) lifted up; the exiting Jeep could pull it up as it left.

The GA Hamilcar was specifically designed to carry the M22 Locust or Mk. IV Tetrarch light tank, or an equivalent load up to 17,500lbs. Entry and exit by hinged nose door.

Historical
Section

Introduction

By the end of World War I, the development of aircraft and parachutes at long last opened the possibilities of a 'third flank' in military operations: neither flank on the ground need be turned, for troops could now be flown directly into the enemy's rear areas. The idea was excellent, the means were being developed, but there would be many problems to solve, however.

In common with several other weapons and types of warfare brought to a practical pitch during this century, airborne warfare can claim a certain historical background, although this is more fanciful than those claimed by military aircraft, submarines and armoured fighting vehicles. Although the balloon invented by the Montgolfier brothers was only six years old at the time of the French revolution, the Napoleonic wars that followed the latter witnessed a crop of ideas for the movement of troops by balloon – usually across the English Channel for an invasion of England. Naturally enough, as the balloons envisaged for such operations would have been entirely at the mercy of the winds as they could not be steered in the slightest, the troops could not have been landed in any real concentration, and the notion was thus visionary rather than practical. Nevertheless, it is interesting to note how quickly after the invention of this totally novel form of transport men were thinking of its use in war, and so the germ of airborne warfare had been sown.

Throughout the nineteenth century, similar ideas cropped up, but the use of balloons for practical military purposes remained confined to the passive tethered type for observation purposes. Only after the invention of the aeroplane by the Wright brothers in 1903, and the development of the aeroplane into a practical means of delivering a worthwhile payload during World War I did the concept of airborne warfare stand any real chance of success.

New concept

What is airborne warfare, however? At first the idea was very strictly limited to the sort of tactical operations that could be carried out by small parties of men dropped by parachute into enemy territory. With the growth of the aircraft's payload capacity, the scope of airborne forces' operations was increased, although they remained essentially tactical, that is an adjunct to the effort of the main land forces. This enlargement of the concept continued as heavier aircraft and gliders were added to the airborne forces' inventory, but though some far-sighted German officers such as Kurt Student saw a strategic role for the new forces, right up to the middle of World War II the airborne arms remained relatively small in numbers, and as specially trained, high-grade troops were clearly destined for special missions tied into the basic plans of the main land forces. Although the Allied airborne forces grew into major combat formations by the end of the war, and although the widespread introduction of gliders had enabled large numbers of conventional infantry with little or no special training to be added to the airborne inventory as air-landed or air-portable troops, little chance was given to the airborne forces to become an independent or strategic instrument of war. Only since the end of World War II, there-

Below: German officers watch men of their embryonic airborne forces make a jump on 4 October 1936. So impressed was Hitler that he ordered a speeding up of the whole airborne programme.

Above: Russian paratroops exit from the dorsal hatch of a G-2 variant of the Tupolev ANT-6 bomber during exercises during the 1930s.

Left: German *Fallschirmjäger*, distinguishable by their special helmets and jumping smocks, parade in honour of Hitler's birthday on 20 April 1939.

fore, have airborne forces emerged from their tactical chrysalis to become a strategic butterfly, albeit a butterfly with considerable muscle. Although, strictly speaking, the term airborne should be reserved for those formations specially trained for deployment from the air, the concept has become blurred, for the nature of the world's alignments, geography and the availability of long-range, high-capacity aircraft have meant that nearly every formation, and most weapons, are air-transportable. This has had considerable strategic repercussions, but it is also worth noting that there has been a tactical revolution too, as the development of the helicopter into a practical and flexible means of transport has brought an extra dimension of battlefield mobility into the picture: conventional ground forces, complete with artillery and light armoured fighting vehicles, can now be shuttled about the battlefield to great effect. Thus although there remain specialist airborne formations in most nations, in many respects the majority of the world's more significant armies have an element of 'airborne' about them in that they are air-portable; and within this concept it is also worthy of note that there are specialist airmobile units, trained to operate in very close liaison with helicopter transports and gunships.

The first practical plan for the use of airborne warfare was developed in 1918 by Colonel William Mitchell of the US Army, with Lieutenant-Colonel Lewis Brereton doing the detailed planning. The two men's notion was for part of the US 1st Infantry Division to be dropped by parachute behind the German front to take the key city of Metz from the rear, in conjunction with a main land force advance. The only aircraft with the capacity and available in any numbers was the Handley Page O/400, a British machine also used by the Americans. The plan was an ambitious one, but it failed to secure the approval of the American commander in France, General John Pershing, and was postponed to 1919, by which time the war had ended. As with all such visionary plans, that of Mitchell appears with hindsight to have been practicable, but when one considers the lack of investigation into the whole practice of airborne delivery, Pershing's hesitation is understandable, and indeed commendable. Popular history tends to laud men such as Mitchell and condemn as too cautious men such as Pershing in these circumstances, forgetting that before any new weapon or method of warfare can properly be used on the battlefield, it must be tested extensively so that the using arm becomes acquainted with its peculiarities and idiosyncrasies, and so that any teething problems may be sorted out. Superficially attractive, Mitchell's plan would have been excellent had all gone entirely to schedule. Had anything at all gone wrong, though, total disaster would almost certainly have ensued.

Progress with airborne forces was slow between the two world wars, with the British at first taking a slight lead in the development and use of air-portable units in trooping aircraft for the suppression of local unrest in the Middle Eastern portions of their empire. In such operations small detachments could be flown into trouble spots to eliminate dissidents with the threat or use of superior firepower and discipline.

The first nation to develop true airborne units, however, was Italy, whose pilots already used the excellent *Salvator* static-line parachute. (A static-line parachute is one in which the canopy is drawn out of its pack by a line attached to the aircraft, and thus opens quickly and automatically as the user exits from the aircraft; the rip-cord parachute, in which the user has to operate the opening mechanism himself, was developed in the United States by Irvin, and eventually proved superior for aircrew. The static-line type, however, remains superior for airborne forces as it ensures quick and consistent opening as a stick of paratroops exit their aircraft.) The Italians made their first mass drop on 6 November 1927 from Caproni Ca 73 biplane bombers. Despite the death of General A. Guidoni in an accident when his parachute failed to open, the Italians pressed on with airborne developments, and by the late 1930s had raised two army airborne divisions, the *Folgore* and *Nembo*, and a naval airborne regiment, the *San Marco*. But although considerable effort had been put into the creation of these forces, they were never to be used in their intended role.

Soviet experiments

The next country to enter the airborne lists was the Union of Soviet Socialist Republics. Under the inspiration of Commissar of Defence Klimenti Voroshilov and Marshal Mikhail Tukhachevsky, the Red Army in 1930 first used a small group of paratroops in the 1930 manoeuvres held between Moscow and Voronezh. Details of airborne progress in the years following this are scarce, but in 1935 a battalion was dropped in the annual manoeuvres, and a year later a regiment was dropped. In both cases the aircraft used was the huge Tupolev ANT-6: the men had to climb out

Soviet Instructor, 1935

A Soviet officer briefs his men prior to a practice jump during the pre-war experiments in airborne warfare. The overalls, helmets and goggles were similar to those worn by air crew, and even the para- chutes were the same. Early Soviet techniques required the man to free-fall away from the aircraft and then open his own parachute with the rip cord. After 1936, however, they adopted the more normal static line method, but with it an unusual square canopy which, although it gave a smooth descent, did not allow the soldier to guide his parachute with any degree of accuracy.

of a hatch on top of the fuselage, clamber out to the wings by means of hand-holds, and then drop freely on receiving a hand signal from the dispatcher, located in another fuselage hatch. But despite the primitiveness of the dropping procedures, the fact that the Russians could drop whole regiments at a time put them clearly into the lead in airborne warfare. Experiments were also made with paradrops of heavy equipment. In 1936, however, Tukhachevsky was executed in the Stalinist purges that characterized that era in Russia, and it seems likely that the airborne forces lost much of their impetus. Certainly the Russian airborne forces were further developed and expanded, but their real value in war must have been doubtful as dropping techniques remained poor. But without a sponsor of Tukhachevsky's seniority to plead their case, the Russian airborne forces were left in a military limbo, and were very seldom used during World War II in the capacity for which they had been so expensively trained and equipped. It should be noted, though, that at the time the Russians also introduced parachuting as a para-military sport, and it seems possible that in June 1941, when Germany invaded Russia, the latter had more than one million trained parachutists. It seems extraordinary that the investment this represented was not used constructively during the war.

Cautious progress

Other nations dabbled their toes cautiously in the still muddy pool of airborne warfare. The United States, for example, undertook some air evacuation of casualties in the 1920s, and in 1931 an artillery battery was airlifted from one side of the Panama Canal Zone to the other under the instigation of Major-General Preston Brown. In 1932, moreover, Captain George Kenney of the US Army Air Corps achieved total surprise, not least on the part of the observers and umpires of the manoeuvres being held in Delaware, when he landed a group of infantry from the air. Small-scale experiments in paratroop drops were also made at USAAC airfields in Texas.

The only other nation to produce major airborne forces before World War II, however, was Germany. Although it is often claimed that Germany's interest in the field was sparked off by the 1936 Russian manoeuvres, this is not the case. Since 1922 Germany had enjoyed access to Russian developments in military science as a result of a secret protocol in the Treaty of Rapallo, and had thus kept a careful eye on Russian progress with airborne warfare. When Hitler announced in 1935 that Germany would abrogate unilaterally the military restrictions of the Treaty of Versailles, the Germans were handily placed to take up where the Russians had left off. And in the Junkers Ju 52/3m transport operated by the national airline, *Deutsche Lufthansa*, the new German air force had the makings of an adequate interim bomber type and more than adequate transport and paratroop aircraft.

Inevitably, the provision of a suitable dropping aircraft for paratroops has been a difficult one throughout the short history of such forces. The Germans were doubly

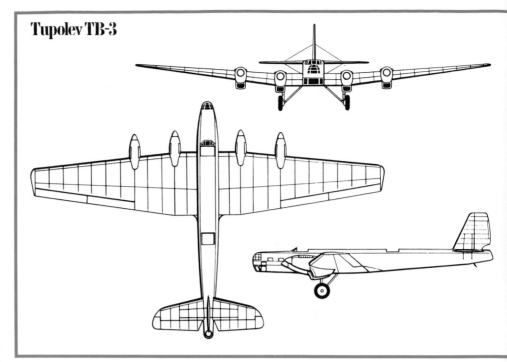

Tupolev TB-3

fortunate in having an adequate aircraft available right from the start. Only after the end of World War II did the British develop a suitable aircraft, and this had severe repercussions. Although it must be admitted that Britain's production capacity would have been hard pressed to mass produce a suitable design during the war, production of combat types inevitably having priority, this meant that the airborne arm never received enough of the types of aircraft necessary from American sources. This of course hampered training, and was to play an important part in operations, the British having again to rely heavily on American aircraft and aircrew. Even with the enormous production capacity of the United States, there were never enough transport aircraft to go round, and airborne operations were thus curtailed by logistic rather than military factors.

Classic transport

With the Ju 52/3m, the Douglas DC-3 was the other classic transport and glidertug for the airborne forces. Like its German counterpart, the DC-3 started as a commercial airliner, and was then pressed into military service in a number of roles. Although not an ideal paratroop aircraft, the exit door being too close to the tailplane and too narrow for the rapid exit of the stick being dropped, the aircraft was nevertheless an excellent one, and stands without real rival as the classic transport of World War II. Some 13,000 of the DC-3 and C-47 military version were built, but this was still insufficient for American, British and other allied needs. Russia, Japan and Italy all failed to develop adequate large transport aircraft during World War II. Since the end of that conflict there has been a revolution in the design of aircraft intended for airborne operations, with rear exits of large dimensions straight out of the fuselage becoming the norm. The United States, USSR, Britain, France and several other countries have all produced excellent designs of this type.

The army at first controlled develop-ment of airborne forces in prewar Germany, with an experimental establishment being set up in 1936. Under the command of Major F. W. Immanns, this had the task of finding the right type of parachute for airborne operations. Immanns' team eventually settled on a back-pack type opened by a static line. By 1937 Colonel Bassenge was in command of the battalion training centre, but as yet no real task had been formulated for the fledgling airborne force. At the same time the *Luftwaffe* wished to get in on the act, with the notion of being able to drop demolition teams on enemy airfields and the like, and two Nazi party organizations, the SA and SS, also wished to get some of the men into the parachute training school. The situation was thus very confused, and in an effort to secure some high command clarification of what he was meant to be doing, Bassenge arranged for the participation in the 1936 manoeuvres of elements of his training establishment. The *Luftwaffe* demolition teams were used properly, and met with mixed success, but the army paratroop battalion was dropped merely as a spectacle. So impressed was Hitler, however, that his interest was firmly attracted, and he earmarked airborne forces for special purposes. At the time, however, little was done to clarify the confused situation. SA men were allowed to join the *Luftwaffe* regiment under training, and an army regiment was allocated for training in the air-landing role.

Ambitious commander

The situation was now too complex for one man to handle, and Bassenge recommended that another officer be appointed to command the airborne forces operationally, while he kept control of the training establishment. The authorities concurred, and Major-General Kurt Student, a *Luftwaffe* officer, was appointed to command. Realizing that it was from the *Luftwaffe* that he could obtain most support, particularly as Hermann Göring wished to expand his empire, Student almost immediately after assuming his command on 4 June 1938 agitated for the

Type: heavy freight and paratroop transport. Engines: four 1,280hp AM-34RNF inlines. Speed: 179mph (288kph). Range: 1,550 miles (2,495km). Service ceiling: 25,365ft (7,750m). Span: 137ft 1½in (41.8m). Length: 82ft 8¼in (25.2m). Height: about 18ft (5.5m). Payload: up to 12,790lb (5,800kg) of freight or paratroops. Weight empty: 26,450lb (12,000kg). Weight loaded: 54,020lb (24,500kg). Armament: three or four 7.62mm ShKAS machine-guns. The basic design of the TB-3 started as

the 1926 ANT-6, which first flew in 1930. For its time it was an advanced design, with clean lines. Of Junkers construction (corrugated but unstressed skinning on a substantial metal frame), the aircraft was intended as a bomber, and was given periodic new leases of life by new engines of higher power and a more streamlined undercarriage. In the late 1930s, however, its obsolescence led to its adoption as a freight and paratroop aircraft. In the latter capacity, its

main failing was that the paratroops had to exit from a hatch in the upper fuselage just aft of the wing, where they were in danger from the tailplane.

airborne forces to come under *Luftwaffe* control. This was quickly implemented, and Student became commander of the 7th *Fliegerdivision.* Student's theories were tested in the Sudeten crisis of September 1938, when some 250 of his aircraft made an exercise landing in Czechoslovakia. But the army and SA then pulled out of the airborne arm, leaving Student with few men but much equipment. This suited Göring, who now decided on an airborne corps within the *Luftwaffe,* which at the end of 1938 was given official as well as practical control of the airborne arm. This now consisted of the 7th *Fliegerdivision,* which was turned into a full parachute formation, and the 22nd Infantry Division from the army, which was to be employed in the airlanding role. Intense and constructive training followed, but although the corps was put on call for the takeover of Czechoslovakia in March 1939 and the invasion of Poland in September 1939, it was not sent into action.

Yet by the beginning of World War II the Germans had the makings of a useful airborne arm, whose potential and abilities the rest of the military world seemed content to ignore. This oversight was ultimately to cost the Allies dear.

What, however, are the advantages of

airborne forces over conventional forces? And why or how should such forces be raised or used? The basic answer to these questions is that airborne forces give back to warfare much of the strategic and tactical mobility it lost in World War I. Throughout history, armies have sought to outmanoeuvre their opponents to secure the best position from which to attack them, causing them the maximum casualties at the cost of minimum casualties to the attacking side. The best way of doing this is to find the enemy's flank and attack there, concentrating one's own strength against the enemy's weaker points. In two-dimensional land warfare, though, there are only two flanks, both of which can be relatively easily guarded.

The airborne concept

The development of airborne forces was the response to a realization that the invention of the aircraft had made possible a third flank: using the third (vertical) dimension, aircraft could fly over the enemy's line and thus 'envelop vertically' the third flank, the enemy's rear areas, which were difficult to defend because of their very area. The airborne landing could be made anywhere in the rear areas,

Above: The shape of things to come as Russian paratroops begin to form up after a mass drop during the 1936 exercises near Kiev.

key positions being taken against negligible opposition until the arrival of relief forces, whose advance would have been facilitated by the disruption of supplies and men to the enemy's front line force by the block in their rear.

In this respect, therefore, airborne operations offered the possibility of restoring the type of mobility, in a tactical sense, that had been lost in the Russo-Japanese War and World War I. Although the airborne forces at the beginning of World War II were small, the capabilities of air transport and supply offered tempting strategic goals, in which the success of airborne forces acting on their own could alter the whole course of the war. The German assault on Crete is a clear example, and in many respects the Allied effort in Operation 'Market' in the Arnhem area can be considered in such a light.

These were still some time in the future, though, and it was with a number of adventurous small-scale tactical operations that the Germans started the ball rolling in World War II.

Denmark and Norway

The seizure of Denmark and Norway in April 1940, just before the opening of the great campaign in the West, was a bold gamble by Hitler, and provided the German airborne arm with its first taste of combat. Despite difficult conditions, the airborne forces performed well, but met with some of the problems that were to beset them very seriously in later years.

In the spring of 1940, Norway was a tempting prize for both Germany and the Allies. There were a number of reasons for this, but the most telling one was naval. In Allied, or more particularly British hands, Norway offered an excellent eastern base for the naval blockade of the North Sea by which the Allies hoped to strangle Germany economically, and the country's 'loss' to the Allied cause would also place the German armaments industry in a difficult position for lack of high-grade iron ore, originating from the Swedish mines near Lulea but transported by rail to Narvik and thence by sea down the 'leads' to Germany in the winter when the Baltic was frozen over. In German hands, Norway offered a convenient and safe passage for this essential iron ore, but also offered the interesting possibility of outflanking the British blockade of the North Sea for both merchant and naval vessels, and also of providing useful U-boat and air bases for attacks on British shipping, ports and other targets.

Both sides had considered the possibility of taking over Norway for some time, but British vacillation on the best course of action had been matched by an apparent German indifference. But then by one of those strange quirks of fortune, both sides decided to do something about Norway. The British, spurred on by their seizure of the supply ship *Altmark* in Norwegian territorial waters while she was carrying some 300 Allied merchant seamen captured by the commerce-raiding German pocket-battleship *Graf Spee*, finally decided to mine the leads against further use of this otherwise safe channel by German shipping. The Royal Naval mining force, escorted by destroyers, left for Norway on 8 April 1940.

Strike to the north

Hitler, meanwhile, had with that great impetuosity that sometimes marked his military actions, decided that Norway would be seized by German forces. General Nikolaus von Falkenhorst was given only a few days with which to prepare the operation, which would necessarily involve a descent on Denmark *en passant* to secure this intermediate country. Codenamed *'Weserübung'* or Weser Exercise, the operation involved seaborne landings at strategic points along Norway's long coastline, after which the landing forces would move off inland and link up, destroying any opposition from the Norwegian Army. The main landing points were to be Oslo, the Norwegian capital, Kristiansand, Stavanger, Bergen, Trondheim and Narvik in the north. So far the German plan could be considered conventional, although the use of major landings was new to the Germans. There was, however, to be one completely novel element: for the first time airborne forces were to be used in combat. Denied by the very speed of the armoured/infantry successes against Poland of any chance for combat in September 1939, Major-General Kurt Student's 7th Air Division was to land several parachute detachments beyond the seaborne invasion forces to secure vital airfields and other points, minimizing the chances of their use against the invasion forces, and keeping them intact for later German use. As there were only

a few such points worth airborne attack, and as the concept of airborne warfare was as yet untested in combat, the German planners allocated only one battalion of airborne troops to Falkenhorst: the 1st Battalion, 1st Parachute Regiment. With planning completed in a great rush, the seizure of Denmark and Norway was slated for 9 April – the day after the British mining forces had left for their operation in the leads.

Denmark falls

The first indication that the Allies had of the impending attack on Norway came during the night of 8–9 April, as the naval forces of Germany and Britain clashed in Norway's coastal waters. Wide-ranging actions were fought, in which both sides suffered heavily, but in every case the convoys carrying the invasion forces got through and landed their men and equipment on or shortly after 0500 on 9 April. The airborne forces, who were intended to land some three hours after the amphibious forces, had meanwhile been preparing for this their first combat jump. Captain Erich Walther's 1st Battalion had four tasks: the main body of the 4th Company was to take and hold the 2 mile (3·2km) bridge linking the Danish islands of Falster and Seeland; the remaining platoon of the 4th Company was to take the two airfields at Aalborg in northern Denmark, a task for which only 20 minutes were allocated before air-landed troops were scheduled to arrive; the 3rd Company was to jump on Sola airfield near Stavanger in Norway so that air-landed and *Luftwaffe* forces could be flown in; and the rest of the battalion was to fulfil the same function on Fornebu airfield just outside

Oslo, so that the 163rd Infantry Division could be flown in to secure the capital before the government and royal family could be evacuated. The scale of the German airborne operation, of which the actual parachute part was relatively small, may be gauged more accurately from the size of the air element involved: some 500 troop-carrying aircraft, made up of 10 *Gruppen* of Junkers Ju 52 tri-motor transports and one *Gruppe* of heavy

Below: Men already on the ground pause to watch a further stick of paratroops descend from their Ju 52/3m transport aircraft over some of Norway's bleaker country.

Above: A snowy drop zone for paratroops landing to reinforce the German force in Narvik under the command of the redoubtable Lieutenant-General Eduard Dietl.

Left: A scene typical of military operations throughout World War II, as men wait anxiously as their transport, in this case a Ju 52, flies in towards the front.

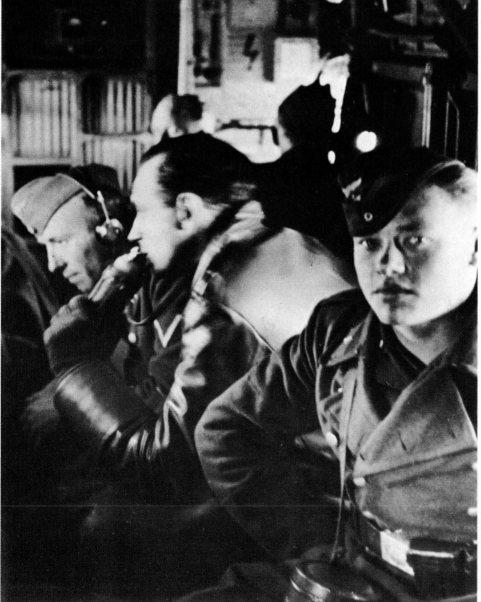

Junkers Ju 90 and Focke-Wulf Fw 200 four-engined converted airliners.

Little needs be said of the descent on Aalborg, as all went according to plan, and within 20 minutes the air-landed troops were pouring out of their aircraft, no resistance having been met. At the Vordingborg bridge matters might have gone very sour as the Danes had a defence force on the bridge. But the tactical novelty of the airborne landing amazed the Danes, who were swiftly rounded up by Captain Gericke's men, armed only with pistols. Only after the Danes had been made prisoner did the Germans bother to seek out their weapons containers and break out heavier weapons. Gericke's men were not counterattacked, and were soon relieved by the arrival of the 305th Infantry Regiment, which had advanced overland, and now pressed on with all speed towards Copenhagen, the Danish capital.

The minor part of the airborne aspect of *Weserübung* concerned with the overrunning of Denmark had been a complete success, and the whole German operation seemed well set up when Denmark capitulated on the day of her invasion.

Right: A paratrooper makes his final preparations before attempting the standard rolling landing in the snow outside the key northern port of Narvik.

KAR 98K

Calibre: 7.92mm. Operation: turn bolt. Overall length: 43.6in (1.1075m). Barrel length 23.6in (60cm), Weight: 8.6lb (3.9kg). Feed: 5-round staggered row detachable box magazine. Front sight: barley corn. Rear sight: tangent with V-notch. Muzzle velocity: 2,476fps (755mps) on date of adoption.

9mm P38 (Walther)

Calibre: 9mm Parabellum. Operation: recoil, semi-automatic. Overall length: 8.6in (21.8cm). Barrel length: 4.9in (12.5cm). Feed: 8-round box. MV: 1,115fps (340mps),

MP38 Sub-Machine Gun

Calibre: 9mm Parabellum. Operation: blowback. Length: 32.3in (82cm) or 24in (61cm) with butt folded. Barrel length 8.66in (22cm). Feed: 32-round box. Weight: 8.2lb (3.7kg). Cyclic rate: 550rpm. MV: 1,300fps (400mps).

The 1st Battalion's 3rd Company, destined for Sola airfield, had a harder time of it. Firstly, the weather was vile, and only the excellent piloting and navigation of the first-rate Ju 52 crews brought the force in over their target with pinpoint accuracy. Approaching 'on the deck' at only 33 feet (10m), the Ju 52s formed up into their dropping formation only at the last minute, and then zoomed up to 410 feet (125m) for the paratroops to pour out of the aircraft. But the Norwegian defenders were alert and greeted the paratroops with heavy machine-gun fire. Luckily for the paratroops, however, two Messerschmitt Bf 110 twin-engined fighters had managed to fly through the murk and reach Sola at just the right moment. As the vulnerable paratroops swung down to the ground the Bf 110s suppressed the fire of the airfield's defenders with cannon and machine-gun fire, giving the paratroops just enough time to gather themselves and launch an attack on the machine-gun posts ringing the airfield. The two main defence posts were quickly 'taken out' with grenades, and within 30 minutes the airfield was ready to receive air-landed troops.

Stroke of luck

The attack on Oslo, however, was a near disaster: the seaborne landing had been severely handled by the Norwegian coastal defences, and the heavy cruiser *Blücher* had been sunk by coastal batteries in the Drobak narrows. The delay to the main part of the assault force therefore placed greater emphasis on the need for success in the airborne part of the operation. But the same appalling weather conditions that had affected the transports flying in towards Stavanger also hit the Oslo transport force, some 29 Ju 52s. After two of his aircraft had collided in the thick overcast, the transport force commander reluctantly decided to turn for home without dropping his paratroops. A considerable wrangle ensued back at base when this information was radioed in, but eventually the air commander ordered all his forces to turn back. At that moment, though, Captain Wagner, in command of the leading element of the transport force, arrived over Fornebu airfield. Suspecting perhaps that the turn-back order was a Norwegian trick, Wagner decided to press on with the original plan. But as his aircraft came in to land it was hit by machine-gun fire and Wagner was killed. The co-pilot took over and decided to turn back. Thus the whole assault force was now on its way back to Germany, despite the fact that one part of it at least had attempted to land the paratroops rather than drop them. But over Fornebu were six Bf 110 fighters, which had been intended to support the airborne forces and then land on the captured airfield. Now desperately short of fuel, their commander decided that they would land and allow their rear gunners to attempt to hold off the Norwegians with machine-gun fire until another force could be

Left: *Fallschirmjäger* after being awarded Iron Crosses on 14 April 1940 for their part in the first successes in the lightning campaign in Scandinavia.

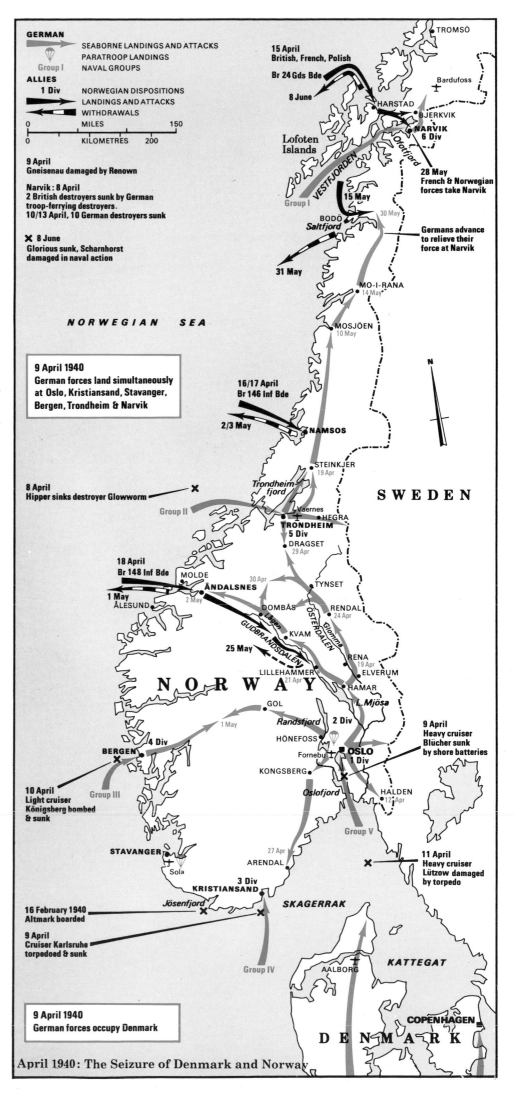

April 1940: The Seizure of Denmark and Norway

flown in once the weather had improved. One Bf 110 crashed on landing, but the other five got down successfully and adopted the best defensive positions they could. To the amazement of their crews, however, they found that the Norwegians had pulled out, leaving the airfield in the hands of the German fighters. By 0915 some Ju 52s arrived and disgorged their paratroops, and throughout the morning other transports arrived after refuelling to bring in more paratroops. Yet the German garrison on the airfield was terribly vulnerable by any objective standards, and was saved from destruction only by the paralysis the new tactics had inflicted on the Norwegians. As the first elements of the 324th Infantry regiment began to arrive, the German hold on the airfield began to look more assured, but the German commander then decided to take the bull by the horns and advance on Oslo with some six companies of infantry – again, by any objective criteria, a hopelessly inadequate force. But moving swiftly, and with a military band giving the force the appearance of assured conquerors, the force took Oslo against no opposition.

The first failure

Thus the four initial German paratroop operations, despite some tense moments, had been completely successful. For this the courage and perseverance of the local commanders must take most of the credit. The next German airborne operation, though, was a total failure. Four days after the initial landings, the 1st Battalion's 1st Company was dropped at Dombas at the upper end of the Lägen river north-west of Oslo to try to block one of the routes being used by the retreating Norwegians. The drop was too widely dispersed, and the Norwegians were able to capture the

Germans before they could muster and make their presence felt. The operation was also hampered by the fact that many of the paratroops were dropped at too low an altitude, giving their parachutes no time to open before the men plunged into the ground.

Airlift to battle

The Norwegian campaign was, however, to see one last airborne operation, in the far north of Germany's offensive. Here Lieutenant-General Eduard Dietl's mountain troops were fighting a desperate battle against the British and French troops firmly ensconced in the town. Short of men, Dietl was reinforced by the available paratroops and by a number of mountain troops, who volunteered to jump into the German-held area with no previous experience. But Dietl also needed artillery support, and there was no way that the special 7·5cm mountain guns could be dropped from the Ju 52s that would have to be used. It was decided, therefore, that a number of these vital aircraft would have to be sacrificed: loaded with the guns and ammunition, they would land on a frozen lake to deliver their supplies. But unable to take off again, the Ju 52s remained on the lake until the spring thaw, when they sank into the water. Yet the artillery reinforcement helped Dietl to hold on until the Allies pulled out after the German invasion of the Low Countries and France.

Auspicious start

Thus ended the German airborne arm's blooding in combat, with an overall impressive performance in difficult circumstances. During the Danish and Norwegian campaigns the *Luftwaffe* had delivered 29,280 men, 259,200 gallons (1,178,778 litres) of aviation spirit and 2,376 tons

Above: Paratroops gather up their parachutes and link up into a combat unit before striking off to find and engage the Allied forces in northern Norway.

(2,414,152kg) of supplies by air. But the cost had been heavy, in aircraft rather than in men. Some 100 Ju 52 transports had been lost. Bad as this was for the airborne arm, it was worse for the *Luftwaffe* in general, for these were the aircraft used for bomber crew training, blind flying training and navigational training. Because the air needs of the airborne arm had not really been thought out, the *Luftwaffe* had to use these vital aircraft for both training and operational purposes, with the result that operational losses played an important part in hampering the production of future aircrews. Yet the campaign had proved the ability of the airborne concept, and future German plans were to incorporate provision for further ambitious use of the airborne element. On the Allied side, the use of paratroops and air-landed forces had come as a very considerable shock, and contributed considerably to a general nervousness about the scope to which the Germans might in the future go in the use of such forces. *Coup-de-main* tactics had worked well, if dangerously, in the four main landings at the outset of the campaign, and from this time onwards the Allied commanders were constantly looking over their shoulders at major targets of a similar nature.

Right: Junkers Ju 52 trimotors, such as these seen on a Norwegian airfield with a Junkers Ju 87 dive-bomber, were used to fly in mountain troops as well as paratroops. Air opposition from the remnants of the Norwegian Air Force and from the RAF was negligible.

9mm P08 (Luger)

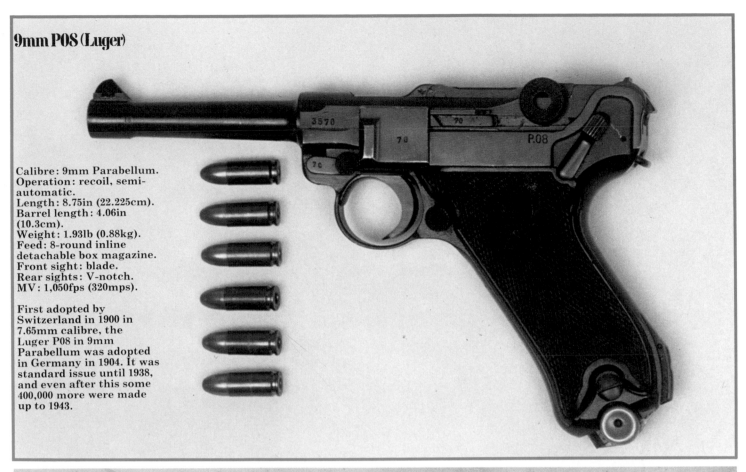

Calibre: 9mm Parabellum.
Operation: recoil, semi-
automatic.
Length: 8.75in (22.225cm).
Barrel length: 4.06in
(10.3cm).
Weight: 1.93lb (0.88kg).
Feed: 8-round inline
detachable box magazine.
Front sight: blade.
Rear sights: V-notch.
MV: 1,050fps (320mps).

First adopted by
Switzerland in 1900 in
7.65mm calibre, the
Luger P08 in 9mm
Parabellum was adopted
in Germany in 1904. It was
standard issue until 1938,
and even after this some
400,000 more were made
up to 1943.

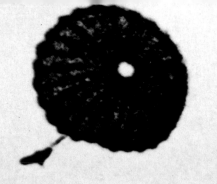

Eben-Emael and Holland

The daring German use of airborne forces in the Scandinavian campaign had amazed and alarmed the Allies. But the use of similar forces, on a larger scale, was to play an even more important part in the German assault on the West in May 1940, though only the gliderborne attack on Eben-Emael could be regarded as wholly successful.

Although the German airborne arm had received its baptism of fire in the Danish and Norwegian campaigns of April 1940, it was in the great German offensive against Holland, Belgium and France, which started on 10 May 1940, that the whole concept of airborne operations was to be given its first real test, and it was for its part in this offensive that the bulk of Lieutenant-General Kurt Student's forces were reserved. Germany's plans for the offensive had been long in the making, but the final version, suggested by Lieutenant-General Erich von Manstein, for an armoured punch through the 'impenetrable' Ardennes region to drive through to the English Channel and cut the Allied forces into two manageable portions, resulted in the airborne arm being given an important role. As the revised German plan meant that only one *Panzer* division would be available for the attack on central Holland, and one for the drive through the Maastricht appendix in

southern Holland during the advance in Belgium, securing the vital crossing points for these advances would be the primary responsibility of Student's forces. While small detachments secured and held three bridges over the Albert Canal in Belgium, just over the border from Maastricht in Holland, the bulk of the two divisions available to Student would attack the Hague and hold the bridges needed for the *Panzer* division moving up from the south to relieve the force.

The key to a successful crossing of the Albert Canal lay in the fortress of Eben-Emael, reckoned by the Belgians and the Allies to be the best modern fortress in the world. With excellent defensive positions and thick concrete walls, this fort commanded the three bridges the Germans would need in their drive to outflank, to the north, the French Maginot Line and the complex of Belgian forts around Liège. Running north-west from the fort at Eben-Emael were the bridges at Canne,

Vroenhofen and Veldwezelt. These three would have to be captured intact, and a *coup-de-main* party would have to take Eben-Emael to prevent its guns from destroying the bridges. A plan of exceptional boldness and originality was therefore devised: while assault parties codenamed Iron, Concrete and Steel would be flown in by glider to take the Canne, Vroenhofen and Veldwezelt bridges respectively, another party, codenamed Granite, was to land in gliders right on top of the fortress and take the Belgian defenders, some 1,000 strong, from above by a surprise attack.

Assault on Eben-Emael

Considering the importance of the attack, the forces allocated appear ridiculously small: Assault Group Koch, commanded by Captain Walter Koch, consisted of only one company of the 1st Parachute Regiment and a parachute engineer platoon led by Lieutenant Rudolf Witzig. The parachute company was split into three detachments with the task

Below: Paratroops tumble from a Ju 52 over Belgium as part of the reinforcements for the assault groups which had landed by glider on and around the Eben-Emael fort.

of taking the bridges, while Witzig's engineers would land on and take Eben-Emael, which was rightly considered to be the crux of the defensive strength of the area. Aircraft allocations for Assault Group Koch comprised 42 Junkers Ju 52 transports and glider tugs, and 42 DFS 230 gliders.

Early on the morning of 10 May 1940 the assault group set off in its gliders from Köln-Wahn towards Maastricht. Surprise was of the essence, so the operational plan called for the Ju 52 glider tugs to climb to over 8,200 feet (2,500m) over Germany, and to release their gliders while still over German airspace. The gliders would then fly silently to their objectives. This was the first time that such an operational tactic had been tried, and although the men of the assault group had been undergoing intensive training since the previous November, the tension in the gliders was great. It was also a cold night, and in the draughty gliders the men wrapped themselves tightly in blankets in their efforts to keep warm. At first the flight was uneventful, but then one of the gliders broke its tow and came down in Germany. As fortune would have it, the glider was the one with Witzig and part of the engineer section in it, and this alone could have ruined the whole German plan. Such was the strength and efficiency of the training, and the initiative of the rest of the engi-

neers though, that the plan continued virtually without a hitch. One other glider was lost *en route* when its pilot cast off his tow too soon and failed to reach his objective. Two other gliders also failed to reach the bridges when their pilots came down at the wrong objectives by mistake.

Bitter fighting

The rest of the glider force approached their target areas correctly and touched down close to the bridges, the paratroops pouring out as soon as they could, often before the glider had come to a complete halt. Although some of the towing aircraft had crossed into Dutch airspace and been fired on by the Dutch AA defences, this does not seem to have alerted the Belgian bridge garrisons. Nevertheless the Belgian defenders were not taken completely by surprise, and the paratroops had to fight their way up to the bridges with small arms fire, flamethrowers and grenades. Once they had reached the bridges, the Germans were able to knock out the defending pillboxes with hollow charges (charges with a cavity at the front of the explosive to focus the force of the explosion). Each bridge was attacked by a detachment consisting of five parachute infantry and four engineer sections, and the Germans moved in swiftly. Veldwezelt and Vroenhofen fell into German hands with little trouble,

Above: A classic combat photograph shows German paratroops storming the approaches to the Moerdijk bridge over the Maas river shortly after 0530 on 10 May 1940.

and the demolition charges were hastily but carefully removed. Realizing what was happening, the Belgian garrison at Veldwezelt asked for permission to blow the bridge just as the Germans were taking it. The local Belgian headquarters, refusing to believe that German troops could have got on to the bridge without their knowing it, refused to allow the demolition, and so it fell intact into German hands.

At Canne, however, the Belgians fared better. The German gliders had landed slightly too far away, and the defences were able to hold off the attackers just long enough to ask for permission to blow the bridge. Being the bridge farthest south, this was controlled by Eben-Emael's commander, who realized the implications, especially as he knew of the fighting on the roof of his fortress, and so gave the bridge garrison permission to blow their charge. Here alone, therefore, the Germans failed, principally because they had landed just too far away from their objective.

The key to the whole operation, though, was Eben-Emael itself, where nine of Witzig's gliders had landed in good order on the roof. The engineers stormed out, and

42

immediately set about destroying the 12 gun emplacements that threatened them and the bridges. Next the six most important roof emplacements were blown open with large hollow charges, against which the Belgians had no defences. Killed or knocked unconscious by the blast of these charges, the Belgians could offer no resistance as the German engineers then blasted their way through into the emplacements and secured the top level of the fortress, effectively trapping the majority of the garrison in the rest of the fortress, from where they could do little damage.

Paratroops hold on

Now completely in control of the situation unless the Belgians brought up massive reinforcements and heavy artillery, the Germans on the bridges and in the fortress waited for supplies, reinforcements of their own and the arrival of the relief forces. At 0610 reinforcements and supplies arrived in the form of parachute drops of men, ammunition, and other necessities for the bridge garrisons and fortress group. Naturally enough, though, the Belgians were now fully alert, and caused the paratroops and their transport aircraft some casualties. Having assessed the situation, the Belgians launched a number of counterattacks to try to retake the Vroenhofen and Veldwezelt bridges, but the paratroop reinforcements received by the Germans included elements from the heavy machine-gun company, whose guns ensured the repulse of the counterattacks. The Canne group, also reinforced, finally managed to fight its way on to the remnants of the bridge and drive off the Belgian garrison. Then at 0830 Witzig finally arrived to join the survivors of the 55 men who had made the original landing – landing in Germany, he had called for another tug aircraft, which had landed in a field and managed to tow the laden glider off.

Koch's men now had to hold on until the conventional forces of Army Group 'A' linked up with them. Koch, firmly established in his headquarters near the Vroenhofen bridge, was in radio contact with these forces, and knew that it should not be too long a time before relief arrived. Yet the Belgians were counterattacking, and his own forces lacked heavy weapons. This situation was improved slightly after 1015, when radio contact was made with a pair of 8·8cm batteries on the flanks of the advancing ground forces. These batteries were able to provide some useful support fire. At 1300 a forward artillery observer reached the most northerly bridge, and 90 minutes later the first ground forces, an infantry platoon, linked up with the airborne soldiers.

Koch was in radio contact with the 51st Engineer Battalion, which was charged with the task of relieving Witzig's men at Eben-Emael, and from this source knew that delays had been encountered. The battalion of the Brandenburg 'Special Service' Regiment that should have taken

Right: During the final run in towards the drop zone, a German paratrooper clips his static line to the fixed line in the fuselage of the Ju 52 transport.

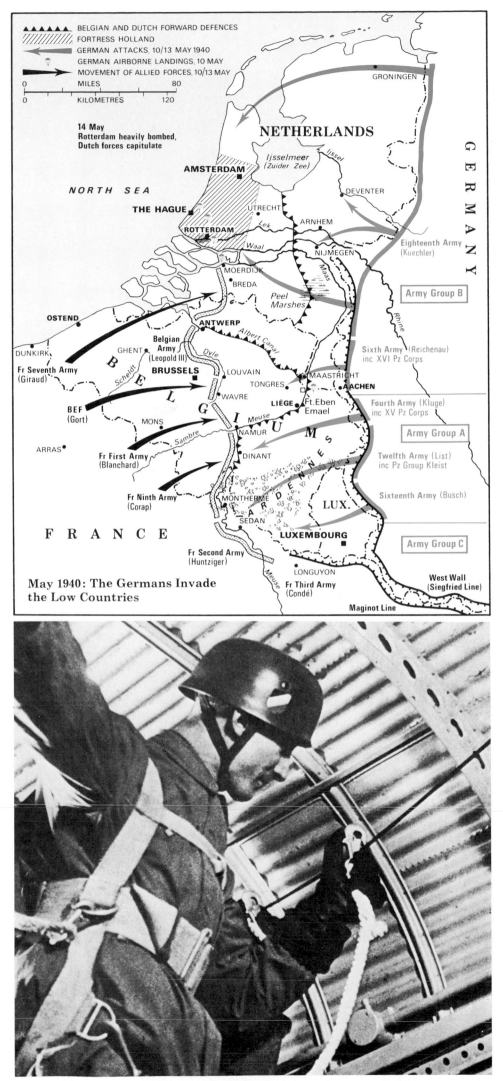

May 1940: The Germans Invade the Low Countries

BELGIAN AND DUTCH FORWARD DEFENCES
FORTRESS HOLLAND
GERMAN ATTACKS, 10/13 MAY 1940
GERMAN AIRBORNE LANDINGS, 10 MAY
MOVEMENT OF ALLIED FORCES, 10/13 MAY

0   MILES   80
0   KILOMETRES   120

14 May
Rotterdam heavily bombed,
Dutch forces capitulate

GERMANY

NETHERLANDS

NORTH SEA

GRONINGEN

Ijsselmeer (Zuider Zee)

AMSTERDAM

DEVENTER

THE HAGUE

UTRECHT

ARNHEM

ROTTERDAM

Lek

NIJMEGEN

Waal

Eighteenth Army (Kuechler)

MOERDIJK

Maas

BREDA

Peel Marshes

Army Group B

OSTEND

ANTWERP

Albert Canal

DUNKIRK

GHENT

Belgian Army (Leopold III)

Dyle

Sixth Army (Reichenau) inc XVI Pz Corps

Fr Seventh Army (Giraud)

Scheldt

BRUSSELS

LOUVAIN

MAASTRICHT

AACHEN

Rhine

WAVRE

TONGRES

BEF (Gort)

MONS

LIÈGE

Ft.Eben Emael

Fourth Army (Kluge) inc XV Pz Corps

Meuse

NAMUR

Army Group A

ARRAS

Sambre

DINANT

Twelfth Army (List) inc Pz Group Kleist

Fr First Army (Blanchard)

ARDENNES

Sixteenth Army (Busch)

Fr Ninth Army (Corap)

MONTHERME

LUX.

SEDAN

LUXEMBOURG

Army Group C

FRANCE

Fr Second Army (Huntziger)

LONGUYON

West Wall (Siegfried Line)

Meuse

Fr Third Army (Condé)

Maginot Line

the bridges over the Maas at Maastricht had failed to do so, and the Dutch had blown them. Nevertheless, Koch was informed by the 51st Engineer Battalion, the 4th *Panzer* Division and the 151st Infantry Regiment were making good progress across the Maastricht appendix. Witzig's men were now in the uncomfortable position of being shelled by Belgian artillery, but luckily for them no counterattack on Eben-Emael was launched. Cut off on the roof of the fortress, the German engineers were much relieved to see the leading elements of the 51st Engineer Battalion approaching Eben-Emael at 0700 on 11 May. The battalion had fought its way across the Maas river and Albert Canal, and was soon joined by the 151st Infantry Regiment. The Germans outside the fortress launched a major attack on the main gates of the portion still held by the Belgians, who finally surrendered at 1200. By 1600 Witzig's men were able to pull out to rejoin the bridge parties, who had been relieved earlier, in Maastricht. The way was open for the 4th *Panzer* Division to drive deep into the Allied defence line in Belgium.

Reward of boldness

The attack on Eben-Emael remains a classic example of what can be achieved by boldness combined with initiative and thorough preparation. The Germans had seen the fortress's blind spot and taken full advantage of this. Only six of Witzig's men had been killed, with a further 20 wounded, while the Belgian defenders of Eben-Emael had lost some 70 men, with the remaining 1,100 effectively locked up and impotent in their own fortress. *Mutatis mutandis*, the same lessons can be drawn from the attacks on the three bridges over the Albert Canal: where the gliders landed sufficiently close to their objectives, *coups-de-main* were possible and indeed fully practical. But once surprise had been lost, as at Canne and in the arrival of parachute reinforcements, the vulnerability of the airborne forces, lacking heavy weapons, was very clear. Nevertheless, the whole operation had gone remarkably smoothly and successfully, to the delight of Hitler, who personally decorated most of the survivors.

Airlandings in Holland

The Albert Canal operation, though, was only a minor affair compared with the scheme devised for the rest of Student's airborne forces. Organized into an extemporized Airlanding Corps under the overall command of Colonel-General Albert Kesselring's 2nd Air Fleet, the corps was made up of two divisions and their transport aircraft, formed into 11 *Gruppen*. Student himself, apart from commanding the corps, also commanded the 7th Air Division, which could field four parachute battalions and three battalions of the army's 16th Infantry Regiment in the airlanding role; also part of the Airlanding Corps was the 22nd Infantry Division, commanded by Lieutenant-General Graf von Sponeck, which had three battalions from each of the 47th and 65th Infantry Regiments in the airlanding role, and one battalion of the 2nd Parachute Regi-

Above: The moment of truth as the jumper leaves the aircraft, his static line trailing behind him. Already another man is waiting his turn at the door.

ment in the parachute role. Both divisions had their own divisional troops, the 7th Air Division's all being capable of parachute deployment.

Student's plan for the two divisions was a bold one, perhaps too bold in the circumstances. Fixed before the invasion of Norway, the plan might have worked but for the fact that the element of tactical surprise, so essential for such an operation, had been 'blown' by the use of airborne forces in the Norwegian campaign. Reduced to its basic elements, Student's plan was for the 22nd Division to airland around The Hague, the Dutch capital, after parachute troops had captured the necessary airfields, move on the capital, capture the government and royal family, and then hold the area to prevent the airfields being used by the Allies and to prevent the free movement of Dutch troops. At the same time the 7th Air Division was to use its parachute capability to take and hold the bridges at Moerdijk, Dordrecht and Rotterdam so that the 9th *Panzer* Division could sweep north to Rotterdam and then on to The Hague to relieve the 22nd Division. Over Kesselring's very legitimate objections, Student decided to lead the 7th Air Division personally rather than stay behind and control the efforts of his corps. This lack of adequate commanders was to have dire results for the whole operation, and there can be little doubt that Student should have sacrificed his own personal desires to the more important command task. Two other major failings are also discernible in the German plan: for a variety of reasons, the approach route was to be direct from bases in Ger-

many to the target areas, across Dutch territory, so that the 22nd Division could not hope for tactical surprise; and the decision to employ virtually the whole strength of the two divisions (4,000 paratroops and 12,000 airlanded troops) in the initial attacks meant that Student had no real reserve. This second failing meant that as Dutch resistance strengthened, as it inevitably would, the Germans would be unable to fly in reinforcements, and that any delay by the relieving forces would pose the real threat of destruction for the airborne forces. On the credit side, it must be pointed out that as overall control of the operation was a *Luftwaffe* responsibility, tactical air support was likely to be first class. This certainly proved to be the case in the Eben-Emael operation. Student was very aware of the difficulties posed by his divisions' lack of organic heavy weapons (ie weapons that are part of the division's normal complement of arms), and had emphasised the importance of full and effective use of *Luftwaffe* tactical air support, from Junkers Ju 87 dive-bombers and Messerschmitt Bf 109 fighters for the most part,

Right: Having taken the Moerdijk bridge, the paratroops had then to hold it until the *Panzers* arrived. Here an MG34 machine-gun crew pins down a counterattack by the Dutch.

MP40 Sub-Machine Gun

Calibre: 9mm Parabellum.
Operation: blowback, full automatic.
Length: 32.8in (83.3cm) or 24.8in (63cm) with stock folded.
Barrel length: 9.9in (25cm)

Feed: 32-round staggered row detachable box magazine.
Weight: 8.87lb (4kg).
Front sight: hooded barley corn.
Rear sight: notched flip-over leaf.

Cyclic rate: 500rpm.
MV: about 1,300fps (400mps).
The MP40 was basically the MP38 re-engineered for ease of manufacture and cheapness, with a new ejector and magazine release assembly, the ribbing removed from the receiver and a formed rather than cast grip frame. Over one million MP40s were made by Erma, Haenel and Steyr in the years 1940–1944. The weapon

illustrated is the MP40/I variant, with a two-piece bolt handle and a stamped, ribbed magazine housing. The variant was far more common than the original.

in all aspects of training and preparation.

Preceded by heavy air bombardments, carefully planned to avoid the airborne forces' objectives, the Airlanding Corps flew into action early on 10 May, directly from its base in Westphalia in some 580 Ju 52 transports. At the southern end of the 'airborne carpet' it was hoped to secure for the German armour, Captain Prager's 2nd Battalion of the 1st Parachute Regiment landed at both ends of the bridge across the Holland Deep at Moerdijk, one company at each end. The Dutch were taken completely by surprise, and Prager's men smashed the defence ruthlessly and quickly, rushed the bridge and removed the demolition charges. Prager reported this to the regimental commander, Colonel Bruno Bräuer, who had dropped with the headquarters and staff of the regiment just to the north, and prepared to defend his prize.

Crisis at Dordrecht

Bräuer's headquarters had been dropped in a sensible place, for located between the Moerdijk and Dordrecht objectives, he could co-ordinate the activities of the forces in both these areas. But at Dordrecht, where the bridge over the Oude Maas was to be taken, the lack of suitable dropping zones (DZs) meant that only Lieutenant von Brandis's company of the 1st Battalion, 1st Parachute Regiment, could be dropped. The force proved insufficient for the task, and the company could take only part of the bridge. The action at Dordrecht was very severe, the Dutch holding on with considerable tenacity. Unfortunately for the Germans, von

Brandis was killed in the strenuous fighting for the bridge, and the Dutch succeeded in recapturing the rail bridge the Germans had taken in their first rush. Yet although they had retaken the bridge, the Dutch did not blow it, for it was essential in their plans for bringing forward reserves from the 'Fortress Holland' area around The Hague.

The Germans enjoyed greater success at the northern end of the 7th Air Division's corridor, where the twin bridges over the Nieuwe Maas in Rotterdam were the objective. The ingeniously devised plan worked perfectly, yet again demonstrating the advantages of surprise and originality in small-scale military operations. Under the command of Lieutenant Schrader, the 11th Company, 16th Infantry Regiment (attached to the 7th Air Division from the 22nd Division) was flown into Rotterdam by 12 Heinkel 59 floatplanes, which taxied right up to the bridges before disgorging their loads of infantry. These immediately leapt on to the bridge, and before the astounded Dutch could react, the bridges had been taken and the demolition charges disarmed. At the same time a party of paratroops, about 50 strong, had landed in a stadium south of the bridges, seized some trams and driven to reinforce Schrader's infantrymen. Dutch fire had made movement across the bridges difficult, and soon after the arrival of Lieutenant Horst Kerfin's paratroops had raised the garrison at the northern end of the bridge to 60, movement became impossible. The Germans set up their defences at each end of the bridges and waited for the inevitable Dutch counterblows. The promise of support was, how-

Above: Hitler invests some of the paratroops involved in the fighting round Rotterdam with the Iron Cross. In this area the paratroops fared better than those at The Hague.

Above: Assault pioneers paddle along the Albert Canal near one of the key bridges dominated by the great fortress of Eben-Emael, taken by classic *coup-de-main* tactics.

ever, close to hand. While the initial fight for the twin bridges was in progress, Waalhaven airfield to the south-west of Rotterdam had fallen to a neat ploy. The 3rd Battalion of the 1st Parachute Regiment, led by Captain Karl-Lothar Schulz, jumped just to the east of the airfield. The Dutch airfield defence force immediately

DFS 230

Type: 10-seat tactical assault glider.
Span: 72ft 1⅓in (21.98m). Length: 36ft
10½in (11.24m). Height: 8ft 11¾in (2.74m).
Maximum towing speed: 130mph
(210kph). Maximum gliding speed:
180mph (290kph). Empty weight:
1,896lb (860kg). Loaded weight: 4,630lb
(2,100kg). Optional armament: one
flexible 7.92mm MG15 and two fixed
7.92mm MG34 machine-guns.
The DFS 230A was first used in combat
during the Eben-Emael operation of
May 1940, where its main tactical
failings were seen to be a long landing
run and lack of armament with which
to keep the defences' heads down
during the final approach. These were
cured on the DFS 230B-1, which had a

braking parachute under the tail and
optional forward-firing armament. The
wheeled undercarriage was
jettisonable.

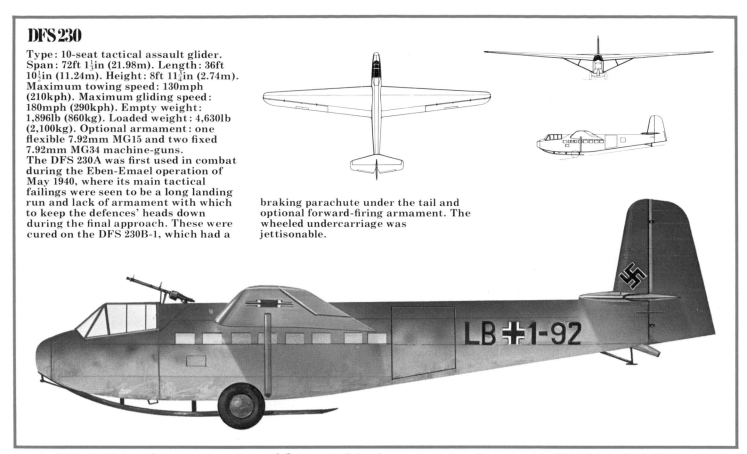

attacked the paratroops, but as soon as it had started to do so the 3rd Battalion of the 16th Infantry Regiment began to airland on the field. Caught between two forces, the Dutch were overwhelmed in a sharp action, leaving the Germans free to move on the Nieuwe Maas bridges in Rotterdam, where they reinforced the garrison at the southern end. The Germans were now in full control of two of the three bridges they had set out to take, and in partial control of the third one, that at Dordrecht. So far, then, the 7th Air Division's plan was going reasonably well.

Northern disaster

Farther to the north, though, the 22nd Division was having a very rough time of it. With only one reinforced parachute battalion, the 22nd Parachute Regiment, to take three airfields, the 22nd Division's timetable quickly went wrong, and the transports carrying the airlanding infantry arrived before the paratroops had been able to secure and clear the airfields. In the '1st Landing Area' at Valkenburg, up the coast from the Hague, the Ju 52s carrying the 47th Infantry Regiment found the airfield still under Dutch fire. The aircraft that managed to get down were greeted by intense fire and then stuck in the soft surface of the field, preventing other aircraft from landing, and so forcing them to turn back home without landing their troops. At the '2nd Landing Area' at Ockenburg, just down the coast from The Hague, the story was the same, with the airfield covered by wrecked Ju 52 transports. Worst of all, perhaps, was the '3rd Landing Area' at Ypenburg, between Delft and The Hague, where von Sponeck was due to land. This airfield had been chosen for the 65th Infantry Regiment's landing, but after 11 of the first 13 aircraft to arrive had been despatched by Dutch AA fire, von Sponeck abandoned the site

and flew on to Ockenburg, where his aircraft was hit by AA fire and forced to crashland. Pilots were forced to come down wherever they could, and the whole of the 22nd Division's plan was in disarray. Von Sponeck was able to contact Kesselring by radio and report the disaster. In the absence of Student, Kesselring took it upon himself to cancel the plan for an attack on The Hague, but instead ordered von Sponeck to gather as large a force as he could and strike out south-east towards Rotterdam, where he might be able to link up with the most northerly elements of the 7th Air Division. Some 2,000 men of the 22nd Division had landed, while another 5,000 had been unable to get down, but von Sponeck was able to gather only part of those in Holland under the command of his extemporized 'Battlegroup von Sponeck'. Those elements that were unable to link up with von Sponeck dug in where they could and prepared to sell their lives in as costly a way as possible, so that Dutch reserves would at least be held up from moving south towards the main front.

Farther south, though, the battle in the airborne carpet area was gathering momentum as Dutch forces arrived, and the Germans strove to build up their forces in the region. Although under constant fire, Waalhaven airfield was kept operational, allowing two battalions of the 16th Infantry Regiment and the 3rd Battalion of the 1st Parachute Regiment to be landed. Bräuer commandeered Dutch vehicles to rush forward reinforcements to Dordrecht, and after some very severe fighting the bridge fell into German hands. Fighting in all of the 7th Air Division's bridgeheads continued unabated until the morning of 12 May, when the forward elements of Lieutenant-General Alfred Ritter von Hubicki's 9th *Panzer* Division pushed through the corridor after relieving the Moerdijk bridge garrison at first light. Yet

the 7th Air Division's task was not yet over, for with the arrival of the ground forces it became part of General Rudolf Schmidt's army corps, part of whose task was to push on through Rotterdam and relieve the remnants of the 22nd Division, cut off in Overschie on the Hague-Rotterdam road after fighting their way back from the Hague. Progress to Rotterdam was slow, however, and on the 14th, with the Germans ground forces on the outskirts of the city, there took place the bombing of the city's old quarter, which finally persuaded the Dutch authorities of the futility of continued resistance. Holland surrendered at 2030 on 14 May.

Dire losses

For the German airborne arm, though, there was still one near tragedy to come. Student had occupied a Dutch military headquarters where a group of Dutch soldiers was turning in its weapons. An SS regiment arrived on the scene, saw armed Dutch troops, and opened fire. In the following firefight Student, who had rushed over to a window to see what was happening, was hit in the head by a bullet and seriously injured. Major-General Richard Putzier, who commanded Student's air support formations during the Dutch operations, succeeded Student as temporary head of the airborne forces. Gradually things settled down in Holland, and the survivors of the 22nd Division began to appear in dribs and drabs just as the two airborne divisions were pulled back to Germany for rest and rehabilitation. The severity of the 22nd Division's ordeal may be gauged from the casualties among those who actually managed to land: 40 per cent of the officers and 28 per cent of the men. Aircraft losses were also high, with 170 completely destroyed and a further 170 badly damaged. Aircrew losses had also been severe, with adverse effects

Above: Against a background of the road and rail bridges over the Maas, paratroops gather in the supplies and weapons dropped to them in special containers.

Right: Still grimy after their triumph over the Belgian garrison of Eben-Emael, nearly 1,000 strong, men of Demolition Party Granite relax and have a smoke.

Above: Covered by fire from an MG 34 medium machine-gun, Oberleutnant Tietjin doubles along the Moerdijk bridge with another of his men on the other side.

on future operations and on *Luftwaffe* training programmes.

On the whole, therefore, the 7th Air Division had been successful: dropping near the Dutch/German frontier, it had enjoyed tactical surprise, and was well within the reach of tactical air support and the relieving ground forces. The 22nd Division, on the other hand, had fared very badly, and for this the plan devised by Student was largely to blame: no tactical surprise had been possible, the parachute forces allocated were insufficient, and long-range tactical air support was all but impossible. Even so, something might have been achieved by the division had Student been on hand to control matters, rather than on the ground controlling the

7th Air Division from his headquarters near Waalhaven.

It was clear to the politico-military heads of the German war machine, though, that airborne forces had much to offer, as demonstrated by the Albert Canal and 'carpet' operations, and so it was decided to enlarge and reorganize the airborne force. The 22nd Division was retained in the airlanding role, the 7th Air Division was expanded into a full three-regiment formation, and the Assault Group Koch was improved into a full Assault Regiment. The command problems of the Dutch operation were appreciated, and it was decided to form *Fliegerkorps* XI, with Student as commander as soon as he had recovered, to control all airborne operations.

Student's wound proved quite serious, and it was January 1941 before he could take over his upgraded formation. Student, therefore, had about two months before his forces were once again to be committed in the invasion of Greece and Crete.

MG34 Machine Gun

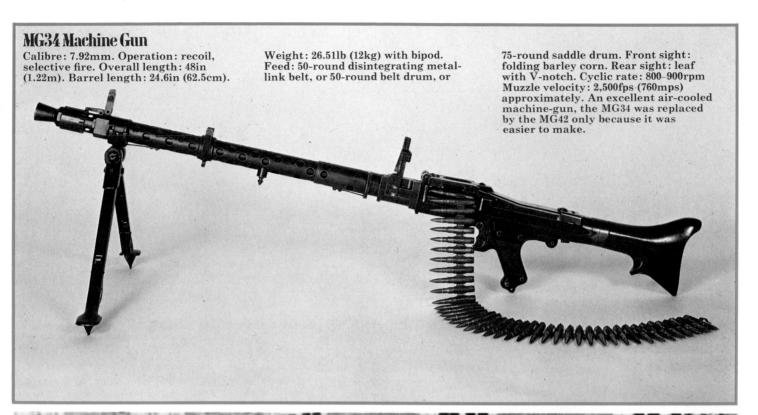

Calibre: 7.92mm. Operation: recoil, selective fire. Overall length: 48in (1.22m). Barrel length: 24.6in (62.5cm). Weight: 26.51lb (12kg) with bipod. Feed: 50-round disintegrating metal-link belt, or 50-round belt drum, or 75-round saddle drum. Front sight: folding barley corn. Rear sight: leaf with V-notch. Cyclic rate: 800–900rpm Muzzle velocity: 2,500fps (760mps) approximately. An excellent air-cooled machine-gun, the MG34 was replaced by the MG42 only because it was easier to make.

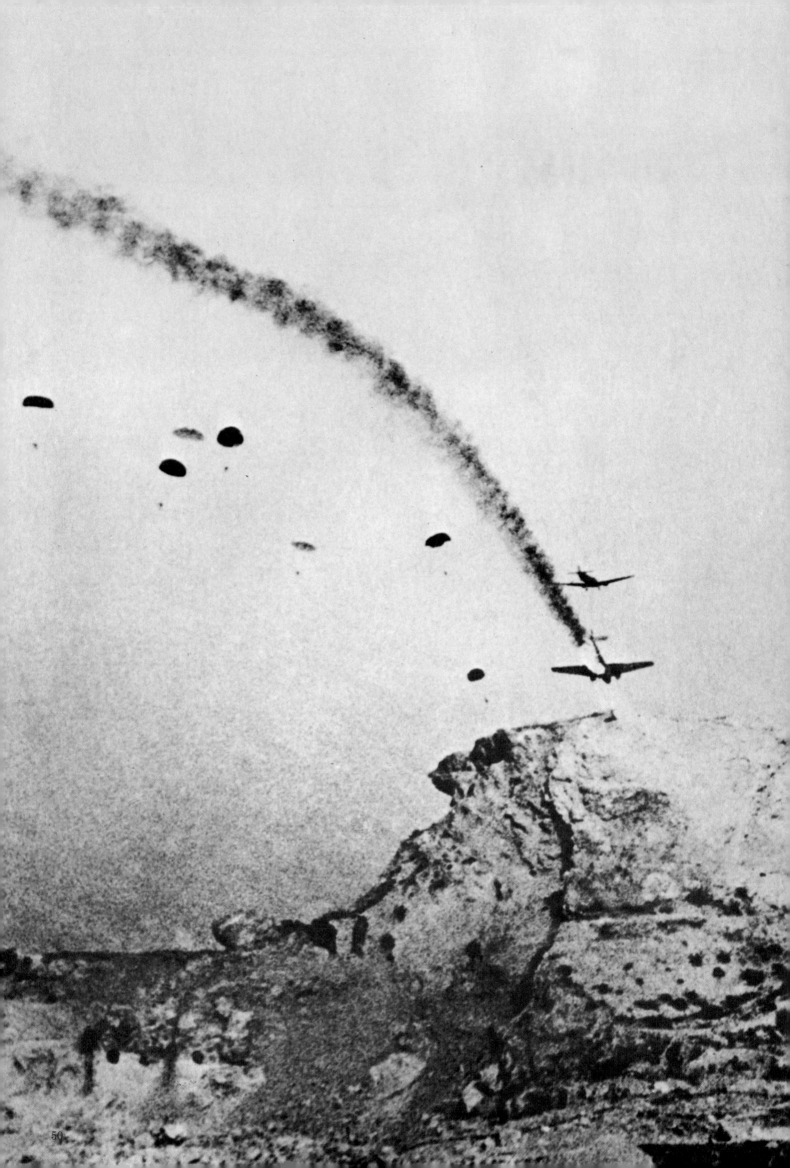

Operation Mercury - the Invasion of Crete

To the Allies and to historians, the German invasion of Crete in May 1941 has always been a classic of airborne warfare. But the fate of the invasion for some time hung in the balance before German daring and Allied ineptitude swayed the issue in favour of the Germans, and so high were the airborne units' losses that Hitler determined never again to allow so large an operation.

The German descent on Crete in May 1941 is a landmark in the history of airborne warfare. So far airborne operations had been petty operations, closely linked with and subordinate to the objectives of the conventional ground forces and against a weak or unprepared opponent. They resembled those of old-fashioned mounted cavalry: to raid, or to seize and hold some objective like a bridge until ground troops could come up and consolidate it, or to harry a beaten enemy. The capture on 26 April 1941 of the bridge over the Corinth Canal with the aim of cutting off the British and Commonwealth troops who were retreating into the Peloponnese after their defeat in Greece was in this last category, but Operation *'Merkur'* (Mercury), named after the Greek god with the winged heels, to invade Crete was the first and, indeed, the only purely airborne offensive against so large and important an objective. It was inspired by Lieutenant-General Kurt Student, a fanatical proponent of the airborne arm who believed that it should operate in its own right and not

be the handmaiden of the army on the ground.

By way of a curtain raiser there had been the Corinth Canal action, undertaken by Colonel Alfred Sturm's 2nd Parachute Regiment of the 7th Air Division. One escape route for the defeated Commonwealth troops retreating from Greece was from Megara across the Corinth Canal where its deep gorge was spanned by a large iron bridge. This, the Germans knew, was guarded by a 'close bridge garrison' of British troops from a ground attack from either side of the canal, while the Royal Engineers had already laid and connected the charges to demolish the bridge as soon as the last of the Australian troops had finished using it and were on their way to their ports of embarkation. The operation was extremely well done. The Germans delayed considerably in deciding to mount it but, in their usual German fashion, once they started they displayed all their ability to 'lay it on' with only verbal orders, maximum speed and without any of the endless joint planning and argument

which bedevilled similar British operations. This may have been due to the fact that German airborne troops were part of the *Luftwaffe* (Student was a *Luftwaffe* man) and there was no competition for control as was apt to occur when the transporting agency and the fighting troops were in separate services.

The British defenders were, numerically at least, sufficient for the task and well posted, with a small covering force on the Greek or north side and the equivalent of a battalion of infantry, supported by a few light tanks, on the south side. They were well dug in and organized. Anti-aircraft defence was provided by a troop of Bofors 40mm light AA guns sited to provide close defence of the bridge itself.

The right DZ

The constant problem facing the planners of an airborne operation is the choice between landing at some distance from the objectives so that the troops can form up, collect their weapons and assault in proper form, or dropping on top of the defenders and relying on the effect of surprise, the subsequent confusion of battle and

Left: A Ju 52 plunges in flames after being hit by British anti-aircraft fire. Losses of these vital aircraft were very heavy in the Crete campaign.

the characteristic dash of the parachute troops to win the ensuing *mêlée*. Colonel Sturm chose the second method, and it may be that his success influenced the tactics of Operation '*Merkur*'. The attack was timed for the early morning of 26 April, in daylight, the airborne force taking off between 0500 and 0530, preceded by a saturation bombardment of level- and dive-bombers which paid particular attention to the AA gun defence. There can be no doubt that the British defenders were tired and discouraged at the end of a disastrous campaign and were to some extent understandably cowed by the wearing experience, which has to be experienced to be understood, of fighting when the enemy has control of the air. The German airborne vanguard consisted of three DFS 230 glider loads of parachute engineers, who were combat troops fully equal to their infantry. These were landed crisply, accurately and unscathed at each end of the bridge, which they proceeded to capture before setting about the neutralization of the demolition charges.

Astride the defence

Before the defenders had had time to react accurately to this piece of impudence a stream of 200 Ju 52 transports arrived in the wake of the bombers and dropped one parachute battalion to the north of the canal and another to the south, each right on top of the defenders. The northern battalion had a quick success: the southern a short but sharp fight before the defence was eliminated. All was over by mid-day. Boldness had paid off. Sturm's total casualties were some 60 killed and 180 wounded, a small price for an operation of this kind. The 'Number One' of a British Bofors LAA gun, a deadly weapon when used like a heavy machine-gun at ground targets, turned his gun on the engineers attacking the bridge and actually hit the pile of disconnected charges and touched them off. The resulting explosion broke the back of the bridge which saved those who had already crossed from pursuit, but a number of Allied soldiers were cut off and captured as a result. A large number of Australian, British, Greek and New Zealand troops, mostly infantry who were still full of fight in spite of their reverses in Greece, escaped. They went not to Egypt, as the German high command wrongly guessed, but to strengthen the defences of Crete.

Slow build-up

It took some time to assemble the airborne troops and aircraft for '*Merkur*' because they were scattered across the breadth of Europe, for no previous thought had been given by Hitler, who dominated German planning down to details, of using the airborne troops in one concentrated blow. As a result D-day for '*Merkur*' was not to be until 20 May, which enabled the scrappy defences of Crete to be put into some kind of order.

The German force was a powerful one. In command was Colonel-General Alexander Löhr, although the driving force was his subordinate, Kurt Student. Löhr's 4th *Luftflotte* was made up of *Fliegerkorps* VIII, the strike component with 716

Above: Men of Colonel Alfred Sturm's 2nd Parachute Regiment drop onto the approaches to the Corinth Canal bridge, destroyed by an explosion at the end of the battle.

Left: Men of Sturm's command break out a machine-gun and other munitions from a container parachute dropped to them during the short fight for the Corinth Canal bridge.

fighter-bombers, 205 dive-bombers and 228 medium level tactical bombers, of which 514 were serviceable on 17 May. *Fliegerkorps* XI was a joint command with Major-General Conrad in command of the troop lift of 500 Ju 52 transports and 72 DFS 230 gliders, and Student of the corps of airborne troops. These were his 7th Air Division, of three parachute regiments each of three battalions with divisional artillery, engineers and signals, and the Airborne Assault Regiment of three parachute battalions and a gliderborne battalion. These could muster a fighting strength of some 8,100 from a total of 13,000. As a follow-up force the 5th Mountain Division, with three mountain rifle regiments and a motor-cycle battalion, was added to the assault force. Mountain units with light equipment were well suited to air-transported operations, and were also elite troops. This was a very powerful force, but Löhr and Student correctly perceived that an exclusively airborne operation on this scale was by way

German Paratrooper, Crete 1941

Dressed in the old style smock this German paratrooper wears the kit issued to the men who jumped over Crete. A quartermaster's error caused the Germans to be wearing the same uniform they had worn for Norway in the late winter of 1940 when they attacked Crete in the spring of 1941. It consisted of a serge battledress suit, plain or camouflaged close-weave cotton smock, padded gloves and rubber-soled, side-lacing boots. After a few days fighting, the Germans discarded everything except boots, smock and equipment. The rifle is a Kar 98K while the paratrooper also carries a P08 pistol in a holster and a bandolier of rifle ammunition.

of being experimental, and that there were inherent dangers in relying solely on a combination of infantry and strike aircraft without *Panzer* and heavy artillery support. It was important not to fail, and the best chance of success lay in deploying maximum strength as early as possible. This was just as well, for German intelligence had badly underestimated the numerical strength and fighting quality of the garrison of Crete and the difficulties of the assault.

Over-extended resources

The defence of Greece and Crete was one of the many operations General Sir Archibald Wavell, then commander-in-chief of the Commonwealth forces in the Middle East, was compelled to undertake with inadequate forces all round the vast perimeter of his command. The controversy over the extension of British strategy in 1941 to the Balkans need not be discussed here, nor the contention that if Crete could not be adequately defended it should not have been defended at all, and the loss of many brave men and good ships, essential to the prosecution of future operations, avoided. The crux of the matter was that with airfields on Crete the *Luftwaffe* was just so much closer to the great British base in Egypt, while if it was in British hands the RAF could interdict the shipping route along which the Axis forces in the desert were supplied. With Malta, Crete was regarded as one of the bastions of the northern British perimeter, despite the shortages of aircraft, weapons and equipment of all kinds. These were certainly crippling. To begin with the most basic, there was a lack of 'defence' stores of all kinds: picks, shovels, sandbags, barbedwire and mines. There was a severe shortage of transport. In those days only the infantry were fully armed. Many troops likely to be involved in combat in a kind of battle without a front line, in which the

enemy would come down from the clouds, were like HQs and artillery in being without personal weapons, there being just a few rifles in each unit. The field artillery consisted of a few obsolete captured French and Italian pieces without transport (all the 25pounders had been lost in Greece) and the AA artillery of a troop or so of obsolete 3in 30cwt medium guns, without proper fire-control instruments, and some 40mm Bofors L/56s There were a few obsolete British Mark VI light tanks armed with a machine-gun only, and some slow 'infantry' (I) tanks. The infantry battalions, the majority of which had been evacuated from beaches or small ports in Greece, were short of their organic heavy weapons. Above all there was one serious shortage of a commodity without which it is impossible to wage modern war, however well off in terms of weapons: a good radio network. By contrast the Germans were well equipped in this respect, and so were able at the most desperate periods of their hazardous operation to exercise full command and control.

Keys to Crete

Altogether there were 32,000 Commonwealth troops in Crete: 6,000 of the original garrison, of whose existence the German intelligence was aware, and another 21,000 from the wrecks of the formations evacuated from mainland Greece and some fresh reinforcements from Egypt. Owing to the shortage of small arms in the whole command, some thousands of administrative troops who were perforce non-combatants were wisely evacuated. It proved impossible to operate aircraft from the island, and all effective air support had to come 300 miles (480km) across the eastern Mediterranean from fields in Egypt.

Crete is an extraordinarily difficult place to defend against an attack, especially from the north, because it is geo-

Above: The Junkers Ju 87 divebomber provided excellent tactical support for the airborne forces, as for other forces, but suffered heavy losses in the process.

graphically speaking a long thin mountain range some 170 miles (275km) from end to end and 20 to 30 miles (32 to 48km) wide, sticking out of the sea, steep-to on the south, open with a narrow coastal plain on the north, along which ran a single road. There was no depth in the defensive positions it offered and any movement of reserves had to be from east to west or vice versa along what was inevitably the front line. The only way to defend the island was to establish a chain of defended localities covering the likely points of entry: the little fishing ports, the sheltered bays and the landing strips. To operate north of Crete and intercept any seaborne invasion the Royal Navy had to sail through either the Kithera or Kaso straits and then accept a hostile air situation.

The order of battle of the garrison of Crete in outline was as follows, reading from east to west: in Heraklion, Brigadier R. H. Chappel and the British 14th Infantry Brigade (7th Leicesters, 2nd Black Watch, 2nd York and Lancasters, reinforced by 2/4th Australian Infantry and a Greek battalion); in Retimo Lieutenant-Colonel I. R. Campbell's 19th Australian Brigade (2/11th and 2/1st Australian Battalions and two Greek battalions); Brigadier G. A. Vasey and two Australian battalions were retained as a counterattack force; in the area of Suda Bay and the town of Canea, Major-General E. C. Weston, Royal Marines, with a composite force of army troops, Royal Marines and the Royal

Right: Junkers Ju 52/3m transports over Crete. Note the dorsal gunner in the lower aircraft, and the corrugated skinning so typical of Junkers aircraft up to the mid-1930s.

7.5 cm LG 40

Calibre: 2.95in (7.5cm). Operation: recoilless. Length: 29.5in (75cm). Barrel length: 9.92in (25.2cm). Weight: 321lb (145kg). Elevation: –15° to +42°. Traverse: 360° below 20°; 60° above 20°. Maximum range: 7,435 yards (6,800m). Shell weight (HE): 12.85lb (5.83kg). MV: 1,150fps (350mps). The LG 40 was the same weapon as the LG 1, but mounted on a carriage with solid rather than spoked wheels. It was first used in Crete.

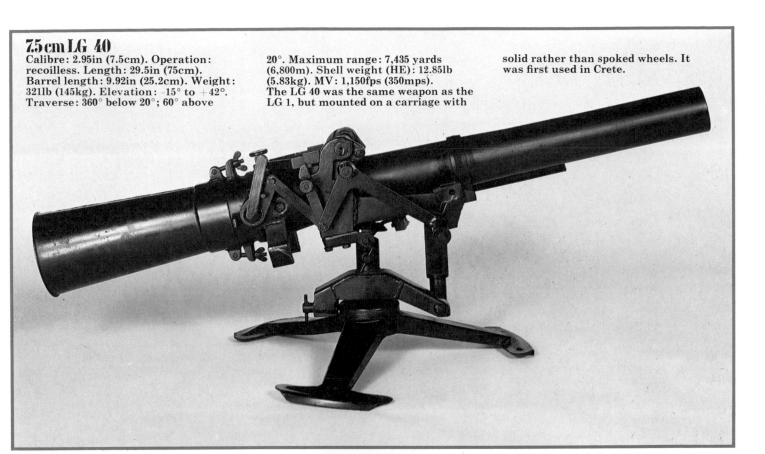

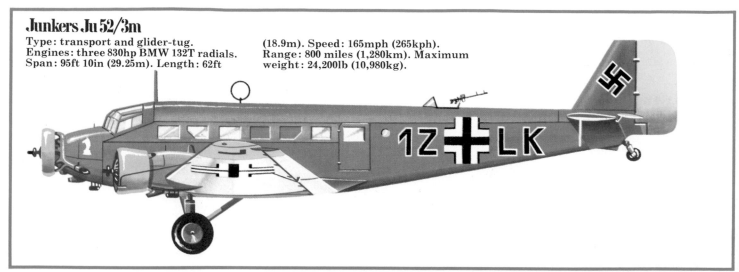

Junkers Ju 52/3m

Type: transport and glider-tug.
Engines: three 830hp BMW 132T radials.
Span: 95ft 10in (29.25m). Length: 62ft
(18.9m). Speed: 165mph (265kph).
Range: 800 miles (1,280km). Maximum
weight: 24,200lb (10,980kg).

Naval Base Defence Organization (Marines and RN). The decisive sector proved to be west of this: Galata, Maleme and Maleme airfield. Here the 2nd New Zealand Division, temporarily commanded by Brigadier E. Puttick, was positioned with the 10th Brigade around Galata, two Greek battalions to the south and astride the so-called 'Prison Valley', and Brigadier J. Hargest's 5th New Zealand Brigade, 28th Maori Battalion, the divisional engineers acting as infantry and the 21st, 22nd and 23rd New Zealand Infantry Battalions. The 22nd Battalion was dangerously spread out with only one company on the airfield: indeed, the New Zealand deployment was weak where it should have been the strongest. Command of the Crete garrison was entrusted to that formidable New Zealander, Major-General Bernard Freyberg, VC.

Compromise solution

Colonel-General Löhr and Lieutenant-General Student proceeded to fall out over the question of the plan of attack. (It seems to have been a characteristic of airborne forces generally that their leaders were all men of strong and even abrasive character, and Student was no exception.) Löhr wanted to concentrate all resources on the Maleme sector, reinforce by air and sea, and then roll up the defences from west to east with a strong, single, properly organized force. Student, who had perceived the essential weakness of the string of isolated strongpoints, wanted to hit them all simultaneously, so blocking the lateral movement of reserves and, as it were, breaking the spine of the snake into bits. A compromise was reached by which there would be two airlifts: to Maleme-Canea in the morning and to Retimo and Heraklion in the afternoon. As soon as the landing fields had been made secure, that is free at least of aimed small arms and machine-gun fire, elements of the mountain division would be brought in to consolidate and extend the operation area either by airlanding, or by sea in local craft commandeered on the Greek mainland and crewed by pressed civilians, mostly their luckless owners, many of whom were doomed to be killed by their own ally.

In detail the German final plan was for the Airborne Assault Regiment (Colonel Eugen Meindl) to take Maleme airfield, landing two companies in gliders on or

close to the runway and a small dominating height, Point 107 (held by a company of the 22nd Battalion). The parachute battalions were to be dropped so as to ring the positions of the 5th New Zealand Brigade to the east of the airfield. The 3rd Parachute Regiment (three battalions) of the 7th Air Division was to jump into Prison Valley, which air reconnaissance had shown to be undefended, accompanied by two gliderborne companies from the Assault Regiment, plus airborne engineer and light AA units, and then develop an attack north-west. This was to be under command of the divisional commander himself, Major-General Süssman, who would jump with the first wave.

Dispersed assault

In the second phase Colonel Sturm with his 2nd Parachute Regiment, less the 2nd Battalion, hoped to repeat at Retimo their success at the Corinth Canal bridge. The 1st Battalion was to attack the airstrip directly while the 3rd was to drop west of the airstrip and attack Retimo town from the east.

Above: A paratrooper examines the wreckage of a DFS 230 glider that has ended its landing-run up against the raised approach to a Cretan river bridge.

The initial assault on Heraklion was curiously dispersed, but it was not known to the German planners how tight a perimeter of good battalions had been drawn round the vital airport (a concrete runway and best on the island, as opposed to the dirt strips at Maleme and Retimo). Colonel Bruno Bräuer's 1st Parachute Regiment with Sturm's 2/2nd under command, was to jump (from left to right): the 2/2nd well west of the town, the 3rd rather closer in on its western outskirts, the 2nd 2 miles (3.2km) and the 1st 4 miles (6.4km) to the east of the airport, while the 1st had the crucial task of dropping on the airport directly and securing it as rapidly as possible. Here the dangers of compromise planning are seen. Student clearly wanted to put the weight on Heraklion, not Maleme, as the proposed development of his plan shows. As soon as the airfield was secure and the harbour accessible the

5th Mountain Division, less 100th Mountain Regiment which was earmarked to follow up success in the Canea-Suda Bay sector, was to come in by air and sea and the Heraklion sector would come under operational command of Lieutenant-General Julius Ringel, the division's commander. If Heraklion was so important, why was it not attacked in the first lift? But this and other speculations are irrelevant besides the command decisions and the hard fighting on which the outcome of the fierce battle about to begin were so narrowly to turn.

Sturdy resistance

What proved a terrible shock to the attackers in both phases was the strength of the defences and the violence of their reaction. Only the iron nerve of the German parachute commanders, from Student down, enabled them to survive and ultimately to overcome this. At Maleme the plan was to use 200 men of the glider battalion to land immediately east of the airfield and secure the bridge over a small river, and for the parachute batta-

lions to land west, south and east of the objective and along the beach north of the 5th New Zealand Brigade's positions. The drop was preceded by intense preliminary bombing by the strike aircraft of *Fliegerkorps* VIII. It was a near disaster. The glider detachment lost half its strength within a few minutes of landing and the battalion commander was wounded. Misjudgement on the part of the Ju 52 pilots, who were afraid that they might drop the troops destined for the beach in the sea, allowed too great a margin, and the bulk of the 3rd Battalion landed on the heads of the alert 21st and 23rd New Zealand infantry and the engineers. On the way down and at the helpless moment of landing the German parachute infantry came under intense and accurate rifle and machine-gun fire, the battalion commander being killed and 400 of all ranks killed or wounded out of 600. This left Meindl only the survivors of the glider troops and his 3rd Battalion as effectives, plus his heavy weapons battalion, to take on four unshaken and well dug in enemy battalions. He saw that the strength of the immediate airfield defence was Point 107, and imme-

diately ordered his 2nd Battalion, which had collected itself having dropped unscathed to the west, to send two companies to drive 'A' Company/22nd Battalion off it, while the glider troops dug themselves in on the airfield's western perimeter. Then Meindl was severely wounded.

The attack by the 3rd Parachute Regiment group in the Canea sector went rather better but was equally unsuccessful. Of the two other glider companies from the battalion in the Assault Regiment one was completely destroyed, but the other was able to round up the unarmed gunners of the field artillery battery. The engineer troops who had, so they hoped, landed in the clear in Prison Valley were roughly handled by the Greek battalion dug in there and lost some 100 men. The 3rd Battalion, with objective Galata village, was landed piecemeal and badly scattered and was briskly counter-

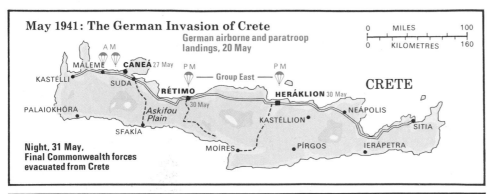

May 1941: The German Invasion of Crete
German airborne and paratroop landings, 20 May

Night, 31 May, Final Commonwealth forces evacuated from Crete

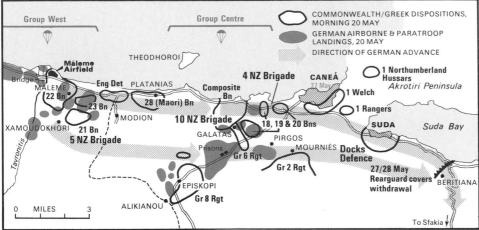

COMMONWEALTH/GREEK DISPOSITIONS, MORNING 20 MAY

GERMAN AIRBORNE & PARATROOP LANDINGS, 20 MAY

DIRECTION OF GERMAN ADVANCE

attacked, as were the remnants of the glider troops, by the Royal Marines. Its scattered remnants were told to rally on the 1st Battalion.

At Retimo the combination of a bad plan and a wildly dispersed drop was almost redeemed by the initiative of the commander of the 1st Battalion of Sturm's 2nd Parachute Regiment, aided by the very inaccuracy of the drop. The 19th Australian Brigade plus a Greek battalion were aligned along the high ground south of the coastal road with the 2/1st Battalion covering the airfield itself, and another Greek battalion 1 mile (1·6km) to the south. Major Weidmann's 3rd Battalion landed more or less in the clear, formed up and set off westwards for the insignificant objective of Retimo town, as ordered. Sturm and his regimental HQ fell on top of the 2/11th Australians and many were either killed or captured, losing the big radio set which was their rear link to Student. Two companies of the 1st Battalion landed close to the eastern edge of the 2/1st Australians position and although badly shot up courageously got to

Above: Paratroopers attack a smoke- and dust-enshrouded British position. Such positions were often lost because of poor medium-level command decisions.

grips with the Australians. Major Kroh, the battalion commander, and the rest of his battalion were scattered away to the east, fortunately, for they were able to assemble unhampered by enemy fire, and Kroh led them without delay into the attack on the 2/1st's position, gaining a foothold on the vital high ground overlooking the east end of the runway and repelling the Australian's immediate counterattacks.

Germans driven back

Colonel Campbell, the acting Australian brigade commander, however, was not to be denied his aim. 'Almost alone amongst the Allied Commanders in Crete,' says a leading British historian of airborne warfare, he realized that defence was not enough and he had to destroy the

enemy and to do this he must attack him. Early next morning he launched another attack which failed, but thinned out his other positions to raise another counterattack force and try again. He succeeded, driving Kroh off the vital hill. Then during the day he went over to the attack everywhere, taking a large number of prisoners including Colonel Sturm himself. The 3rd Battalion of the 2nd Parachute Regiment had run into unexpected resistance from the armed Cretan police defending Retimo and were pinned between them and the 2/11th Australians. Campbell's third battalion had been retained for the force reserve, and he simply lacked sufficient men to finish off the job completely. Nonetheless, in the Retimo sector the Germans were well beaten.

One consequence of relegating the attack on Heraklion to the second phase was that as the transport aircraft had to fly back to Greece, refuel, reload and fly back again to Crete, and the strict timetable became upset by inevitable delays: the time of fly-in was spread out and also fell behind the time programme of the

preliminary bombardments by *Flieger-korps* VIII, which seriously reduced their value. Like artillery preparation, the assault must follow the bombing closely and before the troops in the target area have had time to recover. The Black Watch noted with exactitude that the dive-bombing began at 1612, but that the drop, on a scale which staggered the onlookers, began at 1730. Part of the garrison of the defended areas, such as the Leicesters, were not hit at all. Like the other battalions of the 14th Brigade, the Black Watch were regulars, fresh, full of fight and good shots with good fire discipline. Two companies were sited at the eastern end and along the southern edge of the runway itself, and two more on the nose of a ridge commanding it from the south. Part of the 2nd Battalion, 1st Parachute Regiment dropped amid the fields at the western end of the runway, where they were received by a crossfire from C Company, the Black Watch and the 2/4th Australian Battalion, or below the ridge east of A and B Companies. Large numbers of Germans were written off by aimed fire which

killed the men in the air or on the ground before they could collect their weapons containers. The few who were able to form up were promptly counterattacked by the 2nd Leicesters. The Germans were surprised to find themselves opposed by Bren carriers and also by tanks, admittedly only two slow old 'I' tanks, but to which the parachute infantry without anti-tank guns were dangerously vulnerable. The 3rd Battalion was shot up by the York and Lancasters and by the Greeks dug in around Heraklion, but was able to form up and began to fight its way east into the town and to the harbour beyond it. Only the 2nd Battalion, 2nd Parachute Regiment, short of two companies still in Greece, and safely down west of Heraklion, and the 1st Battalion, 1st Parachute Regiment, miles away to the east, were unscathed, although they arrived late and spread out in time and it took both some time to develop an attack. In the meantime Brigadier Chappel counterattacked into Heraklion, where the defenders were assisted by the Cretan civilians – a notably tough and aggressive

breed – with such weapons as they could muster and the town was cleared. Chappel was later reinforced by the 1st Argyll and Sutherland Highlanders, who had been landed in the south of the island and had marched across to join him.

Poor situation

The outlook for the Germans, therefore, after the first day's fighting was extremely bleak, and it was to become bleaker still when ships of the Royal Navy, patrolling at considerable risk without air cover and under constant attack from *Luftwaffe* bombers, found the fleet of local craft on the night of 20–21 May on the way to Crete carrying the seaborne components of Ringel's mountain division, and sank them with great slaughter, the flicker of incessant gun-flashes out to sea being visible to watchers along the north coast. Those who escaped sinking turned back. This was not immediately known, nor could its consequences be assessed. Bleak as the German prospects were, the situation did not look exactly summery to the defence. General Freyberg was not a man to be easily daunted, but he was perhaps too conscious of the difficulties of his position, and there can be little doubt the constant hammering from the air and the spectacle of a sky full of hundreds of opening parachutes, the fact that all his garrisons were under heavy attack at once – just the impression Student, in defiance of the maxim of concentration, had wanted to give – and the difficulty of mounting a formal counterattack in force all weighed heavily on his mind.

Student's dilemma

Student was personally in an unhappy position. Having overborne his own commander's plan he had to succeed, and as far as he could find out everything had gone wrong everywhere. If his plan failed he, and the cause of airborne warfare, to which he was passionately wedded, were ruined. Heraklion had held. There was no news, which meant bad news, from Retimo where he had sent a staff officer in a light aircraft, in default of radio contact, to discover the situation and who had been promptly captured by the Australians. All he had left in the way of a parachute reserve was four companies, including two left over from the second lift for phase two. There was no secure point of entry open for the introduction of the mountain regiments. Student did not falter, and stories that he was contemplating evacuation or surrender seem to be without foundation. In his 'appreciation', if he ever reasoned so formally, the debits were perfectly clear, but so were his assets. The enemy guns, both AA and field, had been largely silenced. As for ground fire, had the defenders possessed some active batteries of 25pounders or 4·5in and 5·5in medium guns with radio control, observed indirect fire would have made Student's next move suicidal, but most of the botched-up battery of out of date guns in the western sector had been captured, or its crews shot down, although a few guns, gallantly served, remained in action. Above all, in *Fliegerkorps* VIII the attackers had a trump card to play against any counterattack by day. The only possible place where there seemed to be an opening was the Maleme airfield where the Assault Regiment had a finger-tip hold at the western end and also a lodgement at the foot of the commanding Point 107, and there the situation was confused, with the most senior surviving officer at Meindl's command post a captain, but one full of initiative who continued to attack.

Vital reconnaissance

Student sent a staff officer in a Ju 52 to test in the most practical manner if it was possible to land at the Maleme strip, and find out and report on the situation. As luck had it north-west of the runway there was flat, hard ground, mostly dead to the New Zealanders except those on Point 107. Captain Kleye landed successfully at

dawn, was briefed and took off again. Encouraged by this six aircraft with badly needed ammunition and resupply landed at 0800 on 21 May.

Student made his mind up. His *Schwerpunkt* – his point of maximum effort – must be switched from Heraklion to the Maleme sector. Half his last remaining parachute infantry were to drop well clear to the west of the strip and reinforce the troops trying to clear the airfield and the others about 2 miles (3·2km) east on the beach, with a view to taking the defenders of the airfield in the rear. A new commander whose name, Colonel Hermann Bernard Ramcke, was to become better known, was flown in to relieve Meindl and retrieve the situation. Once again the companies committed to the direct assault landed on top of the New Zealand defenders and only 80 survived, but they went to ground in a small village on the road between the airfield and Canea and were to prove a nuisance.

Then came the first stroke of luck, which seems so often to be the prize of boldness in war, to reward the weary attackers. At dawn there was silence from Point 107, and the German infantry at its foot, resuming the attack, found that the defenders had gone in the night.

Crux of the matter

The night of 20–21 May was the turning point of the whole battle of Crete. The air bombardment, the novel form of warfare, the absence of good communications and the presence of the scattered survivors of the 3rd Battalion, Assault Regiment, still aggressive and determined to make a nuisance of themselves, paralysed the defence. The defenders remained glued to the ground, and the flow of information and orders was so interrupted that it made rapid reaction impossible. What the Germans feared most, what they themselves would have done, and what the Australians did in fact do at Retimo, was not done: there was no strong, local counterattack back on to the airfield by the 21st or 23rd New Zealand Battalions, who had only 1 mile (1·6km) or so to go and that through ground still secured by the 22nd Battalion. East again were the Maoris. If

Above: A full medium machine-gun crew provides sustained fire support for an attacking unit with its MG34 mounted on a tripod for extra stability.

there was ever a moment for individual initiative it was then. Certainly the Germans feared more than anything else an immediate counterattack against their exhausted troops, who were tired, without water and running short of ammunition. It might at that moment have been possible to slam the third door, at Maleme, in Student's face.

Initiative lost

Instead the defenders pulled back, and a ponderous counterstroke was mounted, which involved moving two Australian battalions from the Retimo sector and a slow and deliberate hand-over of their responsibilities there. They were sent west along the coast road but, what with one thing and another, including clashes with parties of isolated parachute infantry, only two companies arrived, and these were finally blocked by the 80 men dug in around the village of Pirgos and they got nowhere near the airfield.

The commanding officer of the 22nd New Zealand Battalion had been uneasy about his task. He had been given not only the airfield but a much wider area to defend, some 2,000 yards (1,830m) from north to south, and to secure both the airfield itself and the commanding ground he had been forced to spread his companies out so far that they could not support each other and he had no reserve. He had had a hard fight all day on 20 May without any help from his brigade, and his counterattack to restore his grip on the west edge of the runway (and so effectively stop any adventurous landings by Ju 52s) had been made with only one platoon and two tanks, and had failed. He was only following an infantryman's sound instinct when he decided to withdraw slightly to contract and tighten his perimeter and to avoid his scattered positions being overrun one by one. In doing this he, fatally, abandoned Point 107 and all the positions from where aimed fire could be brought on the runway.

Above: A patrol of paratroopers moves cautiously up towards an olive grove under the protective cover of a typical Cretan dry-stone wall.

As soon as it was light on 21 May the *Luftwaffe* strike aircraft concentrated on the positions east of the airfield, effectively squelching any further attempts by the New Zealanders to restore the position. By the late afternoon it was possible to begin landing a battalion of the 100th Mountain Regiment. Crete was lost.

All through 22 May the airlift of the mountain division continued, with orders to the pilots to fly in and land regardless of crashes or of enemy fire, which continued, but perforce blind, from the surviving guns, whose numbers finally dwindled to zero under the remorseless battering from the air. Two more battalions were flown in and a deliberate attack commenced with an encircling movement to the south to cut in via the Prison Valley and into the Canea/Suda Bay defences from the south. General Ringel, now in command, had discerned that Galata village was the key of those defences, and was now the primary objective. Both the mountaineers and the paratroopers concentrated on it, but it took four days to reduce the position.

It was the strange feature of this battle that while the New Zealanders and General Weston's force were being ground down, Retimo and Heraklion were not only held, but their garrisons were on top of their opponents. Student, or to give credit where credit was due, Löhr, had either by luck or a good tactical eye, chosen the right place for the main effort, and when the western defences cracked, or were seen to be cracking, the Commonwealth troops in the western sector were ordered to pull out and make for the tiny harbour of Sphakia on the south coast. Fortunately for them the invaders were too tired to pursue effectively.

Evacuation ordered

The Australians and the British, completely in the dark about the course of the battle, heard the orders to abandon their

positions and evacuate the island with amazement and indignation. In fact it is doubtful that Colonel Campbell, the Australian commander at Retimo, ever received the orders at all. Many of his men were forced to surrender; others made for the coast. Colonel Sturm and a battalion's worth of men were released from the 'bag' as the Australians went into it; such was the irony of the battle. The Royal Navy took off the 14th Brigade (but not, unhappily, the Greeks, for whom there was no room) from Heraklion harbour. They were to suffer more casualties on the voyage to Egypt than in the fighting in Crete.

Dire losses

Of the Commonwealth forces 23,000, including 1,500 wounded, reached Egypt. In all 1,742 were killed, 1,737 were wounded and prisoners of war and 11,835 were captured. The Royal Navy lost *Greyhound, Gloucester, Fiji, Kashmir, Kelly, Juno, Imperial* and *Hereward,* and *Naiad, Warspite, Carlisle, Orion* and *Valiant* were among the 17 valuable ships badly damaged, all by air attacks by *Fliegerkorps* VIII pressed home with the utmost determination. For the British it was a great military disaster, made more painful by the fact that gradually emerged: only a hairsbreadth had separated victory from defeat and all the sacrifice of men and ships was wasted.

Above: During the mopping up operations on 31 May, German paratroops round up three British infantrymen unable to get to the evacuation beaches.

Useless, that is, in terms of immediate advantage but not in the long term. Crete effectively wrote off the German airborne arm. Of the 8,100 men of the 7th Air Division and the Air Assault Regiment who landed, a minimum of 1,520 were killed, 1,500 wounded, and 1,502 missing, a total of 4,522 or 56 per cent. The most severe battle casualties a good unit can tolerate is 25 per cent and 33 per cent is in effect a write-off until a major reorganization and reinforcement with fresh troops. The 5th Mountain Division, exclusive of those lost at sea, suffered 1,156 casualties, or about a third of those engaged.

After Crete Hitler would agree to no more airborne enterprises and his parachute troops continued to function only as elite infantry on the ground. The loss and gain of Crete, as it turned out, however, was only theoretically important, and had little effect on the final outcome of the war in the Mediterranean. There was one important consequence, though. What the Germans read as Pyrrhic victory, the British and the Americans read as a bitter but valuable lesson. Both armies began to organize powerful airborne forces of their own which were to play a vital part in the campaigns that lay ahead.

Paratroops at Cassino

If no other campaign had done so, the bitter battle for Cassino monastery would serve on its own to confirm the magnificence of the German airborne arm where defensive fighting was required. Here, under the command of General Heidrich, the 1st Parachute Division checked greatly superior Allied forces and then finally pulled back in good order.

As the new year of 1944 opened, Field-Marshal Albert Kesselring, commanding the German forces in Italy, could review the fighting of the last four months with considerable satisfaction. He had slowed down and halted the advance of the Allies since their invasion of Italy on 9 September 1943; German troops still stood firm in central Italy, dominating the peninsula from coast to coast and denying Rome to the Allied 5th and 8th Armies. And this autumn campaign was only the curtain-raiser. The real fight had yet to come, and it would be on ground of Kesselring's own choosing – the carefully-reconnoitred and strengthened positions of the 'Gustav Line' which dominated the Liri valley, leading direct to Rome, with the heights of Monte Cassino at the hub of the defence.

Since the Allies landed in Sicily none of Kesselring's units had seen harder or more successful action than the 1st Parachute Division of Major-General Richard Heidrich. From Sicily to the Gustav Line, Heidrich's men had been living proof of the paratroopers' inbuilt paradox: that, however they may be delivered to the battlefield, the true quality of airborne

forces is tenacity in defence rather than heroics in attack. By 1943 Heidrich's paratroopers, at least those who had survived the vicious fighting in Crete and Russia, certainly ranked among the world's experts in staying alive to fight again tomorrow, inflicting maximum damage and yielding minimum ground in the process, and generally making a nonsense of the numerical and material odds against them.

The Cassino problem

The 1st Parachute Division ended 1943 in the Adriatic sector, on the Sangro river front, whither it had withdrawn from Apulia before the advance of General Sir Bernard Montgomery's 8th Army. During the retreat the paratroopers had perfected the art of defending smashed villages and towns, using the principle that a heap of ruins creates splendid cover for the defenders while only adding to the problems of the attackers. During the fight for Ortona (20–27 December) the paratroopers blew up buildings to make their own ruins. It was the last time they would have to take the trouble for many weeks, thanks to sluggish strategic and tactical thinking on the Allied side. Churchill claimed that Ortona 'was our first big street-fighting battle, and many lessons were learned'. If they were learned at the time (and the evidence is scanty) they were certainly not applied during the three main battles for the Gustav Line at Cassino. Never have defending troops been given so many advantages by the clumsy errors of their opponents.

The Cassino fighting is best explained as follows.

To keep the Allies out of the Liri valley, and prevent them taking the *Via Casilina* (Route No 6) highway that runs up the valley to Rome, the Germans had to hold the commanding hills around Cassino, and Cassino town itself.

To crack the Cassino position, the Allies had to get the Germans off the hills. There were two ways of doing this: head-on uphill attacks with the Germans holding all the cards of tactical defence, or flanking manoeuvres through the hills which would compel the Germans to pull out. It was the choice between smashing a snail with a sledgehammer or easing it out of its shell. The Allies chose the former, landing themselves with 4 months of murderous losses for no result and achieving Kesselring's defensive strategy for him.

Kesselring's position at Cassino was

Below: Perched in the mountains overlooking Cassino town, the 1st Parachute Division had magnificent positions from which to fight its great defensive battle.

Above: Two men of the 1st Parachute Division gaze down into the Rapido valley. The view gives a good idea of the steepness of the slopes up which the Allies had to fight.

all front line and no reserves, particularly after the abortive Allied landings at Anzio and Nettuno in his rear on 22 January. He had constantly to shift 'fire-brigade' units from his best divisions from quieter sectors to the most desperately threatened ones; and it was in this capacity that the 1st Parachute Division entered the first battle of Cassino (17 January–18 February 1944).

By 15 January the Germans' withdrawal to the Gustav Line was complete and Lieutenant-General Mark Clark's 5th Army, generously reinforced from the 8th Army over on the Adriatic sector, was preparing to attack Lieutenant-General von Senger und Etterlin's XIV *Panzer* Corps and break into the Liri valley. Clark planned a three-stage assault, first against the German right (the coastal sector), then centre (the Rapido river) and as a last resort the left (the Cassino heights north of the Liri valley), beginning with the coastal sector attack on 17 January.

Verge of victory

By 24 January Clark had nothing to show for the first week's fighting but a shallow bridgehead across the Garigliano river on the coastal sector, and a bloody repulse on the Rapido. He ordered in the third attack: General Alphonse Juin's French colonials, backed by every avail-

able unit in the sector – American, British, New Zealand and Indian.

Their opponent on the heights north of Cassino was Lieutenant-General Dr Friedrich Franek's 44th *Hoch-und-Deutschmeister* Infantry Division, the 'High and Mighties', who had been severely knocked about in the preliminary fighting. After 10 days of incessant action the 44th Division began to crack, with American spearheads looking straight down on the Liri valley and preparing to tackle the last two obstacles: Height 593 (Calvary Mount) and Monte Cassino itself. Cassino town, also heavily assaulted, was now at the tip of a dangerous salient, at the edge of a deep dent hammered into the Gustav Line north of – and perilously close to – Highway No 6. By 5 February it seemed that the Allies were on the verge of a crushing victory.

Ad hoc defence

But over the next 10 days the balance tipped in Kesselring's favour. The Allied landing at Anzio on 22 January had failed to draw off troops from the Cassino front. On the contrary, the Anzio sector was now so secure that German units could be switched east to the Cassino front – and the first to arrive, in the nick of time to save the 'High and Mighties', were Heidrich's paratroops.

Kesselring had expected some kind of Allied amphibious operation, but when it came on 22 January (co-ordinated with the Rapido attack at Cassino) he was caught on the wrong foot. His forte, however, was always lightning reaction and

Above: A paratrooper typical of those who held Cassino monastery. He is young, fit, well trained, dedicated and more than adequately equipped in clothing and weapons.

this time he was doubly helped by excessive Allied caution.

To meet the Anzio threat Kesselring hijacked every available German unit in central Italy, from battalion strength to platoon – *Panzergrenadiers*, assault artillerymen, AA battalions (with or without

German Paratrooper, Casino 1944

A grounded eagle—this German paratrooper fighting in Cassino is wearing one of the later pattern camouflaged smocks, cut rather like a three-quarter length coat with press studs for gathering around the thighs. He is armed with the unique FG42, a P38 and a *Stielhandgranate*—stick grenade. At Cassino the German paratroops survived a very heavy pounding from artillery and tactical bombers and fought back with such energy that Hitler was moved to say that they fought better than the Waffen-SS. By 1943 they had been in action from Norway, via Holland and Crete to the Eastern Front and though they had no more major operational jumps after Crete, they had become an elite force.

their AA guns), heavy artillery sections, and reconnaissance, special duties, guards and headquarters platoons – and formed them into *ad hoc* battlegroups to rope off the Anzio beach-head. They included a battle group from 1st Parachute Division (Group Schulz) and another, Group Gericke, from a new 'parachute division' which had not been in existence a month before.

The 4th Parachute Division, commanded by Major-General Heinz Trettner, came into being in January 1944 largely through the example set by the 1st Parachute Division in the previous months' fighting. *Luftwaffe* field divisions and ground organizations provided the raw man-power, with veteran survivors from Holland, Belgium and Crete as the foundation. Four days before Anzio, Lieutenant-Colonel Walter Gericke was ordered to hold three battalions of his most experienced troops ready for 'fire-brigade' duties, and with this advantage in readiness the 4th Parachute Division was in position on the western sector of the beach-head by the 26th. It took part in the furious attempts to drive the invaders back into the sea which began on 3 February and continued until 1 March, when Kesselring accepted that his motley collection of forces could do no more and reverted to siege tactics.

But even before the Anzio counter-attack began, the position there was clearly so secure, and that at Cassino so desperate, the Group Schulz was with-drawn and rushed east into the battle for the Cassino heights.

Paratroops arrive

The paratroops entered the Cassino fighting in the second week of February. They came in the nick of time, for Calvary Hill had already changed hands twice. But on 10 February Major Kratzert's 3rd Battalion of the 3rd Parachute Regiment flung the Americans off Calvary Hill again – and this time this key feature was to remain in German hands until May.

Newly arrived from the Anzio front, Group Schulz was pasted like a wafer on the precipitous slopes dropping down to the Liri valley. Lieutenant-Colonel Karl-Lothar Schulz's men (1st Machine-Gun Parachute Battalion) had no depth, let alone prepared positions; above all they were barred, by Kesselring's order of December 1943, from occupying terrain within a 437yard (400m) circle outside the walls of Monte Cassino abbey on the top of its hill. Yet they held the lower slopes and halted all American and Indian attempts to clear the heights and plunge down into the Liri valley. Meanwhile the exhausted 'High and Mighties' were pulled out and replaced by the 90th *Panzergrenadier* Division and the 1st Parachute Division, with the groups of Kratzert and Schulz already in position as the latter's advance guard.

The sudden stiffening of the German defences in the Cassino salient caused by the arrival of the paratroops had fatal results for the abbey. It seemed to confirm the Allied commanders in their totally erroneous belief that German forces had occupied the abbey – the best vantage-point in the whole sector – and were using it as the cornerstone of their defence.

Lieutenant-General Sir Bernard Freyberg of the New Zealand Corps flatly refused to attack Monte Cassino until the abbey had been bombarded, and the result was the brutal and senseless destruction of the abbey on 15 February, which enabled the Germans to fight the Allies to a gory standstill and emerge with their front severely dented but intact.

Allied blunder

The bombing certainly shook the defenders of Monte Cassino, but it was not followed up at once by a massed attack. What it did do was convert the abbey into a sea of rubble and craters with the outer, massive walls still partially intact – perfect for defence by the paratroops with their high allocation of light and heavy automatic weapons. The paratroops easily coped with the gallant but lightweight attacks of 16–17 February (Freyberg did not attack until 18 hours after the bombing, and then only with 6 out of his 24 battalions); and on the 18th General Sir Harold Alexander, commanding the Allied forces in Italy, called off the battle to re-group and reinforce for a second assault after a bombardment 'worthy of the name'.

Above: Germans in the ruins of the monastery, whose destruction by totally misguided Allied bombing gave the paratroops the makings of superb defensive positions.

The ensuing lull enabled Heidrich's division to complete its takeover of the 8mile (13km) Cassino sector, and, moving largely by night, to begin to construct proper fire positions. Colonel Ludwig Heilmann's 3rd Parachute Regiment took over the defence of Cassino town, Rocca Janula to the north-east, and Monte Cassino itself, aided by the 2/8th 3rd *Panzergrenadier* Division. Major Grassmehl's 4th Parachute Regiment took over Calvary Hill and Colle Sant'Angelo, with Schulz's 1st Parachute Regiment further out to the north-west.

The division's order of battle included the 1st Parachute Reconnaissance Section (one wireless and one telephone company) and the 1st, 3rd and 4th Parachute Regiments. Each of these had a pioneer platoon, a cycle platoon, a mortar company and an anti-tank company supporting its three infantry battalions, each made up of three rifle companies and a machine-gun company. In addition there

Above: Paratroops in a forward position at Cassino watch for any signs of activity that might herald yet another Allied attempt to winkle them out of the area.

was the 1st Parachute Artillery Regiment (three batteries of 7·5cm mountain guns and three of 10·5cm light paratroop guns); the 1st Parachute Pioneer Battalion (three pioneer companies and a machine-gun company); and the 1st Parachute Anti-Tank Section (four motorized 7·5cm anti-tank gun companies and one 7·5cm self-propelled anti-tank gun company). Finally there were the 1st Parachute Machine-Gun Battalion of three machine-gun companies and the Parachute Medical Section of two companies.

Classic resistance

Worn down as it was after 220 days of continuous action, the 1st Parachute Division nevertheless retained a high percentage of firepower which paid full dividends when the second phase of the Cassino battle opened on 15 March. In this the Allies compounded all their previous errors and reverted to classic World

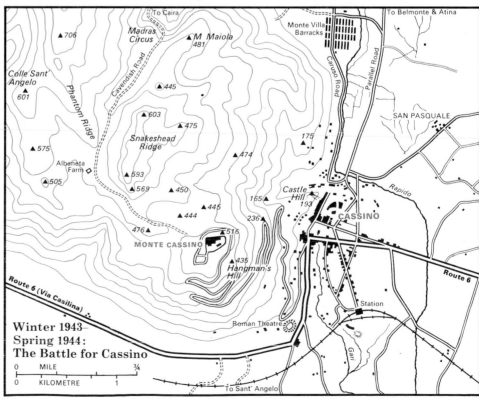

Winter 1943– Spring 1944: The Battle for Cassino

War I sledgehammer bombardments. The results were exactly the same as on the Somme in 1916. The unbelieving assault troops found the surviving defenders still in position and as deadly as ever with their machine-gun and artillery fire.

On 15 March Heidrich's men endured the biggest mass raid delivered by the Allies in the Mediterranean theatre: 750 fighter-bombers, medium and heavy bombers dropped at least 1,250 tons of bombs into an area 1,500 by 500 yards (1,640m by 545m), followed up by an artillery bombardment of nearly 200,000 shells from 746 guns. Only one company from the 2/3rd Parachute Regiment was left intact to halt the New Zealanders' push into the choked, heaped ruins of Cassino town.

Below: A paratrooper and lavish equipment, including an FG42 automatic rifle (in use), a sub-machine gun (probably an MP40/I) and two crates of 'stick grenades'.

This time, however, the monastery ruins were left untouched and the summit remained in German hands.

The fighting down in the ruined town was a murderous affair: a troglodyte war waged amid ruined cellars and tottering walls. Obsessed with clearing the town, Freyberg continued to neglect Monte Cassino. After a week most of the ruins of Cassino town were in Allied hands but there was no question of a breakout along the choked Route No 6. The German front was still intact; and on the 22nd Alexander called off the assault again.

The paratroopers in the front line had suffered terribly. Companies were down to handfuls of survivors and scanty reinforcements could only be got through at night. But despite casualties of nearly 50 per cent (well over this in the case of the 2/3rd Parachute Regiment) the paratroopers not only held on but ended '2nd Cassino' by hitting back, with local counteroffensives against Rocca Janula

and the centre of Cassino town, over which they reestablished control.

The second lull at Cassino (23 March–11 May) saw the failure of the Allied bombing offensive, Operation 'Strangle', to prevent wide-ranging German troop redeployment and reinforcement both at Cassino and Anzio. The 4th Parachute Regiment took over the front-line defence of Cassino town and Monastery Hill. Almost incredibly, however, Heidrich's division was weakened by having one-third of its manpower weeded out and packed off to France as nucleus troops for new units forming there. This left the 1st Parachute Division with only two understrength battalions per regiment, each battalion with an average strength of 200–300 men. But no changes were made to the division's firepower in anti-tank guns and artillery, which remained high.

1st Parachute holds out

For his third Cassino offensive, Alexander hauled the bulk of the 8th Army across to Cassino and radically overhauled his strategy. This time the main effort would be made against the German right, with Juin's French colonials making an enveloping breakthrough across the hills. The assault on town and abbey would be made by General W. Anders' II Polish Corps, making its debut. There was to be no repetition of the huge air bombardments which had failed so dismally in the first two Cassino battles.

The story of the last act is briefly told. Between 11 and 17 May the 1st Parachute Division repulsed every attack launched against it while the German front col-

Below: Paratroops wait in the courtyard of a counting house on 21 April 1944 to make a counterattack. Note the machine-gun with its ready-use belt, and 'ammo box'.

lapsed spectacularly to the south. Not an Allied soldier set foot on the summit of Monastery Hill until the paratroops pulled silently out on the night of 17–18 May to escape certain encirclement. In the ensuing fortnight, as the German 10th and 14th Armies escaped annihilation as a result of the American preoccupation with Rome, the 1st Parachute Division served as the 10th Army's rearguard, savagely punishing every 8th Army unit that came within reach during the long retreat to the Gothic Line in the north.

The very best

The superb stand of the Cassino paratroops ranks the 1st Parachute Division with the toughest fighting units known in military history. They were the best, the hard-core professionals, who were prompt to exploit every extra card dealt them by Allied ineptitude. All the units they defeated at Cassino – the 4th Indian Division, New Zealand Corps, British 78th Division, US 34th Division and Polish II Corps – were high-quality troops themselves.

The paratroops of Cassino fought the model defensive battle and emerged from it undefeated. But the men who did it were irreplaceable and their loss – as the German paratroop arm had already experienced after Crete – could not be made good, certainly not in the 12 months of life remaining to the Third Reich.

Right: British infantry make use of a temporary lull to rush forward. The man nearest the camera is carrying a .45in Thompson submachine gun.

Below: Although most of the 1st Parachute Division, or what was left of it, got away at the end of the battle, some units were taken by the British, Indians and Poles.

Defeat in the West: the Last Paratroop Operations

With Germany forced ever more on the defensive from 1943 onwards, the elite airborne formations found that they were increasingly used in a 'conventional' role as high-grade infantry, charged with the holding of key areas such as Brittany and its ports, or 'fortresses' such as Breslau. Only in the Battle of the Bulge were they used, disastrously, as airborne forces.

By June 1944 the bulk of the *Wehrmacht* stood on the defensive in western Russia, looking apprehensively over its shoulder in anticipation of the inevitable Allied landings in France. There was no question that the Eastern Front remained top priority: by 6 June 1944 there were only 59 divisions in the West to the 157 in the East. But troops would have to be found

from somewhere to defend the new Western Front when it was opened, and *Luftwaffe* ground forces were only one of many sources to be greedily rifled in the creation of new 'armies', 'corps', 'divisions', and 'brigades', most of them far under their paper strength and with little value in combat.

The new 'parachute divisions' were different. They had rather more than the memories of remote victories to sustain them. The *esprit de corps* of the German airborne arm was higher than ever in 1944 and this was largely due to the exploits of the superb 1st Parachute Division at Cassino. Another new parachute division, the 4th, had been hastily formed in January 1944 and had also done well, at Anzio. As Hitler and his sycophants continued to lose touch with military reality, they could at least point to the successes at Cassino and Anzio and claim that further experiments with new 'parachute' units were worthwhile. For once, events were to prove them correct.

Veteran of Crete

By the spring of 1944, with Field-Marshal Erwin Rommel, commanding in northern France, on the Atlantic coast moving heaven and earth to create viable defences against the coming invasion, it was decided to repeat the recent successful creation of 4th Parachute Division to bolster the garrison in France. In the lull before the final storm at Cassino – 23 March to 11 May – the three magnificent regiments of 1st Parachute Division were denuded by a third to provide nucleus troops for the new units in France.

The new II Parachute Corps was com-manded by Lieutenant-General Eugen Meindl, a veteran of Crete, and consisted of the 2nd, 3rd and 5th Parachute Divisions. It was stationed in Brittany to help defend the Atlantic ports and act as reserves for the Normandy sector – but this role certainly reflected the tendency of the *Wehrmacht* high command, by 1944, to draw false parallels with earlier successes, stick flags in maps and try to forget the real position. Field-Marshal Albert Kesselring had been able to whisk his troops about like magic at Anzio and Cassino largely because the distances were short (about 100 miles/160km at most) and

Below: A scene typical of the confused fighting in the Ardennes during the 'Battle of the Bulge', where the Germans last used their airborne forces as such.

the Allies did not know how to use their air power to stop him. But Meindl's corps would have to cover at least 200 miles (320km) from Brittany to the invasion sector. It would find this very difficult because it had no transport, let alone protection from the comprehensive Allied air programme aimed at slowing down German reinforcements.

Within 48 hours after D-Day in Normandy, II Parachute Corps was under orders to quit Brittany for Normandy. Rommel wanted it to plug the ominous gap opened between the British and American spearheads (Caen/St Lô), but by 10 June Meindl only had one regiment, the 6th, east of St Lô. The rest of the division was still struggling eastward out of Brittany. It failed to arrive in time to prevent the American investment and capture (29 June) of Cherbourg, but the corps – the bulk of the 3rd Parachute Division plus 352nd Infantry Division – was finally in the line on the western beach-head sector, entrusted with the defence of the vital road junction of St Lô.

Ideal terrain

The terrain north of St Lô was ideal for defence: the *bocage* country, a mesh of high banks topped with hedges that cancelled out nearly all the massive American advantages in manpower and *matériel*. By 18 June the Americans had pushed to within 5 miles (8km) of St Lô; it took them precisely a month, until 17 July, to crawl forward until Meindl's paratroops and infantrymen were threatened with encirclement in the ruins of St Lô. Then, and only then, Meindl asked for permission to withdraw just to the south of St Lô, immediately bringing the Americans to another frustrating halt.

This was a splendid piece of work by any standards, and it shook the Americans. St Lô cost them nearly 6,000 dead, and their enemies were still very much in the field. 'The Germans haven't got much left, but they sure as hell know how to use it,' was one grudging tribute. '[They] are staying in there just by the guts of their soldiers' was another. St Lô, June–July 1944, certainly ranks with Cassino among the last battle honours of the German airborne arm.

Paratroops bypassed

Lieutenant-General Omar Bradley, the American 12th Army Group commander in western Normandy, was as deeply impressed by the defence of St Lô as his combat commanders. It was no accident that 'Cobra', the breakout operation launched the week after St Lô was taken, was aimed west of II Parachute Corps' front. Bradley was looking for rapid results from a narrow-fronted assault, and the painful crawl towards St Lô had led him to search further west for easier opposition as well as faster terrain.

'Cobra' was a runaway success, flooding down the seaward coast of the Cotentin peninsula and reaching Avranches, 50 miles (80km) to the south, in a week (25–31 July). But the exultant Americans, though on the move at last, were unable to widen the breach inland. II Parachute Corps held fast, a pillar of solid resistance like

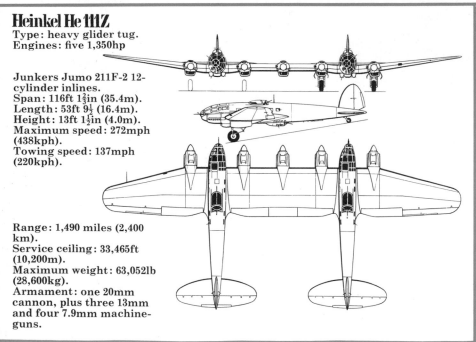

Heinkel He 111Z
Type: heavy glider tug.
Engines: five 1,350hp

Junkers Jumo 211F-2 12-cylinder inlines.
Span: 116ft 1⅔in (35.4m).
Length: 53ft 9½in (16.4m).
Height: 13ft 1½in (4.0m).
Maximum speed: 272mph (438kph).
Towing speed: 137mph (220kph).

Range: 1,490 miles (2,400 km).
Service ceiling: 33,465ft (10,200m).
Maximum weight: 63,052lb (28,600kg).
Armament: one 20mm cannon, plus three 13mm and four 7.9mm machine-guns.

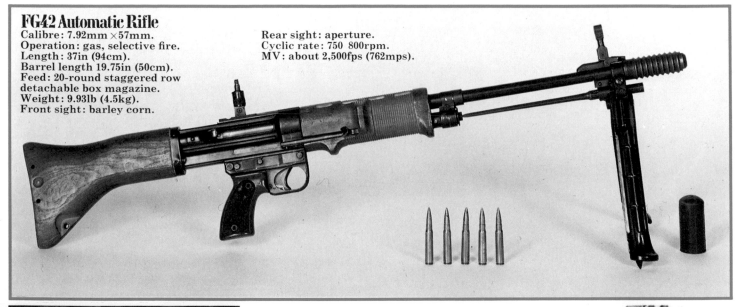

FG42 Automatic Rifle
Calibre: 7.92mm ×57mm.
Operation: gas, selective fire.
Length: 37in (94cm).
Barrel length 19.75in (50cm).
Feed: 20-round staggered row
detachable box magazine.
Weight: 9.93lb (4.5kg).
Front sight: barley corn.

Rear sight: aperture.
Cyclic rate: 750 800rpm.
MV: about 2,500fps (762mps).

Above: Major-General Hermann
Ramcke commanded the excellent
2nd Parachute Division in the
hopeless defence of Brest against
vastly superior US forces.

Left: Seen here in conversation with
Field-Marshal Erwin Rommel,
Lieutenant-General Eugen Meindl
(right) commanded II Parachute
Corps.

Above: General Meindl, always keen
to gain personal experience of his
men's weapons, tests an anti-tank
grenade against invasion obstacles
on the French coast during May 1944.

the 1st Parachute Division at Cassino,
creating the conditions for a *Panzer*
counterstrike westward through Mortain
aimed at sealing off the breach. But after
repeated attempts made on Hitler's in-
sistence (7–11 August) the venture was
abandoned.

This was the last achievement of the
German paratroops in the struggle for
Normandy.

In the following week, II Parachute
Corps was engulfed by the vast American
double-envelopment, east from Avranches
and north from Le Mans, which trapped
the chaotic remnants of seven German
corps in the Falaise Pocket. Meindl's
paratroops began to withdraw from the
western edge of the pocket on 16–17
August, but their cohesion dissolved in
the carnage and *sauve-qui-peut* after the
Allies partially sealed off the pocket on the
19th.

Against a background of 10,000 counted
German dead and 50,000 POWs, the 3rd
Parachute Division was one of the 10
trapped divisions that was wiped out as a

fighting force in the Falaise Pocket.
Ironically, the very success of the paratroops in defending the St Lô axis with
such tenacity had contributed no little to
their own final destruction.

As the bulk of the American forces
wheeled eastward from Avranches, two
US corps pushed west into Brittany, their
objective the Channel and Biscay ports
through which the 'Overlord' forces might
be supplied.

The siege of Brest

After II Parachute Corps quit Brittany
for Normandy, General Wilhelm Fahrm-
bacher was left with a scattering of static
forces with which to defend the Breton
ports. Their role was grim and simple:
hold out as long as possible, destroy the
port facilities when the time came and
deny the Allies those ports. To defend
Brest he made the masterly choice of
Major-General Hermann Bernard
Ramcke, one of the toughest leaders produced by the German airborne arm, and

his 2nd Parachute Division, which Ramcke
had forged into a formidable fighting unit.

Ramcke was immensely helped by the
resolute defence of St Malo by General
von Aulock, who did not surrender until
17 August, tying down a whole division for
over a week with only 12,000 men. As St
Malo was wrecked before the surrender,
the Americans had no choice but to push
on to Brest and try to eject Ramcke's
garrison.

The siege of Brest began in earnest on
25 August, by which time the 2nd Parachute Division had been reinforced by the
266th Division from Morlaix, giving
Ramcke some 35,000 combat troops. He
also had the benefit (a surprising phe-
nomenon in modern warfare) of massive
stone defences of mediaeval vintage, plus

a hard core of paratroops who knew all about street fighting and mediaeval defences from their experience in Italy.

Even the 15in guns of the battleship *Warspite*, brought up to pound the German positions, failed to bring about a rapid solution. Ramcke's men made the battle for Brest a miniature version of Stalingrad and Cassino rolled into one, with every room of every building a strongpoint. 'Fortress Brest' held out until 18 September. Like the 6th Army at Stalingrad it had fulfilled its duty nobly, in this case keeping over 50,000 US troops pinned down more than 300 miles (480km) behind the main front. With the Allies already halted on the frontier of the Reich, the ruins of the town and harbour of Brest were an utterly useless acquisition for them.

Ramcke's defence of Brest was the last operation by a cohesive German airborne division on the Western Front. As far as the German airborne arm was concerned, the last months of the war added up to a story of frantic improvization, deluded expectation of performance, and constant, foredoomed failure.

Above: The LG 40 recoilless gun on its wheeled carriage. In action, the LG 40 rested on a tripod mounting (see page 55) made up of the three trail legs. The carriage of the otherwise similar LG 1 had spoked rather than disc wheels and two trails.

As the Allies approached the frontiers of Germany and Holland, Colonel-General Kurt Student's 1st Parachute Army was created. A ragbag of 'odds and ends' from all over north-west Europe and Germany, it was an army only in name and a 'parachute army' in even less. Allocated to Army Group 'H' in Holland on 4 September, within a fortnight it was in action at Arnhem, where it played an emphatic second fiddle to the SS *Panzer* units in smashing General Sir Bernard Montgomery's airborne gamble. Student was forced to watch helplessly as the awesome tug and glider fleet roared over his HQ, and to lament 'Oh, if I'd ever had such means at my disposal.' After Arnhem, the 1st Parachute Army retreated steadily over the Rhine and across northern

Germany. Its grandiloquent title reflected the syndrome which in 1943 had created Army Group *'Afrika'* only when the German and Italian forces were penned helplessly in the Tunisian bridgehead.

Gamble in the Ardennes

The last actual operation by German airborne troops was reserved for that supreme gamble: the Ardennes offensive of December 1944. Colonel Friedrich-August von der Heydte was intended to drop with 800 paratroops and cut all roads menacing the advancing *Panzer* troops from the north. It was a night drop, badly executed over unsuitable terrain in the early hours of 16 December, and it was a fiasco. Only 300 confused paratroops met at the assembly-point; their only radio was smashed, depriving them of contact with the main forces; and they were forced to hide, watching impotently while three American divisions rolled right through their position. The scattered troopers were soon rounded up and von der Heydte himself was captured on the 18th.

Utter failure though this was, the reputation of the German airborne forces was still so high that a 'paratroop scare' was flashed to all Allied units coming to grips with the crisis around the 'Bulge'. Unfounded reports of new paratroop drops added mightily to the chaos and confusion of the first week in the Ardennes. And so it was that this last fiasco – although, this time, there were no actual reports of paratroops disguised as nuns – did resurrect a flicker of the triumphs of 1940 and 1941. The decisive difference was that by December 1944 the German ground forces had already lost the war.

Right: German paratroops, armed with sub-machine guns and a *Panzerschreck*, plus rifles, pause to look at a knocked-out tank.

FG42 Automatic Rifle

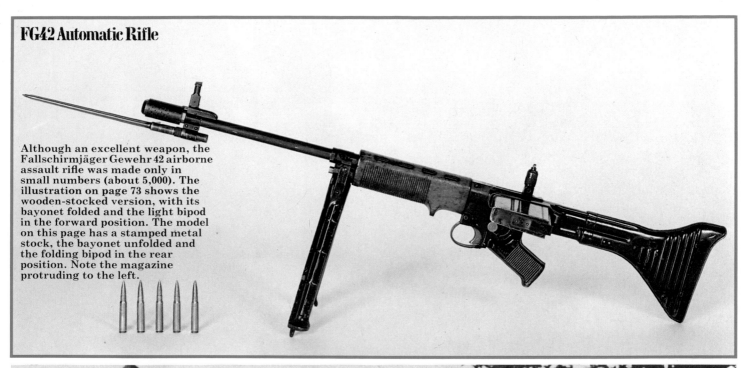

Although an excellent weapon, the Fallschirmjäger Gewehr 42 airborne assault rifle was made only in small numbers (about 5,000). The illustration on page 73 shows the wooden-stocked version, with its bayonet folded and the light bipod in the forward position. The model on this page has a stamped metal stock, the bayonet unfolded and the folding bipod in the rear position. Note the magazine protruding to the left.

Tunisia 1943

The first Allied use of airborne forces on any scale took place after the 'Torch' landings of November 1942. Lack of practical experience and any real concept of how to use airborne forces reduced their effect considerably, however, and they were wasted in useless operations that caused high casualties but did provide invaluable tactical information.

The seaborne invasion of Morocco and Algeria, codenamed 'Torch', took place in November 1942 while the 2nd Battle of El Alamein was still raging. The Allied aim was to take the Axis forces in Tripoli and Libya in reverse and so between Alexander's and Eisenhower's commands to secure the whole African shore of the Mediterranean and clear the way for the invasion of Europe from the south. The operational goal was the north-east tip of Tunisia, where there were the good all-weather airfields outside Tunis and the naval base and port of Bizerta, and the prize would be carried off by the side who could arrive there first. Given that both sides

were equally efficient and determined, as they were, the brief campaign was really a competition between two troop movement schedules.

The Allies had a long haul by sea and then, for political reasons as well as the need for avoiding the Axis air threat, they were forced to land at points hundreds of miles to the west of their objectives. In consequence the Tunisian task force, initially two British infantry brigades reinforced by British and American armoured units, were faced with a long approach march. By contrast the Germans had only the short sea and air crossing from Italy and a still shorter distance to

go to establish a defence line far enough to the east to secure their supply ports, like Gabès, where the local French garrison, officially neutral, attempted a *coup* on behalf of the Allies. At Gabès the German troops simply landed in Ju 52s on the airfield after preliminary bombing and successfully suppressing the French. German parachute troops did indeed fight with distinction in Tunisia, notably their 5th Parachute Regiment under Lieutenant-Colonel Walter Koch and the parachute engineer battalion commanded by Major Rudolf Witzig, but the German reaction to the Allied advance on Tunis, speedy as it was, was merely a conventional manoeuvre using air transportation.

On the Allied side the nature of the problem presented to Eisenhower and by him to Lieutenant-General K. A. N. Anderson,

Below: Men of a British airborne unit prepare to repack one of their camouflaged parachutes. On the whole, though, such units operated as high-grade infantry.

the commander of the British 1st Army, offered valuable rewards for the correct use of parachute troops in the 'seize and hold' role. This conclusion was not easily reached. There had been a great deal of strenuous debate about the utility of airborne forces, much of which, especially in Britain (where there was a natural propensity to view any new idea with suspicion and also the reluctance of the Royal Air Force to be distracted for any reason from offensive air operations) centred on the provision of suitable aircraft. The consequence was that instead of forward planning there was delay, which led to inadequately trained pilots and lack of jumping practice and of exercises in the whole business of mounting airborne operations. Certainly in 1943 some sections of the planning staffs of all the services had but the haziest notions of what airborne troops could achieve or how they should be used, which led in Africa to the mishandling of the British 2nd Parachute Battalion and severe and unnecessary casualties. Nevertheless, these difficulties were overcome, in England by the persistence of Winston Churchill, in the forces committed to 'Torch' by Eisenhower, and in the field by the high qualities of the parachute troops and their leaders.

Basically four separate airborne missions were carried out by the battalions which took part in the operation, the first being one by the 2nd Battalion, US 503rd Parachute Infantry Regiment.

One of the perplexing factors of 'Torch' was the possible reaction of the French authorities in North Africa. Many French-

Above: Intense concentration marks the faces of American paratroopers on their way by Douglas C-47 transport from Algiers towards a combat jump in Tunisia.

men felt that they still had a score to settle with Nazi Germany, but officially the two countries were not in a state of war and the Allied invasion was a serious breach of neutrality and a *casus belli*, likely to be resisted by force by the French. The role of Lieutenant-Colonel E. D. Raff, commanding the 2/503rd, was to capture an airfield near Oran using alternative drop zones according to whether his reception was friendly or hostile. He was despatched in 39 Douglas C-47 aircraft from England to fly the 1,500 miles (2,400km) to his target, and navigation was such that the lead pilot, in whose aircraft Raff was flying, at the end of the journey knew only that he had hit the African coast broad on the beam. Such was the adaptability of US pilots and the ruggedness of the C-47, however, that Raff was, unbelievably, able to land, enquire the way to Oran and take off again. He then led his stream of aircraft to the target airfield, but being greeted by anti-aircraft fire wisely turned away to his alternative DZ, the dry bed of a salt lake or *sebkra*, where his fleet landed. In fact it was almost out of petrol, but an advance party of three aircraft was sent off to attempt a drop on another airfield, secured by the seaborne forces but under French attack, while Raff set off leading the rest of his battalion on a forced march on

foot. French resistance soon crumbled, but sadly not before their over-zealous fighters had shot down the three C-47s attempting the drop.

The 3rd Battalion of the British 1st Parachute Brigade, also carried in C-47s of the USAAF all the way from England, had a less adventurous journey via Gibraltar and landed at Algiers, from where it mounted an operation to seize the small but useful harbour at Bône and the adjacent airfield, some 300 miles (480km) nearer Tunis. (The correct title for the battalion is the 3rd Battalion, The Parachute Regiment, the British having decided to create a distinct new regiment from the volunteers for the new service. Battalions for the glider brigades were drawn from the county regiments and retained their ancient titles, as did the units of Royal Artillery and Royal Engineers, even though trained and used as paratroops.) The Bône operation went smoothly without any opposition from the French, although there were a number of casualties due to accidents on landing. There was a belief at the time that the Germans were on the way to jump on the same objective, which would have provided an interesting confrontation.

Left-right punch

The next airborne operation was designed to assist the dash for Tunis by the British 78th Infantry Division and its attached American and British armoured units. The plan was for one brigade to advance by the northern route via Mateur and another farther south via Medjez-el-Bab and the Medjerda valley, while the little armoured task force moved between them to strike right or left depending on the success of the flanking brigades. The 78th Division could not use its full strength but it was the most the road network and the logistics could support. Nevertheless, the force pushed forward boldly; the US 1/1st Armoured Battalion, equipped only with light tanks, alone and unsupported, motored to Djedeida, 20 miles (32km) from Tunis and shot up 37 German aircraft on the airfield there. In riposte the Axis commander on the spot, General Walther Nehring, pushed out his own troops as they arrived from Italy out in small hastily assembled battlegroups to seize key points like the bridge at Medjez-el-Bab with equal speed.

A harassing force

The part of the British 1st Parachute Battalion in the plan was to fulfil what might be termed the 'cavalry' role of bygone days: to go as far forward as possible to meet and harry the enemy's advance guards and act as a screen for their own. Lieutenant-Colonel J. Hill (later to command a parachute brigade in Normandy) was ordered to seize the road junction and airfield at Béja, contact the French garrison there and establish friendly relations and with them then to act as he saw fit.

Preliminary planning and preparation for airborne operations in Tunisia was virtually non-existent: both the air and the army staffs seemed to believe that all that was necessary was to pack some para-

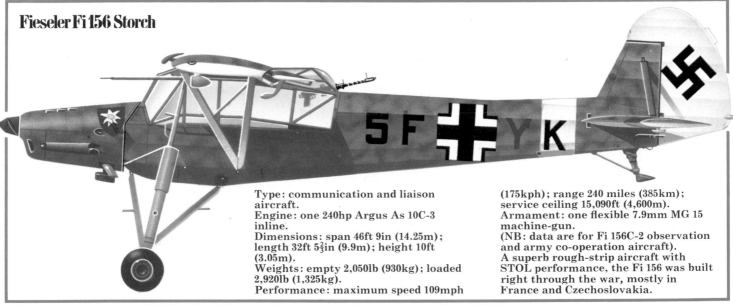

Fieseler Fi 156 Storch

Type: communication and liaison aircraft.
Engine: one 240hp Argus As 10C-3 inline.
Dimensions: span 46ft 9in (14.25m); length 32ft 5⅜in (9.9m); height 10ft (3.05m).
Weights: empty 2,050lb (930kg); loaded 2,920lb (1,325kg).
Performance: maximum speed 109mph (175kph); range 240 miles (385km); service ceiling 15,090ft (4,600m).
Armament: one flexible 7.9mm MG 15 machine-gun.
(NB: data are for Fi 156C-2 observation and army co-operation aircraft).
A superb rough-strip aircraft with STOL performance, the Fi 156 was built right through the war, mostly in France and Czechoslovakia.

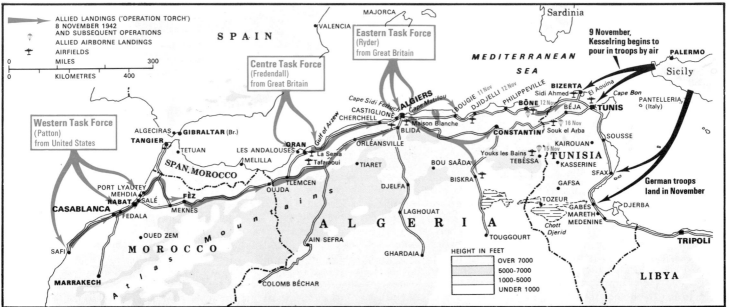

November 1942: the Dash to Tunisia

chute soldiers into an aircraft and despatch them into the blue. The USAAF pilots had no notion of what was required and had never attempted a tactical drop: they were a purely passenger and cargo carrying force. There were no maps and no one had bothered to check on the Tunisian weather, which by November was vile. At the first attempt the aircraft were turned back by dense clouds and rain over the mountains. On 16 November the battalion was flown off again with orders to drop where they could and march to Béja on foot. Mistrusting the navigational ability of the pilots, Colonel Hill ordered them to fly in line astern while he guided the leading pilot by visual map reading, using a quarter-inch French motoring map. He intended to choose the DZ himself from the air, and as soon as the following aircraft saw him jump they were to despatch their sticks to the same area.

Hill found a suitable DZ at Souk-el-Arba in the Medjerda valley. There the French proved more than friendly and gave Hill's men a great welcome, lending the battalion some motor transport for the 30 mile (48km) journey to Béja. There again the French commander rallied to the Allies and Hill made this his base for a series of daring little operations which, had it been possible to follow up in strength, might

have shortened what was to prove a long and dour campaign.

Hill's chosen area was the Béja-Mateur road and he moved out to Sidi Nsir where he obtained as an ally a company of West African French colonial infantry. The first contact with the enemy was with an armoured patrol of three armoured cars and three scout cars which were skilfully ambushed by Major Cleasby-Thompson with two of his platoons and

Above: American troops move with great caution through a Tunisian town, wary lest the Germans should have left any snipers in concealment to hamper the Allied advance.

some parachute Royal Engineers. The road was mined with the small man-portable Hawkins devices, with other sappers in hiding ready to push out some more in rear of the last car as soon as the

first had struck, and a fire party of Brens and a mortar, carefully sited, as were two officers ready with Gammon bombs (simple bombs of plastic explosive with a time fuze and an adhesive cover used against armour or for small demolitions) to attack from close range, crouched in the road-side ditch, one so close that he was wounded by the explosion. The whole German patrol was killed or captured and a scout car taken intact. This little success and the whole of this phase indicates both the high degree of training of the British parachute infantry – ambushing requires both skill and strict discipline – and the emphasis on irregular or commando-type warfare; later the airborne troops were to be used more conventionally and in large formations able to play their part in a major battle.

Airborne panache

Another patrol was less successful, but memorable for the subsequent exploits of a prisoner the battalion lost there, who escaped in Italy to bicycle to Rome and take refuge in the Vatican City. A more ambitious operation was a night attack on a small outpost near Sidi Nsir manned by German and Italian troops, in prepared positions strengthened by three light tanks, also dug in. A silent approach was betrayed by an accidental explosion of the mines carried by the sappers, and heavy firing broke out, much of it in the German practice of that time with tracer bullets, which revealed the weapon pits. A combined charge by the British and French Senegalese, put in immediately on Colonel Hill's order, carried the position. Two of the tanks surrendered to the imperious Hill's knocking on the turret with his walking-stick, as did two of the crew of the third, but the last man out, a German, refused and shot down Hill and one of his captains at short range with a pistol. The German was bayoneted for his pains, together with his companions. Both British officers were severely wounded, but survived. The resourceful paratroops found a motorcycle and sidecar into which they put the two officers and drove them along

the railway track 11 miles (18km) to the battalion medical aid post.

The rest of the patrol exploits of the battalion read more like adventure fiction than sober operational reports. There was no front line behind which to operate, the area being dotted with small units of both sides, and the 1st Battalion took full advantage of this situation. Its patrols penetrated deep into enemy-dominated areas in small numbers – on two occasions only a solitary officer – ruthlessly shooting and killing enough of the enemy to tie up numbers of men in local guard duties, but suffering ambushes and casualties in their turn from their equally tough opponents. On 25 November the battalion came under the orders of the armoured task force and continued in a normal infantry role.

In the end the dash for Tunis failed, if only by a narrow margin, and after the return of the survivors of the 2nd Parachute Battalion from their operation no more airborne operations were attempted and the whole brigade was used to hold the line.

Unfair judgement

Sober military historians tend to regard the early phases of this campaign as an example of muddle, lack of foresight, hasty improvisation and the dissipation of effort in all directions. This is unfair. The one approach to Anderson's mission which would have guaranteed ignominious failure would have been a long delay to make meticulous arrangements and build up a force level to avoid all risk. The 1st Army plan was the boldest and therefore the best in the circumstances. Nevertheless there were moments when boldness became reckless gambling, and when this was compounded with poor staff work and poor intelligence it proved costly and to no unit was it more costly than to the 2nd Parachute Battalion, commanded by Lieutenant-Colonel John Frost.

By late November the 10th *Panzer* Division had almost completed its assembly of 100 tanks and was ready to counterattack in strength on 1 December. On the Allied

Above: The Douglas C-47 military derivative of the DC-3 airliner was one of the Allies' most useful aircraft in World War II, serving in a multitude of capacities.

side, the British decided to try to force the Tebourba gap, just west of Tunis, on 29 November, using only one battalion of infantry and one of US Grant tanks. This hopelessly inadequate force made barely any ground as the tanks were halted by the effective German anti-tank artillery. On the same date Frost was ordered to drop in daylight out in the blue at a deserted airfield at Depienne, and from there march to another airfield at Oudna and destroy the aircraft and stores there, presumably with a view to covering the attack at Tebourba, although this could have been done more economically by the very strike aircraft detailed to cover the fly-in of the C-47s. How so stupid a plan came to be made remains a mystery, but the parachute commanders characteristically attempted it without question. After this Frost was expected to march west or north-west and join the ground troops who, it was hoped, would be advancing on Djedeida. As it turned out the airfield was deserted and non-operational, but not unoccupied: a reception committee of tanks was waiting for the battalion.

Gruelling march

Frost followed Hill's example in travelling in the lead plane and navigating until he could see a suitable DZ, when he jumped with his stick as the signal for the rest to follow him down. The battalion then set off on a gruelling march which lasted all night, carrying all the 'clobber' of the parachute soldier plus rations for five days, listening meanwhile to the calling of the Arabs in the villages passing the news of their progress along, whence it reached the Germans. (It is the Arabs' custom to shout the news from hamlet to hamlet, or from field to field. The Parachute Regiment heard these cries as 'Ho--o--o--o Muhammed!' and adopted the words as a battlecry). Frost reached Oudna airfield

SAS Officer, Tunisia 1942

This bearded Lieutenant in the Special Air Service sports the wings peculiar to the regiment on his shirt. He is armed with a .38 in Webley and his belt has a battered holster, ammunition pouch and compass pouch. Despite his comfortable mix of issue and native dress, including tank crew gauntlets, he has suffered from the almost inevitable desert sores and bandaged his left knee. The beard and the sores were the result of living without water in a dry and dusty environment. The armed Jeeps in the background include twin Vickers K machine-guns, with their distinctive 96-round flat pan magazines, and large numbers of German and American Jerricans of fuel and water.

Messerschmitt Me 321

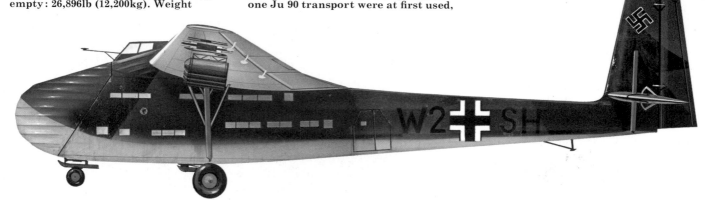

Type: heavy transport glider. Power-plants: up to twelve 1,102lb (500kg) rocket-assisted take-off units under the wings. Span: 180ft 5½in (55.0m). Length: 92ft 4¼in (28.15m). Height: 33ft 3½in (10.15m) on take-off dolly. Towing speed: 137mph (220kph) with He 111Z tow aircraft. Gliding speed: 87mph (140kph). Payload: 130 troops or up to 21,500lb (9,750kg) of cargo. Weight empty: 26,896lb (12,200kg). Weight

loaded: 86,860lb (39,400kg). Armament: two 7.92mm MG15 machine-guns, plus two 7.92mm MG34 machine-guns when in use as a troop transport.

The Me 231 was one of the largest aircraft of World War II. It was designed in 1940, and made its first flight in March 1941. To tow the glider, three Bf 110 twin-engined fighters or one Ju 90 transport were at first used,

though later the five-engined He 111Z composite aircraft was used. The A and B series differed only in cockpit layout, the latter allowing for two pilots. Extensive RATO arrangements were possible.

---

in the afternoon, driving off some infantry and then coming under fire of four medium tanks in addition to attack by aircraft. The strip was empty of aircraft; even its 'buildings' proved to be hayricks. He could raise no one on his rear-link radio. Frost accordingly withdrew a short distance and set up a perimeter defence, where at least he could rest his men, tired by 24 hours of marching and fighting. Next morning the radio came alive and Frost was told that the Tebourba attack had failed. He was now faced with a 50 mile (80km) rear-guard action, entirely on foot, without artillery or anti-tank weapons except the almost useless Boys rifle and with no means of calling for air support, while pursued by a mechanized column of all arms. Indeed at that very moment his position was being reconnoitred by armoured cars and at about 1000 a typical German battle-group of tanks and lorried infantry hove in sight. After some skirmishing and being heavily mortared it withdrew to mount an organized attack. The German commander returned a captured British NCO with a suggestion that Frost should surrender, a suggestion which he naturally refused. His present position was untenable, however, and with great skill he broke contact and withdrew in daylight – a most difficult manoeuvre – and re-established himself on a commanding ridge farther back. From 1500 to dusk he was strongly attacked by tanks with artillery support, standing his ground but losing a company. Unfortunately for the German attackers the direct air support they summoned mistook the target and bombed and strafed their own side, which afforded the defenders a welcome relief.

Fighting retreat

At 1830 that evening Frost once again was able to slip away across country, but was forced to leave 150 wounded behind with his battalion medical officer under the care of an armed guard to protect them from the Arabs, who were hostile to the French and their Allies and, moreover, had the barbarous habit of murdering and stripping the wounded. The going was very

difficult, but this at least was equally an obstacle to the pursuers, who stumbled after them, eventually to find the battalion once more in a close perimeter defence round a farm where it had been forced to halt from sheer exhaustion. There it sat tight, surrounded, and on Frost's orders holding its fire until the expected assault. This materialized late in the evening and was repelled at close range with Sten gun fire and showers of bombs. When it was dark the survivors were concentrated and on a blast from Frost's hunting horn – his highly individual means of signalling – burst out of the ring and began their retreat once more to reach Medjez-el-Bab and the Allied positions without further contact with the enemy the next evening. Sixteen officers and 250 NCOs and other ranks were killed

Above: British infantrymen help unload paratroopers' equipment from a C-47. Note that only half of the double cargo door has been opened for the small items visible.

or wounded or missing, leaving 180 undaunted effectives. A small number of resolute men, some wounded, escaped either by stealth or by killing their guards and rejoined later.

Wasted opportunity

Such was the unnecessary little epic of the 2nd Parachute Battalion. The operations in Tunis marked the end of the wildly amateur attitude of the planning staffs, who confused the potentially decisive role of the new arm with raiding and clandes-

Above: Paratroops check their jump equipment en route to Tunisia by C-47 Dakota. Static-line drops from the Dakota were slightly dangerous because of the small size of the door and its proximity to the tail.

Left: Although the paratroopers arrived from England by air, their heavier equipment and supplies arrived over the landing beaches together with everything else. This operation is near Algiers.

tine operations behind the lines. The air-borne assault in Sicily was to be marred by serious faults in execution, but at least it was conceived as a proper operation of war and an integral part of the whole land-air plan.

The Airborne Assault on Sicily

The scene for the first major Allied airborne operations of the war was Sicily, where Allied paratroops and gliderborne troops were given important tasks in Operation 'Husky' in July 1943. But lack of experience and forethought resulted in a near disaster, redeemed only by the flexibility and courage of the troops, and the lack of real Axis power in southern Sicily.

By May 1943 two full airborne divisions had been assembled in Tunisia: the US 82nd, commanded by Major-General Matthew B. Ridgway, and the British 1st, commanded by Major-General G. F. Hopkinson. Both were elite formations with officers of the highest quality in command positions from the top down, as the subsequent careers of men like Ridgway himself, Gavin, Lathbury, Hackett and Frost were to show. A great deal of argument and inter-Allied rivalry was to bedevil the planning for Operation 'Husky', as the invasion of Sicily from the African mainland was codenamed, but one decision seems to have been clearly decided from the beginning: the airborne forces would play a full part closely coordinated with the main forces. The mission of the US 82nd Airborne Division was to block off any immediate counter-attack against the US beaches while the landings were being consolidated, always the most dangerous moment of an amphibious operation. Thereafter it would provide a reserve. The British role was more ambitious: it was to seize and hold bridges lying on the axis of the 8th Army's northward advance.

Allied plans

The ground plan (itself not finally settled without violent differences in opinion, not only between the Allies but between rival services) was in essence for the US II Corps of Lieutenant-General George Patton's 7th Army to land on the south-western shore of the island, and for the leading divisions of XIII and XXX Corps of the renowned 8th Army under General Sir Bernard Montgomery to land astride Cape Passero and in the Gulf of Noto. Once the bridgehead had been secured, the 8th Army was to swing north and thrust along the coast with objective Messina, while the Americans took the minor but important role of a measured advance to cover Montgomery's left flank.

There were also disagreements among the airborne forces, and between them and the planning staffs. The British were in the disagreeable position of being largely dependent on the Americans for air transport. The RAF was reluctant to deflect bombers or their trained aircrews in any quantity to airborne warfare, so the resources of the US Troop Carrier Command had to be shared.

The British Lieutenant-General F. A. M. 'Boy' Browning, the nominal commander and adviser on airborne forces, was frustrated because General Hopkinson tended to ignore him and to deal direct with the imperious Montgomery to plan his side of the operations. When the commander of the British glider pilots (army personnel) expressed his well-justified doubts on the proposed method of using his gliders, he was told to comply or accept dismissal.

Once more, insufficient time was given to combined training of the troops and aircrews and glider and Douglas C-47 pilots. This was a serious deficiency as the pilots of the Troop Carrier Command, USAAF, were able only to fly from field to field in peace conditions, ignorant of operational flying, and quite unable to navigate accurately in the dark and not very well by day if away from easily recognizable landmarks. Many pilots did not maintain the rigid course and altitude for a successful drop when faced by anti-aircraft fire.

Inherent faults in troop training cannot be corrected by written orders for their discontinuance, but only constant practice backed by discipline until the correct reaction to danger when under stress is second nature is effective. This applied not only to the pilots but to the crews of land and naval anti-aircraft artillery, whose fire discipline, judged by the standard achieved later, was lamentable.

Shortage of transport

These were some of the disadvantages, inevitable perhaps, when the armed forces of two allies attempt for the first time anything so complex and dangerous as a combined operation against a coast held by a first-class enemy equipped with armour and an unsubdued air force. On the credit side was the excellence of the troops and the formulation of a plan designed to use them concentrated in the maximum numbers the air resources would allow and one closely linked with the ground forces.

There was sufficient lift for two brigades. On the American side the role allotted to Colonel J. Gavin's 505th Regimental Combat Team of three infantry battalions, with attached artillery (equipped with the 75mm light airborne howitzer) and parachute engineers, was to drop behind the centre of II Corps' landing beaches in the area of Gela. Gavin's mission was to secure the Piano Lupo, hold off any counterattacks and hang on until the units from the beachhead could join him.

Initial fiasco

Hopkinson's mission was to land the two battalions of his 1st Airlanding Brigade (1st Borders and 2nd South Staffords) on or near the road to Syracuse, the first of the 8th Army's objectives. The bridge at Ponte Grande was to be captured by a *coup-de-main* group carried in ten gliders, while the rest of the brigade landed on a suitable landing zone (LZ) 2 miles (3·2km) away with the tasks of consolidating the hold on the bridge, dealing with a nearby coast artillery battery and advancing on Syracuse. The link up with the 8th Army vanguards was planned for 1000 on D-day, 10 July. The landings, like those of the 505th Regiment, were to be under cover of darkness. The subsequent tasks of the 1st Airborne Division would be similar and planned on a contingency basis as the advance of the 8th Army dictated.

The airborne troops were concentrated around Kairouan in Tunisia, where they were served by a cluster of airfields on which were based the 51st and 52nd Troop Carrier Wings of XII Troop Carrier Command. Each division at that time consisted of two parachute brigades or regiments and one airlanding brigade or regiment, each of three battalions (although the British were a battalion short), so virtually there were four brigades of excellent infantry in reserve for the whole enterprise.

It is sad to relate that from the airborne point of view the operation began as a fiasco and ended in disaster. Equally, it is inspiring to relate that it was redeemed by the extraordinary initiative and courage of the airborne soldiers themselves, who in fact did almost all they were asked to do. This was also to be the saving of the airborne operations in Normandy 11 months later.

The 505th Regiment began its flight at 2200 on the night of 9 July, 3,400 strong, carried in 226 C-47s of the 52nd Troop Carrier Wing flying in threes in V formation in groups of three Vs, a long column of nine abreast. Only the leading aircraft in each nine carried a competent navigator, the rest following the leader. The drop zones (DZs) were to be identified by eye from air photographs: no pathfinder parties dropped by skilled navigators, light markers or radio beacons were to be used. For one reason and another direction was lost and the regiment was dropped all over southern Sicily, a spread of 65 miles (105km). Only some 200 men were dropped on the Piano Lupo; Colonel Gavin was himself dropped some 30 miles (48km) from his correct destination. Many of the 505th Regiment were badly injured by being dropped too low on rough ground in the high wind that had sprung up in the night. Some men eventually found their way back, but many others were captured. The commanders, however, wherever they landed, collected groups of men, rallying more after it was daylight, and set about seeing what mischief they could do. The commanding officer's group of

Below: A Sicilian airfield, with the crew of a 40mm anti-aircraft gun standing watch over a C-47 transport awaiting attention on the runway in July 1943.

the 1st Battalion found itself near a forti- fied farmhouse deep in enemy territory with a garrison of 60 men and took it by assault with grenade and tommy-gun. Other parties captured, or took part in the capture of Ragusa, Noto and Avola, the last actually in the 8th Army sector. Another group harassed an anti-aircraft battery. One impudent lieutenant on being taken prisoner convinced his cap- tors that their best course was to surren- der, which they did, but those were Italians, whose heart was not in the fight; the vil- lagers were all turning out to welcome their liberators. The Germans were by contrast their usual formidable selves. On the Piano Lupo the 200 men dropped in the right place made a remarkable stand against the German armoured counter- attack. One of the airborne howitzers actually engaged and destroyed a *PzKpfw* VI Tiger firing direct. As far as is known, this is one of the few, if not the only in- stance of the little 75mm M116 engaging a tank, but the *Panzers* were in fact stopped partly by direct fire from the field artillery landed on the beaches but chiefly by some astonishingly accurate and concentrated shooting by the guns of the US Navy. As far as the plan was concerned, the 505th Regiment achieved something short of their official objective, but their wide- spread aggression certainly confused the defenders for some time about the weight and direction of the 7th Army's thrust.

Inaccurate drop

The next American airborne phase was completely disastrous, and can be briefly told. It was decided on 11 July to reinforce the American bridgehead by dropping the whole of the 504th Regimental Combat Team of the 82nd Airborne Division on territory already gained in the bridge- head. Every step was taken to ensure that the naval guns and the anti-aircraft artil- lery ashore would hold their fire. Orders were widely disseminated, General Ridg- way himself visited the island in advance to warn artillery units and the aircraft were routed through a known corridor, 2 miles (3·2km) wide at an altitude of 1,000 feet (305m), running east to west along the coast. These precautions were all in vain. During the day of the drop, 11 July, the anchorage had been under heavy air attack, ships had been sunk or damaged and nerves everywhere were stretched. When the first flights came into the gun-defended area at about 2340 they were allowed to pass safely but then as the sky seemed to fill with hundreds of planes, the crew of a single gun on one ship fired a few shots and in a surge of panic the whole fleet opened up. The casualties were bad enough. Of 144 aircraft 23 were destroyed and 81 men were killed and 148 wounded or missing. Some men were shot down after landing by their own side under the impression that they were part of a German airborne counterattack, but worse, once again the resultant scatter in landing wasted the effort. Only one company and one light battery landed on the correct DZ and by the evening of the 12th only 37 officers and 518 men had been assembled.

The two battalions of the British 1st Airlanding Brigade suffered similar mis-

Willys Jeep

The Willys Jeep was one of the Allies' most important 'weapons' in World War II, and served in a wide variety of roles. It had a capacity of up to four men, a speed of 55mph (89kph) and a range of 225 miles (362km).

fortunes. The pilots of the tug aircraft were sufficiently off course between their check point at Malta and their release points to have a 25-mile (40km) lateral spread from Cape Passero to Cape Murro di Porco. In addition there was a strong westerly wind of some 30 knots (56km/h) which would cause the gliders to land short if slipped at the planned points, which were over the sea; in addition to which anti-aircraft fire made frighteningly visible by tracer undoubtedly deterred a closer approach to the coast. Sixty-nine gliders landed in the sea and some 500 men were drowned.

Only one glider of the *coup-de-main* party landed accurately near the Ponte Grande. In it were Lieutenant Withers and his platoon of the South Staffords.

Undaunted by the fact that the only other glider to arrive had crashed on landing and blown up killing everyone on board, Withers gathered his platoon, ordered half to swim the river and then assaulted the bridge garrison, who were Italians, from both ends. In half an hour he was in possession and had lifted the demolition charges. Daylight brought reinforcements as parties from the scat- tered gliders marched to their objective and from then on a weak company held off the counterattacks of an Italian bat- talion until it was down to 15 unwounded men without ammunition, also without artillery or air support. (Close air support for ground troops at that date was slow, crude and primitive in both the Allied armies and air forces.) Withers' platoon was overrun at 1530, however. A bare hour later the leading battalion of the 8th Army hove in sight and recaptured the bridge, intact.

Battle for Primasole

The 8th Army rapidly broke through the crust of the coastal defences, never very strong. The 7th Army had drawn the main weight of the German armour, the greatest threat to the landings, away from

Right: Container-dropping apparatus under the centre-section of a C-47 Skytrain transport receives careful attention from US airborne personnel in North Africa.

the east coast and on to itself. The British 50th Division was now advancing against only light opposition, but it was about to run into trouble. It was faced by a tough German battlegroup and no less than the German 1st Parachute Division, which was dropped on 12–13 July accurately and compactly behind the Axis line of defence on the plain south of Catania. The line of the Simeto river and the important bridge at Primasole were firmly held. There a confrontation was to take place between the parachute troops of both sides, for the

Right: US paratroopers check their equipment before moving off to their transport aircraft. Note the weapon bag over the left shoulder of the man on the right.

Armstrong Whitworth Albemarle

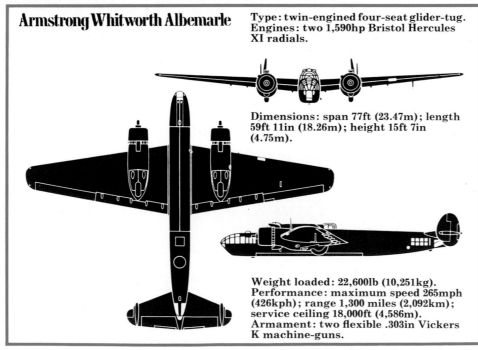

Type: twin-engined four-seat glider-tug.
Engines: two 1,590hp Bristol Hercules
XI radials.

Dimensions: span 77ft (23.47m); length
59ft 11in (18.26m); height 15ft 7in
(4.75m).

Weight loaded: 22,600lb (10,251kg).
Performance: maximum speed 265mph
(426kph); range 1,300 miles (2,092km);
service ceiling 18,000ft (4,586m).
Armament: two flexible .303in Vickers
K machine-guns.

8th Army plan called for the British 1st
Parachute Brigade to capture the bridge
at Primasole which lay on its main axis to
its next objective: Catania.

Brigadier Gerald Lathbury's plan was to
seize the bridge itself on the night of the
13th by direct assault, using the 1st Parachute Battalion and a squadron of the
Royal Engineers, while the 3rd Parachute
Battalion eliminated a neighbouring anti-
aircraft battery and established itself to
the north of the bridge and the 2nd Parachute Battalion on commanding ground to
the south. The 1st Airlanding Anti-Tank
Battery, Royal Artillery, was to be brought
in by glider, as close to the bridge as possible. This would present the enemy with
a solid defence on the bridge itself and

against an attack from either direction,
but it was essential to the plan that the
British 50th Division, advancing from the
south, should join up with them without
delay during the next morning and so
open the road to Catania, which Montgomery hoped to reach before German
resistance had time to stiffen.

Lathbury's force was carried in 96 aircraft of the 51st Troop Carrier Wing and
11 Armstrong Whitworth Albemarles of
the RAF, 17 of the powered aircraft towing
gliders. The 21st Independent Parachute
Company was to precede the force and
mark the glider LZs and position radio
beacons ('Eureka-Rebecca') for the DZs.
The USAAF pilots had been persuaded to
abandon their rigid formation of 'Vs of
Vs' in favour of a loose stream as used by
Bomber Command, but this placed too
great reliance on individual navigators
who were not up to the task, with the awful
consequence that the stream became
badly scattered after passing the check
point at Malta. Then a number of aircraft
were seen by the light of a three-quarter
moon by the gunners of the Royal Navy
flying off course through a 'Gun Free'
area where the supporting fleet was

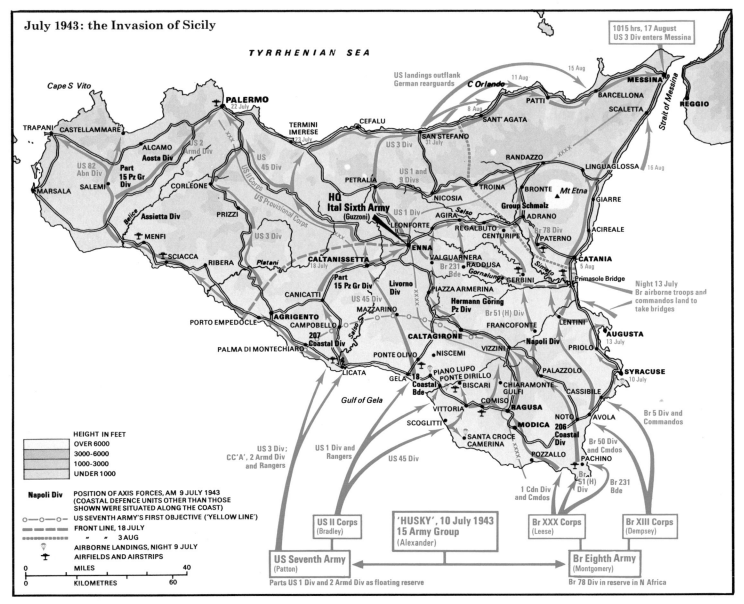

TYRRHENIAN SEA

1015 hrs, 17 August
US 3 Div enters Messina

US landings outflank
German rearguards

Night 13 July
Br airborne troops and
commandos land to
take bridges

HEIGHT IN FEET
OVER 6000
3000-6000
1000-3000
UNDER 1000

Napoli Div POSITION OF AXIS FORCES, AM 9 JULY 1943
(COASTAL DEFENCE UNITS OTHER THAN THOSE
SHOWN WERE SITUATED ALONG THE COAST)
○─○─○─ US SEVENTH ARMY'S FIRST OBJECTIVE ('YELLOW LINE')
━ ━ ━ FRONT LINE, 18 JULY
············ 3 AUG
⚐ AIRBORNE LANDINGS, NIGHT 9 JULY
✈ AIRFIELDS AND AIRSTRIPS

MILES 40

KILOMETRES 60

US II Corps
(Bradley)

'HUSKY', 10 July 1943
15 Army Group
(Alexander)

Br XXX Corps
(Leese)

Br XIII Corps
(Dempsey)

US Seventh Army
(Patton)

Br Eighth Army
(Montgomery)

Parts US 1 Div and 2 Armd Div as floating reserve

Br 78 Div in reserve in N Africa

---

anchored near or standing off and on the 8th Army beaches. The aircraft were instantly engaged. Eleven aircraft were shot down, 39 achieved a reasonably accurate drop, 48 dropped wide, some as far off as Mount Etna, the pilots having lost their bearings after taking violent evasive action, three crashed. Only four gliders arrived safely and 26 pilots decided, prudently perhaps, to return to base. At least their elite troops survived to fight again and were not dropped so low that their parachutes did not open properly, or into the sea.

Confused fighting

Altogether some 540 men of the brigade had arrived safely in the area of the objective, including Brigadier Lathbury and Lieutenant-Colonels John Frost of the 2nd Battalion and Alastair Pearson of the 1st, with some sappers and three 6pounder anti-tank guns. Captain Rann, who had collected 50 men of the 1st Battalion, correctly judged his task, ignored his original orders and rushed the bridge, and when Lathbury and Frost arrived with some 40 men with the same goal it was already secure and the sappers were removing the demolition charges.

There was a good deal of confusion. The brigadier was wounded during an exchange of grenades when a lorry seen dimly in the dark proved to contain the aggressive crew of an 8·8cm *Flak* gun limbered up, and there were a large number of Italians eager to surrender milling about. Most of the command radio sets were missing or not working and Lathbury was not in touch with the 50th Division or with Frost, who was in fact digging himself in on his correct objective, having found another of his companies there. There was no sign of the 4th Armoured Brigade, which was leading the advance of the 50th Division and on whose timely arrival the success of the whole operation depended.

In the meantime the Germans reacted with their usual admirable speed and skill in the face of an emergency. The German 4th Parachute Regiment was by this time south of the river, some joining the armoured battlegroup facing the 50th Division, while others set themselves to recapture the bridge. Lathbury, although wounded, remained there observing its defence by 120 men of the 1st and 3rd Battalions under Pearson. Frost, with his battalion headquarters and one of his companies, was firmly in position, Lathbury discovered. The German attack developed from the south side of the river, and for some time the skeleton 2nd Battalion was hard put to hold its ground, being gradually hemmed in on three sides and kept under heavy fire. Fortunately Frost had with him his naval bombardment liaison officer, Captain Vere Hodge

of the Royal Artillery, whose radio set was intact, so when the German attack developed it was engaged by the accurate and devastating fire he was able to call for from the 6in guns of HMS *Mauritius,* which broke it up completely. While the position of the 2nd Battalion continued to be painfully harassed by enemy fire from mortars and armoured cars, no more attacks were pressed against it for the rest of the day.

Heroic defence

The defenders of the bridge were attacked first by fighter aircraft, then infantry and tanks and subjected to continuous mortar and artillery fire. As casualties mounted Pearson had to concentrate his unwounded men at the southern end. Some of his people were ensconced in the concrete pillboxes built as part of the bridge defences. They were only driven from these when the German gunners, in the bold way they would handle artillery, brought up an unwieldy 8·8cm *Flak* gun to engage them at close range over open sights, while the paratroops replied with small arms to pick off the crews. 'I swear that as each round solid shot struck it [the pillbox] it heeled over and bounced up again,' recalled one officer. It could not last. Lathbury who, although wounded had remained in command, ordered that at nightfall the survivors should dis-

Sten Mk 1 Sub-Machine Gun

Calibre: 9mm. Operation: blowback, selective fire. Length: 35.25in (89.5cm). Barrel length: 7.75in (19.7cm). Feed: 32-round detachable box. Weight: 7.8lb (3.5kg). Front sight: barleycorn. Rear sight: fixed aperture. Cyclic rate: 540rpm. Muzzle velocity: 1,280fps (390mps). The Sten Mark I was adopted in 1941, and was an easy to manufacture but effective sub-machine gun.

Sten Mk V Sub-Machine Gun

Data are the same as the Sten Mark I with with the following exceptions—Length: 30in (76.2cm). Barrel length: 7.8in (19.8 cm). Weight: 8.5lb (3.86kg). Cyclic rate: 575rpm. Note the wooden stock and pistol grip.

SMLE No 4 Mk 1 Rifle

Calibre: .303in (7.7mm). Operation: turn bolt. Length: 44.43in (1.13m). Feed: 10-round detachable box magazine. Weight: 9lb (4.1kg). Front sight: protected blade. Rear sight: adjustable aperture. Muzzle velocity: 2,465fps (751mps).

engage and slip back to the vicinity of Frost's position. This they managed to do, and the little party sat out the night wondering how the 4th Armoured Brigade were faring.

No relief

The brigade, with its attached battalion of the Durham Light Infantry, was in fact resting in harbour no more than 1 mile (1·6km) away! The German capacity for defence among the narrow lanes, broken ground and stone walls of Sicily was immense, as they were to demonstrate repeatedly on the Italian mainland and in the Normandy *bocage*, while the 50th Division and the tank regiments were the tired and wary veterans of the long desert campaign, determined to advance only step by step with caution and maximum covering fire. Its commanders were severely criticised for remaining active that night when their infantry could have reinforced Frost, or even reached the vital bridge in time, but in all fairness they could claim they had marched 20 miles (32km) and fought most of the way. Fortunately the airborne engineers had disposed of the demolition charges so thoroughly that they could not be replaced and the bridge remained intact. It was, however, now firmly in the German grasp.

Next morning Lathbury, hearing the sounds of tanks, went back himself on foot and brought them and the infantry up to mount an attack on the bridge, which was repulsed, but they were able to keep the bridge under fire. That night Pearson himself guided the Durham Light Infantry across the river at a point upstream and they were able to take the defence in reverse, so by 14 July it was in British hands

once more, but too late. The chance of pouring an armoured brigade across it on to the plain of Catania had gone. Montgomery had to switch his main axis of advance and Catania eventually fell, not on 13 July as he had hoped, but on 5 August.

Airborne arm disbanded?

So many mistakes had been made that voices were roused, certainly in the United States, to advocate disbanding the airborne divisions, but on analysis it was

Above: A scene typical of World War II airborne operations—C-47 glider-tugs prepare to pick up their tows, in this case Waco CG-4 Hadrians, at Comiso in Sicily.

not the concept but the staffwork and inter-arm co-ordination that had been at fault. The correct decision was to read the lessons of Sicily and obviate the faults. This was supported by Eisenhower, with results that were to be seen in Normandy.

US Airborne Soldier, Sicily 1943

This soldier from the US 82nd Airborne shows the sort of load that was worn by American troops who jumped during World War II and Korea. With no leg bag they were obliged to carry weapons, ammunition and personal kit with them—in addition to the main and reserve parachutes. Their parachutes, however, were less porous than the British ones and also larger, so letting their owners down more gently. The wearing of knives or bayonets attached to the ankle, though an additional hazard when landing, did allow the soldier to reach a knife reasonably quickly if he had to cut himself free from a parachute tangled in a tree. The Germans incorporated a pocket in their trousers for a special gravity blade knife. The distinctive insignia of the 82nd Airborne Division can be seen.

The Airborne Assault on France

The Allied invasion of France in June 1944 made daring and large-scale use of airborne forces: in the west the US 82nd and 101st Airborne Divisions, and in the east the British 6th Airborne Division. These three formations had vital tasks, and despite the serious handicaps of a night drop and considerable dispersion, most of the units achieved their missions.

No operation of war in military history has ever been prepared with such thoroughness as the invasion of German-occupied France in June 1944. Some believed that the undertaking was too dangerous to attempt at all, and that other routes into Europe should be considered as the basic plan involved a frontal attack by sea on one of the most powerful and skilled armies in the world sitting in elaborate defences. Everyone believed it to be a most difficult exercise and that every resource of science and of modern tactics had to be brought to bear if it was to be successful. One of these, it was clear, was that new arm, the airborne forces, and their new tactics of vertical envelopment. Even in that branch of planning there were fears of failure, or at least of heavy casualties, although not among the air-borne officers, who collectively were as daring and imaginative a body as could be found, but rather among the airmen who would have to deliver the troops to their objectives.

There were also considerable differences of opinion on the airborne forces' correct role. The early planners favoured a series of scattered raids, each directed at a strong-point which might hold up the landing of the divisions by sea. From the United States Army Air Force came a bolder suggestion, with a strong flavour of Major-General Orde Wingate's theory of 'long-range penetration', for a mass drop far behind the coastal defences. This would be developed into an airbase and fortified area, towards which the seaborne half of the invasion forces would fight its way. This was pressed hard by no less than

General George Marshall, US Army Chief-of-Staff, on General Dwight Eisenhower, commanding the Allied invasion forces, but that excellent general was too hard headed and practical to fall for such a scheme, or at the other extreme to pay attention to the fears of disaster expressed by Air Chief-Marshal Leigh-Mallory of the RAF, his air commander.

The Allied plan

In the planning, the air forces and the navies concerned were naturally pre-occupied with their responsibilities for the safe delivery of the armies by sea and air and supporting them with supplies and firepower thereafter. They were, therefore, carefully counting their resources in ships, strike aircraft and, essential for the airborne effort, trained pilots who could deliver the 'sticks' of parachute troops and the gliders accurately by night. The army commanders, the 'passengers', wanted above all to make the first landing so strong that they could not be driven back into the sea before they could deploy and exert their full strength. This was the basic lesson of Crete, of Sicily, of Salerno and of Anzio. As soon as General Sir Bernard Montgomery was appointed to command the initial landing and had looked at the plans, he demanded that the assault should be increased to a front of five divisions. This was to extend from Ouistreham near the mouth of the Orne river in the east to les Dunes de Varreville on the base of the Contentin peninsula in the west; the British-Canadian forces would land on the left (east) and the Americans on the right, straddling the estuary fed by the Vire and Merderet rivers, with their extreme right, or western flank, on the beach codenamed 'Utah'. Inland from 'Utah' was marshy, close country ideal for delaying tactics. The US 4th Infantry Division on 'Utah' beach was separated from the rest of the US 1st Army and good routes for German counter-attacks led into its sector. Here was the right place to drop the two powerful US airborne divisions, the 82nd and the 101st. Similarly, the left flank of the British 3rd Infantry Division, landing on the most easterly 'Sword' beach, was exposed to attack and the main task of the British 6th Airborne Division was to secure the crossings over the Orne river and Caen canal, and to fight a holding operation in the area immediately to the east. In sum, the airborne assault added approximately the strength of three divisions to the initial blow of five arriving by sea. It was just sufficient to break through the crust of the coastal defences and make a lodge-ment powerful enough to repel any promptly delivered counterattack and deep enough to give elbow-room for the troops to deploy.

This solution was not arrived at simply or easily: there had to be endless and repeated balances struck between opera-tional necessities on the ground and the availability of aircraft. The British, for instance, planned initially to use only one brigade, but this was increased to two, with the third to follow up. Similarly, early in 1944 it looked as if only one US airborne division could be used initially, but by great efforts sufficient transport aircraft and gliders were assembled and the pilots trained for the final plan. Some idea of the numbers involved is given by the fact that it required 822 aircraft to trans-port the main body of the 82nd and 101st Airborne Divisions, totalling some 13,000 parachute infantry, artillery, engineers, HQ and communication units. The USAAF Troop Carrier Command was standard-ized on Douglas C-47 aircraft, having some 1,200. The RAF had a mixed bag of con-verted bombers and 150 C-47s. Over 2,500 gliders were available.

Below: In a later, but comple-mentary mission, the Allies also landed in the south of France. In this photograph, US paratroops descend behind the German lines.

The problem of delivery was one of considerable complexity. First, there was the question of navigation. The opponents of large-scale airborne operations pointed to the scattering of sticks by the Germans in Crete and the Allies in Sicily and the subsequent loss of control and heavy casualties. If an airborne assault on such a scale and against such an enemy was to succeed, the accuracy of the drop had to be improved enormously, especially as the three divisions were to be dropped at night. Pilot training was crucial. Aids to accuracy were devised, which included 'pathfinder' paratroopers whose sticks were to be delivered by experienced pilots. The pathfinders were to carry markers and radio beacons – the 'Rebecca' and 'Eureka' devices – but even with these aids, only excellent navigation and map-reading by eye in the final run-in proved of any use. All three divisions were to suffer intensely from the confusion resulting from scattered landings, to be corrected only by the courage and instinct for offensive action shown by the airborne troops once they had dropped.

Careful flight paths

Second, there was the whole question of routing. The invasion of Normandy saw the greatest concentration of military aircraft of all kinds in the history of warfare, so the flight plans of these great streams of aircraft had to be adjusted to fit in with the others, and also to avoid the areas where anti-aircraft fire might be dangerous. Plans for the use of gliders, in many ways more useful than landing by parachute, had to be altered or discarded when it was found that many possible landing zones had been blocked by arrays of telegraph-poles, some with explosive devices and connected by wires, known to the Germans as 'Rommel's asparagus'. Plans had to be made to fly in parachute engineers and bulldozers to knock these down. This caused the whole of the British 6th Airborne Division's plan, which was to lead with the glider troops brigade, to be altered.

Initiative the key

It has been well said that once units have to get down to planning in earnest for a real operation, 'tactics' are not so much concerned with ingenious schemes of manoeuvre, which any amateur can concoct by looking at a map, but with the timely arrival (in the right order) of men with the correct tools and weapons for the various tasks that the mission will present. Radio communication is all important. For instance, the 9th Battalion of the British Parachute Regiment was given the mission of silencing the important German coast defence battery at Merville, whose guns were protected by steel and concrete casemates and surrounded by barbed-wire 10 feet (3m) high and 6·5 feet (2m) deep in places, as well as a ditch and a mine-field, exactly 30 minutes before the main landings on the beaches it threatened were due to start. To achieve this the arrival of the assault parties in gliders who were to crash land on top of the guns; the drop zone (DZ) control party; the covering party to prevent external interference to the

Above: A British paratrooper with typical kit, but without his parachute and harness. Note the special helmet and the airborne 2in mortar across the top of the haversack.

Above: The American equivalent, complete with main and emergency parachutes, boards his aircraft. Note the knife and the .45in Thompson sub-machine gun.

Right: British paratroops on their way to Normandy. Note the large canvas equipment bags, which will touch down first.

assaulting troops; the assault party attacking from outside; the assault engineers who were to lift the mines and blow gaps in the wire; the collection and issue of the scaling ladders and duraluminum bridges for crossing the ditch; and every event in sequence up to final capture of the battery had to be timed carefully and the programme rehearsed in exercises on a full-scale model of the fort built in England. As it happened, there as elsewhere, everything possible went wrong, in spite of which those fragments of the battalion the commanding officer could rally from a drop scattered over 50 square miles (160sqkm) actually captured the battery.

Well had Brigadier S. J. L. Hill, commanding the 3rd Parachute Brigade, said in his final talk to his officers: 'In spite of your excellent training and orders do not

be daunted if chaos reigns. It undoubtedly will.' This statement was true of all the airborne operations, British and American, and like the assault on the Merville battery, universal success was plucked out of chaos by the initiative of the airborne soldiers and their officers, even though, as in the US 1/501st Battalion, the commanding officer was killed and all the company commanders missing. Gradually as the many small and desperate fights were won the desired pattern began to emerge. The only way to describe what was 24 hours of confusion is to highlight the crucial fights in each divisional area.

The tasks given to Major-General R. Gale, commanding the British 6th Airborne Division were, in order of importance: first, to capture the bridges over the Orne and the adjacent Caen Canal intact;

Airspeed Horsa

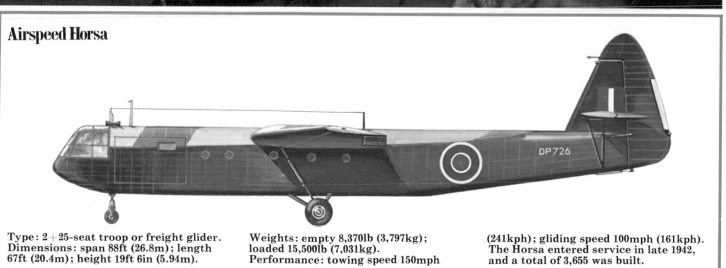

Type: 2+25-seat troop or freight glider.
Dimensions: span 88ft (26.8m); length 67ft (20.4m); height 19ft 6in (5.94m).

Weights: empty 8,370lb (3,797kg); loaded 15,500lb (7,031kg).
Performance: towing speed 150mph

(241kph); gliding speed 100mph (161kph).
The Horsa entered service in late 1942, and a total of 3,655 was built.

second, to silence the Merville battery 30 minutes before it was light enough for observed fire on the 'Sword' beach where the 3rd Division was due to land; and third, to capture and blow four bridges over the Dives river which runs parallel to and east of the Orne, offering approaches to the 3rd Division's east flank and the flank of the whole bridgehead area. When these were completed General Gale, reinforced by a second flight bringing in the third brigade of his division and his heavy anti-tank guns and the 1st Special Service Brigade (Commandos) who, with his last gliderborne battalion were to come in by sea on D + 1, was to engage any enemy entering the quadrilateral between the sea, the two rivers and the town of Caen. The final assignment was a formidable task in view of the high probability of a *Panzer* counterattack in this sector, but the wooded nature of the terrain suggested that elite troops like Gale's could successfully fight a delaying action there while the seaborne build-up continued and more heavily armed troops with tanks and artillery could take over.

Coup-de-main tactics

Gale's plan is reminiscent of the attack on the Corinth Canal bridge by the German parachute engineers in April 1941. Two *coup-de-main* parties each of three platoons of the 2nd Battalion, The Oxfordshire and Buckinghamshire Light Infantry (the 52nd Foot, as they liked to be called) carried in six gliders, were to crash land as close as possible to the two bridges. The gliders directed on the canal bridge were released at 5,000 feet (1,525m) over the coast and in a miraculous piece of navigation landed within 20 yards of each other with the lead glider's nose actually pushing through the perimeter wire of the bridge defences. The two forward platoons dashed into action immediately, to find the garrison in their firing positions. One platoon commander was killed charging across the bridge and the other wounded, but the company commander was with this party and throwing in his third, reserve, platoon secured the bridge after a short, sharp fight, mopped up and established a bridge garrison. It settled down to await the rest of the division and news of the fortune of the other party on the river bridge. Of the other three gliders one was lost completely and came down not on the Orne but the Dives 5 miles (8km) away. The two others landed 300 and 400 yards (275 and 365m) off, not as close as the first party, but close enough for the two platoon commanders to reach the bridge, where a less alert garrison was asleep in its billets and the fire positions empty. R. L. Howard, the major commanding the company, had now secured both his objectives and was able to organize his defences in time to receive visitors, who proved to be a small patrol, some officers in a staff car and later a single tank, and knocked them all out. It was now after 0100 and the night was alive with shooting and the roar of the aircraft

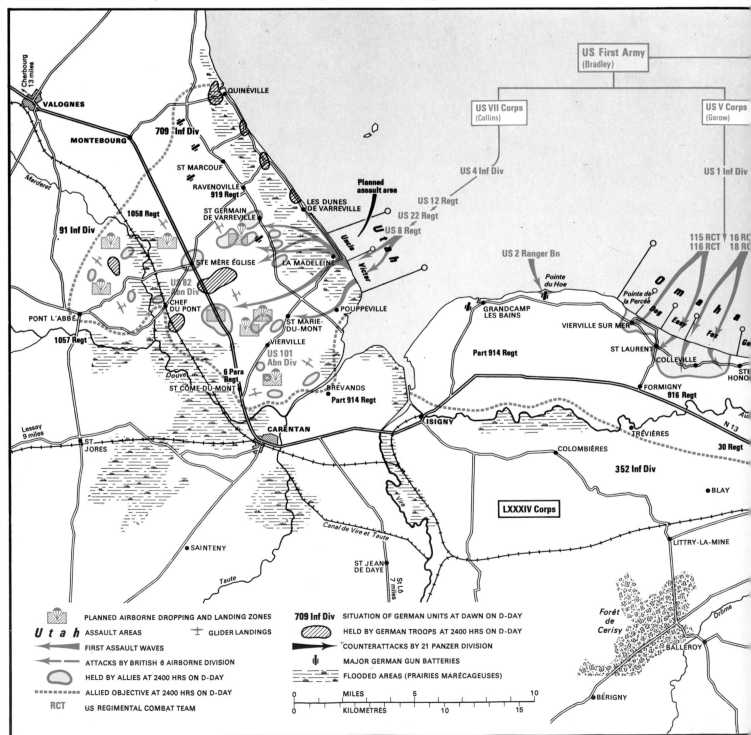

Browning Automatic Rifle

Calibre: .30in (0.76mm). Operation: gas, selective fire. Length: 47.8in (1.21m). Barrel length: 24in (61cm). Feed: 20-round staggered row detach- able box magazine. Weight: 19.4lb (8.8kg). Front sight: blade. Rear sight: leaf with windage-adjustable aperture. Cyclic rate: slow mode 300–450rpm; fast mode 500–650rpm. Muzzle velocity: 2,805fps (855mps). A unique weapon combining the roles of the infantry rifle and LMG.

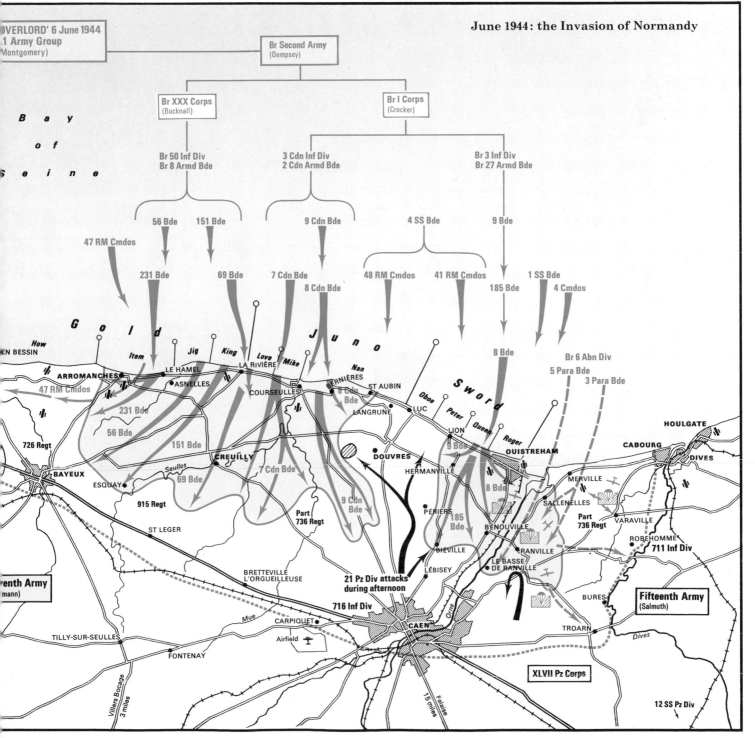

June 1944: the Invasion of Normandy

'OVERLORD' 6 June 1944
1 Army Group
(Montgomery)

Br Second Army
(Dempsey)

Br XXX Corps
(Bucknall)

Br I Corps
(Crocker)

Br 50 Inf Div
Br 8 Armd Bde

3 Cdn Inf Div
2 Cdn Armd Bde

Br 3 Inf Div
Br 27 Armd Bde

56 Bde   151 Bde   9 Cdn Bde   4 SS Bde   9 Bde

47 RM Cmdos

231 Bde   69 Bde   7 Cdn Bde   48 RM Cmdos   41 RM Cmdos   1 SS Bde
8 Cdn Bde   185 Bde   4 Cmdos

8 Bde

Br 6 Abn Div
5 Para Bde
3 Para Bde

Bay of Seine

Gold   *Juno*   *Sword*

How   EN BESSIN
Item   Jig   King   Love   Mike   Nan
Oboe   Peter   Queen   Roger

ARROMANCHES   LE HAMEL   LA RIVIÈRE   BERNIÈRES   ST AUBIN   HOULGATE
ASNELLES   COURSEULLES   9 Cdn   LANGRUNE   LUC   CABOURG
47 RM Cmdos   Bde   LION   DIVES
231 Bde   9 Bde   OUISTREHAM
56 Bde   DOUVRES   MERVILLE
726 Regt   151 Bde   HERMANVILLE   8 Bde   SALLENELLES
BAYEUX   CREULLY   7 Cdn Bde   VARAVILLE
Seulles   PÉRIERS   185   Part
ESQUAY   69 Bde   BENOUVILLE   736 Regt   ROBEHOMME
915 Regt   9 Cdn   Bde   RANVILLE   711 Inf Div
ST LEGER   Bde   BIÉVILLE   LE BASSE   BURES
Part   DE RANVILLE
736 Regt
Seventh Army   BRETTEVILLE   LÉBISEY   Fifteenth Army
(mann)   L'ORGUEILLEUSE   TROARN   (Salmuth)
21 Pz Div attacks   Dives
during afternoon
716 Inf Div
Mue   CARPIQUET   CAEN   XLVII Pz Corps
TILLY-SUR-SEULLES   Airfield
FONTENAY   Villers Bocage   Falaise   12 SS Pz Div
3 miles   15 miles

Above: A patrol of men from the US 82nd Airborne Division moves with extreme caution through the churchyard of Saint Marcouf, to the north of 'Utah' Beach, on D-Day.

bringing in the 5th Parachute Brigade, due to land some 1,000 yards (915m) east of the river. At 0300 the brigade commander, N. Poett, arrived leading the 7th Parachute Battalion, who now made good the first priority objective. This very neat little operation was the only one to go according to plan in the whole airborne assault.

Lieutenant-Colonel T. Otway's 9th Parachute Battalion, whose mission it was to silence the Merville battery, suffered every form of navigational mischance. It was the business of the battalion reconnaissance parties to land ahead of the battalion to position the radio beacons on the drop zone and mark the routes and rendezvous points for the companies on their way to their objective. They were correctly dropped and carried out their various tasks, but after that nothing went right. As a preliminary, heavy bombers of the RAF were to bombard the battery, a target 500 yards (455m) in diameter, and while they certainly hit it, most of their hail of 4,000lb (1,814kg) bombs fell well to the south and narrowly missed the reconnaissance parties. The dust from the bombardment was to obscure the drop zone of other brigades. Two gliders, in spite of determined efforts to land in the correct

place and undeterred by anti-aircraft fire which at least gave one glider pilot a clue that he was near the battery, were unable to land on target on top of the casemates. The other broke its tow and came down in England. The *coup-de-main* against the battery therefore never took place. As for the paratroopers of the 9th Battalion, various reasons (the pitching of the aircraft as the pilots strove to avoid anti-aircraft fire which threw the sticks waiting to jump off their feet, the difficulty of picking up the ground navigation lights put out by the reconnaissance parties and the failure of the 'Rebecca-Eureka' equipment) led to delayed jumping and a wide scatter of the sticks. It must always be remembered that the delivery of troops from aircraft in the dark of the night, in cloudy weather, at 200mph (322km/h) and low altitudes, while being shot at was at best never anything better than a chancy affair. After all, it is perfectly possible to lose one's way using a map travelling on the ground by daylight at 25mph (40km/h).

The net result was that only some 150 men arrived in or near the drop zone, and it took over an hour for them to discover where they were and assemble. However, it was not simply a question of numbers. The whole battalion, and its attached

troops with their specialized equipment such as mine detectors and bangalore torpedoes – long metal pipes full of explosive – and the heavy support weapons, were all detailed for separate tasks in a carefully co-ordinated plan, and most of them were missing, including gliders due to land after the drop carrying anti-tank guns and jeeps. There was only one medium machine-gun, and a few of the vital bangalore torpedoes to blow gaps in the perimeter wire.

German confusion

Fortunately Colonel Otway had dropped close to the drop zone and was able to exercise command. He decided to go for the battery with what he had. Luck favours boldness. As Otway's little band filed silently along the route to the battery they were unnoticed either by the garrison of a hamlet lying on it or by a strong German patrol crossing the head of the column, whose members froze until it was out of sight. The reconnaissance party

had an equally narrow escape, hiding in a roadside ditch. They had done wonders. All the German garrisons in the area were now thoroughly awake and alarmed with the noise of the RAF bombing, the fire of anti-aircraft guns and the continual roar of aircraft engines in the sky above, but the reconnaissance party succeeded in penetrating the outer belt of wire, locating pathways through the minefield by touch and marking them, leaving guides in position. They then made contact with the battalion as arranged.

There was now another fortunate diversion. One only of the three *coup-de-main* gliders, lost, without sight of the ground marking lights or response from the radio beacon, reached roughly the correct area and circled six times in the face of light anti-aircraft fire which hit the glider and wounded four men. The pilot spotted the battery but could not make it and crash landed, as it happened, in such a position as to cover the rear of the battalion as it went into the attack. The glider disintegrated and the platoon tumbled out to meet an enemy force following in the battalion's tracks; this German force had come probably from the garrison in Gonville village which Otway's main body had successfully bypassed. Parachute

troops have always claimed to be a special breed and, to take a single small incident from many, it is easy to see how their legend has been created. With some men wounded, all dizzy with endless circling in an air-tossed glider amid flak and half-stunned by a crash which tore off the wings, broke the airframe into three pieces and then set the glider alight, only vaguely aware of the situation, position and orientation, Lieutenant H. Pond, the platoon commander, heard the sounds of approaching men. He identified them as enemy, deployed, engaged them and drove them to ground. There the two parties faced each other, and Pond had effectively secured Otway's rear.

Total success

Otway, meanwhile, had rapidly simplified and mounted his assault. Two parties using the 20 bangalore torpedoes available, were to use them to blow two holes in the inner wire, while a third, following the old plan, 'demonstrated' noisily at the main entrance. While he was doing this three enemy machine-guns to his left and three to the right sited outside the battery unexpectedly opened an enfilade crossfire along the south face of the battery de-

Above: British airborne troops practise disembarkation procedure from the small door in the fuselage of a General Aircraft Hotspur II training glider.

fences which Otway was about to assault. He detached a small party to each flank from his already attenuated force to suppress them. The bangalore torpedoes were joined together and pushed through the wire and duly exploded. The assault parties rushed in, the demonstration party yelled and opened fire and threw grenades, and then succeeded in breaking in as well. It can be assumed that the garrison had been already badly shaken by the bombing (for although the bulk of the bombs missed, some 40 craters can be counted in the air-photo of the position) and further unnerved by the assault. They surrendered after a short but sharp fight. The guns were then wrecked using 'Gammon' bombs, simple devices made up from a woollen stocking full of plastic explosive and a fuze. It was 0500, 30 minutes before the deadline laid down for silencing the battery.

Otway's worries had by no means ended, however. A safety clause in the original plan allowed for the bombardment of the

M1 Rifle Calibre .30
Calibre: .30in (7.6mm). Operation: gas, semi-automatic.
Length: 43.6in (1.11m). Feed: 8-
round staggered row non-
detachable box magazine.
Weight: 9.51lb (4.3kg). MV:
2,805fps (855mps).

Colt .45 M1911A1 Pistol
Calibre: .45in (11.43mm).
Feed: 7-round box.

Thompson M1 Sub-Machine Gun
Calibre: .45in (11.43mm).
Operation, blowback,
selective fire.
Length 32in (81.3cm).
Feed: 20- or 30-round
detachable box.
Cyclic rate: 700rpm.
MV: 920fps (280mps).

M1 Carbine Calibre .30
This weapon was intended
for the use of NCOs, company-
grade officers and special
troops, as a pistol replacement.
It was very popular, and some
3,707,645 of the four models
were made.

M1A1 Carbine Calibre .30

Calibre: .30in (7.6mm).
Operation: gas, semi-
automatic. Length: 35,5in
(90.1cm) (stock extended).
Barrel length: 18in (45.7cm).
Feed: 15- or 30-round
staggered row detachable

box magazine. Weight:
6.19lb (2.8kg). MV: 1,970fps (600mps).
M1A1 Carbine. This model
was intended for use by
special troops, and had a
folding butt, reducing length
to 25.4in (64.5cm).

battery from seaward by the cruiser HMS *Arethusa* if no signal reporting success was received by her, and the bombardment liaison officers whose business it was to spot, and their naval signallers, were still missing. Otway had, therefore, to get well clear, pick up and care for his wounded, 40 all told and 20 unable to walk, including his adjutant, find a defensible position somewhere, collect the rest of his battalion and continue to play his part in the larger operation. In the course of his march he fought two more actions before he found a haven in which to reorganize.

Aggression wins

To a certain extent, it can be supposed, an airborne assault benefits from a wide scatter, frustrating though it may be. It was seen in Crete, notably near Canea, and later in Sicily, that the presence of small aggressive groups of men can interfere seriously with essential movement of messengers and staff officers in what they could reasonably hope to be a safe area, and even the movement of reserves. The one thing the defending commander wants to perceive are the main DZs and the enemy objectives so that he can arrange his counterstrokes, and the appearance of enemy everywhere fogs his view. This is really the difference between airborne or 'three-dimensional' fighting and the conventional kind: there are no fronts or

Left: Roman Catholic men of the US 1st Airborne Task Force attend mass before boarding their Waco CG-4A glider for the invasion of southern France on 15 August 1944.

flanks and the effect cuts both ways. Gale's well-considered plan with its tidy 'goose-eggs' drawn on the map around his DZs had become blurred by the dispersion that had in fact taken place. Confusion reigned. One brigade commander, Hill, and his party walked into the target area of Allied heavy bombers; many were killed and he was severely wounded. The same confusion possibly assisted one of the units detailed to capture and blow the bridges over the Dives, the 8th Battalion and the 1st Canadian Parachute Battalion. Much of the operational area was flooded. Vital stores and vehicles were dropped or landed in the wrong place, or worse, in the water. The adventures of the airborne Royal Engineers who collected enough stores and men to carry out their mission is a saga in itself. One astonishing feat was that of the engineer squadron commander who with a jeep and trailer loaded with explosive and a few armed sappers drove through the enemy lines to Troarn, and after some armed clashes with the surprised enemy actually succeeded in blowing up the bridge there as planned and withdrawing unscathed except for one sapper who fell off the jeep and was captured. All the bridges were in fact attacked and blown, some by sappers on foot pulling their loads of explosives in hand trolleys long distances.

So D-Day wore on, with much sharp fighting and confusion, but the fragments of the 6th Airborne Division, like well-trained soldiers, were gradually coalescing into their ordered units and making for the objectives. The divisional commander and his staff had arrived early that morning by glider and Gale had soon established

his headquarters, riding there on a horse, it is recounted, as his jeep was jammed in his glider. He was soon visiting the captured positions and gathering up the threads of the situation. By the evening of a very long day this was as follows. Brigadier Poett's 5th Parachute Brigade had had a good drop, and the 6th Airlanding Brigade (in gliders) had arrived and the primary objective, to form a strong flank astride the Orne extending westward, had been gained. Further east the 3rd Parachute Brigade was ready to fight a mobile delaying action. The German counterattacks were about to begin, and much bitter fighting and many casualties lay ahead, but the airborne phase of Gale's battle was over: from then on it was part of the battle of the bridgehead.

Scattered drop

Gale and his brigade and battalion commanders had to cope with scattered sticks and confusion, but their flight was mild compared with the impending ordeal of Major-Generals Maxwell Taylor (101st Airborne Division) and Matthew Ridgway (82nd Airborne Division). The American operation was a much bigger enterprise, the pilot errors were bigger, the confusion worse and therefore the effort required to create order out of chaos correspondingly greater. The stretch of coast extending some 13 miles (21km) north from the Vire on which 'Utah' beach was located was separated from the road running parallel and 2 miles (3·2km) inland by a stretch of inundations. There were wider and deeper floods in the valley of the Merderet to its confluence with the Douve and thence to

Carentan. The airborne mission was to secure the area inland between the coastal floods and the inner river line on a front of some 8 miles (13km) plus a salient 4 miles (6·4km) square east of the Merderet, securing key bridges and villages within it. The area was divided by an L-shaped boundary giving the important objective of Ste Mère-Eglise and the tract west of the river to the 82nd Division and the beach exits and the crossings over the Douve and Vire in the south to the 101st Division. It was a saturation plan. Each division was to drop three regiments initially, totalling 18 battalions plus, in the 101st, a battalion of light artillery and a company of engineers. The remainder of the divisions was to be flown in by glider as soon as the operational area had been secured.

Mixed results

The flight plan for this operation required air corridors from Grantham, past Bristol and Portland Bill south-west to a point north of the Channel Islands and thence across the Cotentin peninsula from the west, while the glider corridor branched off to come in over 'Utah' beach. By way of deception the RAF scattered 'window' (or 'chaff'), to obstruct radar observation along a false corridor. The 82nd Division was to drop astride the river, the 505th Parachute Infantry Regiment to the east of it and the 507th and 508th to the west. The 101st Division had a more mixed drop pattern, but briefly they also had three DZs, the 502nd Regiment and 377th Artillery Battalion in the north, the 1st and 2nd Battalions of the 506th, the 3/501st and division HQ in the middle, and the 1st and 2nd Battalions of the 501st Regiment and 3/506th and a company of engineers in the south. From these DZs the various battalions were to radiate out to their separate tasks: dealing with known enemy positions and batteries in their areas, securing the important river crossings and Ste Mère-Eglise. It was the particular task of the 101st Division to secure the inland end of the tracks which gave access from the 4th Infantry Division's beach. The 4th Infantry Division, for whose benefit the whole operation was, had to push into the airborne area as far as the Vire and Merderet and then develop its offensive northward in the direction of Montebourg. This was achieved. By the evening of D-Day it had taken over with trifling casualties from the two airborne divisions all their objectives bar a few bridges, and these were blocked.

In the *United States Army in World War II* (their official history) two maps show with coloured dots where all the sticks of the two divisions landed, and the result is like a diagram of an attack of measles. The divisional areas were well peppered, but some of the 82nd Division were dropped into the 101st Division's area and vice versa, and some sticks were landed as far as 20 miles (32km) to the north and 25 miles (40km) to the south of their DZs. Of the gliders carrying heavy weapons and equipment delivered shortly after the parachute drops few reached their targets and many crashed into natural or man-made obstacles. Only the 505th Parachute Infantry enjoyed a fairly accurate drop. The 501st in the south of the 101st Division's area was fairly concentrated

in the DZ but sustained heavy casualties from enemy action. Two of its sticks were dropped 8 miles (13km) to the south.

The causes, which were to be the subject of considerable bitterness and searching enquiry, can be summarized as due to the rapid expansion of the carrier command and lack of adequate training for the pilots; attempts to evade anti-aircraft fire leading to departure from straight and level courses; inaccurate delivery of some of the pathfinder teams; enemy ground interference; and thick cloud which obscured ground detail and prevented visual navigation during the final approach. A whole mass of men and equipment fell into the marsh and floods along the Merderet valley. Many radios were lost. It appeared, or would have appeared if the whole horrid picture had been visible at the time, that Leigh-Mallory's worst forebodings of 75 per cent losses were about to come true. Eisenhower, who had taken so many hard decisions, including this one, confessed to feeling understandable relief when during D-Day he heard that the divisions were in being and fighting a winning battle.

Complicated plan

In the 82nd Division mission the crucial tasks were to seize Ste Mère-Eglise, to block the Cherbourg road where it entered the divisional area at Neuville and to secure the bridge carrying the road leading from the west into Ste Mère-Eglise. Its German garrison were already alerted by the noise of aircraft, the fire of their own anti-aircraft guns, a fire caused by an incendiary bomb and finally by the arrival of stray parachutists who fell, to be killed or captured, into the village square. One who survived was suspended by his parachute from the spire of the village church.

The village was the objective of the 3/505th, commanded by Lieutenant-Colonel Edward Krause. An hour after the drop he had collected about a quarter of his battalion and without further delay marched off. In another hour he was poised to attack. He put stops on each of the five roads radiating from the village and sent an assault group directly into it, with orders to use only steel or grenades so that

Above: The glider landings in the south of France. The latest touchdowns are marked by the dust raised by the Hadrian's wheels and skids.

any small-arms fire could be identified as hostile. Krause quickly cleared his objective with little loss and then organized all-round defence. He sent two runners off to his regimental commander to report success, neither of whom got through. That officer was marching with the CO of the 2/505th, Lieutenant-Colonel Benjamin Vandervoort, who had assembled his battalion in strength and was about to establish the block at Neuville. It was about 0930 when Colonel William Ekman, without news from Krause, heard firing from Ste Mère-Eglise, so he ordered Vandervoort to leave only a platoon at Neuville and countermarch to help Krause, who by then was under attack by infantry supported by light tanks and SP guns from the south. These he repulsed but Vandervoort's arrival was welcome as it enabled him to strengthen his defences and later to mount a counterattack which, although it failed, discouraged any further attempts against his southern perimeter.

As soon as it was daylight the Germans with their characteristic aggression and quick reaction ordered all their adjacent units to counterattack at once. It was not long before a company of *Panzergrenadiers* was in contact with the platoon commanded by Lieutenant Turner Turnbull at Neuville. It took the Germans eight long hours of fighting to dislodge him, in the course of which his solitary 6pounder anti-tank gun knocked out an SP gun and a *PzKpfw* IV tank. At last, when Turnbull was down to 16 men able to handle weapons out of 42, another platoon was sent up to help him disengage, but the main northern route and the nodal junction of roads at Ste Mère-Eglise was now firmly gripped. Krause and Vandervoort, and especially the gallant Lieutenant Turnbull, who was to be killed the following day, had secured the keystone of the tactical arch.

The struggle to secure the road bridges over the Douve and the Merderet was less

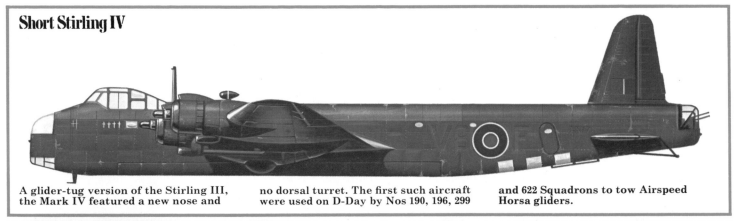

A glider-tug version of the Stirling III, the Mark IV featured a new nose and

no dorsal turret. The first such aircraft were used on D-Day by Nos 190, 196, 299

and 622 Squadrons to tow Airspeed Horsa gliders.

Above: The cockpit of an Airspeed Horsa glider during the flight to Normandy on D-Day. Note the 'home made' dive/climb indicator marked on the pilot's windscreen.

successful. The 508th Regiment had been dropped all over the place; eight of its sticks 1 mile (1·6km) from 'Utah' beach. Of the 508th, the bulk of the sticks usefully near the correct DZ were close to the bridge at La Fière, but the men were struggling to emerge from the floods into which they had splashed and in which most of their equipment had sunk to the bottom. Here as elsewhere, but more critically, the lack of radio sets reduced command and control to personal contact by the leaders and the classic formula of 'marching to the sound of the guns', but as this was heard everywhere it led to mistakes. Brigadier-General J. A. Gavin, to

become famous in his turn as a divisional commander, personally rallied as many men as he could. Mindful of the need to seize the bridges as soon as possible he tried at first to work down the eastern limits of the inundations, but ran into heavy fire, turned away and found a way east across via the railway bridge and so to La Fière, leaving one group there to attack the bridge and taking another 75 men on to the one at Chef-de-Pont. Meanwhile General Ridgway, happy that Ste Mère-Eglise was secure, made his way to La Fière, found the colonel commanding the 508th and ordered him also to collect the various groups and secure the bridge.

The net result of a number of barely co-ordinated moves was as follows. A mixed party under Captain R. E. Creek, unexpectedly reinforced by a lost glider from the fly-in of the afternoon of D-Day carrying an anti-tank gun, reached the Chef-de-Pont bridge, beat off a furious counterattack supported by a field gun firing over open sights, and finally seized

and consolidated a fingertip hold at the western end. Captain F. V. Schwartzwalder with three companies captured the La Fière bridge but, uncertain whether to stay put and consolidate or to press on into the area where they should have dropped, were caught by a well-supported armoured counterattack and driven off in some disorder. Schwartzwalder himself and his own company following the instinct of good soldiers to rally, joined up with his commanding officer of the 2/507th. The latter and the commander of the 2/508th had decided independently to dig in with the men they had west of the Merderet and hang on, and so from these strongpoints be able to assist in the next moves to secure the western portion of the divisional objective.

Inaccurate drops

The primary role of 101st Airborne Division was to make absolutely certain that the 4th Infantry Division had clear routes inland from 'Utah' beach. Four tracks across the marsh had been selected and numbered from the south: No 1, Pouppeville; No 2, Houdienville; No 3, Adouville; No 4, St Martin-de-Varreville. Each of these was to be taken in reverse. At the northern end of the divisional area the flank was to be secured by capturing St Germain de Varreville and in the south, a much tougher nut as it turned out, the bridges over the Douve north of Carentan.

There was a complication of bad drops and enemy action to upset the prearranged plans. The 2/506th, whose objectives were the Nos 1 and 2 exits, instead of being delivered opposite them arrived at Foucarville 5 miles (8km) to the north, but some

200 men were rallied by 0330. The battalion's approach march now ran along the front and it bumped into fire and pockets of resistance causing much delay. Eventually it arrived at Exit No 2, but so late that the 4th Infantry Division had taken it. The commanding officer of the 506th Regiment was close to his objectives but in an awkward fix, as his headquarters were established in the gun area of three batteries of German 10·5cm field guns, and every move drew fire. His entire 2nd Battalion was missing and he had no news of it, so he sent off what there was of his 1st Battalion, numbering some 50 men and the commanding officer. They, when they finally arrived at Pouppeville, found themselves forestalled by the divisional reserve battalion, the 3/501st, sent on the same errand by General Taylor himself, who had landed nearby and established his headquarters, lacking all communications as the radios were lost. Lieutenant-Colonel Julian Ewell had only some 50 men and Pouppeville was doggedly held by 70 infantry who had to be winkled out of the houses, a task he completed at last by mid-day. He was relieved to meet the leading elements from the 4th Infantry Division at last coming up from the beach.

Local aid

Lieutenant-Colonel G. Cole, who had landed some way to the west of his proper DZ near the inter-divisional boundary, collected 75 men, including some from the other division, and set off on his way to Exit No 3, not before an initial error which led him into Ste Mère-Eglise, where he was put on the right road by a Frenchwoman. He encountered a small party of

Above: The 1st Airborne Task Force was a formation of mixed nationalities, as indicated by these British and US troops of the 509th Parachute Infantry Battalion.

Germans, who were rushed, and then picked up some more of his own men. Cole was able without further difficulty to secure Exits Nos 3 and 4 by 0730. At 0930 he was able to ambush and shoot down some 70 Germans retreating in front of the 4th Infantry Division fighting their way up from the beach, and all without casualties.

All four of the primary objectives were thus attained, but the capture of the hardly less important blocks against immediate counterattack from the flanks were to require much harder fighting.

Brilliant action

Lieutenant-Colonel P. J. Cassidy, like all the other parachute commanders, had only a fraction of his battalion on hand for a mission more than enough for a whole one. He had to clear three villages, cover a front almost 2 miles (3·2km) long and make contact with the 82nd Airborne Division, if possible, and to make things worse the group assigned to contact the 82nd Division mistook its objective and went to the village of Haut Fournel where it became involved in a prolonged fight. Cassidy's load was lightened, however, by an individual action which, judged even by the standards of parachute troops whether German, British or American, was outstanding.

Cassidy despatched a tiny force, made up of 18 strays collected after the drop, under Staff Sergeant H. Summers to clear

Mesières village, which was occupied, although somewhat passively, by a large number of what appear to have been artillery headquarters personnel. None of his men were known to Summers by name or sight, and nothing he could say or do would persuade more than one private with a machine-gun to join him in the attack. At the first round of fire all the rest huddled in a ditch. These attacks of collective paralysis are not uncommon in battle, one man infecting another, but are unusual among elite troops. Sergeant Summers, at the other extreme, behaved as if he were immortal. In an action lasting over an hour, probably more, for he gave himself half an hour's rest before resuming his berserk course, Summers cleared the buildings by the simple method of ignoring all enemy fire, going up to one door after another, kicking it open, and shooting everyone he found inside with his sub-machine gun. Private Burt with his machine-gun gave him covering fire, and he was joined, one after another, by two officers, one of whom was wounded and one killed in a short time. His paralysed followers did make one dash from their ditch, only to return to it after some were shot down, but it was Summers' single-handed battle, supported only at the end by help sent up by Cassidy. It was he who won the day.

White flag

The determined pressure of Cassidy's detachment at Haut Fournel and company at Foucarville was rewarded unexpectedly at the end of the day by the Germans pulling out of Fournel and at Foucarville actually asking for terms

Above: Men of the 1st Airborne Task Force wait in a ditch near La Motte in southern France for the order to move up and engage the German rearguards.

under a white flag. Eighty-seven surrendered and another 50 were shot down when they tried to bolt to temporary safety. Cassidy dug in on a shortened line and the right-hand regiment of the 4th Infantry Division, having taken its time to cover some 4 miles (6·4km), arrived to link up after darkness had fallen.

Vindication

It is not to disparage the feats of the US airborne troops on the northern shoulder to say that by 1944 many German units were drained by the terrible casualties on the Russian front and their dilution by pressed non-Germans, but tough resistance was met by the group of three battalions delivered on the southern DZ. The German troops on the spot were well commanded and well prepared and inflicted many casualties at the moment of drop. Also, unknown to the Americans, a German parachute regiment had arrived in Carentan and was advancing north up the main road and were deploying around St Côme-du-Mont.

In the fighting for the Carentan bridges the same picture was repeated of commanders at all levels, energetically collecting what troops they could in the confusion and making their own way to their objectives, or fighting the first opponents they met as the fortunes of the battle dictated. The regimental commander of the 501st Regiment led a party

Above: A US paratrooper exits from his aircraft over southern France.

Top: A US trooper passes a wrecked glider. Another prepares to land.

to the bridge and lock at La Barquette, Captain Charles Shettle another in an attempt on the Vire bridges leading to Brevand, Major Richard Allen, the operations officer of regimental headquarters, and Lieutenant-Colonel R. A. Ballard, 2/501st, each with his little group making for the most important objective, the main road bridges between Carentan and St Côme. They ran into stiffer resistance than expected and very heavy fire from the German parachute troops. Fortunately the US Navy bombardment team was safely with them, and although they were unable to push on or even approach the bridges, an accurate and heavy bombardment from the cruiser USS *Quincy* enabled these four handfuls of men each under their aggressive leaders to hold on to the southern shoulder.

Universal initiative

So, as night fell on 6 June, ended the purely airborne phase of the operation. The total casualties on D-Day for both US divisions were 2,499 killed, wounded and missing out of 13,000, and so the critics were confounded and the airborne concept proved after the severest possible test.

Operation Market-Garden

The airborne part of Operation 'Market-Garden', the descent by British and US forces on Arnhem and the corridor stretching up to it from the Allied front line, was the largest Allied airborne effort of the war, and the only attempt at a semi-strategic airborne operation, but failed in its efforts to secure a Rhine bridge because of poor planning and intelligence.

The strategic potential of airborne forces was neither fully developed nor exploited during World War II. Such forces are extremely expensive in men and material. Large numbers of picked men have to be given special training and kept out of battle for long periods; a great many parachutes, gliders and other specialist equipment have to be provided and men trained to operate and maintain them; hundreds of four-engined bombers to tow the gliders and transport aircraft to drop the paratroopers had to be diverted from other tasks and their crews given special training; and a large base organization is necessary to launch and maintain the force.

High-level disputes

Among senior Allied commanders opinions were divided on the proper use of airborne forces. Some, such as Lieutenant-General George Patton, believed that airborne forces should be confined to the tactical role with airborne brigade groups assigned as corps troops for quick reaction. Others believed that the great cost of such specialist forces could only be justified by their being used to carry out deep and strategically significant penetrations of

enemy territory, though the threat which airborne forces held in reserve posed to the enemy was also a valuable bonus.

To promote planning for the strategic use of airborne forces, General Dwight Eisenhower, Supreme Commander, Allied Expeditionary Forces, established in August 1944 the 1st Allied Airborne Army Headquarters, under Lieutenant-General Lewis H. Brereton, United States Army Air Force. The raw material for their planning was provided by three American and two British airborne divisions, the 1st Polish Parachute Brigade and the 52nd (Lowland) Division as an airtransportable follow-up and consolidation formation. For air transport they had the United States IX Troop Carrier Command and Nos 38 and 46 Groups, RAF.

The establishment of this headquarters did not immediately alter the essentially tactical nature of the tasks assigned to airborne forces. Of these the most successful, so far as British forces were con-

Below: American paratroops dash through the mess thrown up by the explosion of a German artillery shell just beside them. The US airborne divisions fought successfully.

cerned, were the set-piece operations of the 6th Airborne Division in the Normandy invasion and at the Rhine crossing. Because the 1st Airborne Division, in general, and the 1st Parachute Brigade, in particular, had had greater operational experience prior to the invasion, they were held in reserve for use against targets of opportunity. By the time of 'Market-Garden' the 1st Airborne Division had been involved in the plans for 16 abortive operations. This had led to a great deal of frustration, best summed up by the men who had the arduous task of loading their heavy equipment, jeeps and guns, into Airspeed Horsa gliders by small side doors, an operation which became known as 'into the - - - - - gliders, out of the - - - - - gliders!'.

Trying times

The cancellations were nearly all the result of the Allies advancing more rapidly than expected or from the strength of the enemy, for one reason or another, appearing too great for the risk involved to be acceptable. The main limitation on the rapid launching of airborne operations was the time required to collect and disseminate briefing material and orders down to the level of the individual soldier. The air photographs provided for one cancelled operation were largely of month-old clouds, while for another there were only nineteenth-century French hachured maps with only the dolphins missing!

The British 2nd Army crossed the Seine on 30 August and were in Antwerp and Brussels on 4 and 5 September respectively after an advance of some 250 miles (400km). On 1 September Eisenhower took over command of all the forces in the field in North-West Europe. The very rapid advance had put a tremendous strain on the logistic system. While the initial delay in enlarging the Normandy bridgehead had assisted the administrative planners, once the breakout started the rates of advance on which they had been told to plan proved wildly pessimistic. The Seine was reached 11 days ahead of schedule, and Allied forces were approaching the German frontier by D + 96 days while the logistic plans were based on their doing so about D + 300 days. Moreover, until the lower Scheldt had been cleared and Antwerp opened as a port, the armies were still being supplied through Cherbourg and over the Normandy beaches.

Narrow or broad front?

These important logistical considerations entered into the disagreement between Eisenhower, who favoured an advance on a broad front, closing up to the Rhine along the whole front before crossing it to break into the heart of Germany, and General Sir Bernard Montgomery, who advocated an advance on a narrow front launched from the 21st Army Group area and designed to carry the Allies deep into the North German plain with the chance of ending the war in 1944.

Montgomery tried to persuade Eisenhower to give the 21st Army Group absolute priority in additional formations and in logistics to support this single-front thrust. Eisenhower was not to be persuaded, but was sufficiently impressed

Above: Major-General Roy Urquhart, general officer commanding the British 1st Airborne Division in Operation 'Market', seen outside his headquarters in Holland.

with the advantages of a northern advance to give Montgomery what was in effect the whole of the strategic reserve, the forces available to the 1st Allied Airborne Army. 'Market-Garden' was the child of this concept and of Montgomery's singleness of purpose.

'Market-Garden' and its immediate predecessor 'Comet' were brilliant in concept. After occupying Antwerp and Brussels, XXX Corps, under Lieutenant-General Sir Brian Horrocks, had reached the Meuse-Escaut Canal. Montgomery aimed to use airborne forces to seize the bridges over the Maas, Waal, and Neder Rijn, at Grave, Nijmegen, and Arnhem respectively, and establish an airhead at the Deelen airfield just north of Arnhem into which to fly an airportable division and supplies (Operation 'Market'), thus enabling XXX Corps to 'bounce' the Rhine and advance to the Zuider Zee ('Garden').

The tactical prizes for the success of such an operation were great: the German 15th Army and its forces in Holland would have their lines of communication cut, as would the V-2 missiles sites, the elimination of which was of high priority, and the Siegfried Line would have been turned to the north.

The strategic prize was yet more glittering: the ending of the war in 1944. Not only would this have saved enormously in lives and money, but it would have altered the whole pattern of postwar Europe. The occupation zones in Germany had yet to be agreed. The Russians were advancing in the Balkans but were halted east of Warsaw, refusing even to aid the

Allies in aiding the citizens of Warsaw who had risen against the Germans. The outstanding courage of the citizen army of Warsaw was not finally overcome until 2 October. Had 'Market-Garden' been successful, the Western Allies would have entered Berlin and Prague and the Yalta Conference would have been a very different affair from that which it turned out to be. But strategic concepts can only be sealed through tactical success. In 'Market-Garden' this was denied the Allies and it is with the causes of this failure, in particular that of the British 1st Airborne Division, that we are here concerned.

Abortive plan

The prevalent optimism at the beginning of September is well illustrated by the plans for Operation 'Comet', which was to have been put into effect on 8 September. This operation had the same objectives as Operation 'Market' but was to be executed by the 1st Airborne Division and the 1st Polish Parachute Brigade alone. The 4th Parachute Brigade was to drop south of the Maas and capture the bridge at Grave, the 1st Parachute Brigade was to drop north of the Neder Rijn (or Rhine) and capture the bridges at Arnhem, and the remainder of the 1st Airborne Division and the Polish Parachute Brigade were to

drop and land between the Maas and the Waal and capture the bridge at Nijmegen.

Major-General Roy Urquhart, GOC 1st Airborne Division, has been accused by some of showing a lack of imagination in his 'Market' plan, in not planning to take the Arnhem bridges by glider *coup-de-main*, as had been done by the 6th Airborne Division in Normandy. It is therefore of interest that his plan for 'Comet' included provision for a reinforced company from each of the airlanding battalions (1st Borders, 7th KOSB and 2nd South Staffords) each being allotted six Horsa gliders with the task of taking the bridges at Grave, Nijmegen and Arnhem by *coup-de-main*.

New optimism

The forces were all assembled at Harwell, where were the author's regimental tactical headquarters (1st Light Regiment, RA), and the author well remembers getting ready to take off on this adventure, only to have it postponed for 24 hours just before midnight on 7-8 September and finally cancelled about the same time on the 9th. When for 'Market' three instead of one airborne divisions were assigned for the same task, it is not surprising that optimism prevailed.

Another effect of the very rapid advance of the 2nd Army from the Seine was the increasing difficulty of getting reliable intelligence of the enemy. Successive postponements of 'Comet' were partly due to the realization that enemy resistance was again hardening and that not only might

Above: Men of the 1st Airborne Division make their last-minute checks before embarking in their Airspeed Horsa gliders. Behind the men are Short Stirling tugs.

Below: British paratroops emplane in a C-47, one of the 149 such aircraft of the US Troop Carrier Command allocated to the transport of the British airborne formation.

the 1st Airborne Division find the enemy too strong for it to carry out its very dispersed mission, but that it would need a deliberate attack, strongly supported by artillery, to enable XXX Corps to breakout across the Meuse-Escaut Canal to the north.

The plans for Operation 'Market' were very similar to those for 'Comet', but used divisions where before there had been brigades to seize five major bridges, three over the Maas, Waal, and Neder Rhine, laying what was called an airborne carpet, more accurately a series of mats that would enable XXX Corps to 'bounce' the Rhine.

Operation 'Market'

I British Airborne Corps (Lieutenant-General F. A. M. 'Boy' Browning) commanded the airborne force until it had landed and came under British 2nd Army (Lieutenant-General Sir Miles Dempsey). The forces available were: the British 1st Airborne Division, the US 82nd and 101st Airborne Divisions and the 1st Polish Parachute Brigade, the last under command of the 1st Airborne Division. Aircraft and gliders were provided by Nos 38 and 46 Groups, RAF, and the US IX Troop Carrier Command. The last also provided the pilots for gliders towed by American aircraft, those towed by British aircraft coming from the Glider Pilot Regiment.

Air support and air escort was provided by the 2nd Tactical Air Force, Nos 2 and 11 Groups RAF and the US 8th Air Force (fighters and bombers), all under the control of Headquarters Allied Expeditionary Air Force. The 1st Allied Airborne Army made all arrangements for air escort and for air/sea rescue and dummy parachute drops.

Operation 'Garden'

'Garden' was to be carried out by XXX Corps, under Lieutenant-General Sir Brian Horrocks (Guards Armoured Division, 43rd and 50th Infantry Divisions) with VIII Corps on its right and XII on its left keeping up what pressure they could with limited ammunition supplies. The Guards Armoured Division was to lead on what was virtually for much of the way a one-tank front along the main road Eindhoven – Uden – Grave – Nijmegen – Arnhem – the Zuider Zee. Distances in miles from the start line being: Eindhoven 13 (21km); Uden 32 (52km); Grave 43 (69km); Nijmegen 53 (85km); Arnhem 64 (103km); and Zuider Zee 94 (151km).

The 52nd (Lowland) Division was to be ready to be flown in north of Arnhem. On the assumption that Operation 'Market' was successful, it was estimated that XXX Corps might reach the Zuider Zee between two to five days after crossing the Belgian-

Dutch border. The corps was expected to join the 1st Airborne Division at Arnhem between D+1 and D+3 days.

In drawing up its plans XXX Corps gave too little credence to Dutch warnings on how easy it would be for quite small parties of Germans to hold up the advance or interrupt the lines of communication along the single road, much of it on an embankment from which, along considerable stretches, tanks could not deploy. Nor do the warnings of the Dutch resistance of increasing German strength in the area seem to have been given the weight they deserved. On the other hand, the 1st Airborne Division in its planning paid too much attention to Dutch advice that much of the low-lying parts of the area were too marshy and intersected by ditches and canals to be used for parachute drops or glider landings. Let us turn now from the general to the particular and consider the task of 1st Airborne Division and its plan to fulfil it.

Browning's briefing

On 10 September, immediately after the cancellation of Operation 'Comet', the commanders of the three airborne divisions were summoned to Montgomery's headquarters to be briefed by Lieutenant-General Browning, who was both deputy commander of the 1st Allied Airborne

Above: Waco CG-4A gliders regained after the operation reveal varying degrees of damage, typical of such airborne operations.

Army and commander of the British Airborne Corps, and in the latter capacity in charge of the planning for Operation 'Market'.

When given his orders by Montgomery, Browning was told that the 2nd Army would be up to Arnhem in two days. Feeling some reservation about this optimism he made the reply made famous by Cornelius Ryan's 'best seller': 'We can hold the bridge for four days but I think we may be going *a bridge too far*' (editor's italics).

This reply should not be interpreted to mean that Browning favoured an airborne operation which stopped short after crossing the Waal at Nijmegen. That would have been to forgo the prize of ending the war in 1944 at which the whole operation was aimed, and to have turned a potentially decisive strategic stroke into yet another airborne operation for limited tactical ends, a use to which at this juncture the author feels sure airborne forces would never have been put, for if the Rhine was not to be 'bounced' the 2nd Army would surely have been directed to clearing the estuary of the Scheldt, opening up the port of Antwerp.

The concept of 'a bridge too far' meant

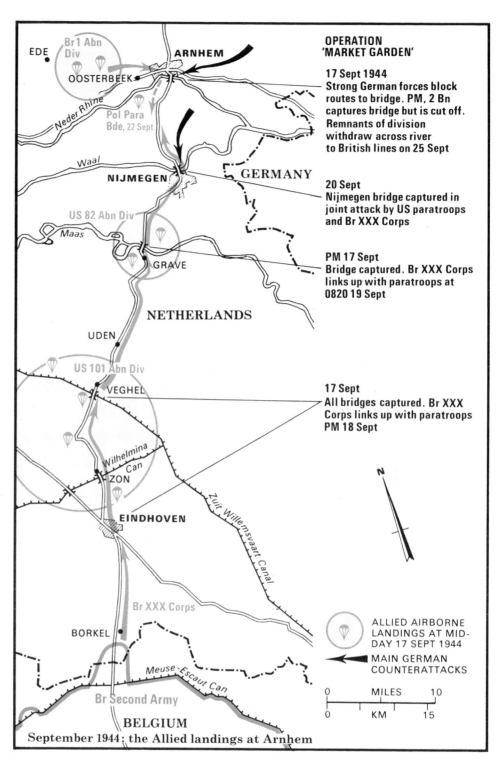

OPERATION 'MARKET GARDEN'

17 Sept 1944
Strong German forces block routes to bridge. PM, 2 Bn captures bridge but is cut off. Remnants of division withdraw across river to British lines on 25 Sept

20 Sept
Nijmegen bridge captured in joint attack by US paratroops and Br XXX Corps

PM 17 Sept
Bridge captured. Br XXX Corps links up with paratroops at 0820 19 Sept

17 Sept
All bridges captured. Br XXX Corps links up with paratroops PM 18 Sept

⊛ ALLIED AIRBORNE LANDINGS AT MIDDAY 17 SEPT 1944

◀ MAIN GERMAN COUNTERATTACKS

September 1944: the Allied landings at Arnhem

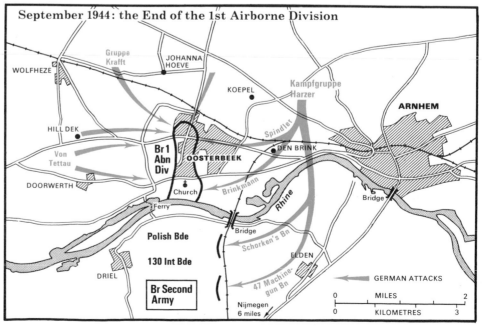

September 1944: the End of the 1st Airborne Division

◀ GERMAN ATTACKS

that the Allies were paying the penalty for not having a strong advocate of the strategic use of airborne forces at a sufficiently high level of command to ensure that when the great opportunity arose, those forces were adequate to seize it. The belated formation of the 1st Allied Airborne Army, a planning organization outside the normal chain of command and planning, was no answer.

Too little airlift

The problem of making a success of 'Market-Garden' was not that there were too many bridges but rather too little airlift. This meant, as will become clear, that the 1st Airborne Division's plan had of necessity to run counter to the two most important principles of airborne operations: the achievement of surprise and concentration of force. Had it been possible to put the 1st Airborne Division down in one lift success would almost certainly have been assured; had it been possible to use a fourth airborne division success could have been guaranteed, for in the planning it had been recognized that it was unlikely that the US 82nd Airborne Division would be able to take the Nijmegen bridge as well as the bridge at Grave and the vital high ground south of the Waal and east of Nijmegen. This proved correct and when the Guards Armoured Division reached Nijmegen the carpet had yet to be extended beyond the Waal.

American advantages

The shortage of airlift capacity presented the corps planners with a problem. While the 1st Airborne Division was clearly going to be in the most exposed position and would need to hold out the longest, to deprive the 82nd and 101st Airborne Divisions of the necessary forces to capture the bridges which alone would ensure their timely relief by XXX Corps would be doing them no service.

In the end the allocation of aircraft to divisions was as follows: 481 to the 1st Airborne; 530 to the 82nd Airborne; 494 to the 101st Airborne; and 38 to the Airborne Corps headquarters. All the aircraft allotted to the American divisions were American-piloted Douglas C-47s. The British lift was made up of 149 American and 130 RAF C-47s, and 494 converted RAF bombers, mostly four-engined. Although the 1st Airborne Division had fewer aircraft, the capacity of their Horsa and Hamilcar gliders gave them a larger lift in men or tons of equipment.

This allocation meant that each division could fly in only about two-thirds of its strength with the first lift – in the case of the 1st Airborne Division, which had the Polish Parachute Brigade under command, only half. To reduce this handicap as much as possible, the soldiers pressed for two lifts on the first day but this was turned down mainly because there was no moon and the American pilots were not considered to have the capability of carrying out airborne operations at night under these conditions.

As soon as Urquhart had received his orders, planning for 'Market' started in the stately club house at Moor Park which

was the headquarters of the British Airborne Corps and the tactical headquarters and briefing centre for the 1st Airborne Division when operations were in course of preparation. Units of the 1st Airborne Division and the Polish Parachute Brigade remained at their airfield assembly camps after being stood down from Operation 'Comet'. The division's administrative tail with, among other things, personal kit had already crossed to the continent by sea.

Triple tasks

General Urquhart translated the divisional aim into three tasks. The primary task was to capture the Arnhem bridges or a bridge; the secondary task was to establish a sufficient bridgehead to enable the follow-up formations of XXX Corps to deploy north of the Neder Rijn; lastly, during operations immediately following the landing of the first lift, everything was to be done to ensure the safe passage of subsequent lifts by destroying anti-aircraft positions in the vicinity of the dropping and landing zones and of Arnhem.

To accomplish these tasks the battle-experienced 1st Parachute Brigade, under Brigadier Gerald Lathbury, was given the

Above: A Waco CG-4A, towed by a Douglas C-47 Skytrain, lifts off from an English airfield—just two of the 1,543 gliders, tugs and transport aircraft involved.

job of seizing the rail and road bridges at Arnhem. The 4th Parachute Brigade, under Brigadier 'Shan' Hackett, was to occupy the high ground on the northern outskirts of Arnhem with the 1st Polish Parachute Brigade, under Major-General Stanislaw Sosabowski, holding the eastern perimeter, and the 1st Airlanding Brigade, under Brigadier 'Pip' Hicks, the western.

But what of the enemy? Ever since a, fortunately abortive, plan to drop the 1st Airborne Division in the Orléans gap in the path of German armour escaping from the Falaise-Argentan pocket, the redoubtable and experienced commander of the Polish Parachute Brigade, which first came under command of the 1st Airborne Division for that operation, showed a good deal more concern about enemy strengths and dispositions than did the British. His realism in this has rightly been praised, but it was also coloured by a strong desire not to get his brigade pinned down in western Europe, for he was dedicated to the liberation of Warsaw. The

British 1st Airborne Division, on the other hand, had a natural tendency to play down the enemy in its intense desire to get into battle.

The expectation at the time of 'Market-Garden' was that, though German resistance on the Meuse-Escaut Canal was stiffening, it was expected that once that crust was broken, there would be little to hold up the advance of XXX Corps. The airborne divisional commanders were led to expect no more opposition, at most, than a brigade of German infantry with a handful of tanks. Reports of German armour re-forming in the vicinity of Arnhem began to come through from 10 September onwards, but though these were taken seriously by the intelligence staff they were largely discounted by commanders.

Poles in reserve

Intelligence suggesting that the Germans were beginning to recover from their crushing defeat in Normandy and that stronger resistance might be expected was not allowed to influence the operational plans of the ground forces, though Lieutenant-Colonel Charles Mackenzie, Urquhart's principle operational staff officer, strongly represented that the

number of anti-tank guns should on no account be reduced, when the quantity of aircraft allotted to the division's first lift was cut.

On the other hand, reports that there had been a 30 per cent build-up in the German anti-aircraft defences around Arnhem and the Deelen airfield, north of the city, were taken very seriously by the RAF. It ruled out all thought of a *coup-de-main* by gliders on the bridges and led to a disagreement between Air Vice-Marshal Leslie Hollinghurst, air officer commanding No 38 Group RAF and responsible for the 1st Airborne Division's air movement plan, and Urquhart as to the position of the dropping and landing zones.

Urquhart was prepared to accept the dry heathland some 7 miles (11·25km) west of Arnhem for the mass glider landing, but he pressed Hollinghurst hard to drop the 1st Parachute Brigade on both sides of the river and as near to the Arnhem bridges as possible. The RAF, however, believed that to do so would invite unacceptable losses and it was decided that the drop should take place in the same area as the glider landing but with different zones.

This decision seriously prejudiced the tactical success of the division. Short of airlift, members of the division begrudged

Above: Cheerful faces among men of the 1st Airborne Division waiting for take-off in their C-47, known to and admired by the British as the Dakota.

the 38 glider loads allotted to the Airborne Corps HQ, for this already meant that only half Urquhart's command would be available to exploit the initial surprise. On top of that the decision to drop and land 7 miles (11·25km) from the objective again divided the remaining forces as one brigade would be needed to hold the DZs and LZs until the second lift came in, leaving only one brigade to go for the Arnhem bridges.

Intelligence ignored

It was decided that the 1st Parachute Brigade would on landing go for the final objective, the bridges, leaving the 1st Airlanding Brigade to guard the landing area until the fly-in of the 4th Parachute Brigade on D + 1. The Polish brigade would be held in reserve with the expected role of being dropped immediately south of the Arnhem road bridge on D + 2, provided that the anti-aircraft fire covering the area around the bridge had been eliminated. A landing zone east of the main divisional landing zone had been selected for the gliderborne portion of the Polish brigade due to land on D + 2.

This plan, forced on the 1st Airborne Division's commander by circumstances, ran counter to the principles of war of greatest importance in airborne operations – surprise and concentration of force. These required that the force be landed on or as near as possible to their objective, taking into account enemy strength and dispositions. The plan as it stood was a perfect receipt for defeat in detail.

The author has heard General Jim Gavin, the dynamic commander of the American 82nd Airborne Division, say that the British should have been prepared to accept a 10 per cent increase in casualties in order to land nearer their objectives. He was, however, unaware that the RAF had at the briefing at Moor Park, predicted up to 40 per cent casualties on the fly-in according to the adopted plan. Urquhart can hardly be expected to have suggested making it 50 per cent.

Divided command

In any case there was no way in which Urquhart could have influenced the RAF plan except by persuasion, the War Office and the Air Ministry having formally agreed that 'Airborne operations are air operations and should be entirely controlled by the Air Commander-in-Chief.' Why then, ask some critics, did Urquhart not refuse to go?

The author believes there were two fundamental reasons. Firstly, given the correctness of higher commands' estimate of the strength and condition of the enemy, and given that all went according to plan, then despite the plan's very serious weaknesses there was still a reasonable chance of success, and success held out the best hope of ending the war in 1944. In these circumstances it would not seem reasonable to expect the 1st Airborne Division's commander to refuse to carry out his superiors' orders.

There was, however, a second reason which those who were not directly involved may find difficult to comprehend. The morale of the 1st Airborne Division was high, but it had become increasingly brittle as a result of the frustration felt from planning and getting ready for 16 abortive operations. Officers and men had joined airborne forces to see action in novel and exciting circumstances, but instead they had been held back on the side lines, spectators while others fought.

Limited experience

There were units in the division that had seen hard fighting in North Africa and Sicily but a considerable part of the division had only seen limited action in Italy and some none at all. In September it looked as if the war would be over without their having heard a shot fired in anger, let alone demonstrated the *élan* which had come to be associated with the Red Beret. It is significant that when the RAF predicted up to 40 per cent casualties on the fly-in, no one appeared to be listening. In these circumstances another cancella-

tion would most probably have destroyed the division's morale, it would certainly have destroyed the acceptance of Urquhart's leadership.

As we now know, things did not go according to plan, nor was luck on the side of the 1st Airborne Division. Before turning to a broad consideration of the 'Market-Garden' operation as events unfolded, attention should be drawn to one more serious weakness from which the 1st Airborne Division suffered and which, like others, stemmed largely from the failure at the highest levels of command to appreciate the strategic potential of airborne forces and the organization and equipment required to exploit it.

Light artillery only

The organic artillery of an airborne division was strictly limited by the airlift required for carrying guns and ammunition, particularly the latter. The 1st Airborne Division's field artillery consisted of only 24 75mm pack howitzers, firing 15lb (6·8kg) shells, and organized into three batteries, each affiliated to one of the brigades. For the 1st Parachute Brigade's operation in Sicily, *ad hoc* arrangements were made to enable an airborne gunner officer to control the fire of the artillery of the link-up forces as they came within range, so no field artillery accompanied the brigade.

Between Sicily and the Normandy invasion the Royal Artillery paid great attention to this problem, and the two British airborne divisions were each supplied with a FOURA (Forward Observation Unit, Royal Artillery) made up of officers with signallers and wireless sets designed to control the fire of the link-up artillery and supplement the limited number of OP parties the divisional artillery regiment could provide.

When airborne forces were used tactically in close support of the ground forces, these arrangements were adequate as the airborne forces either landed within range of the longer-ranged link-up artillery or would become so very soon after landing. In a strategic role, such as that of the 1st

Above: Men of the 82nd Airborne Division stream down to the ground near Grave. In the foreground are the gliders that brought in the division's advance parties.

Airborne Division at Arnhem, it must be expected that a considerable time would elapse before the fire of the divisional artillery regiment could be supplemented by that of artillery from outside the division. During this time the division would be heavily dependent for close fire-support on the air forces. One of the unanswered questions about the Arnhem operations is why the arrangements for close air support were so inadequate.

The need had long been recognized and shortly after the Normandy landings a staff officer from divisional headquarters was sent over to study the problem at first hand but no ASSU (Air Support Signal Unit) was developed. In consequence the arrangements for ground to air communications for the support of the 1st Airborne Division had to be improvised. The normal British wireless set used by an ASSU for ground-to-air communications was not airportable. The Americans had a set that could be carried in a British General Aircraft Hamilcar or American Waco CG-4A glider. Unfortunately one of the two sets allotted to the 1st Airborne Division was damaged on landing and no more than one contact was made with the other. The American signallers who accompanied the sets were unfamiliar with them and untrained in operating ground-to-air communications.

No air support

No 83 Group RAF was responsible for providing the 1st Airborne Division with close air support. In this, apart from the failure of the ground to air communications, the group was severely handicapped by fog over its airfields most mornings and by their aircraft being kept out of the area whenever aircraft of the US 8th Air Force were providing fighter cover for the air transport force bringing in troops or supplies. In consequence, not only were

Vickers .303 Machine Gun

Calibre: .303in (7.7mm). Operation: recoil with gas boost, automatic only. Length: 43in (1.09m). Barrel length: 28.4in (72.1cm). Feed: 250-round canvas belt. Weight: 33lb (15kg) without water; about 40lb (18.1kg) with cooling water. Tripod weight: 50lb (22.7kg). Front

sight: hooded blade. Rear sight: leaf with aperture. Cyclic rate: 450–550rpm. Muzzle velocity: 2,440fps (744mps).

The Vickers Mark I machine-gun was introduced in 1912 and served the British army with distinction to 1960.

Below: The Projector Infantry Anti-Tank (PIAT). Length: 39in (99.06cm). Weight: 32lb (14.4kg). Grenade weight: 3lb (1.35kg). Combat range: 100 yards (91m). MV: 450fps (137mps).

the airborne forces largely deprived of close air support, but also of the salutary effect which the continual presence of Allied aircraft overhead would have had on enemy morale. It was an admitted serious error that all aircraft flying in the battle area had not been placed under the control of the local air commander, the air officer commanding No 83 Group, with a senior liaison officer having direct communications with the 8th USAAF at his headquarters.

Having cleared out of the way some of the structural weaknesses and inadequacies which militated against the effective use of airborne forces in a strategic role, let us turn our attention to the development of events.

It was decided that Operation 'Market-Garden' would start on Sunday 17 September, and that the airborne drop and glider landings would take place at about the same time for all three airborne divisions: the 1st Airborne Division at 1250, with the Independent Parachute Com-

pany responsible for marking the dropping and landing zones dropped 20 minutes ahead of the main body; and the 82nd and 101st Airborne Divisions at 1230.

RAF fears

A second lift was to go in on 18 September, with the first arrivals at 1000. This lift was held up by bad weather, and finally came in four hours late. For the 1st and 82nd Airborne Divisions there was to be an important third lift on D + 2, bringing in the 1st Polish Parachute

Brigade and 325th Glider Infantry Regimental Combat Team for the British and Americans respectively. In all, some 34,000 troops were flown in, 20,190 being dropped by parachute and 13,781 landed by glider; of the paratroopers 16,500 dropped on 17 September.

As noted already, the RAF believed that the build-up of German anti-aircraft defences on barges as well as on land presented a serious threat to the vulnerable air transport trains. To reduce this to a minimum 821 Boeing B-17s of the 8th USAAF dropped 3,139 tons of bombs on

117 sites, Bomber Command attacked German fighter airfields during the night of 16-17 September, and in daylight raids against coastal batteries in the Walcheren area 85 Avro Lancasters and 15 de Havilland Mosquitoes dropped 535 tons of bombs.

The air trains were provided with escort and anti-flak patrols by 550 8th USAAF Lockheed P-38 Lightnings, Republic P-47 Thunderbolts and North American P-51 Mustangs, and by 371 Hawker Tempests, Supermarine Spitfires and de Havilland Mosquitoes of the Air Defence of Great Britain command, while 166 fighters of the US 9th Air Force gave umbrella cover over the dropping and landing zones.

No concentration

Early on 17 September 84 Mosquitoes, Douglas Bostons and North American Mitchells of the 2nd TAF attacked barracks in Nijmegen, Cleve, Arnhem and Ede. That evening dummy parachute drops were made west of Utrecht, and east of Nijmegen and Emmerich.

Splitting the airborne forces into two or more lifts not only ran counter to the principle of concentration but made the whole operation hostage to the weather, forecast as good for the whole period of the operations. The weather over Holland on 17 September was excellent, though low cloud over England caused some gliders of the 1st Airborne Division to run into slip-stream trouble and mainly for this reason 24 of those in the first lift parted company with their tug aircraft over England.

The aerial armada of transport and tug aircraft took off from two groups of airfields. The southern group, mainly in Wiltshire and Oxfordshire, comprised eight British and six American airfields; the eastern group, in Lincolnshire, eight American airfields. The armada crossed the channel in two streams, each stream being divided into three sub-streams 1·25 miles (2km) apart.

Unhindered drop

The northern stream crossed the coast at Aldeburgh, made landfall at the western end of Schouwen Island and flew on to a point near 'sHertogenbosch, where it split to deliver the men and equipment of the British 1st and US 82nd Airborne Divisions to their landing areas. The southern stream, carrying the US 101st Airborne Division, crossed the coast at the North Foreland flew almost due east to Gheel before turning north-east to the divisional DZs and LZs north of Eindhoven. The C-47s carrying the paratroops flew in close formations of nine aircraft (Vics of Vics); the Handley Page Halifax, Short Stirling and Armstrong Whitworth Albemarle glider-tugs flew in loose pairs. It took 65 minutes for the northern stream to pass overhead. Between 1025 and 1155, 1,534 transport aircraft (including the Pathfinders for marking the DZs and LZs), 491 of them towing gliders, took off for Holland.

By the time the English coast had been crossed the weather was perfect. The author's Horsa was flying rather lower than the rest, its altimeter reading 1,200

feet (366m), and standing between the two pilots the author had a wonderful view of the ships set out at regular intervals for rescue purposes, and of the stream of aircraft ahead. One felt a little anxiety as the glider crossed the formidable-looking German coast defences. The leading aircraft were fired on from a barge as they crossed the coast but this fire was immediately suppressed by the anti-flak escort.

Some aircraft encountered a little heavy anti-aircraft fire, but for most all that could be detected was a squirt or two from light weapons. From neither were there any losses. The fly-in and landing was outstandingly successful, and the disembarkation into a field of wheat stubble seemed more like an exercise than an operation of war. Had the plans anticipated how completely successful the Allied air forces' anti-flak plan was to prove how different would subsequent events have been.

The 1st Airborne Division started landing at 1240, some 10 minutes early; the 82nd Airborne Division at 1230, as planned; and the 101st Airborne Division at 1300, some 30 minutes late. By 1400 the first lift had been delivered. At 1435 XXX Corps started its advance (Operation 'Garden'), but encountered strong opposition. By Sunday evening it had moved forward only 7 or 8 miles (11·25 or 13km) and had not broken the enemy's main defences. Its leading troops spent the night at Valkenswaard, some 6 miles (9·5km) south of Eindhoven. Who were the Germans in front of them?

Model's reaction

Following the *débâcle* west of the Seine, Hitler had ordered Field-Marshal Gerd von Rundstedt once again to take overall command of the Western Front, with

Field-Marshal Walter Model commanding Army Group 'B' in the north. Model ordered a new defence line to be established behind the Meuse-Escaut Canal. For this he asked for reinforcements from Germany and ordered General Gustav von Zangen to hold the southern bank of the Scheldt while disengaging and ferrying back units from his 80,000-strong 15th Army, many locked up defending the Channel ports, to the northern side of the Scheldt via Walcheren Island.

To provide reinforcements Colonel-General Kurt Student was ordered from a staff and training appointment, on 4 September, to take command of some 10,000 troops, made up of units from all over Germany, only a few well trained and battle experienced, and to deploy them behind the Meuse-Escaut Canal with the title of the 1st Parachute Army, with headquarters at Veghel, north-east of

Eindhoven. It was an army with very little transport, artillery or armour.

Amid the chaos of retreat, one of the German generals to keep his head was the commander of the 85th Infantry Division, Lieutenant-General Kurt Chill. Bringing together the remnants of his own and two other divisions he established 'reception stations' along the Meuse-Escaut Canal. These stopped and took under control the numerous parties of demoralized German servicemen 'going home'. All these became a part of Student's army which by 17 September had created defences in some depth behind the canal.

German armour

Model had ordered similar reception stations to be established by military police and local training units along the other waterlines. More important for the

Above: David Shepherd's depiction of the battle for Arnhem bridge between the Germans and Lieutenant-Colonel John Frost's 2nd Parachute Battalion Group.

1st Airborne Division, he had ordered Lieutenant-General Willi Bittrich, commander of II SS *Panzer* Corps, to move north from the Mosel to Doetinchem, due east of Arnhem, on 6 September and there to re-form the excellent but much battered 9th and 10th SS *Panzer* Divisions in the area north and east of Arnhem. The unconfirmed reports from the Dutch underground of armour assembling in the Arnhem area were only too true.

On 17 September there were some 6,000 German troops in the area. Besides the *Panzer* divisions there were three quite good battalions forming the reception stations along the Neder Rijn. The

Above: British Airspeed Horsa gliders lie at the ends of the tracks they have made while landing in grain fields on the western outskirts of Arnhem.

rest were of inferior calibre. At the time of Bittrich's move, Model established his own headquarters in Oosterbeek, displacing companies of the local reception battalion, composed of men from the SS depot and NCO school at Arnhem, and commanded by *Sturmbannführer* Krafft, which encamped between Oosterbeek and Arnhem.

Total surprise

The airborne assault on 17 September took the Germans completely by surprise. Model and his headquarters had to flee to Bittrich's headquarters to avoid capture. Bittrich, as soon as he heard where the landings were taking place, ordered the tracks which had been removed from the 9th SS *Panzer* Division's armour to be replaced. He appreciated that the Allies' objective must be the bridges at Nijmegen and Arnhem and therefore ordered the 9th SS *Panzer* Division to move as soon as possible to secure the Arnhem bridge by intercepting and destroying the airborne troops west of Arnhem. The divisional reconnaissance regiment was to send patrols out toward Oosterbeek and one squadron over the Arnhem bridge toward Nijmegen. Model approved these plans, disapproved Bittrich's suggestion that the bridges at Nijmegen and Arnhem be blown, and ordered the 10th SS *Panzer* Division to be sent to Nijmegen as soon as it was ready.

Apart from a little sniper fire, the 1st Airborne Division's first lift formed up without molestation. The 1st Border, 7th KOSB and 2nd South Staffords (less two companies) took up positions to secure the landing and dropping zones. It had been intended that Major Freddie Gough's Reconnaissance Squadron should rush the Arnhem road bridge, taking it by *coup-de-main*. A number of the unit's glider loads had not arrived, however, and the reconnaissance cars that went forward were ambushed near Wolfhezen. The plan miscarried but Gough with some of his squadron later joined Lieutenant-Colonel John Frost's 2nd Parachute Battalion at the bridge.

Arnhem entered

The 1st Parachute Brigade Group (Brigadier Gerald Lathbury), less the guns of the 3rd Airlanding Light Battery RA, which deployed near the landing zone, set off for Arnhem by three routes which converged in the city centre. The 2nd Parachute Battalion Group, led by Lieu-

Above: The Headquarters Group of the 1st Airborne Division's Artillery Regiment gathers its vehicles and equipment from the interlocked wreckage of two Horsa gliders.

tenant-Colonel John Frost, whose task was to secure the rail and road bridges at Arnhem, took a secondary road close to the river; the 3rd Parachute Battalion Group moved on the central route with the 1st Parachute Battalion Group to the north of them heading for the high ground on the city's outskirts. Lathbury, with brigade headquarters, followed Frost. All three battalions ran into opposition but the 2nd, though checked on a number of occasions, was able to establish itself on the approaches to the Arnhem road bridge by dark, though the railway bridge was blown up just as Frost's men reached it.

The other two battalions came up

British Paratrooper, Arnhem 1944

Dressed in his Denison smock over a set of serge battledress, a British paratrooper runs to his RV at the dropping zone. His web equipment is the almost universal '37 pattern while his personal weapon is a Lee Enfield No 4 Mark 1 rifle. The scabbard for the unpopular spike bayonet is just visible on his left hip. Around his neck is a face veil, a square of camouflaged netting intended for quick personal camouflage, but used as a scarf, sweat rag, and towel. This type of uniform and web equipment was worn, with some local variations, throughout the war and even now the smock and helmet with some improvements are still in use.

119

Above: Watched by Dutch civilians, a British paratrooper escorts German prisoners to a temporary holding area. Quick successes were soon to end, however.

Left: The strain of seven days of combat is reflected in the faces and clothing of a British patrol in the ruins of Oosterbeek during 23 September 1944.

against increasing resistance. *Sturmbannführer* Krafft subsequently claimed credit for imposing these delays. It was, apparently, his men who ambushed the Reconnaissance Squadron, but the main opposition was coming from the Reconnaissance Battalion of the 9th SS *Panzer* Division, one squadron of which crossed the Arnhem bridge heading south just before the 2nd Parachute Battalion gained control of the northern end.

Radio failure

More serious than these delays was the fading of wireless communications between the 1st Parachute Brigade and divisional headquarters as the brigade entered the tree-clad suburbs of Arnhem. Bereft of all information, Urquhart had no alternative to setting out in his jeep to make personal contact. On reaching the 2nd Parachute Battalion he learnt that Lathbury had gone to visit the 3rd Parachute Battalion on the centre route. Here Urquhart found him and after confused and sporadic fighting in the outskirts of the

town both became besieged in a house and incommunicado with the outside world.

Away to the south, by last light, the 101st Airborne Division had occupied Zon, St Oedenrode and Veghel, and was fighting for Best. The bridges they held had been captured intact, except that over the Wilhelmina Canal south of Zon, though a regiment had crossed the canal from the north on an improvised bridge and had reached Bokt.

The 82nd Airborne Division and Airborne Corps headquarters had also landed successfully. By last light the division had seized intact, and was holding, the bridges over the Maas at Grave and over the Maas-Waal Canal at Heuven. The remainder of the division was moving north and north-west to dominate the high and tree-clad area south-east of Nijmegen, vital to cover the flank from German counter attacks from the Reichswald forest.

For the 1st Airborne Division 18 September was to be a crucial day. With the arrival of the second lift, carrying the 4th Para-

chute Brigade, it would no longer be necessary to hold the DZ and LZ area. Urquhart would therefore have in hand two-thirds of his division with which to influence the situation as he thought fit.

Unfortunately, at this vital time the divisional commander was still holed up in Arnhem and no one at divisional headquarters knew whether he was dead or alive. Shortly before the arrival of the 4th Parachute Brigade, which had been delayed for four hours by bad weather, Hicks had assumed command of the division in accordance with the wishes of Urquhart conveyed to his GSO I, Charles Mackenzie, a decision unknown to Hackett, commanding the 4th Parachute Brigade, who though much younger was the senior. The only news of the 1st Parachute Brigade coming into divisional headquarters was of the 2nd Parachute Battalion via the regimental net of the 1st Airlanding Light Regiment RA.

Second lift delayed

The 2nd Parachute Battalion had successfully ambushed several lorries loaded with infantry making for the Arnhem bridge, and almost annihilated the reconnaissance squadron of the 9th SS *Panzer* Division, which tried to rush the bridge as it returned from the south and lost 16 armoured vehicles. But pressure on Frost's men was increasing from the east as more tanks and SP guns were brought into the battle. Casualties were mounting and ammunition dwindling.

During the morning David Dobie switched his 1st Parachute Battalion from the northern route to that along the river bank in a fresh attempt to reach the bridge. Hicks, on hearing of the delay imposed on

Bren Mk3 LMG

Calibre: .303in (7.7m).
Operation: gas, selective fire.
Length: 45.5in (1.16m). Barrel
length: 25in (63.5cm). Feed: 30-
round staggered row detachable
box magazine. Weight: 23.18lb
(10.5kg). Cyclic rate: 540rpm.
MV: 2,440fps (744mps).
This first-class light machine-gun
was widely used by all British
ground forces.

the second lift, ordered the 2nd South Staffords, less two companies not yet arrived, to reinforce the efforts to get through to Frost.

The second lift for the Airborne Corps comprised 1,360 troop-carrying aircraft and 1,203 gliders. The 1st Airborne Division's lift started arriving at 1500 and was met by AA and German fighter opposition. Hicks had decided that as soon as they could be assembled, the remainder of the 2nd South Staffords and the 11th Parachute Battalion would be despatched in a further attempt to get through to the bridge. At Hackett's request, the 7th KOSB replaced the 11th Parachute Battalion under command of the 4th Parachute Brigade, which made preparations for an attempt to take the high ground at Koepel, 1 mile (1·6km) north-west of the outskirts of Arnhem, early next day. Rumours of some 60 German tanks moving toward Arnhem from the north were confirmed by the Dutch underground.

XXX Corps held up

During the 18th XXX Corps advanced slowly against considerable opposition, with the fighting for most of the day centred around Aalst. The 101st Airborne Division's capture of Eindhoven helped matters and at about 2100 the Guards Armoured Division reached the southern bank of the Wilhelmina Canal below Zon where a bridge was constructed during the night.

The 101st Airborne Division held its ground but was unable to capture Best, which the Germans had reinforced. By an outflanking movement Eindhoven was captured with its bridges intact and by dark control had been established throughout the town.

The 82nd Airborne Division continued to control the vital high ground south-east of Nijmegen through vigorous offensive action. It attacked along the Maas-Waal Canal, capturing the bridge for the main Grave-Nijmegen road, intact but damaged. The Germans counterattacked vigorously from the Kranenburg and Reichswald forest areas. When the second lift arrived it was subjected to anti-aircraft fire. Despite the fact that the LZs were being fought

over, the landings were successful.

Time, however, was running out and, in retrospect, Tuesday 19 September was the last chance of snatching victory from defeat. At the bridge at Arnhem the 2nd Parachute Battalion Group was still giving as good as it got, but the pressure and the casualties continued to rise as German tanks and SP guns began systematically to destroy and set fire to the buildings from which they fought. Their stubborn defence prevented the 10th SS *Panzer* Division from using the bridge to reinforce the Germans holding on to the Nijmegen bridge, and so forced them laboriously to ferry their armoured vehicles across farther up the river.

From now on the lack of any ground-to-air communication not only deprived the 1st Airborne Division of effective close air support but combined with lack of effective communication with Airborne Corps to make it impossible to alter the pre-planned dropping zones for resupply to conform with the shrinking divisional perimeter – with tragic results. While bad weather and operational restrictions combined with communication failure deprived the 1st Airborne Division of close air support, good weather over the German airfields enabled German fighters in increasing numbers to strafe the divisional area.

British pull back

About 0730 Urquhart managed to get back to his divisional headquarters. He immediately sent the deputy commander of the 1st Airlanding Brigade, Colonel Hilary Barlow, to co-ordinate the action of the 2nd South Staffords, 11th Parachute Battalion and any other available troops in a further attempt to break through to the bridge. Barlow was never seen again. The 4th Parachute Brigade's attack to take and hold Koepel failed. Pressure on the western side of the division's perimeter built up and threatened to isolate the 4th Parachute Brigade north of the railway.

Urquhart decided to pull back this brigade and use it to stabilize the eastern perimeter roughly on the line of the

branch of the railway that crossed the Neder Rijn, and to use this as a start line for still another attempt to relieve Frost. The disengagement of the brigade in daylight entailed considerable casualties and a lot of confusion. The gliderborne part of the Polish Parachute Brigade landed in the face of heavy anti-aircraft fire only to be caught in the cross fire of the land battle.

Matchless courage

The weather was again bad over England and the drop of the rest of the Polish Parachute Brigade south of the river had to be postponed, as had the landing of the 82nd Airborne Division gliderborne regimental combat team (RCT). Anti-aircraft fire was intense and the *Luftwaffe* having, unlike the Allies, good weather over their airfields sent out more than 425 Messerschmitt 109s and Focke-Wulf 190s against the air escort alone.

Many members of the 1st Airborne Division witnessed an unsurpassed example of bravery and devotion to duty under tragic circumstances. Failing wireless communications, every effort had been made to indicate to the re-supply aircraft a change of dropping zone, but without avail. When the daily re-supply aircraft came under intense anti-aircraft fire, Flight-Lieutenant David Lord had his Dakota hit and the starboard engine set on fire; he nevertheless held his course at 900 feet (275m) to drop his load with accuracy then turned for a second run to discharge the remainder of his cargo, being all the time under intense fire. Just before his wing collapsed he ordered his crew to bale out while he remained at the controls. He was awarded a posthumous Victoria Cross.

Thirteen of the 163 aircraft taking part in the re-supply were lost and 97 damaged. Tragically nearly all the 380 tons of ammunition and supplies dropped into German hands.

At 0830 the Guards Armoured Division started to cross the Grave bridge and at 1700 a battalion of the 82nd Airborne Division and one of the Grenadier Guards made an unsuccessful attack on the

Nijmegen bridge, while a battalion of the Coldstream Guards was sent to support the 82nd Airborne Division on the Reichswald forest front.

Not only had bad weather deprived Urquhart of a fresh reserve, but it deprived Gavin of his gliderborne RCT which would have enabled him to take the Nijmegen bridge without diverting the Guards Armoured Division from its primary task of linking up with the 1st Airborne Division. In the 101st Airborne Division's area a sharp German attack on Zon stopped movement on the main axis of advance for several hours.

Wednesday 20 September saw the end of one great martial exploit, the 2nd Parachute Battalion Group's stand at Arnhem bridge, and the performance of another, the crossing of the Waal at Nijmegen, by the 504th Parachute RCT of the 82nd Airborne Division supported by the Guards Armoured Division. The former by holding back the 10th SS *Panzer* Division made the latter possible.

Battle on the bridge

At Arnhem bridge Frost was wounded and command devolved on to Gough. More and more houses were set on fire or were reduced to rubble. The number of wounded in the cellars multiplied and were in danger of being burnt to death. The last attempt to break through with three Bren carriers filled with ammunition was defeated. By 21 September all resistance had ceased.

The rest of the 1st Airborne Division consolidated on a reduced perimeter. By the evening the eastern side, nearest the river, was held by a mixed force of the 2nd South Staffords and the 11th Parachute Battalion, with some men of the 1st Parachute Brigade, under Major Dickie Lonsdale, with positions in line with and between the forward guns of the 1st Airlanding Light Regiment RA. To the west the perimeter still included the ferry at Heveadorp; on the north it extended only 1,000 yards (915m) beyond divisional headquarters. In the defensive battle of what the Germans called 'the Cauldron' the Glider Pilot Regiment played a notable part, for which they had been trained. For instance it was standard practice for the glider pilots with each Airlanding Light Battery to form a platoon for local protection. The 180 glider pilots who had flown in the Airlanding Light Regiment formed four platoons commanded by Major Bob Crout, who was killed, and remained under command of that regiment throughout.

Nijmegen bridge

The 82nd Airborne Division was under pressure from the Reichswald forest area. General Gavin believed that the Nijmegen bridge must be captured this day at all costs and that this could be done only by capturing both ends of the road and rail bridges simultaneously. He therefore ordered the 504th Parachute RCT, under Colonel Reuben H. Tucker, to cross the wide Waal in British assault boats covered by fire of artillery and tanks of the Irish Guards, and seize the northern end of the bridge. Tanks of the Grenadier Guards

Above: The vital Arnhem road bridge, seen just after the end of the battle. Frost's men held the north end (at the top), destroying the German vehicles visible there.

Right: For much of the way, the Guards Armoured Division led XXX Corps' drive towards Arnhem. Here one of its lorries, already on fire, is seen exploding.

and a battalion of the 505th Parachute RCT stood ready to rush the bridge from the south.

Major Julian Cook's 3rd Battalion was selected to lead the amphibious assault. This they did in British assault boats with which they were totally unfamiliar and which, because of traffic congestion and a German bombing raid on Eindhoven, only arrived at the last moment. There were enough boats for only a two-company lift without heavy weapons.

American success

At 1430 air attacks were made on the German position on the farther bank, at 1440 artillery and tank gun fire opened on the enemy positions, and at 1500 the first wave of boats, rowed by sappers and infantry using their rifle butts, started to cross the wide river 1 mile (1·6km) below the bridge and in the face of intense German fire. Beyond the farther bank lay 200 to 800 yards (180 to 730m) of flat and open country terminating in a sloping dyke some 15 to 20 feet (4·5 to 6m) high which carried a roadway open to view from a fortified building some 800 yards (730m) beyond.

The first wave of Americans rushed the embankment, routing the Germans after strong resistance. The remainder of the 3rd Battalion was ferried across, cleared the ground beyond the embankment and swinging right rushed and secured first the north end of the railway and then of the road bridge. The 3rd Battalion had suffered about 50 per cent casualties. The Guards then rushed the bridge from the south while Lieutenant Tony Jones of the Royal Engineers methodically cut the wires connecting the bridge demolition charges, while under fire. Of this magnificent action by the 504th Parachute RCT the British official report reads: 'Desperate resistance of a strong and deter-

mined enemy, with every advantage of position, had been insufficient to stop these men.'

The last bridge before Arnhem was taken intact just as that at Arnhem was about to fall into the hands of the enemy. The higher command continued to act as though success were still a possibility. On Thursday night, plans were made to fly in supplies and possibly the 52nd (Lowland) Division, an air portable formation, to an LZ near Grave, instead of at Deelen, north of Arnhem, and on Friday the 2nd Army limited XXX Corps advance to Apeldoorn, halfway between Arnhem and the Zuider Zee! It seems certain that neither the precarious position of the 1st Airborne Division nor the remarkable recovery made by the Germans had yet been fully appreciated. German pressure against both sides of the corridor and against the 1st Airborne Division continued to grow, with serious interference in the flow of traffic as more and more men and equipment belonging to Zangen's 15th Army were ferried across the Scheldt.

Communications restored

Early on Thursday Captain McMillan established wireless communication from the headquarters of the 1st Airlanding Light Battery, near Oosterbeek church, with the 64th Medium Regiment RA. From now on the 1st Airborne Division enjoyed a reliable line of communications with

Enfield .38 No2 Revolver

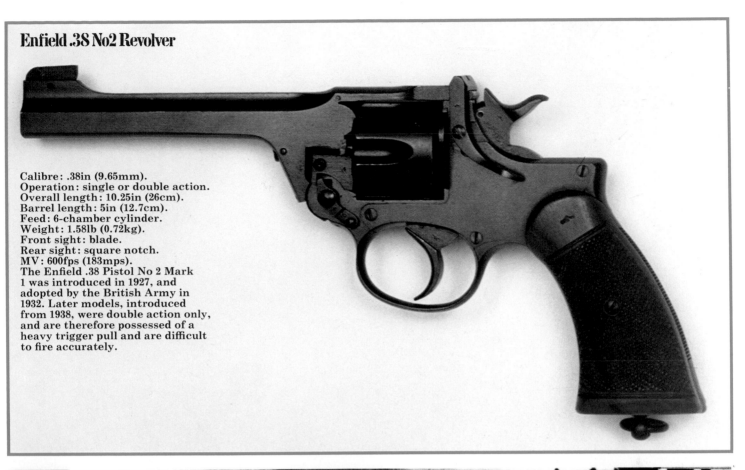

Calibre: .38in (9.65mm).
Operation: single or double action.
Overall length: 10.25in (26cm).
Barrel length: 5in (12.7cm).
Feed: 6-chamber cylinder.
Weight: 1.58lb (0.72kg).
Front sight: blade.
Rear sight: square notch.
MV: 600fps (183mps).
The Enfield .38 Pistol No 2 Mark 1 was introduced in 1927, and adopted by the British Army in 1932. Later models, introduced from 1938, were double action only, and are therefore possessed of a heavy trigger pull and are difficult to fire accurately.

Douglas C-47 Skytrain

Type: troop and supply transport, paratroop transport and glider tug. Engines: two 1,200hp Pratt & Whitney R-1830-92 Twin Wasp radials. Span: 95ft 6in (29.1m). Length: 63ft 9in (19.4m). Height: 17ft (5.2m). Speed: 230mph (370kph). Range: 1,600 miles (2,575km). Service ceiling: 24,000ft (7,315m). Payload: 27 troops or up to

10,000lb (4,536kg) of cargo. Weight empty: 18,200lb (8,255kg). Loaded weight: 29,000lb (13,154kg). Named Skytrain by the Americans and Dakota by the British, the C-47 was one of the most important aircraft of World War II. Its civil counterpart, from which it was derived, is the celebrated and ubiquitous Douglas DC-3 airliner.

The military version differed mostly in having a larger door, a strengthened floor and lashing points for cargo.

XXX Corps both for fire support and for operational messages; it had been through to the 2nd Army on the 'Phantom' net for some time.

The weather at last allowed the Polish Parachute Brigade to take off, which it did at 1400, its dropping zone being changed from south of Arnhem bridge to south of the Heveadorp ferry. The 110 Dakotas carrying the Poles encountered bad weather *en route* and were attacked by German fighters with some loss of aircraft. In all, 41 Dakotas returned without dropping, 13 were missing, 3 landed at Brussels and only 53 reached the dropping zone, discharging some 750 men from whom Major-General Sosabowski formed two weak battalions.

It was intended that the Poles should join the 1st Airborne Division via the ferry, but unfortunately the Borderers were driven from the high ground commanding the ferry. The 1st Airborne Division was coming under increasing pressure from small parties of Germans supported by SP guns, while heavy mortar and gun fire took their toll within the shrinking perimeter. Ammunition for the British was getting low and no supplies were being received. On the other hand, morale was boosted by the demonstrated ability of the 64th Medium Regiment RA, with a heavy battery under command, to bring down accurate and effective fire on infiltrators within the divisional perimeter. On occasion the 1st Airlanding

Light Regiment deliberately brought this fire on to its own gun positions.

It was soon realized that the capture of the Nijmegen bridge had not opened the way for a swift dash to Arnhem by the Guards Armoured Division. The road ahead, through Elst, lay along the top of a causeway with steep banks, and on both sides, off the causeway, the country was not favourable to the use of armour. Horrocks therefore decided that the 43rd Infantry Division should take over the lead. Unfortunately it was not until nightfall on the 21st that the division had arrived in strength in the Nijmegen area.

At first light on Friday 22 September an enterprising armoured car squadron of the Household Cavalry crossed the Waal

Above left: A Vickers machine-gun crew of the 1st Airborne Division engages German snipers in a house on the edges of Arnhem during 18 September 1944.

Above: A German patrol stops under the cover of a hedge to consider its next move in the battle in Arnhem. Only after severe street fighting did the British surrender.

and, moving north-west on secondary roads, got through to the Poles about Driel, and subsequently damaged a German steamer and sank three German barges on the Neder Rijn. At 0830 the 214th Infantry Brigade of the 43rd Division attacked along the main axis towards Elst, which was strongly held by units of the 10th SS *Panzer* Division. Held up halfway to Elst, the brigade attempted to pass a battalion mounted on tanks to the west through Oosterhaut with DUKWs to ferry supplies and the Poles across the Rhine. They were held up in Oosterhaut for six hours and only reached Driel in the evening.

Black day

Urquhart was convinced that XXX Corps did not appreciate the precarious situation of the 1st Airborne Division. He therefore decided to send Lieutenant-Colonel Charles Mackenzie and Lieutenant-Colonel Eddie Myers, commanding the Royal Engineers, across the river to report directly to XXX Corps. They were with the Poles at Driel when the 5th DCLI

and a squadron of Dragoon Guards arrived. The DUKWs could not be launched and the only Poles to cross were some 50 who got across that night on rafts.

Friday was a black day. The weather again prevented effective air support, no supplies reached the 1st Airborne Division, and a strong German attack in the Veghel area cut the Allied line of communications. The 32nd Guards Brigade was sent south to support the 101st Airborne Division in restoring the situation, but the road remained closed for 24 hours.

Defeat accepted

On Saturday came a break in the bad weather. Gliders carrying the remainder of the 101st Airborne Division's 327th Glider Infantry RCT, and the 82nd Airborne Division's long overdue 325th Glider Infantry RCT were flown in, a very welcome reinforcement. By the end of the day the 43rd Infantry Division had its 130th Infantry Brigade established about Driel and the 214th Infantry Brigade fighting in Elst, but a plan for the 1st Airborne Division to regain control of the ferry had to be abandoned and the 5th DCLI was unable to make the river crossing to enlarge the bridgehead.

By Sunday all intention of getting through to the bridge at Arnhem had been abandoned, but the 214th Infantry Brigade continued to clear Elst against strong opposition. The 130th Infantry Brigade ordered the 4th Dorsets to cross the river that night. With great difficulty 300 to 400 men got across, but drifting down river they landed well outside the 1st Airborne Division's shrunken perimeter;

early on Monday morning an OP party from the 43rd's divisional artillery arrived in the 1st Airlanding Light Regiment's gun area. The pounding of the 1st Airborne Division continued, and the division was now out of food and very short of ammunition.

Brian Horrocks remained determined and optimistic, but he was overridden by the 2nd Army commander, Lieutenant-General Sir Miles Dempsey, who with Browning's support finally secured Montgomery's permission to withdraw the 1st Airborne Division during Monday night, 25 September, D+8 days. The division's withdrawal was covered by intensive artillery fire from XXX Corps, which the wounded optimistically believed to herald a river crossing by the Allies. The division withdrew through the 1st Airlanding Light Regiment's gun position near the Oosterbeek church. The gunners were the last to go, having first rendered their guns useless. Only 2,163 out of the 10,095 who took part in the battle got across, though some more came out later.

No 1944 end

Thus ended, with dire historical results, the dream of ending the war in 1944.

At the start of this chapter we examined some of the organizational weaknesses in the 'Market-Garden' plan, weaknesses which were accentuated by the speed with which this complex inter-Allied operation had to be mounted. The effects on the operations of the inadequacy of the signals equipment for the tasks required of it; the unexpectedly bad weather; the rapidity with which the German generals were able

to reorganize and instil renewed fighting spirit into their beaten and demoralized soldiery; and the effects of this recovery on a plan which depended for success on a rapid advance of over 60 miles (95km) along a narrow corridor and across major water obstacles are brought out in the narrative. The author also believes that it is not unfair to say that whatever the sense of urgency at the higher levels of command this did not in every case communicate itself to the individual soldier after the widespread euphoria which followed the rapid advance to the Dutch frontier.

The technical failures of the past are of little interest for the future but the spirit of man is eternal and it is in study of human reactions under conditions of great stress both individually and in units that the main interest in these operations lies.

Great gallantry

Individual's actions speak for themselves. Four members of the 1st Airborne Division were awarded the Victoria Cross: Captain L. E. Queripel, The Royal Sussex Regiment, attached to the 10th Parachute Battalion; Lieutenant J. H. Grayburn, the 2nd Parachute Battalion; Lance-Sergeant J. D. Baskeyfield, the 2nd South Staffords; and Major R. H. Cain, The Royal

Northumberland Fusiliers, attached to the 2nd South Staffords. All but Cain's were posthumous, and all were awarded for acts of great gallantry and self sacrifice.

Fighting efficiency

There were, of course, many acts of gallantry that went unrecognized. Courage is an expendible commodity, and it is interesting to note at Arnhem examples of men fighting with great tenacity or having suffered some shattering experience early in the battle then finding themselves drained of courage but who nevertheless got, as it were, their second wind and so came back strongly in the last days, in one case to win a well-deserved Victoria Cross. This is something worth noting for it is the responsibility of leadership to aid such recovery.

Though individual bravery is a precious asset, what counts above all in fighting efficiency, particularly where infantry is concerned, is the ability of a unit to maintain cohesion under seemingly intolerable pressure. Cohesion is the result of many factors; pride of regiment, previous success in battle, good leadership, good training, and discipline.

It is difficult to generalize. Units of the 1st Parachute Brigade had enjoyed great success in North Africa and Sicily, but

Above: Consolidated B-24 Liberator heavy bombers of the US 8th Air Force drop supplies to the American airborne divisions. The British were not so lucky in their drops.

they had also received many casualty replacements. Their reputation and the realistic training which sprang from their combat experience stood them in good stead. On the other hand, the 7th KOSB with no previous battle experience fought remarkably under most difficult circumstances.

Combat cohesion

Some may wonder, despite the difficulties already pointed out, why only the 700 who comprised the 2nd Parachute Battalion Group, out of more than 10,000, reached their objective. In judging the performance of other units the difficulty of the task and the fact that they included many young and inexperienced soldiers must be taken into account. No form of fighting puts a greater strain on unit cohesion than offensive action in a heavily built-up area against a determined enemy. Street fighting requires special training and, so far as the author knows, the units trying to fight their way through to the Arnhem bridge had had little or none.

Above: The end of the road for British paratroops, rounded up by German infantry at the end of the battle after those who could had swum across the Rhine to safety.

Right: Major-General Stanislaw Sosabowski (with map) of the 1st Polish Parachute Brigade, was one of the few senior officers to voice dissent with the basic Arnhem plan.

The 2nd Parachute Battalion got through with skill, and before resistance had hardened.

Moreover, the Dutch habit of putting high and strong steel-mesh fences around their gardens provided an additional difficulty, and the prevalence of cellars was a ubiquitous temptation in situations of danger. Not all soldiers wearing the Red Beret were courageous, few perhaps were courageous all the time, but the division as a whole would endorse Major-General Roy Urquhart's report, made in January 1945, in which he wrote: 'The losses were heavy but all ranks appreciate that the risks were reasonable. There is no doubt that all would willingly undertake another operation under similar conditions in the future.' The author, for one, would add: 'providing the lessons learned in "Market-Garden" had been applied.'

The Defence of Bastogne

The German airborne arm had acquired an enviable reputation for dour defensive fighting at Cassino and in Brittany. The British had won a similar reputation in the closing stages of the desperate fighting for Arnhem. And in the Battle of the Bulge the US 101st Airborne Division, 'resting' after the rigours of 'Market', won similar fame for the defence of Bastogne.

In their short history the airborne forces of the world have with some justification acquired a reputation as first-class fighting troops, and no little part of this reputation has been earned in defensive fighting under the most adverse conditions, as in the magnificent efforts of the German 1st Parachute Division in front of Cassino and of the British 1st Airborne Division at Arnhem. Elite units, confident in their own basic superiority, airborne troops seemed capable in World War II of achieving far more than they should have been able to, especially in defensive fighting when all else appeared to have been lost, and the epic of the US 101st Airborne Division's beleaguered stand at Bastogne fully deserves to be included with the other great feats of airborne forces.

Late in 1944, the backs of Germany's armies were firmly against the wall: to the east the Russians, in vast, well equipped numbers, were pounding their way forward towards Germany; and to the west the Allies were forging forward towards Germany's last real defence, the Rhine river. Hitler, adventurous as ever, refused even to consider the possibility of surrender, and decided to gamble all on one last throw against the Western Allies. Germany's last major armoured formations, heavily reinforced, were to be gathered secretly in the Ardennes, from where they were to strike out in the direction of Antwerp, a major Allied supply

port. With the Allied forces thus split in two again, as in 1940, the armies cut off to the north of the German corridor would be destroyed piecemeal. The plan was wildly over-ambitious, but had everything gone smoothly the Allies would have been very severely jolted. Hitler's plans for what was to become the 'Battle of the Bulge', however, were entirely dependent on three factors: a quick initial breakthrough, the immediate capture of the great Allied fuel dumps and centres of communication between St Vith in the north and Bastogne in the south, and then the widening of the breach so that the necessary German forces could debouch up into Belgium. None of these prerequisites was to be met, and it was the sterling defence of Bastogne by the 101st Airborne Division that cost the Germans the second one.

The German offensive, which was launched by eight *Panzer* divisions from the 6th SS and 5th *Panzer* Armies, smashed through weak American defences on 16 December 1944. Allied intelligence had in general discounted the possibility of a major German push, especially in the Ardennes, and the sector was held by inferior grade formations and units resting from their efforts in the previous Allied offensive. The inadequacy of the defences, which had little in the way of heavy weapons, allowed the initial German breakthrough to move forward swiftly. In these dire first hours, only the sturdy defence of the US V Corps in the north and the US 4th Infantry Division prevented the Germans from widening the breach as they had intended.

Germans flood west

Lieutenant-General Omar Bradley, in whose 12th Army Group sector the offensive had started, rushed in two armoured divisions to stem the German flood, and at the same time General Dwight Eisen-

Below: Men of the 101st Airborne Division move out of Bastogne on 29 December 1944 to help push the Germans back east towards their original start lines.

hower, commanding the Allied forces in western Europe, released from his theatre reserve XVIII Airborne Corps, resting in the Rheims area after their exertions in the 'Market-Garden' operations. The corps' two divisions immediately moved into the Ardennes by truck: the 82nd Airborne Division, under Major-General Matthew Ridgway, to the northern flank of the German salient, and the 101st Airborne Division, under the temporary command of Brigadier-General Anthony McAuliffe, to Bastogne, key to the southern flank. Other Allied forces were hurriedly allocated new tasks, but their movement would take some time, and so the defence of the salient initially rested with these scratch reinforcements. The 101st Airborne Division arrived in Bastogne on 19 December, and immediately set about preparing its defence. Major-General Troy Middleton, commanding the US VIII Corps in the area, visited McAuliffe on the 19th and succinctly ordered him to 'Hold Bastogne'.

Outposts pushed back

First into action was Lieutenant-Colonel Julian Ewell's 501st Parachute Infantry Regiment, which was instructed on 18 December to move out at 0600 on the next day from Bastogne to try to link up with US outposts to the east, and develop the situation there. These outposts, from the 9th and 10th Armored Divisions, were already pulling back under extreme pressure from the *Panzer Lehr* armoured division, which had in fact bypassed several of them. The Germans knew of the arrival of the airborne division at Bastogne, and were hoping to destroy it before an adequate defence could be organized. Of the three German divisions heading in the general direction of Bastogne, though, only two had a direct interest in the town: while the 2nd *Panzer* Division made for the Meuse bridges, the *Panzer Lehr* was to attack Bastogne from the east and the 26th *Volksgrenadier* Division from the north. One problem for the Germans, however, was that the *Volksgrenadier* division was exhausted from keeping up with the mechanized elements of the *Panzer Lehr*, and would have to wait for its rear echelons to catch up before it could participate in the planned concerted attack on the American bastion.

Main thrust held

The 501st Regiment had meanwhile moved out and met the Germans at Neffe, some 2,000 yards (1,830m) east of Bastogne. Confused fighting raged through the day as the paratroops strove to find suitable defensive positions, the armoured divisions' outposts fell back and the Germans tried to push on through. There were heroic moments: Private Bernard Michin, of the attached 158th Engineer Combat Battalion, halted a German thrust towards Neffe by blasting the leading German tank at a range of only 10 yards with his bazooka; and in Wardin, south-east of Neffe, one of the SP guns the Germans were using to clear the town was knocked out by a paratrooper who calmly stepped out into the street, fired and was then cut down by machine-gun fire. By the end

of the day, however, the 501st Regiment was in position astride the main road into Bastogne from the east, and the various American outpost forces were straggling into the perimeter that was forming. With the arrival of these detached units, McAuliffe eventually had some 18,000 men under his command.

What the Americans failed to realize on the 19th, though, was that as yet they had not been contacted by the main strength of the *Panzer Lehr* and 26th *Volksgrenadier* Divisions, which were busily engaged destroying Combat Command R of the 9th Armored Division to the north-east between Mageret and Longvilly. Thick fog had hampered the efforts of both sides during large parts of the day, making it difficult to try to make any sense of the confused fighting, and this was to be the case in the next few days as well.

German build-up

Throughout the 20th and 21st the Germans continued to close in round Bastogne, launching a series of strengthening attacks. McAuliffe's men managed to beat these off, however, and a defensive perimeter gradually formed round Bastogne at an average of some 3,000 yards (2,750m) from the town centre, although there was an excrescence some 2,000 yards (1,830m) long running to the north-west from Mande-St Etienne, west of Bastogne. Armour support for the 101st Airborne Division was promised, in the form of a combat command from the 4th Armored Division of Lieutenant-General George Patton's 3rd Army, which was racing north. But this failed to arrive before the German ring had been closed round Bastogne, leaving McAuliffe with only a few armoured vehicles from a team of Combat Command B of the 4th Armored Division, led by Captain Bert Ezell. McAuliffe was also led to believe that major elements of VIII Corps would cooperate on his flanks, but by the 20th this was manifestly not the case. Although no one on the American side realized it until the day afterwards, from 20 December Bastogne was cut off from the outside world and on its own.

Above: A blanket covers the body of a member of the 101st Airborne Division killed in his billet by the explosion of a German shell during the attack on Bastogne.

Above right: Apparently unconcerned by the buildings set on fire by German artillery fire, two Americans ride through Bastogne on the glacis plate of an M4 Sherman.

Below right: With the improvement in the weather, a C-47 of the US IX Troop Carrier Command parachute drops supplies to the beleaguered troops in Bastogne on 23 December.

The 501st Parachute Infantry Regiment held the eastern side of the perimeter, and then running clockwise round this were two battalions of the 327th Glider Infantry Regiment in the south, with the 3rd Battalion, 327th Regiment holding the salient out to the west, the 502nd Parachute Infantry Regiment manning the northern perimeter, and the 506th Parachute Infantry Regiment occupying the north-eastern sector between the 502nd and 501st Regiments. In Bastogne itself were the headquarters of the 101st Airborne Division, Combat Command R of the 9th Armored Division and Combat Command B of the 10th Armored Division.

Bastogne encircled

During the 20th the battle for the town grew in intensity, with both the *Panzer Lehr* and 26th *Volksgrenadier* Division attacking. None of these attacks succeeded, but the growing intensity indicated what was to come. By the end of the day, the two German divisions had encircled the town, *Panzer Lehr* basically to the south-east of a line running from south-west to north-east through the town, and the 26th *Volksgrenadier* to the north-west of the line. Fighting continued on the 21st, but then on the 22nd the Germans made a considerable blunder.

General Heinrich Freiherr von Lüttwitz, commanding XLVII *Panzer* Corps which was controlling the battle, thought the American position hopeless, and at about

Above: Armoured fighting vehicles of Lieutenant-General George S. Patton's US 3rd Army begin to group on the outskirts of Bastogne to relieve the 101st Division.

Left: German prisoners taken at Bastogne dig a mass grave for some of the 101st Airborne Division's dead, the whole time under armed American supervision.

midday sent in four officers under a flag of truce. Coming in through the lines held by the 2nd Battalion, 327th Glider Infantry Regiment, the Germans gave the Americans an ultimatum: unless the 101st Airborne Division agreed to the 'honourable surrender of this encircled town' within two hours, the American garrison would be 'annihilated' by the massed fire of the German artillery. McAuliffe's answer to Lüttwitz's ultimatum has secured him a special niche in military history: 'Nuts!' Lieutenant-Colonel Ralph Harper, commanding the 327th, failed to find an idiomatic translation for McAuliffe's answer, and told the Germans to 'Go to Hell!'

Morale booster

Realizing that this could be a useful boost to morale if properly handled, Lieutenant-Colonel Paul Danahy, the divisional head of intelligence, reported in his daily account that 'The Commanding General's answer was, with a sarcastic air of humourous tolerance, emphatically negative.'

22 December, which finally saw the end of Germany's effort elsewhere in the Ardennes salient, was marked by the return of excellent weather. Although this was important for the battle in other sectors, allowing Allied fighter-bombers to play a decisive part in the blunting of the German armoured spearheads, it was a mixed blessing for the 101st Airborne Division. Admittedly vital supplies could be airdropped in, but it also allowed German aircraft to bomb the town, and gave the assault forces excellent fighting weather, despite the snow and cold. Some 241 aircraft dropped supplies on the 23rd, 160 on the next day, none on Christmas Day because of poor weather, and on Boxing Day 289 aircraft flew in supplies. Most of the tonnage dropped was ammunition for the artillery, without which the survival of the garrison would at best have been problematical. Fighter-bombers also operated with great success against the German besiegers, dropping general-purpose and fragmentation bombs, as well as using napalm and machine-gun fire to suppress German movements.

The fighting of 23 December was a desperate affair, with the *Panzer Lehr* making serious inroads near Marvie on the southern flank before being halted by the 327th Regiment. Lieutenant-Colonel Harry Kinnard, head of the divisional operations section, informed his VIII Corps opposite number: 'In regard to our situation it is getting pretty sticky around here. They [the 4th Armored Division] must keep coming. The enemy has attacked all along the south and some tanks are through and running around our area. Request you inform 4th Armored Division of our situation and ask them to put on all possible pressure.' This was a masterly understatement of the 101st Division's problems, but appreciated rightly that the garrison's saviour must be the 4th Armored Division pushing up from the south.

Final attacks

Kinnard played a very significant part in the battle, and he realized that the division was overextended, especially in the west. This had had the effect of making co-ordination difficult, especially between the paratroops and the armoured units. During the 24th, therefore, Kinnard instituted a reshaping of the defence perimeter, which was brought in closer to Bastogne in the south and west. The reorganization was only just in time, for on Christmas Day the Germans launched their most dangerous attack. Supported on its south-west and north-west flanks by attacks by the 26th *Volksgrenadier* Division, the 115th Regiment of the 15th *Panzergrena-*

M1919 Calibre .30 Machine Gun

Calibre: .30in (7.6mm). **Operation:** recoil, automatic only. **Length:** 41in (1.04m). **Barrel length:** 24in (61cm). **Feed:** 250-round fabric or disintegrating link metal belt. **Weight:** 31lb (14.1kg). **Tripod weight:** 14lb (6.35kg). **Front sight:** blade. **Rear sight:** leaf. **Cyclic rate:** 400–550rpm. **Muzzle velocity:** 2,800fps (853mps).

dier Division, an armoured reinforcement just arrived, would attack towards Hemroulle, north-west of Bastogne. Supported by a *Luftwaffe* raid, the attack at first went well, and looked as though it might succeed in advancing as far as Bastogne itself, as planned.

The defence holds

The American frontline positions were overrun, and it was only after heroic efforts by the US reserve, parts of the 1st Battalion, 502nd Parachute Infantry Regiment, that the German push was halted in Hemroulle and Champs. Brought to a standstill, the Germans attempted to dig in, but were unable to do so because of the frozen ground. They then stood and fought it out, being virtually wiped out in the process. It was a last despairing effort by the local German commander, Major-General Heinz Kokott of the 26th *Volksgrenadier* Division, who now had only his own formation, the remnants of the 15th *Panzergrenadier* Division's 115th Regiment and 901st Regiment of the *Panzer Lehr* Division.

Relief arrives

Bastogne had held out in dire circumstances, and during the afternoon of the 26th the gallant American garrison was to be relieved. But first the Germans launched one last 'desperate effort', or perhaps desperation move might be a better description. An assault force from the 26th *Volksgrenadier* Division, supported by 10 tank-destroyers, drove into the US lines at Isle-la-Hesse, south of Hemroulle. At first steady progress was made, but then the German force was caught in the open by fire from the American howitzers west of Bastogne. The infantry were wiped out, and six tank-destroyers knocked out, the remaining four pressing on alone. Trapped in front of a large ditch, however, these last four were blown apart by artillery fire and the efforts of American tank-destroyers.

The 5th Parachute Division, which had been trying to halt the US 4th Armored Division south of Bastogne, was now swept aside, and at 1645 the 326th Airborne Engineer Battalion reported contact with 'three light tanks believed friendly'. The siege was over. Bastogne had held out, thanks to the efforts of the 101st Airborne Division and its attached units, materially hindering the 5th *Panzer* Army's westward advance. The Germans made desperate attempts to cut the 4th Armored Division's corridor to the south in the next few days, but all to no avail, and the German hold on Bastogne was finally crushed on 2 January 1945. Because of the conditions

Above: German prisoners head for the rear and POW cages under the escort of 3rd Army men, whose arrival greatly speeded the final dissolution of the German attacks.

during the siege, which made it impossible ever accurately to assess the number of personnel trapped at Bastogne, casualty lists are tentative. The 101st Airborne Division, however, lost 105 officers and 1,536 other ranks, and Combat Command B of the 10th Armored Division, which had played a notable part in stopping the German armoured attacks, 25 officers and 478 men.

The Rhine Crossings

The eventual failure of the Arnhem operation had the immediate effect of halting Allied plans for further 'strategic' airborne moves, but in the spring of 1945 two whole airborne divisions were launched in one of the war's most successful tactical operations: landings just in the Germans' rear areas beyond the Rhine to facilitate the Allied crossings of that great river.

In the spring of 1945 the three great Western Allied army groups were poised to invade Germany proper across the Rhine. Yet this formidable river barrier, forming Germany's geographical frontier, posed the Allies very difficult problems, principally because of its size and the speed of its current. Moreover, the skill of the decimated German armies in defensive fighting had been proved time and time again since the Allies had landed in Sicily during July 1943, and this skill might now be expected to join with a surge of patriotism to make the actual assault into Germany a very dangerous affair.

If the Allies were to bring the war to a swift and successful conclusion, however, an assault crossing of the Rhine was inevitable. The problem, therefore, was how to maximize the assault forces' chances of success, while at the same time minimizing their casualties from the German positions on the east bank and from counterattack by artillery, armour and reserves moving up from rear areas once the actual crossing points had become clear. The best solution to the problem

Below: Men of a US parachute infantry battalion dig in under the trees of a German orchard, the branches of which are draped with the parachutes used in the landing.

appeared to be an airborne landing between the assault forces on the east bank and the reserves moving up for a counter-attack.

This operation, codenamed 'Varsity', was to be the last great Allied airborne action of the war, but before discussing it, mention should be made of the fact that Lieutenant-General Lewis Brereton's staff at the 1st Allied Airborne Army's headquarters had since the time of 'Overlord' prepared a large number of plans for the airborne forces they controlled. These had been tactical operations for the most part, but in December 1944 this began to alter significantly with the arrival of Colonel Philip Cochran in England. An American air force officer, Cochran had recently commanded the No 1 Air Commando in Burma, with the task of providing air support for Major-General Orde Wingate 'Chindits'. Convinced of the strategic value of Wingate's concepts of air-supplied 'strongholds' deep behind enemy lines, Cochran set about considering similar operations for the 1st Allied Airborne Army. One of his first plans was 'Eclipse', in which two airborne corps were to be dropped on Berlin, but even if the Allied command had been prepared to consider so ambitious a plan, it was ruled out by the decision taken at the Yalta Conference between Roosevelt, Churchill and Stalin that Berlin was to be a Russian objective. Despite this setback, Cochran pressed on, his next scheme being 'Arena', in which no less than 10 divisions (the British 1st and 6th Airborne, the US 13th, 17th, 82nd and 101st Airborne, and four US infantry divisions) were to be landed halfway between Berlin and the Rhine to establish a stronghold. 'Arena' might well have yielded fruitful results, but the Allied high command was not ambitious enough to consider such a plan, and it was dropped. It is interesting to speculate, however, how these two large-scale operations might have fared in a situation as fluid as that prevailing in Germany during the closing months of the war. Certainly the plans might have been looked at with a little more sympathy, for they offered the distinct chance of striking success for minimal casualties.

Tactical operation

Yet the type of bold strategic airborne operation advocated by Cochran and other planners at 1st Allied Airborne Army headquarters failed to find favour, and so this powerful force was earmarked to support Field-Marshal Sir Bernard Montgomery's push across the lower Rhine just north of Wesel. Montgomery's 21st Army Group planned to put across two armies, the British 2nd and US 9th, which between them could muster seven corps containing 6 armoured divisions, 17 infantry divisions, 5 armoured brigades, 1 commando brigade and the specialized 79th Armoured Division, plus supporting troops. Though this was an extremely formidable force, Montgomery and Lieutenant-General Sir Miles Dempsey, commanding the 2nd Army, both felt that the strength of the expected German defences necessitated airborne support. The assault front was defended by the 1st Parachute Army, which had some 150 armoured

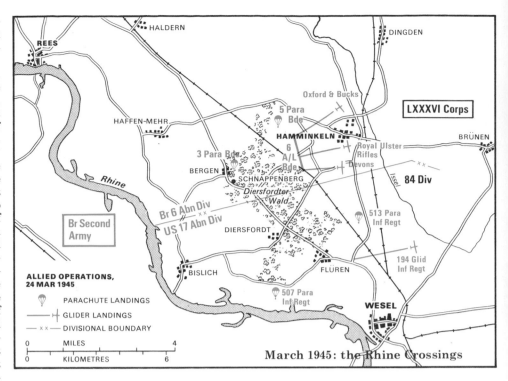

ALLIED OPERATIONS, 24 MAR 1945

PARACHUTE LANDINGS
GLIDER LANDINGS
DIVISIONAL BOUNDARY

March 1945: the Rhine Crossings

vehicles, and XLVII *Panzer* Corps was also in the area with one *Panzer* and one *Panzergrenadier* division, and a battalion of heavy tank destroyers. The fact that the Germans expected an airborne attack was confirmed by the increase in AA guns deployed in the sector: in the middle of March 150 light and 100 heavy guns; a week later 710 light and 115 heavy guns.

Assault crossing first

The British commanders in the 21st Army Group expected two tasks to be fulfilled by the airborne forces. Firstly, the high ground east of the crossing point was to be taken to prevent its use by German artillery that might otherwise command the crossing; and secondly the bridgehead area was to be sealed off from the possibility of a rapid German counter-attack from the south-east, from the Wesel direction.

The formation allocated these two major tasks was Major-General Matthew B. Ridgway's XVIII Airborne Corps. Originally intended as a three-division effort, the operation was scaled down to two divisions for lack of the necessary airlift capacity. Ridgway's plan was for his two airborne divisions to jump into the area of the Diersfordterwald, west of Hamminkeln, between the Rhine and Issel rivers. The landing was to be in front of the British 2nd Army, with the British 6th Airborne Division (Major-General Eric Bols) on the left, and the US 17th Airborne Division (Major-General William Miley) on the right. The drop was to be highly concentrated, and the whole formation was to be delivered in one massive lift. This use of only one lift was a tactical novelty, and meant that each division would receive its two parachute brigades (or regiments) and one glider-borne airlanding brigade (or regiment) very quickly, ensuring maximum concentration in a short period. Another tactical innovation of 'Varsity' involved the timing of the airborne operation: whereas other Allied operations in which both

Right: US troops take shelter as a white phosphorus grenade bursts farther down the street which they are clearing. Note the picture of Hitler lying among the debris.

ground and airborne forces were used had opted for the initial deployment of the airborne forces, followed by the arrival of the ground forces, in 'Varsity' this order was to be reversed in the hope of confusing the Germans. The ground forces were first to assault across the Rhine, and only after the Germans had discounted the possibility of an airborne operation and had started to move their forces up against the bridgehead were the airborne divisions to come in.

The US airlift was the responsibility of the US IX Troop Carrier Command, which had reduced the time needed for airborne drops to an absolute minimum: Ridgway was thus able to plan his operation with a tight schedule in mind. The two parachute brigades and two parachute regiments were to drop in the first 20 minutes of the operation, with the British airlanding brigade being delivered by the RAF's Nos 38 and 46 Groups within the next 45 minutes and the US airlanding regiment within 108 minutes.

Impressive sight

By dawn on 24 March 1945 the leading elements of the 2nd and 9th Armies had crossed the Rhine, and in southern England and around Paris the airborne divisions were boarding their aircraft for the flight to the rendezvous and forming up point near Brussels. From this the aircraft would fly in two concentrated divisional streams to the target area. The lift was an impressive sight: 1,696 transport aircraft and 1,348 gliders bringing in some 21,700 airborne troops. About 1,000 Allied fighter-bombers were also employed to ward off German fighters, suppress flak and engage German tanks and artillery. Major-General James Gavin of the 82nd Airborne Division had moved up to the front to watch the great armada fly over

General Aircraft Hamilcar

Type: troop and tank transport glider.
Engines (Mark X): two 965hp Bristol
Mercury 31 radials. Span: 110ft (33.5m).
Length: 68ft (20.7m). Height: 20ft 3in
(6.2m). Towing speed: 150mph (241kph).
Payload: one 7 ton tank or equivalent
load of troops or other freight. Weight
empty: 19,500lb (8,845kg). Loaded
weight: 37,000lb (16,783kg).

The Hamilcar was designed to carry
light tanks to provide the airborne
forces with armoured support, and was
first used as such in the D-Day
landings. Some 390 were built. The
Mark X powered model had a speed of
145mph (233kph) and a range of 1,675
miles (2,696km), but only 20 were made.

Curtiss C-46 Commando

Type: troop and freight transport.
Engines: two 2,000hp Pratt & Whitney R-2800-51 Double Wasp radials. **Span:** 108ft 1in (32.9m). **Length:** 76ft 4in (23.3m). **Height:** 21ft 9in (6.6m). **Speed:** 269mph (433kph) at 15,000ft (4,572m). **Range:** 1,200 miles (1,931km). **Service ceiling:** 27,600ft (8,413m). **Payload:** 50 troops or up to 10,000lb (4,536kg) of cargo. **Weight empty:** 32,400lb (14,697kg). **Weight loaded:** 56,000lb (25,401kg).

Designed as the CW-20 civil airliner, the aircraft which later became the C-46 Commando was not initially a success. In US military service, however, the Commando played an important part in the Pacific campaign, especially in Marine hands, where its good short field performance and good load carrying capabilities were very useful. Doors on each side also made loading easier than on the C-47. The Commando, with its good ceiling, was widely used in mountainous areas. The type was first used in Europe in the Rhine operation, where it proved very vulnerable.

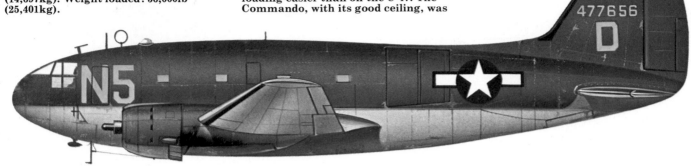

the Rhine: 'It was an indescribably impressive sight. Three columns, each nine ships or double-tow gliders across, moved on the Rhine. On the far side of the river it was surprisingly dusty and hazy, no doubt caused by the earlier bombing and the artillery firing. The air armada continued on and crossed the river. Immediately it was met by, what seemed to me, a terrific amount of flak. A number of ships and gliders went down in flames and after delivering their troops, a surprising number of troop-carrier pilots we saw on their way back were flying planes that were afire. The crew I was with counted twenty-three ships burning in sight at one time.'

The drop had indeed been costly, with 53 aircraft lost and another 440 badly damaged. The high number lost reflects on the use of Curtiss C-46 Commando transports for the first time. Although the type offered tactical advantages over the C-47, in that the aircraft had doors on each side of the fuselage, allowing the paratroops to drop in half the time, the Commando was effectively a death-trap. If a fuel tank were punctured, the spirit ran into the fuselage, where one spark would set it on fire. After this operation Ridgway decided that the C-46 would not again be used for combat operations with paratroops.

One faulty drop

Otherwise the landing went smoothly, all the units but one being dropped on target. On the left, in the 6th Airborne Division's sector, the 3rd Parachute Brigade was dropped just east of Bergen, the 5th Parachute Brigade west of Hamminkeln, and the 6th Airlanding Brigade just to the south of the 5th Parachute Brigade. On the right, in the 17th Airborne Division's sector, the 507th Parachute Infantry Regiment came down on the southern edge of the Diersfordterwald, the 194th Glider Infantry Regiment west of the Issel river south of Hamminkeln, and the 513rd Parachute Infantry Regiment alongside the 6th Airlanding Brigade. This last American drop was the only inaccurate one, and was the result of the C-46s' inadequacies. Colonel James Coutts nevertheless moved straight into action with his men alongside the British glider troops.

Only after helping the British did Coutts's regiment contact its own artillery support and helped by this break out to the south in the direction of its own objectives, all of which had been secured by dusk on 24 March.

Despite the losses to aircraft, casualties to the airborne troops were relatively small, for the swift delivery of the two divisions had given the Germans little time with which to do much damage. Many men, though, became victims on the ground as they struggled to free themselves from their parachute harnesses after they had landed in the trees of the Diersfordterwald. A notable casualty of this type was Lieutenant-Colonel Jeff Nicklin, commander of the 1st Canadian Parachute Battalion in Brigadier James Hill's 3rd Parachute Brigade.

Losses to flak

The brigade, which had come down in the right target area between Bergen and Schnappenburg, was immediately engaged by the Germans and suffered moderately heavy losses to German light flak guns used in the anti-personnel role. Leaving the 8th Parachute Battalion to deal with opposition on the DZ, though, Hill struck off with the 1st Canadian and 9th Parachute Battalions to take his objective, the village of Schnappenburg. By the middle of the afternoon the 3rd Parachute Brigade had been reached by the leading elements of the 2nd Army's overland advance from the Rhine.

The 6th Airlanding Brigade, though, had suffered far more heavily. Intended for the most easterly landing, to seize bridges over the Issel and the large village of Hamminkeln, the gliders of Brigadier R. H. Bellamy's brigade had been released by their tugs at an altitude of 2,500 feet (760m). This meant that the gliders were in the air for some time and they lined up for their LZs and came in, giving the German flak gunners easy targets. Some 27 per cent of the Glider Pilot Regiment's personnel involved were killed, and the losses in the troops being carried were also heavy. The landings were accurate, however, and by the late morning the 6th Airlanding Brigade had secured all its objec-

tives. The 2nd Oxfordshire and Buckinghamshire Light Infantry took the Issel bridges, while the 12th Devons and 1st Royal Ulster Rifles took Hamminkeln. The glider troops were aided in this last task by the 513rd Parachute Infantry Regiment, which had landed in the wrong area.

Objectives taken

Brigadier Nigel Poett's 5th Parachute Brigade landed to the north of the British divisional area, and dropped from slightly too high an altitude. This meant again that the German gunners had time to cause some considerable casualties with small arms and automatic weapons fire before the three battalions reached the ground and set about removing their opponents. The 7th, 12th and 13th Parachute Battalions came down well grouped together astride the road from Hamminkeln to Rees on the Rhine, and moved smoothly against the former, taking all their objectives.

By the late afternoon of the 24th the 2nd Army had linked up with all elements of the 6th Airborne Division. Losses to the division on the ground had not been high, though those in the air had been, to both the parachute and glider troops. This was primarily the result of too high a drop and release point, which gave the German gunners too much time. A passenger in one of the gliders, for example, remembers being released at 2,500 feet (760m) and coming steadily down through a hail of AA fire. His glider contained an engineer section with a jeep loaded with explosives. At 1,000 feet (3·5m) the glider was hit by AA fire which set the petrol tank of the jeep on fire. All the engineers could do was hope that the glider came down before the flames burned through the glider's structure or detonated the load of explosives. All seemed to be going well until the last moment, just as the pilot was lined up on his final approach. The Devons officer's memory then ceases until the moment when he woke up on the ground, or rather on top of a haystack that had broken his fall, to see the wreckage of the Airspeed Horsa glider all around him, together with the bodies of the rest of the glider's

.45 M3 Sub-Machine Gun

Calibre: .45in (11.43mm).
Operation: blowback, automatic
Length: 29.8in (75.7cm); 22.8in
(57.9cm) with stock retracted.
Barrel length: 8in (20.3cm).
Feed: 30-round inline detachable
box magazine.
Weight: 8.15lb (3.7kg).
Front sight: blade.
Rear sight: fixed aperture.
Cyclic rate: 350–450rpm.
MV: about 920fps (280mps).

complement. The fire had reached the explosives just as the Horsa was about to touch down. This experience, although not common, reveals clearly the dangers of too high a release and drop point.

By 1500, however, the division had been relieved by the advancing 2nd Army, and could take stock of its losses: 347 killed and 731 wounded.

The US 17th Airborne Division had flown in from bases around Paris, and throughout used lower drop and release points, the gliders, for example, being cast off at 600 feet (183m). This meant that the airborne troops came down more quickly and so suffered fewer casualties from the German AA fire, but conversely meant that the towing and dropping aircraft suffered correspondingly higher losses.

Successful but unnecessary

Two of the 507th Parachute Infantry Regiment's battalions were dropped in the right place south of the Diersford-terwald, but the third, which included the regimental commander, Colonel Edson Raff, came down almost in the village of Diersfordt itself. Severe fighting broke out in the 507th Regiment's area, and it was only at 1500 that the Germans in Diersfordt surrendered. By dusk, however, the situation had stabilized, and the regiment had made contact with the British commando brigade from the 2nd Army which had entered Wesel to the south-east.

The 513rd Parachute Infantry Regiment, as already mentioned, landed in the wrong area and helped the 6th Airlanding Brigade to take Hamminkeln before breaking out to the south with the support of its artillery component, which had arrived at the right spot. By the time the leading ground forces reached it, however, the regiment had secured all its objectives.

The American glider unit, the 194th Glider Infantry Regiment, landed on the west side of the Issel south of Hamminkeln, and after a short action took its objectives along the river. The 17th Airborne Division's casualties totalled 159 killed, 522 wounded and 840 missing, although some 600 of these last subsequently turned up. Operation 'Varsity' had been success-

ful in itself, but as things turned out it was unnecessary. Opposition to the 2nd Army's Rhine crossing had been minimal, and so the 'airhead' to protect the bridgehead had not been essential. The landings were useful, destroying the rear echelons of two German divisions, and yielding some 3,500 German prisoners, but can hardly be claimed to have been worth the losses. Bad as were the manpower casualties, to both the airborne divisions and their transport and glider-tug aircrew, the *matériel* losses in aircraft were far worse. And although Ridgway was later to claim in support of the operation that the Allied bridgehead over the Rhine had been significantly enlarged and speeded up by the airborne operation, this was manifestly not the case. In areas where no airborne troops had landed the assault forces

Top: US paratroopers link up after dropping in an open field. They were greatly aided by the lack of immediate German reaction from the first available forces.

Above: Near Wesel a British paratrooper who landed in an American zone helps his allies to flush German civilians from a farm house that might contain snipers. One man has already surrendered.

had advanced as far as in the Hamminkeln area, and bridging operations across the Rhine were not materially speeded up, large-scale bridging operations not even starting until the day after the airborne landings.

The Pacific Theatre

During the Pacific campaigns in World War II, there were surprisingly few airborne operations by either side, despite the fact that the success of the few such actions launched, and the nature of the Pacific theatre, argued the case for more airborne landings. In compensation, though, the concept of air mobility was fully pioneered by the Americans in New Guinea.

The Japanese entered the field of airborne warfare late, setting up their forces and the necessary training schools only in 1940. Given the political climate in Japan, it was inevitable that the country they selected to give them guidance in all matters airborne should be Germany: Lieutenant-General Tomoyuki Yamashita, later to be dubbed the 'Tiger of Malaya', had spent the six months following the outbreak of World War II on a tour of inspection in Germany and Italy. Here he had been impressed with the potential of airborne warfare, and on his return he urged Lieutenant-General Hideki Tojo, the Minister of War, to set up military airborne units. It was clear that the Imperial Japanese Navy, which had its own land forces, would follow suit if the army set up an airborne force. Thus in the autumn of 1941 Germany had 100 instructors in Japan, and candidates for the airborne forces were undergoing the two-month courses in batches of several thousand at a time.

Two separate formations

The army's airborne force was the equivalent of a division in size, and was designated the Raiding Group: it consisted of a glider brigade, a parachute brigade and the various support elements necessary for semi-independent operations. Lacking suitable heavy lift aircraft, or even large numbers of medium transport aircraft, the army's airborne force was intended solely as a tactical adjunct to the assault forces for the forthcoming war, with the primary task of seizing airfields in distant parts so that the army's air cover could be provided from the nearest possible base.

The navy's airborne force had exactly the same mission: the capture of airfields so that air cover could be provided for local naval forces operating without the benefit of carrier-based aircraft. At the same time the navy did consider the use of its airborne arm for the capture of important targets deep behind the enemy's lines. The navy's forces were the Yokosuka 1st and 3rd Special Landing Units, each about 1,000 men strong.

Early in the war there was a classic example of the type of mission envisaged by the Japanese for their airborne forces. Setting off from Davao in the Philippines, three companies of the Yokosuka 1st Special Landing Unit dropped on Menado airfield at the northern tip of Celebes island in the Dutch East Indies on 11 January 1942. The airfield defences had

Below: Men of the 503rd Parachute Infantry Regiment drop on the far from ideal drop zone on Corregidor island, controlling Manila harbour, on 16 February 1945.

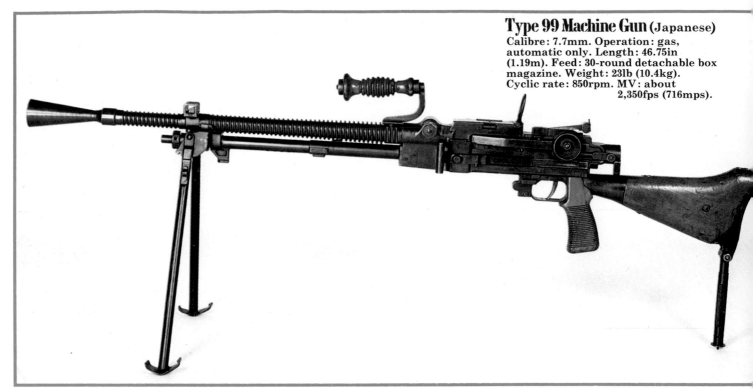

Type 99 Machine Gun (Japanese)

Calibre: 7.7mm. Operation: gas, automatic only. Length: 46.75in (1.19m). Feed: 30-round detachable box magazine. Weight: 23lb (10.4kg). Cyclic rate: 850rpm. MV: about 2,350fps (716mps).

Left: Native New Guinea porters cluster round three newly landed C-47 transports on Nadzab airfield in September 1943. The Japanese could not match Allied air mobility.

already been softened up by naval bombers, and air support for the airborne forces was provided by a number of Mitsubishi A6M Zero long-range fighters. The Dutch defence force, with the exception of 30 men captured, was wiped out in the course of five hours fighting. The Imperial Japanese Navy's air arm, however, now had a useful airfield from which to provide support for Japanese forces fighting in Borneo and in Celebes itself.

Daring raid

The largest Japanese airborne operation of the whole war, however, took place shortly afterwards on the island of Sumatra, south-west of the Malay peninsula. The main objective of the southern push by Japan was the enormously wealthy and important island of Java, but first bases for air support were necessary, and here Sumatra offered excellent pickings. The task of taking Palembang airfield was allocated to the army's Parachute Brigade, commanded by Colonel Seichi Kume. Palembang, moreover, also had an important oil refinery, and Kume was instructed to take this important additional prize intact. The Parachute Brigade was to be dropped on 9 February 1942, take the airfield and refinery as quickly as possible and hold the two until the 38th Division, which was to land on the coast on the same day, arrived to relieve it, supposedly on the second or third day. The Allied defence, under Dutch command, comprised some 1,000 Australian, British and Dutch troops with 16 3·7in and 15

Left: A supply officer explains the unloading procedures to a not wholly attentive audience gathered by a C-47 on an airstrip in the Buna area.

142

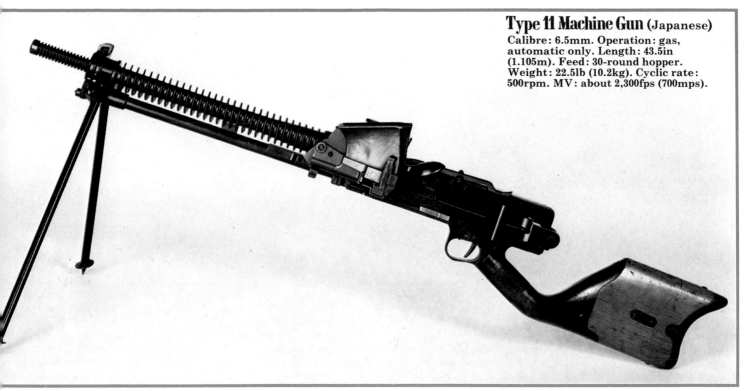

Type 11 Machine Gun (Japanese)

Calibre: 6.5mm. Operation: gas, automatic only. Length: 43.5in (1.105m). Feed: 30-round hopper. Weight: 22.5lb (10.2kg). Cyclic rate: 500rpm. MV: about 2,300fps (700mps).

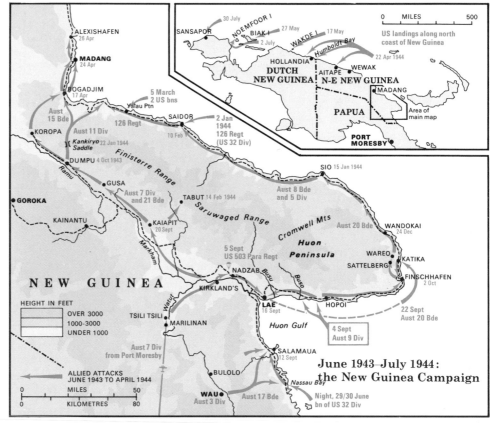

June 1943–July 1944: the New Guinea Campaign

40mm guns.

With his force operating from airfields at Kluang and Kahang in southern Malaya, Kume realized that the task facing him was a difficult one. His brigade was not a large one, and by the time he had pulled out an infantry company and an engineering platoon as reserve, he was left with only 330 men with which to attack and take his two objectives. The Allied defence of Sumatra was proving tougher than expected, so the airborne operation was put back to 14 February to allow the 38th Division to be brought up.

All was finally ready, and the operation got under way. Japanese air attacks had failed to reduce the intensity of the Allied AA fire, and as the Japanese aircraft approached their dropping zones at 1130, two were shot down in flames. The party told off to capture the airfield arrived safely in two groups, 60 men dropping into a clearing in the jungle north of their objective, and another 80 landing in a clearing south of the airfield. As' they prepared to move off towards their target, the men of the second group ran into a party of Dutch reinforcements moving up to strengthen the airfield defences and scattered them with well-controlled small arms fire after killing not a few of their number. Then the two Japanese groups mounted a concerted attack on the airfield. The Allies were ready for them, and although the fighting was vicious neither side could get the better of the other during the afternoon. The Japanese, however, were better trained in night fighting, and during the evening were able to link up and drive the Allies off the airfield into the jungle.

Almost total success

The small group intended for the attack on the refinery fared worse: many of the men, and most of the group's heavy equipment containers, fell into swampland, slowing the group's muster and attack. Only 40 men, therefore, were able to attack the refinery garrison. No conclusion was reached though the fierce fighting continued right through the night.

Meanwhile news of the 38th Division's landing had reached the Allied force, causing them considerable anxiety. Kume, seeing that his forces on the ground needed immediate reinforcement if they were to succeed, accordingly had the reserve force dropped on the airfield at 1340. Thus augmented, the paratroops on the airfield advanced towards Palembang, where they linked up with the refinery attack group and the spearheads of the 38th Division on 16 February. The airfield was intact, some 250,000 tons of oil had been captured, but the Allies had managed to damage the refinery considerably before they pulled out. Yet had the Allied commander, a Dutch colonel, counter-attacked at dawn on the 15th, as he should have done, there can be little doubt that the refinery and oil stocks would have been completely destroyed, and the two parties of paratroops wiped out. Be that as it may, the Allies were very worried by the news of the 38th Division's imminent arrival, and so failed to do what they should have done. None of this, of course, can detract from the success of Colonel Kume's Parachute Brigade, which achieved a considerable feat of arms with wholly insufficient forces.

The Japanese launched only one other airborne operation during the period in which they established their 'impregnable' defensive perimeter. This operation again made use of the skilled Yokosuka 1st Special Landing Unit to take the

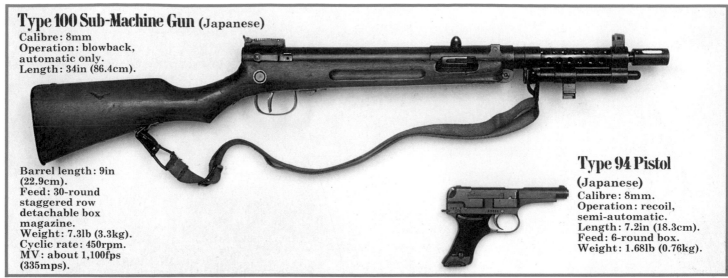

Type 100 Sub-Machine Gun (Japanese)

Calibre: 8mm
Operation: blowback, automatic only.
Length: 34in (86.4cm).

Barrel length: 9in (22.9cm).
Feed: 30-round staggered row detachable box magazine.
Weight: 7.3lb (3.3kg).
Cyclic rate: 450rpm.
MV: about 1,100fps (335mps).

Type 94 Pistol

(Japanese)
Calibre: 8mm.
Operation: recoil, semi-automatic.
Length: 7.2in (18.3cm).
Feed: 6-round box.
Weight: 1.68lb (0.76kg).

airfield at Penjoei, some 15 miles (24km) east of the capital of Dutch Timor, Kupang. As a feint, five aircraft dropped a small number of paratroops on the south-west corner of the island. While the Dutch and Australian garrison was searching for this small party, three companies of paratroops were dropped on the airfield on 21 February 1942, and these were reinforced by a further three companies on the next day. The airfield had fallen to the Japanese quickly, and amphibious landings on the 22nd secured the Japanese hold on the island, although elusive parties of Australians cut off in the interior proved a great thorn in their sides for some time to come.

Final efforts

The course of the war in the Pacific did not thereafter offer the Japanese much scope for airborne operations. The Allies first held the Japanese attempt to extend their perimeter, broke through the perimeter and then drove back toward the Philippines in twin drives, across the Pacific and along the northern coast of New Guinea. The two drives met off the island of Leyte, the first of the Philippine islands to be invaded by the Americans. The landings went in on 20 October 1944, and at first there was little that Lieutenant-General Sosaku Suzuki's 35th Army could do to halt the US 6th Army's conquest of the island. Yamashita, now commanding in the Philippines, ordered as many formations as possible to be moved into the island, at the same time urging Suzuki to retake Burauen airfield from the Americans and destroy the American-held fields at Tacloban and Dulag on the coast. To this end he gave Suzuki the tactical command of the 3rd and 4th Parachute Regiments of the army's Raiding Group. Once Tacloban and Dulag had been 'taken out' by airborne demolition teams, the 3rd and 4th Parachute Regiments would help the advance of the 16th and 26th Divisions on Burauen with tactical airborne operations.

Complete chaos

At the same time as the Tacloban and Dulag raids by small teams, Burauen was also to be raided to destroy American aircraft based there. The whole operation was a disaster. The aircraft flying in the Burauen raiding party was destroyed by AA fire as it tried to land at Buri; another raiding party disappeared after its aircraft crashlanded on the beach at Bito; and the third was wiped out as its aircraft was taken under fire by an American armoured battalion as it landed at Fizal.

The main airborne blow, though, was that in support of the land attack on Burauen, whose defence had been entrusted to the US 11th Airborne Division commanded by Major-General Joe Swing. Japanese infiltrators had already passed through the American lines on 6 December 1944, the day set for the attack, with the intention of linking up with the airborne troops, 350 men of Task Force Katori Shimpei. These were heading for their objectives in 30 transports with minimal fighter escort. The only thing the Japanese had going for them, however, was the fact that many US aircraft had been pulled out of the forward area for overhaul after six weeks in combat. Four aircraft were heading for Tacloban and Dulag once again, but none of these reached their target areas.

No serious damage

The 25 heading for the Burauen area reached the airfields at Buri, San Pablo and Bayug at dusk, and jumped into the utter confusion caused by an earlier air attack. Soon the results of their incendiary work added to the flame and smoke rising from the airfields. Swing's combat regiments were committed in the main land action to the west of Burauen, but when he saw the damage that was being caused at San Pablo in particular, he decided on a counterattack with the support and headquarters forces at his immediate disposal. This force attacked at 1200 on the next day and after a savage battle drove the Japanese off San Pablo field. The Japanese survivors pulled back to link up with the groups on the other two airfields, which held out for another four days. Just before they were about to be overrun by American infantry rushed in to the area, the remaining paratroops pulled out with the aid of a part of the 16th Division which had fought its way through to them. Damage to the American airfields had been confined mostly to stores and fuel, plus a few light aircraft, most of the combat machines having been pulled out earlier to Tacloban and Dulag, the two fields the Japanese had not been able to hit. This marked the effective end of Japanese airborne operations in World War II.

Kenney's vision

The Americans and British also used airborne forces in the Far Eastern theatre, and would have made even more extensive use of such forces had the war continued for much longer. The American-controlled operations in New Guinea, though they might more properly be regarded as exercises in what would in the 1970s be called 'air mobility', were among the most imaginative and stimulating of World War II. Commanding the 5th Air Force in General Douglas MacArthur's South-West Pacific Area was Major-General George Kenney. Although an airman by

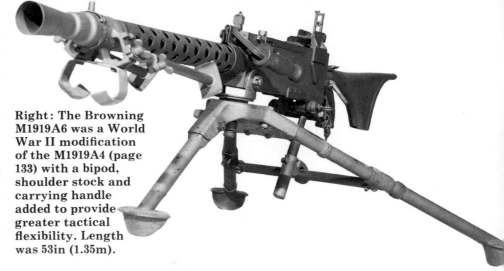

Right: The Browning M1919A6 was a World War II modification of the M1919A4 (page 133) with a bipod, shoulder stock and carrying handle added to provide greater tactical flexibility. Length was 53in (1.35m).

Japanese Naval Paratrooper, Pacific Theatre

Armed with a Type 100 (1940) 8-mm sub-machine gun, this Japanese Naval paratrooper is wearing the special uniform peculiar to his service. It consists of a 50% cotton and 50% silk two-piece uniform and velvet-lined boots with $\frac{1}{2}$ inch rubber soles and 1 inch rubber heels. The Type 100 SMG is of interest since it can be broken down, the butt folding forward, the working parts coming out and the magazine and bayonet detaching to give a compact load that can be fitted into a chest pack with cleaning equipment and sling. Later in the war Japanese airborne forces received far fewer items of specialist equipment, while their uniform became similar to that worn by conventional infantry.

training, Kenney had since 1932 been a devotee of the use of tactical air mobility after conducting a demonstration in the US Army manoeuvres of that year. Kenney realized that New Guinea offered an ideal situation for the strategic use of air mobility: the Japanese lacked the aircraft with which to match the 5th Air Force's capabilities, and the great mobility he could offer the American and Australian ground forces with his aircraft would play a decisive part in defeating the Japanese in New Guinea. MacArthur was impressed by the theories put forward by Kenney, especially after photographic reconnaissance ordered by the latter had shown that there were many places along the northern coast of New Guinea where Douglas C-47 transports could land.

Strategic fly-in

But first Port Moresby had to be secured from the Japanese advance over the Owen Stanley mountains, and it was here that Kenney finally convinced the erstwhile sceptics of air mobility. For while the bulk of the 32nd Division was moved from Australia to Port Moresby slowly by sea, Kenney's aircraft moved one regiment smoothly and swiftly by air. With Port Moresby secured by the arrival of the 32nd Division and the exhaustion of the Japanese in the mountains, Kenney's ideas on air mobility could be put into operation. On 6 October 1942 an Australian battalion was flown in to Wanigela in Collingwood Bay, 65 miles (105km) down the coast from the Japanese base area at Gona and Buna. Joined here by US engineers, the force hacked out a series of airstrips along the coast, and into these, between 14 October and 10 November, the equivalent of a division of infantry was flown, completely outflanking the Japanese to the west. To the north the Japanese positions were also threatened when a brigade of the Australian 3rd Division was flown in to Wau, 30 miles (48km) inland of Salamaua. Attacked by the Japanese, the Australian brigade was able to hold out, thanks to a supply by air. The threat to Salamaua posed by the Wau brigade was finally amplified early in September 1943 when the US 503rd Parachute Infantry Regiment was dropped at Nadzab, just inland from the main Japanese base at Lae, in the Markham valley. With the Americans blocking any advance by the Japanese, the Australian 7th Division was airlifted into Tsili Tsili and then pushed down to the coast to link up with the US paratroops. Combined with amphibious landings in the Huon gulf, these airborne landings left the Japanese with just too much to handle. Serious fighting lay ahead, but the outcome was never in doubt.

Kenney's concept had been fully vindicated, although it contained a number of novel ingredients. Few of the troops moved by air had any previous experience of the method, and the Australian guns had to be specially catered for. The supply of such a force by air posed considerable problems, but as each arose Kenney and his staff coped magnificently. Further landings were made in the Markham valley, keeping the Japanese constantly off balance.

This set the style for the rest of the

Above: Paratroopers fire a Japanese bunker on Corregidor with a phosphorus charge, covered by a 34th Regiment machine gun crew.

New Guinea campaign, with amphibious landings and airborne landings leaving the Japanese wondering which attack pattern would be next used. MacArthur also showed great strategic genius in deciding which Japanese garrisons to ignore while his forces 'leapfrogged' on along the coast of New Guinea to the west. The last airborne operation in New Guinea was that to take Numfoor island on 2 July 1944. The American paratroops were then warned for the Philippine operations, scheduled to start in a few months time.

Not followed up

It is one of the oddities of the American campaign in the Pacific that despite the promise shown by Kenney's air mobility tactics in New Guinea, airborne operations in the rest of the Far Eastern theatre were rarities. What makes this all the odder is the fact that MacArthur had an airborne division, the 11th, at his disposal for the Philippines operations. As it was, the main landings on Luzon, the largest of the Philippines, were undertaken on 9 January 1945 in Lingayen Gulf by the two corps of the 6th Army. Once they had landed, I Corps was to strike out east and south-east, while XIV Corps was to head south towards Manila and its excellent harbour. To meet up with XIV Corps and help it drive on Manila, XI Corps was landed just north of the Bataan peninsula on 29 January, while most of the 11th Airborne Division was landed from the sea at Nasugbu on 31 January to drive up north to Manila. In an extraordinarily over-cautious move, two battalions of the 11th Airborne Division were dropped on Tagaytay ridge, just inland of the rest of the division's landing point, on 3 February to secure this important tactical position. Opposition to the airborne operation was negligible, and it is hard to see what the Americans hoped to achieve with it four days after the amphibious landings. As

it was, the airborne troops jumped on to DZs marked out by pathfinder teams from the amphibious portion of the division, who had arrived with other elements on the ridge before the airborne operation was scheduled!

There was to be a 'real' airborne operation, however, designed to crush the 6,000 Japanese naval troops manning the island fortress of Corregidor. As Kenney put it, the idea was to 'slug the place to death with bombs and then let the paratroopers take it'. The Japanese commander had been warned of the possibility of an airborne attack, but apart from mining the light aircraft landing strip, he had done nothing else to hinder what he thought an unlikely method of attack. The unit chosen for the attack was Colonel George Jones's 503rd Parachute Infantry Regiment. Knowing that the Japanese would be deep in the underground tunnels that honeycombed the fortress island while the American bombers pounded the surface, Jones decided to land on 'Topside', the rocky western headland of the tadpole-shaped island. For a number of physical reasons, though, 'Topside' offered severe problems, and Jones made a courageous decision in choosing it. Only two possible DZs, both very small, were available, so a number of passes would have to be made by the dropping aircraft, releasing only six men on each pass. Fifty-one C-47 aircraft were available, and combined with the low dropping rate this meant that one battalion group would be dropped at 0830, one more at 1200 and the third on the following morning. Lack of space also meant that no weapons containers could be dropped, so everything the paratroops would need in the way of automatic weapons and ammunition had to be broken down into

Type 2 Rifle (Japanese)

Calibre: 7.7mm.
Operation: turn bolt.
Length: 43.9in (1.115m).
Barrel length: 25.8in (65.5cm).
Feed: 5-round staggered row
non-detachable box magazine.
Front sight: barleycorn with
projecting ears.
Rear sight: leaf.
Weight: 8.9lb (4kg).
MV: about 2,360fps (720mps).
To lock the two halves of the
weapon together, a locking key
is inserted through the receiver to
engage a slot in the barrel.

small loads and sent down with the paratroops.

A final heavy bombing raid on the morning of 16 February 1945 made the Japanese keep their heads down as the transport aircraft approached. The actual drop was a nightmare because of the various physical difficulties, but by 0930 the 3rd Battalion was down on Corregidor, although some 25 per cent casualties had been suffered in landing accidents and to Japanese small arms fire. The battalion was quickly brought into action, and by 1030 had secured the area from which its automatic weapons would cover the amphibious landing that would come in at the dock area on the south-west side of the

island. The amphibious landing was effected successfully, as was the delivery of the 2nd Battalion at 1200. By evening the airborne and amphibious forces had linked up, so the 1st Battalion's jump, scheduled for the next morning, was cancelled.

But the battle for Corregidor was by no means over. For 10 days the 503rd Regiment, reinforced by the 1st Battalion brought in by sea, fought a desperate battle with the Japanese defenders. The Americans were forced to pour oil and petrol down ventilator shafts and set fire to it when it proved impossible to winkle out difficult little pockets. The Japanese, on the other hand, often blew themselves

Above: A jeep forges ahead through long grass after emerging from a Hadrian glider of the 11th Airborne Division during the Aparri landings of 23 June 1945.

and their American attackers up when further resistance was impossible. In the closing stages of the battle, just as the paratroops were about to clear the 'tail' of the tadpole on 27 February, the remaining Japanese blew themselves up in a vast arsenal, showering debris for miles around. The terrible battle was over, and US shipping could at last use Manila harbour. US casualties were some 800, and the Japanese known dead totalled 4,700.

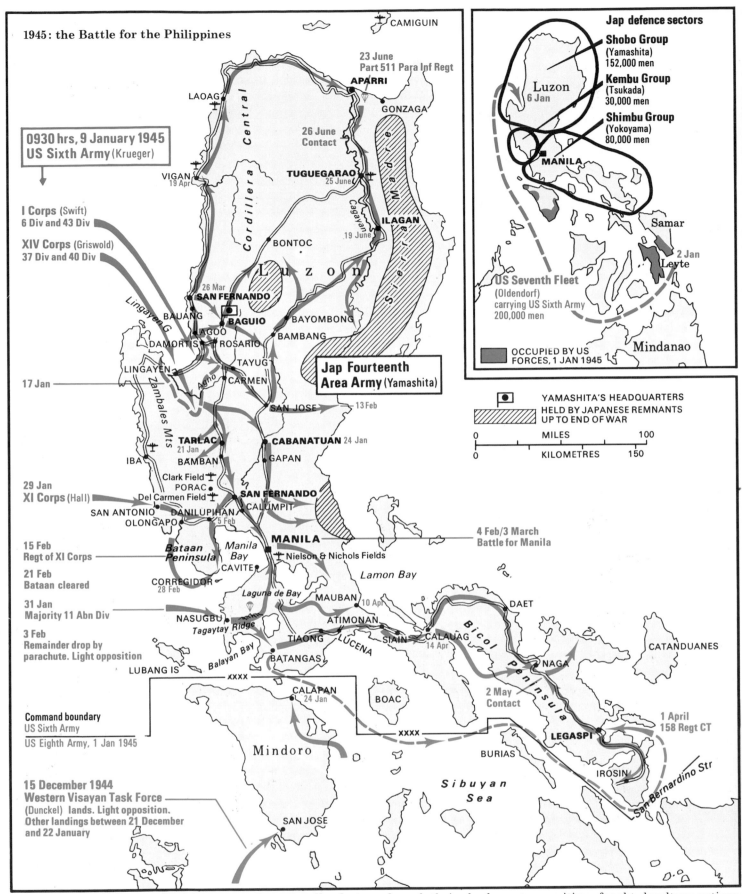

1945: the Battle for the Philippines

23 June
Part 511 Para Inf Regt
APARRI
GONZAGA

CAMIGUIN

LAOAG

26 June
Contact

**0930 hrs, 9 January 1945
US Sixth Army** (Krueger)

VIGAN
19 Apr

TUGUEGARAO
25 June

I Corps (Swift)
6 Div and 43 Div

XIV Corps (Griswold)
37 Div and 40 Div

Cordillera Central

ILAGAN
19 June

BONTOC

Luzon

Sierra Madre

Cagayan

26 Mar
SAN FERNANDO
BAUANG
BAGUIO
BAYOMBONG
AGOO
DAMORTIS ROSARIO
BAMBANG

17 Jan

LINGAYEN
Agno
TAYUG
CARMEN

Zambales Mts
Lingayen G

SAN JOSE — 13 Feb

TARLAC
21 Jan
BAMBAN
GAPAN

CABANATUAN 24 Jan

IBA
Clark Field
PORAC
Del Carmen Field

**29 Jan
XI Corps** (Hall)

SAN ANTONIO DANILUPIHAN
OLONGAPO
SAN FERNANDO
CALUMPIT

5 Feb

**15 Feb
Regt of XI Corps**

**Bataan
Peninsula**
Manila
Bay
CAVITE

MANILA
Nielson & Nichols Fields

4 Feb/3 March
Battle for Manila

**21 Feb
Bataan cleared**

CORREGIDOR
28 Feb

**31 Jan
Majority 11 Abn Div**

Laguna de Bay

Lamon Bay

MAUBAN
10 Apr

DAET

**3 Feb
Remainder drop by
parachute. Light opposition**

NASUGBU
Tagaytay Ridge
TIAONG
LUCENA
ATIMONAN
SIAIN
CALAUAG
14 Apr

Bicol Peninsula

CATANDUANES

Balayan Bay
BATANGAS
BOAC

NAGA

2 May
Contact

LUBANG IS

XXXX

CALAPAN
24 Jan

**Command boundary
US Sixth Army
US Eighth Army, 1 Jan 1945**

XXXX

1 April
158 Regt CT

LEGASPI

BURIAS
IROSIN

**15 December 1944
Western Visayan Task Force**
(Dunckel) **lands. Light opposition.
Other landings between 21 December
and 22 January**

Mindoro

Sibuyan
Sea

San Bernardino Str

SAN JOSE

Jap defence sectors

Shobo Group
(Yamashita)
152,000 men

Kembu Group
(Tsukada)
30,000 men

Shimbu Group
(Yokoyama)
80,000 men

Luzon
6 Jan

MANILA

Samar

2 Jan
Leyte

US Seventh Fleet
(Oldendorf)
carrying US Sixth Army
200,000 men

Mindanao

OCCUPIED BY US
FORCES, 1 JAN 1945

**Jap Fourteenth
Area Army** (Yamashita)

YAMASHITA'S HEADQUARTERS

HELD BY JAPANESE REMNANTS
UP TO END OF WAR

0   MILES   100
0   KILOMETRES   150

The 11th Airborne Division was chagrined that this major task had been given to the independent 503rd Regiment, but while the Corregidor battle was still raging, the division got a chance to acquire some glory. Some 2,200 American prisoners were held in a camp near Tagaytay ridge, and lest the Japanese decide to kill them, B Company, 1st Battalion, 511th Parachute Infantry Regiment was sent in to rescue them. The operation was planned and carried out with superb precision, and only one prisoner was injured. Yet the Japanese defences round the camp had

been totally destroyed, and their dead totalled 247, as compared with six American casulties. The whole operation was a classic of its kind.

The final airborne operation of the Pacific war took place on 23 June 1945, as the Luzon operations were coming towards an end. A task force from the 511th Regiment was instructed to cut off the Japanese line of retreat towards the port of Aparri on the northern coast of Luzon. Approaching 54 C-47s, 13 C-46s and 7 Waco CG-4A gliders (the only time such gliders were used in the Pacific), the force landed with-

out opposition, fought desultory actions against the Japanese for three days and then linked up with the advance guards of the 37th Division.

No more operations were undertaken by the US airborne forces in the Pacific, but they would have played an important part in the planned operations against the Japanese home islands. Considering the success of Kenney's air mobility tactics, though, it must remain a pity that American commanders failed to make more significant use of airborne forces in other Pacific actions.

US Paratrooper, Pacific Theatre

This cigar-chewing US paratrooper is wearing standard OD fatigues and has cut down his web equipment to the working minimum.

On his belt he has an ammunition pouch, water bottle and machete, slung under his left arm on an armoured crew's shoulder holster

is a .45 Colt 1911A1. He is holding an M1 carbine with a 15-round magazine. This was a very popular weapon, 3,700,000 being manufactured.

Operation Thursday

Although not on the same scale as airborne operations in Europe, the fly-in of two Chindit brigades deep into the heart of Japanese-held Burma during March 1944 was expected to yield large-scale results. Here, for the first time, major units would operate for considerable periods of time deep beyond the enemy lines, with air transport as their only lifeline to the outside.

Operation 'Thursday' is the codename given to the fly-in of two brigades of Major-General O. C. Wingate's 'Special Force' to northern Burma on 5–6 March 1944, and by extension to the whole concept of his bold project to wage large-scale war in the heart of Japanese-controlled territory. As an airborne operation it remains unique in the history of warfare, for all the others were predominantly parachute operations and governed by the elitist outlook of parachute troops and, except possibly for the invasion of Crete, they were all subordinate to a larger ground strategy and planned so as to permit a rapid junction with ground troops.

Wingate's strategic ideas altered continually during his brief period in high command. At first what he termed 'long-range penetration' (LRP) went no further than the support by air supply of raiding parties far behind the enemy lines. Later the concept developed into introducing his specially constituted units by air to avoid long and hazardous marches through the enemy lines. Then this was extended to the establishment of safe harbours sited in deep jungle (known as 'strongholds') from which the LRP units could operate. Finally, just before his death, Wingate sketched out a plan for a new radical strategy involving seizing whole areas by air-transported forces of divisional size. 'Thursday' was halfway towards this final concept, with Wingate secretly hoping to alter it to a point three-quarters of the way along if he could coax or pressure the higher command to release to him a complete conventional infantry division to garrison the territory he hoped to liberate.

Large-scale raiding

The orders given to Wingate were: first, to cut the supply routes of the Japanese 18th Division opposing the southward advance of Lieutenant-General 'Vinegar Joe' Stilwell's *Chih Hui Pu* or 'Chinese Army in India', whose mission was to clear a land supply route from India to beleaguered China; second, to create an opening for the Chinese armies in Yunnan to cross the Salween river and engage the Japanese in Burma; and third, generally to cause confusion behind the Japanese lines.

Wingate's force therefore had indirect strategic rather than direct tactical linkage with the other armies: Wingate regarded himself as an independent commander. For this mission he created his own instrument in the shape of the 'Chindits': brigades of regular troops retrained and restructured to his own pattern, and also, it must be added, brought to a high pitch of morale by his own fervent leadership. Not since the days of the Covenanters in 1643 has a British leader effectively used such oratory drawn from

Right: Sporting the diagonal fuselage stripes of No 1 Air Commando, a North American B-25 Mitchell medium bomber provides air support for the Chindits in Burma.

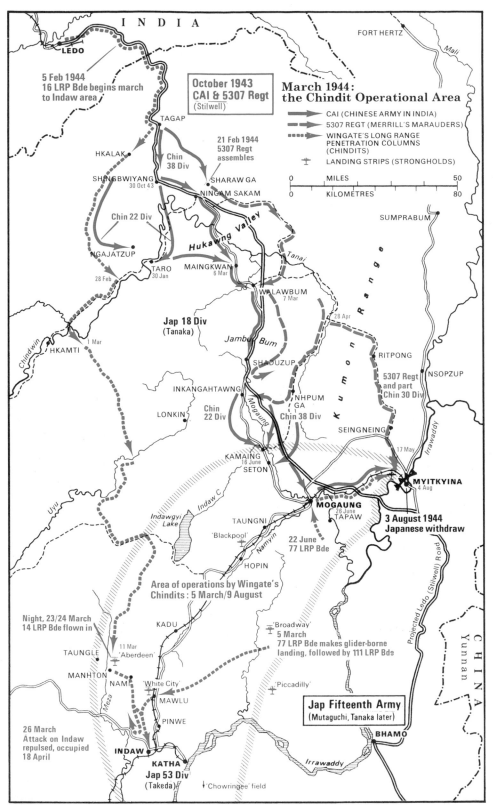

March 1944:
the Chindit Operational Area

- CAI (CHINESE ARMY IN INDIA)
- 5307 REGT (MERRILL'S MARAUDERS)
- WINGATE'S LONG RANGE PENETRATION COLUMNS (CHINDITS)
- LANDING STRIPS (STRONGHOLDS)

October 1943
CAI & 5307 Regt
(Stilwell)

MILES 0 — 50
KILOMETRES 0 — 80

INDIA

LEDO

5 Feb 1944
16 LRP Bde begins march
to Indaw area

FORT HERTZ

Mali

TAGAP

HKALAK

Chin
38 Div

21 Feb 1944
5307 Regt
assembles

SHINGBWIYANG
30 Oct 43

SHARAW GA
NINGAM SAKAM

SUMPRABUM

Chin 22 Div

Hukawng Valley

Tanai

NGAJATZUP

TARO
30 Jan

MAINGKWAN
6 Mar

28 Feb

WALAWBUM
7 Mar

Jap 18 Div
(Tanaka)

Jambu Bum

28 Apr

Kumon Range

RITPONG

Chindwin

HKAMTI
1 Mar

SHADUZUP

5307 Regt
and part
Chin 30 Div

NSOPZUP

INKANGAHTAWNG

Mogaung

NHPUM
GA

Chin 38 Div

LONKIN

Chin
22 Div

SEINGNEING

17 May

KAMAING
16 June
SETON

MYITKYINA
4 Aug

Uyu

Indaw C.

MOGAUNG
26 June
TAPAW

3 August 1944
Japanese withdraw

Indawgyi
Lake

TAUNGNI

22 June
77 LRP Bde

'Blackpool'

Namyin

HOPIN

Projected Ledo (Stilwell) Road

Area of operations by Wingate's
Chindits : 5 March/9 August

Night, 23/24 March
14 LRP Bde flown in

KADU

'Broadway'
5 March
77 LRP Bde makes glider-borne
landing, followed by 111 LRP Bde

CHINA
Yunnan

TAUNGLE

11 Mar
'Aberdeen'

MANHTON

NAM

'White City'

'Piccadilly'

MAWLU

Meza

26 March
Attack on Indaw
repulsed, occupied
18 April

PINWE

Jap Fifteenth Army
(Mutaguchi, Tanaka later)

BHAMO

INDAW

KATHA

Jap 53 Div
(Takeda)

'Chowringee' field

Irrawaddy

---

the language of the Bible to inspire his troops. No 'alien' troops unindoctrinated by him were acceptable and it is possible that this is why he rejected the inclusion of any of the airborne units then under training in India, who could have been of great service. (Wingate alleged that they were inadequately trained, but this seems an unsatisfactory reason.)

Novel organization

Altogether, Wingate acquired a very large force, the equivalent of two and a half divisions in bayonet strength of first class British, Gurkha and West African (Nigerian) battalions. These were organized in brigades of four battalions each divided into two 'columns', each consisting of a strong rifle company with a support platoon of two Vickers medium machine-guns and two 3in mortars, plus specialist platoons for engineer commando, signals and reconnaissance duties. Transport of heavy weapons, large radio sets and reserve ammunition was almost entirely by mule, plus a few ponies; in fact the animal content of the force and its dependence on forage and water was huge. The tactical idea was that the column was smaller and better suited for movement in jungle and guerrilla fighting than a conventional battalion, and that when a real battle, as opposed to guerrilla action, was impending the columns could amalgamate, to disperse again later. There was no divisional headquarters or co-ordinating headquarters in the field above brigade level. Wingate exercised command by visit, and control was by an elaborate

radio-net whose transmitters were located at Special Force Headquarters in India. (Special Force was retitled the '3rd Indian Division' as a cover name. Wingate wanted to call it 'Gideon' Force, but settled for 'Chindit', actually *Chinthi*, which became the accepted title. *Chinthes* are the stone winged lions guarding the entrances to Buddhist temples.)

Quick evolution

The whole Chindit idea evolved rapidly from August 1943, when Wingate persuaded first Prime Minister Winston Churchill and later President Franklin D. Roosevelt and the United States chiefs-of-staff that his methods of warfare could be usefully employed to assist Stilwell in opening land communications with China. General H. H. Arnold, Chief-of-Staff of the United States Army Air Force, in a single imaginative stroke converted Wingate's 'long-range penetration' to an airborne, or air-transported, operation. He sent for two young air force lieutenant-colonels, both fighter pilots, Philip Cochran and John Alison, and in a few words gave them their mission: to fly the Chindits in and their wounded out, supply them, interdict the Japanese air force as far as possible and provide direct air support for the Chindits in place of the field artillery they lacked. Arnold also gave Cochran and Alison *carte blanche* to requisition such aircraft as they might need together with the best of aircrews and maintenance men. The mission was to last only three months. (At the end of this period the Americans were withdrawn, which caused much chagrin in the Chindit command, but Arnold had kept his word and expected others to conform.) There was little or no administrative or logistic back-up, and the ratio of men to aircraft was fantastic: 600 to 300. But they were excellent men: 'We were allowed to take the best,' recalls Alison. The pilots were not specialists; they crewed or piloted the P-51A fighters and B-25 bombers impartially as the operational requirement demanded. The aircraft inventory included 100 Waco CG-4A Hadrian gliders, 100 Stinson L-5 and 12 Consolidated-Vultee L-1 light aircraft for intercommunication and recovering wounded, 12 Noorduyn UC-64 Norsemen transports and a squadron each of Douglas C-47 transports, North American P-51A single-engined fighter bombers and North American B-25 fast medium bombers. (The glider lift and supply drops were assisted by RAF and USAAF transport aircraft. As a matter of historical interest a few of the earliest helicopters were included and performed the first active service missions in their history, but only on a small scale.) Such was the No 1 Air Commando, USAAF, a force as unique and unorthodox as the Chindits themselves.

Airlift problems

The debate on airborne tactics revolved about the question of the distance between the point of landing (the DZ or LZ) and the objective. Every variety had been tried by 1944, from crash-landing gliders on top of the objective to dropping sufficiently far off to avoid small arms fire and to give

Above: Chindit leaders—Colonel Alison (in sweater), Brigadier Calvert (in peaked cap), Major-General Wingate (in topee) and Lieutenant-Colonel Scott (smiling).

time for the airborne troops to assemble themselves and collect their weapons and march in good order to their objective. Wingate's chosen tactics were extreme: he used LZs remote from the objectives and from enemy interference, involving approach marches of up to 150 miles (240km).

Complicated plan

A suitable LZ was chosen in deep jungle otherwise inaccessible to all but lightly armed infantry. This would first be occupied by gliderborne engineers with protective infantry, who would convert it to a dirt strip suitable for C-47s. Into this would be flown the columns who would march off through the jungle to their operational areas. A garrison battalion would follow, with field and anti-aircraft guns, and the whole area would then be converted into a fortress or 'stronghold', which would act as a base for the column in the field.

Wingate's plan was a complicated one which, if it was to come off, required the simultaneous arrival of three brigades in an operational area centred on the little town of Indaw: one marching across mountains and through dense jungles from Ledo, 200 miles (320km) as the crow flies but a great deal more on the ground; one from two landing zones, 'Broadway' and 'Piccadilly', to be carved out of the jungle some 60 miles (97km) to the east of Indaw; and one from an LZ in the bend of the Irrawaddy, 'Chowringhee', also some

60 miles (97km) from its objectives. The route from 'Chowringhee' involved crossing the Irrawaddy, one of the major rivers of Asia, with three battalions of men and mules. To facilitate this, gliders loaded with assault boats and outboard engines were to land on a sandbank at the crossing point. A battalion of Gurkha Rifles (4/9th) was also to land at 'Chowringhee' and march some 150 miles (240km) northeastwards, crossing the Shweli, a large tributary of the Irrawaddy, on the way, and harry the Bhamo-Myitkyina road from sanctuaries in the wild country lying between it and the Chinese border. Also to operate in this area was a small

Above: Waco CG-4A gliders at the 'Broadway' landing strip. These were the only US gliders to see combat service in WWII. Note the aircraft on which the upward-hingeing nose has been pulled off sideways.

force or military mission known as 'Dah' Force (a *dah* is a Burmese sword), whose task was to organize an anti-Japanese guerrilla movement among the warlike Kachins who live in those parts. This was to land at 'Templecombe'.

Wingate's choice of objectives had a double purpose. His official and primary duty was to cut the Japanese lines of com-

Above: Chindit sappers prepare to 'blow' a bridge near Henu ('White City') on the Naba–Mogaung railway, vital to the Japanese defence of northern Burma.

coup by No 1 Air Commando which virtually removed one great danger to the whole enterprise. Shortly before D-day for 'Thursday' an 18-plane fighter sweep spotted a large force of Japanese aircraft assembling on a field near Shwebo and attacked them, at the same time alerting their own base, where six B-25s were immediately bombed up in readiness. The bomber squadron commander and his deputy were actually flying as pilots in the P-51 mission, and as soon as they returned they changed aircraft (this was possible in those non-specialized days) and went once more into the attack in the B-25s. The Japanese had been caught unprepared, without early warning or defences, and in the process of refuelling. They lost 100 aircraft, a figure later confirmed by RAF reconnaissance. 'Murphy', therefore, combined with the zest and skill of the USAAF, first struck a blow for Wingate. Then he changed sides.

Plan compromised?

On D-day, 5 March, photo-reconnaissance, banned until then to avoid compromising the LZs, revealed that 'Piccadilly' was blocked by rows of logs, which caused general consternation. Had the Japanese got wind of the plan, and were the LZs to be ambushed? (They had not: it was a routine commercial logging operation.) Councils of courage prevailed and on Calvert's advice 'Piccadilly' was abandoned and his whole brigade flown in to 'Broadway'. Next, as a result of overloading and lack of rehearsal, many gliders

munication running north to the Japanese 18th Division facing Stilwell, and this duty was met by the force directed on to the Bhamo road, and by Brigadier Michael Calvert's mission, which was to establish part of his 77th Brigade in a strong road-block – a miniature fortress – on the Indaw-Mogaung-Myitkyina road/rail link at Mawlu. But two brigades, Brigadier Bernard Fergusson's 16th marching from the north and Brigadier W. D. Lentaigne's 111th from 'Chowringhee', were to converge in the Indaw area. There the 16th was to capture the little railway town and its two dirt airstrips, while the 111th screened the approaches from the south and south-west to prevent Japanese reinforcement. A fourth LZ, later to be code-named 'Aberdeen', was to be selected near Indaw and converted into a stronghold. There can be no doubt that Wingate's

Above: Chindits engage the defence of a Japanese-held town with the aid of a muzzle-loading 3in mortar's high-angle fire. Ammunition supply was always a problem.

private intention, evidenced by the disposal of 50 per cent of his force to Indaw, was by an initial and stunning success to pressure Lieutenant-General William Slim, commanding the 14th Army, under whose command he was, to release the 26th Infantry Division to garrison Indaw and so create the large liberated area demanded by the most advanced version of his peculiar strategy. War, however, is especially the province of 'Murphy's Law', which states that what can go wrong usually will. There was much to go wrong, and most of it did.

First, however, must be mentioned a

Waco CG-4 Hadrian

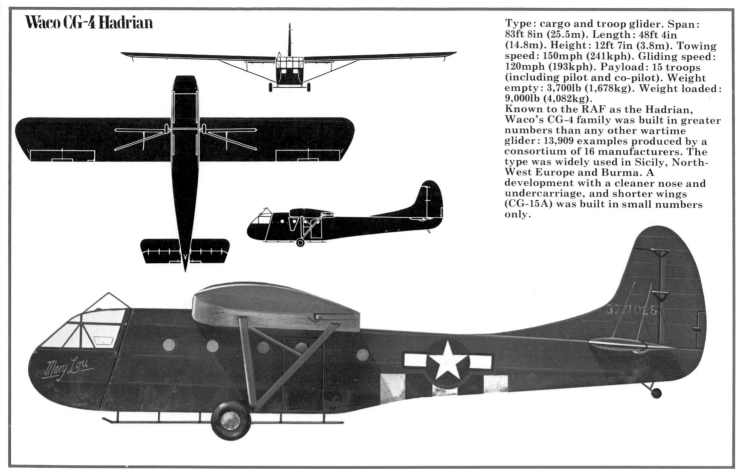

Type: cargo and troop glider. Span: 83ft 8in (25.5m). Length: 48ft 4in (14.8m). Height: 12ft 7in (3.8m). Towing speed: 150mph (241kph). Gliding speed: 120mph (193kph). Payload: 15 troops (including pilot and co-pilot). Weight empty: 3,700lb (1,678kg). Weight loaded: 9,000lb (4,082kg).

Known to the RAF as the Hadrian, Waco's CG-4 family was built in greater numbers than any other wartime glider: 13,909 examples produced by a consortium of 16 manufacturers. The type was widely used in Sicily, North-West Europe and Burma. A development with a cleaner nose and undercarriage, and shorter wings (CG-15A) was built in small numbers only.

broke away from their tows. The leading gliders into 'Broadway' suffered a high accident rate, which led to a temporary halt in the fly-in. However, heroic efforts remedied this and before long the 77th Brigade was being landed in by C-47, together with the 3/9th Gurkha Rifles as stronghold garrison.

Gut reaction

The landings at 'Chowringhee' started well, but the river crossing took a long time and became disorganized. Wingate appeared, had a finger-tip feeling that the Japanese were about to discover the LZ and ordered one column still on the left bank of the Irrawaddy to follow the 4/9th eastwards to Bhamo and the rest of the 111th Brigade to fly into 'Broadway'. He was right: 'Chowringhee' was severely bombed just after it was abandoned.

'Templecombe' proved not to be ready at all, so 'Dah' Force was flown into 'Broadway' as well, also to be faced with a long march to its scene of operations.

In spite of these difficulties, some 9,000 men, 1,300 animals and 223 long tons (226,580kg) of stores were safely delivered to their LZs by 331 RAF sorties, 197 USAAF Troop Carrier Command sorties and a 132 sorties with a further 74 gliders dispatched by No 1 Air Commando.

The Indaw operations went sadly wrong. The 111th Brigade, scattered into columns all over the place, had very little effect on the outcome, although they had some adventurous and successful clashes with stray Japanese elements. Fergusson's attack, planned as a combination of encirclement and frontal assault, ran into a combination of misfortunes. The area north of Indaw proved waterless, except at points firmly gripped by the Japanese. One column allowed itself to be surprised

in bivouac and was written off as a fighting force. Static, combined with the move of Chindit HQ to a new location, blocked radio communications at a crucial period, another column became involved in a fight for a water-point instead of the objective, and after a resolute attack the one battalion which had secured a foothold near Indaw airstrip had to be withdrawn. (A question, unanswered so far, is that if Wingate set so much store by Indaw, why was its capture by *coup-de-main* not attempted? There the true, or parachute, airborne troops could have surely been of use, and the airfields existed on to which the follow-up force of Chindits could have been flown after capture.)

The final blow of fate was the death of Wingate while flying to his headquarters at Sylhet in Assam. Only he, if anyone, could conduct the extraordinary military orchestra he had created.

Brilliant success

The two main goals were brilliantly achieved. Calvert established his fortress at Henu on the railway, repelling the first and frantic Japanese attacks on it with great slaughter, and combined in the old classical manner his static defence with a manoeuvre force orbiting his stronghold to harry the would-be besiegers. The 'White City' was only finally abandoned on a change of plan and the whole garrison and its equipment successfully evacuated by air under the noses of the Japanese.

The campaign of 'Morris' Force, named after its commander Brigadier J. R. Morris, the 4/9th Gurkha Rifles, plus another column, was less spectacular and is hardly known, but was hardly less effective. The Bhamo road was regularly cut but somehow the Japanese managed to sneak up enough reinforcements and supplies to keep the

18th Division going. All the same it was down at one time to three rounds of small arms ammunition per man per day, and the contribution of the two commanders to Stilwell's successes is beyond question, if only grudgingly admitted by American historians.

Superb piloting

The fighting, however, was really a series of land rather than airborne operations, but on the purely land/air side there were some striking features. The establishment of 'Broadway' and its successful defence against ground and air attack is a unique event in the history of warfare. It was virtually an airport of entry into the Japanese rear, defended by infantry, field artillery and anti-aircraft artillery and for a time there was an early warning radar and a fighter defence with Supermarine Spitfires and P-51s. Direct support of ground operations by bombers and fighters was nothing new, but between the Air Commando and the Chindits its methods reached a high level of refinement. It made possible Calvert's theoretically impossible feat of capturing Mogaung by Chindits alone, without the tanks and heavy artillery other troops would have regarded as essential.

Many hundreds of Chindits owe their lives to the dauntless light aircraft pilots of the Air Commando, who evacuated the sick and wounded from boggy strips hacked out of the jungle. To this must be added mention of the daring operation by the RAF of two Sunderland flying boats to evacuate hundreds of casualties from the Indawggyi lake.

'Thursday' remains a prototype of 'three-dimensional war' waged far behind the enemy front and a brilliant, if bizarre, chapter in military history.

Eastern Europe

Although they had pioneered the large-scale use of airborne forces in the 1930s, Russia used such forces in their intended role only rarely in World War II. On the other side of the lines, the Germans used their transport fleet mostly for army support work, the airborne forces themselves being used increasingly as 'fire brigades' in desperate situations.

Soviet Russia had been among the pioneers of the concept of airborne warfare in the early 1930s, but with the execution of Marshal Mikhail Tukhachevsky in the Stalinist purges later in the decade, the airborne arm began to fall into an early decline. Although the forces allocated to airborne warfare remained in nominal existence, no tactical doctrines for their employment were worked out, and the Red Air Force received no large trooping aircraft suitable for the mass-dropping of airborne formations. Obsolete bombers were instead allocated this task, although

they were by no means suitable for the role. The classic aircraft for paratroop operations remained the ungainly Tupolev TB-3 (otherwise designated ANT-6) in its G-2 variant. In this the paratroops had to exit from a dorsal position halfway along the upper side of the fuselage. With such a method it was impossible for tight sticks to be dropped.

In April 1942, as the Germans prepared for the great offensive that was to take their armies deep into the Caucasus and to the tip of a highly vulnerable salient at Stalingrad, the Russian airborne arm was

in disarray. Its major formation, IV Airborne Corps, had been virtually destroyed in a series of small-scale operations that can hardly be designated 'airborne'. During the Russian retreat between June and December 1941, large numbers of broken-up units had been cut off by the advancing Germans. Russian contingency plans called for these forces to operate as partisans behind the German lines, their two main areas of operation being the Pripet marshes and around Smolensk, where there was a good chance of setting up secure bases. The Russians placed great reliance on the efficacy of such partisan units, and indeed by the middle of 1943 they were an important thorn in the side of the Germans, forcing them to deploy field formations in rear areas to guard the *Wehrmacht*'s long and vulnerable lines of communication. But in the spring of 1942 these units could achieve relatively little, as they were as yet poorly organized and led, and

possessed little in the way of the necessary supplies. The relatively small numbers of heavy aircraft possessed by the Russians were widely used to fly in supplies and reinforcements to the partisan forces, and it was in the course of such operations that IV Airborne Corps was destroyed as an effective fighting formation. To disrupt the German preparations for their spring and summer offensives, the partisans in the Smolensk area had been ordered to harass and cut the German lines of communication between Smolensk and Vyazma. But the partisans lacked the ability to do so, and in an effort to bolster them, the Red Army high command decided to provide them with support in the form of IV Airborne Corps. Clearly the partisans had no need of large formations, and so the corps was broken up into small units and spread throughout the partisan forces. The operations against the German lines of communication were not successful, but there was no way in which the now-divided IV Airborne Corps could be reassembled. The Russians had thus lost their major airborne strike force in futile small-scale operations between January and April 1942.

The Russians remained committed to the principle of supporting partisans with elements drawn from the airborne forces, and in this way the airborne force was gradually whittled away. But in the autumn of 1943 the Russians at last had a golden opportunity to strike a major blow with their airborne forces. In the aftermath of the crushing defeat of the 6th Army, trapped in Stalingrad, the German armies were driven pellmell back to the Dniepr river in some disarray. Realizing that if they could keep the Germans off their balance, they stood a good chance of preventing the Axis forces from taking up strong positions in the so-called 'Eastern Rampart', the Russians planned a bold move. As their forces reached the great barrier of the Dniepr, where any other army might be expected to halt, rest and plan an assault crossing after thorough preparation, the Russians decided that an immediate assault crossing without lengthy preparations should be made as the armies arrived. In short, the Russian armies would attempt to 'bounce' across the river before the German defence line could be strengthened.

On 21–22 September 1943 the 3rd Guards Tank and 40th Armies reached the river north-west of Dniepropetrovsk and immediately fought their way across, using any boats they could find, rafts and just about anything that would float. The Germans were indeed amazed by the speed of the Russian assault, but quickly recovered their composure and reacted with the vigour and initiative that characterized German counterattacks right through the war.

Complete ineptitude

As the battle on the western bank of the Dniepr raged, the Russian high command at last saw a golden opportunity for an airborne operation to try once again to knock the Germans off their balance and allow the 3rd Guards Tank and 40th Armies to move forward again. On 24 September, therefore, the 1st, 3rd and 5th Parachute Regiments were dropped at night in the area north-west of Kremenchug, about 25 miles (40km) behind the German lines. The plan was a bold one, and perhaps deserved to be successful. Unfortunately for the Russians, however, the decline into which their airborne arm had

Below: Among other German aircraft on an airfield taken by the 1st Ukrainian Front in 1943 lies a wrecked Gotha Go 242 twin-boom troop and freight glider.

Above: Russian paratroopers, with main and emergency parachutes, emplane in a Lisunov Li-2 (the Russian-built version of the DC-3) for a 1942 training mission.

fallen led to disaster. For although the plan would in all probability not have worked in any case as the airborne operation was poorly co-ordinated with the renewal of the 3rd Guards and 40th Armies' offensive, complete tactical ineptitude on the part of the three airborne regiments finally killed any chance of success. Poorly trained for such an operation, the crews of the dropping aircraft had scattered the three regiments across a wide dropping zone, some 25 miles (40km) across. Instead of regrouping as swiftly as possible, the Russian paratroops merely dug in where they were, in small and relatively ineffective parties, and as such posed no threat to the Germans at all. As the Russian paratroops made no aggressive moves, their elimination was left to security and reserve divisions, and within a few days the paratroops had been wiped out, although some severe local fighting broke out as the Russians held out with their customary strong resistance.

Far Eastern venture

The only other occasion on which Russian airborne troops were used was in the extraordinary campaign undertaken right at the end of the war against Japan's forces in Manchuria, northern China, Korea and the Kurile islands. To help the ground forces keep up a blistering pace of advance, airborne landings were made in a number of major cities on the ground forces' line of advance. As the Russian official source *The Soviet Army* puts it, in typically laconic and uninformative style: 'On August 18 (1945) Japanese troops began to surrender on different sectors, though many units did not know of the surrender or deliberately stalled it. In these conditions a swift advance became of primary importance. It was de-

cided to employ airborne troops to capture big cities . . . Between August 18 and 24, airborne troops were landed in the cities Changchun, Harbin, Kirin, Pyöngyang, Dalny, Port Arthur and others.' In short, the Russians had made extensive use of their airborne forces to ensure that they took the main cities of the area in the period immediately after the Japanese surrender. And although it is not mentioned in *The Red Army*, airborne troops were also used in the conquest of Sakhalin island. Three landings were made: on 23 August at Oshiai, on 24 August at Tojohara and on 25 August at Otomari.

With the exception of the landings in the Far East, therefore, the Russians made little constructive use of their airborne forces in World War II. Nevertheless, the success of the Far Eastern landings combined with the Russian appreciation of German and Western Allied airborne operations to convince them that airborne forces could play an important large-scale part in future wars, and immediately after the end of hostilities they set about building up their airborne capability.

Although the Eastern Front was not to see German airborne operations on a scale similar to those in the West, the German parachute forces were widely used against the Russians as elite infantry, in much the same sort of way as they were used at Cassino and in France. Thus throughout Germany's great campaign against Russia the German airborne forces played an important part.

First into action were units of the 7th Air Division. With the removal of Colonel-General Erich Hoepner's 4th *Panzergruppe* from the German formations of Army Group 'North' attacking Leningrad in September 1941, the Russians counterattacked and retook vital areas around

Schlüsselburg and Volkhov, east of the beleaguered city. To meet these threats to the German position, the 2nd Battalion of the Assault Regiment, part of Lieutenant-General Petersen's 7th Air Division, was flown in, to be followed swiftly by the 1st and 3rd Parachute Regiments, as well as the divisional headquarters. Bitter fighting for the Russian bridgehead over the Neva river followed before the Assault Regiment wiped it out. Major Stenzler, the battalion commander, was killed in the fighting, and every other officer of the battalion was killed or wounded. By the end of November most of the division was in combat, for apart from the units around Leningrad, the 2nd Parachute Regiment and the 4th Battalion of the Assault Regiment were heavily engaged in the south on the lower reaches of the Mius river, and the Parachute Machine-Gun Battalion was operating on the central front. Then between December 1941 and February 1942 the 1st Battalion, Assault Regiment and Battlegroup Meindl, which included airborne elements, played an important part in stemming the Russian drive west from the start line between Moscow and Tula. Thereafter Major-General Eugen Meindl raised an *ad hoc* division which fought with great distinction between March and November 1942 in the region south of Staraya Russa where the Russians were making a major effort to retake Velikiye Luki, Vitebsk and Smolensk. Throughout the desperate winter battles at the end of the first summer's campaign against Russia, therefore, the men of the 7th Air Division were heavily

Soviet Paratrooper, Eastern Front

This Russian paratrooper on a sabotage mission behind German lines is wearing the one-piece mottled suit issued to snipers, combat engineers and other specialists. He has retained his close fitting leather helmet normally worn only during the jump. His weapon is the ubiquitous PPSh 41 sub-machine gun. He has a pouch for a spare 71-round drum magazine on his belt. The combatants on the Eastern Front used captured weapons and equipment, so it was not uncommon for German troops to use PPSh while Russians favoured German binoculars, mess tins and water bottles. In winter both sides went into white overalls, except those unhappy individuals on the Russian side doing penal service at the front who retained their dark uniforms which made them easy targets, but allowed their comrades to locate the German machine-guns.

M1938 Carbine (Russian)
Calibre: 7.62mm. Operation: turn
bolt. Length: 40in (1.016m). Barrel
length: 20in (50.8cm). Feed:
5-round box. Weight: 7.62lb
(3.46kg). MV: 2,514fps (766mps).

committed, and played a notable part in
holding the German line. The cost was
heavy: some 3,000 irreplaceable casualties,
combat veterans of Holland, Belgium,
Greece and Crete. As the situation eased,
the airborne units were in the spring of
1942 pulled back to France for rest and
rehabilitation.

Although an airborne operation against
the Black Sea port of Tuapse was considered in summer 1942, the 7th Air Division's next action was in October of that
year, helping to bolster the German
defences around Velikiye Luki and Orel.
As this fighting drew to a close, the division was redesignated the 1st Parachute
Division and once again pulled back to
France. Under the superb command of
Major-General Richard Heidrich, and
later of Major-General Schulz, the division thereafter fought with enormous distinction in the Italian campaign.

Rapid expansion

The 22nd Division, although nominally
retained as an airlanding formation, was
not used as such again after the *débâcle*
around the Hague in May 1941. It served,
and suffered great losses, in the capture of
Sevastopol, and was thereafter used in
the Balkans.

The 2nd Parachute Division was formed
under the command of Major-General
Hermann Bernard Ramcke in the spring
of 1943 with the 2nd Parachute Regiment
and the 4th Battalion of the Assault Regiment. After service in Italy, the division
was transferred to Zhitomir on the Eastern
Front, where most of the 6th Parachute
Regiment was destroyed. After refitting
in Germany, the division distinguished
itself in Brittany and then in the retreat.

The 3rd, 4th, 5th, 6th, 7th and 8th Parachute Divisions were all formed in the
period autumn 1943–autumn 1944 from
cadres from previous divisions, and fought
with varying degrees of success as infantry
on the Western Front. None of the divisions ever received its proper allocation
of divisional troops, although all but the
8th Parachute Division, which had six

**Above right: German paratroops
neutralize a Russian forward
position with the aid of a wire-
detonated mine during the summer
fighting of 1942.**

**Right: Men of Battlegroup Meindl
receive armoured support in their
efforts to halt the Russian drive
west between Moscow and Tula in
the closing weeks of 1941.**

German Paratrooper, Eastern Front

A German paratrooper on the Eastern Front greets a comrade during a pause in the bitter winter offensives launched by the Russians. He is wearing the popular reversible two-piece snow suit which was issued from 1942–3 onwards (the camouflage pattern inside is just visible). His boots are leather and felt and are a superior version of the Russian felt boot. He is armed with an MP38 and has the special 32-round magazine pouches on his belt. Beneath his helmet he has wrapped a woollen toque scarf around his head and neck, while on the sleeves of his jacket are the coloured bands which the Germans wore in the winter to enable them to distinguish friend and foe in snow suits.

battalions, had their full complement of nine infantry battalions, at least on paper.

The 9th Parachute Division was formed under Major-General Bruno Bräuer in December 1944 from *Luftwaffe* personnel. The division had only five battalions, two of which contributed very considerably to the magnificent defence of Breslau after it had been cut off by the advancing Russians. The German garrison surrendered only at the end of hostilities after one of the classic sieges of modern times.

Airborne *Panzers*

The last parachute division to be raised was the 10th, commanded by Major-General von Hofmann. Formed in Austria during March 1945 from cadres of the 1st and 4th Parachute Divisions, the new formation totalled nine battalions and was heavily engaged with the Russian forces in Austria and the Moravian region of Czechoslovakia, where it finally surrendered in May 1945.

The only other major airborne formation raised by the Germans was the oddly named Hermann Göring Parachute *Panzer* Corps, commanded by Lieutenant-General Schmalz, and formed in East Prussia during October 1944 by the amalgamation of the Hermann Göring *Panzer* and Hermann Göring *Panzergrenadier* Divisions. The corps was in no real sense airborne, and was totally destroyed in the heavy fighting for East Prussia.

Enter the SS

One last German parachute unit to fight on the Eastern Front is worthy of mention, however. This was the SS 500th Parachute Battalion, formed under SS *Hauptsturmführer* (Captain) Rybka in autumn 1943 for special missions. Although half the men were SS volunteers, the rest of the battalion was composed of military prisoners. The battalion's first mission was an attempt to kidnap Marshal Tito, head of the Yugoslav partisan movement, from his headquarters in Bosnia during May 1944. Tito got away, and in a vicious three-day battle in which no quarter was given, the 500th Battalion was reduced to about 200 men. Made up to full strength again, this time only 20 per cent of the 'volunteers' were of disciplinary origins. The battalion fought next in the Kurland campaign against the Russians in autumn 1944 before being transferred to Otto Skorzeny's command. Redesignated SS 600th Parachute Battalion and made up to strength with genuine volunteers, the battalion was used in the 'Battle of the Bulge' to try to confuse the Americans: the battalion was dropped wearing US uniforms. In the closing stages of the war the battalion was used with considerable local success as a 'fire-brigade' unit on the Eastern Front, but finally surrendered, with only 180 survivors, to the Americans.

Above: A young *Fallschirmjäger* on sentry duty during February 1943. Ready to hand on the parapet of the wood-built bunker are three hand grenades.

Right: Loaded with paratroopers, two DFS 230 gliders move sedately across the sky towed by a pair of Junkers Ju 87 by *Seilschlepp* (cable tow) 131 feet (40m) long.

Below right: German paratroops in snow camouflage suits tow an extemporized sledge to bring up supplies. The sledge at present holds only the men's rifles.

Below: The three-man paratroop crew of a 3.7cm Pak 35/36 anti-tank gun prepare to engage the Russian light armoured vehicles in 1943.

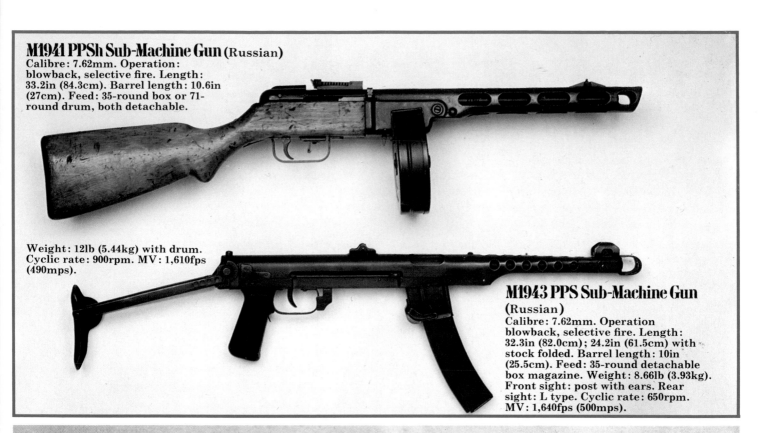

M1941 PPSh Sub-Machine Gun (Russian)
Calibre: 7.62mm. Operation: blowback, selective fire. Length: 33.2in (84.3cm). Barrel length: 10.6in (27cm). Feed: 35-round box or 71-round drum, both detachable. Weight: 12lb (5.44kg) with drum. Cyclic rate: 900rpm. MV: 1,610fps (490mps).

M1943 PPS Sub-Machine Gun (Russian)
Calibre: 7.62mm. Operation blowback, selective fire. Length: 32.3in (82.0cm); 24.2in (61.5cm) with stock folded. Barrel length: 10in (25.5cm). Feed: 35-round detachable box magazine. Weight: 8.66lb (3.93kg). Front sight: post with ears. Rear sight: L type. Cyclic rate: 650rpm. MV: 1,640fps (500mps).

The Korean War

Airborne operations played only a minor part in the Korean War, and then only in a tactical way, despite the fact that the major use of such forces could well have paid handsome dividends for the United Nations Forces. Any ideas of making strategic use of the airborne forces foundered completely on the non-availability of the right aircraft.

Although true offensive airborne operations played only a small part in the Korean War (1950–53), they yet again demonstrated what could be achieved by the tactical surprise and expertise of such forces. On a larger scale, however, the difficulties encountered by the United Nations' forces in trying to build up large conventional forces in a country lacking an adequate road system, let alone rail network, and generally hostile terrain, once again proved the validity of the air mobility concept propounded by General Douglas MacArthur's air chief in World War II, George Kenney. Had the United States, as the main supplier of men and *matériel* to the UN forces, possessed large numbers of transport aircraft, the war in Korea might very well have taken a different and happier course.

As it was, when the North Korean forces swept over the 38th parallel on 25 June 1950, there was little in the short term that the South Koreans, or in the longer term that the Americans could do but fall back as best they could and prepare for the counterblow. By 5 August the UN and

South Korean forces were hemmed into a tight perimeter around the port of Pusan in south-eastern Korea, fighting grimly to prevent the North Koreans driving them into the sea. Meanwhile MacArthur, as UN commander, was preparing for one of the most courageous, and certainly inspired, counterpunches. On 15 September the US X Corps began landing at Inchon, halfway up Korea's western coast. Tidal conditions here are extreme, and the landings could have come disastrously unstuck, but they did in fact work, and this threat to their rear gave the North Koreans a severe jolt. At the same time the Pusan forces, the 8th Army, broke out of their perimeter and started to push the North Koreans back as the two UN forces drove a corridor diagonally across Korea to link up on 26 September. The South Korean capital, Seoul, was liberated on the same day, and MacArthur five days later launched his forces in a general offensive towards the Yalu river separating North Korea and Communist China. Reeling back in disarray, there seemed to be nothing between the North Koreans and complete defeat except United Nations and American political factors.

Tactical blocks

This, then, was the strategic background to the first US airborne operation of the Korean War. As the UN forces moved forward over the 38th parallel, in the west their primary objective was Pyongyang, the North Korean capital. On 16 October, when the fall of this important objective seemed imminent, MacArthur decided to use part of his GHQ reserve, the US 187th Airborne Regimental Combat Team, to drop behind the North Korean lines and cut the only two routes by which they could pull out to the north as the UN forces closed in on Pyongyang.

The best places for such blocks were Sukchon and Sunchon, especially the latter, and Colonel Frank Bowen's RCT, based at Kimpo Airfield outside Seoul, was told to prepare for the operation, which would drop his unit some 30 miles (48km) behind Pyongyang, in two DZs about 12 miles (20km) apart. The order for the operation was given on the 19th, as the US 1st Cavalry Division entered Pyongyang, and as the South Korean 1st Division moved past the city to try to cut the North Koreans' line of retreat up to the Yalu

Below: A Fairchild C-119 Flying Boxcar of the 314th Troop Carrier Group unloads parachute containers as the men of the 187th Regimental Combat Team prepare to jump.

from the south-east, east and north-east. To give the South Koreans time to mount their attack, the 187th RCT was ordered to block the two northward routes. In readiness for the operation the US Combat Cargo Command had cancelled all cargo commitments of the US 314th Troop Carrier Group and the US 21st Troop Carrier Squadron, so that the necessary aircraft would be available for the paratroops. On the morning of the 20th, the paratroops and their equipment were loaded into the 76 Fairchild C-119s of the 314th Troop Carrier Group and 40 Douglas C-47s of the 21st Troop Carrier Squadron. The aircraft were crowded, the C-119s carrying 46 paratroops (two sticks of 23 men), 15 monorail bundles and 4 door bundles. By 1200 the aircraft were all in the air and heading for their rendezvous point over the Han river estuary. As they did so, the DZs were being softened up by attacks by 75 North American F-51 and 62 Lockheed F-80 fighters, and by five Douglas B-26 bombers, which claimed the destruction of 53 vehicles, 5 fuel and ammunition dumps, 23 oxcarts, 4 tanks and 1 piece of artillery. Major-General William Tunner, in command of the operation, was well pleased.

Masses of support

Escorted by 5th Air Force fighters, meanwhile, the transports had been flying north. At 1400 they started to drop their paratroops at Sukchon, 1,470 men being dropped quite quickly. The Sunchon aircraft, with a little farther to fly, started to disgorge their men at 1420, and by 1500 1,390 men had been delivered to this DZ. At the same time some 301·2 tons (306,036kg) of equipment had been drop-

ped. At neither DZ was there any AA fire, a few men being hit by sniper fire. Casualties during the drop totalled one man killed and 46 injured. Once on the ground the paratroops immediately gathered up their equipment, made for the high ground commanding both routes to be blocked, and dug in. To their surprise, the American paratroops found that the preliminary softening up had caused the North Koreans in the area to abandon excellent defensive positions well provided with artillery and ammunition. In the next three days additional drops were made, bringing in an additional 1,095 men and 290·8 tons (295,469kg) of supplies and equipment. This was the first drop in history where large quantities of heavy equipment had been dropped, and losses were slight: two of 12 105mm howitzers, four of 39 jeeps and two of four $\frac{3}{4}$ ton trucks.

Limited success

Bowen had landed with his 1st Battalion, regimental headquarters and attached troops at Sukchon, and immediately took up his position on Hill 97 to the east of Sukchon town. Other elements took Hill 104 north of the town, and after Sukchon had been cleared the road was blocked. The 3rd Battalion, which had dropped on to the same DZ, moved quickly 2 miles (3km) south to seize some hills overlooking Sukchon. By 1700 the Sukchon jobjectives had all been taken and the road and rail link north through the area had been cut.

The 2nd Battalion had dropped 2 miles (3km) south-west of Sunchon, and quickly secured all its objectives: while two companies set up roadblocks west and south of Sunchon, a third moved into the town,

where it met advance elements of the South Korean 6th Division advancing from the south-east.

MacArthur was delighted with the apparent success of the operation, and claimed that some 30,000 North Korean troops had been cut off. Over the next few days, though, the fallacy of this dream became clear. Not many troops had been cut off, and those that had been quietly melted through the UN lines. The North Korean government had left Pyongyang some eight days before the airborne operation started, as soon as the US 1st Cavalry and South Korean 1st Divisions came within striking distance of the capital.

Although the airborne operation itself had produced negligible results, the paratroops were to be involved in one fierce action. At 0900 on 21 October the 3rd Battalion struck out to the south in the direction of Pyongyang. After moving some 8 miles (13km), the battalion's leading unit, I Company, was attacked in the region of Opa-ri by an estimated North Korean battalion, well armed with 120mm mortars and 40mm guns. A hard-fought action lasted for 2 hours, at the end of which two platoons were overrun, and the rest of the company was forced to fall back

Right: Men of Company C, 1st Battalion, 187th Regimental Combat Team, X Corps, clean their weapons and prepare ammunition belts during a lull in the Korean fighting.

Below right: Part of the 3rd Battalion, 187th Regimental Combat Team, move in open order along a road east of Pambol to hit the Communists' right flank.

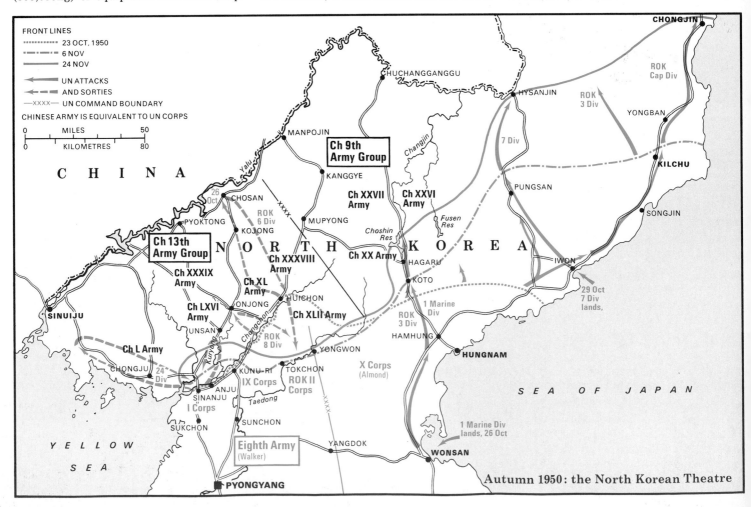

Autumn 1950: the North Korean Theatre

on Hill 281 west of the rail line. Some 90 men were missing. While I Company was suffering on the rail line, K Company was also having a hard time of it on the road, where it was attacked by a North Korean battalion in the region of Yongyu. After a sharp firefight, the North Koreans fell back south and east of Yongyu on to the high ground, and K Company took Yongyu and Hill 163, just to the north of the town. The Americans' problem lay in the fact that the line of hills between Yongyu and Opa-ri formed the best defensive position between Pyongyang and the Chongchon river to the north, and here the North Korean 239th Regiment, some 2,500 strong, had taken up defensive positions to halt the expected UN drive north from Pyongyang. An airborne landing to the north had not been expected, and the regiment was now cut off.

Communist desperation

At 2400 the regiment attempted to break out, but after severe fighting in the K Company sector the attempt was broken off. Two other attacks were launched shortly after 2400, and in these the K Company roadblock near Hill 163 was forced to withdraw. Realizing this, the North Koreans again attacked, this time at 0400. At 0545 the regiment blundered into the 3rd Battalion's command post, suffering heavy casualties. Nonetheless some 300 North Koreans attacked L Company, and 400 others the battalion command post and headquarters company. The situation was now critical, and the battalion called for help. This was forthcoming almost immediately from the 27th Commonwealth Brigade, part of the US I Corps advancing from the south. Early in the morning of the 22nd the Australian Battalion closed up from the south and the North Korean 239th Regiment was all but destroyed in the subsequent fighting.

The operation was over. The 3rd Battalion reported that it had killed 805 North Koreans and captured 681 others, out of a 187th RCT bag of 3,818 prisoners. The RCT had suffered 65 battle casualties, and on the 23rd was relieved by the 27th Commonwealth Brigade.

The disaster that had overtaken the North Koreans in the great UN offensive finally persuaded the Chinese Communists that they must take a hand, and in November 1950 their forces entered the war in a massive counter-offensive. This was augmented in a second offensive in January 1951. In January, February and March 1951, however, the UN forces launched a series of limited offensives designed to retake Seoul, which had been lost to the Chinese, and to cause the Communists heavy casulties. Seoul was abandoned by the Communists on 14 March, but then resistance once again stiffened north of Seoul. The 187th RCT was once again alerted for a drop, this time in the region of Munsan at the mouth of the Imjin river 20 miles (32km) north-north-west of Seoul. Here the North Korean 19th Division was reported to be preparing strong defensive positions, and the airborne operation was needed to provide the anvil against which the US I Corps could hammer the retreating Communists. Led by Brigadier-General Frank Bowen, the 187th RCT, supported by two companies of Rangers, dropped on Munsan at 0900 on 23 March 1951. Although there were still strong Communist forces in the area, most of the enemy had already crossed the Imjin, so the 187th RCT's primary task was impossible. Nevertheless, the drop was a hard one against a determined opposition, and by the time Task Force Crowden arrived from the south to link up, the 187th RCT had suffered 782 casualties in the 9 hours since the landing.

Inefficient use

Thus ended airborne operations in Korea. The 187th RCT continued to play an important part in the land operations, but from this time onwards there was a noticeable swing away from airborne operations towards helicopter ones. Although the helicopters of the time were very limited in their capabilities, and were used mostly for casualty evacuation and rescue missions, the US Marines were quick to realize that they had battlefield potential. This seemed to be borne out on 11 November 1951 when two Marine

Above: M4 Sherman tanks of the 72nd Tank Battalion, 2nd Infantry Division, provide support fire for the 1st Battalion of the 187th at Pambol-ni.

Above right: Further support from a 105mm howitzer of Battery C, the 674th Field Artillery Battalion, the 187th Regimental Combat Team, against Communist hill positions.

battalions were rotated by means only of helicopters. For American service therefore, the helicopter gradually came to replace the aircraft for battlefield use. Korea also taught the United States that its heavy lift capacity was inadequate for long-range strategic operations with heavy loads, and so a new generation of high-capacity aircraft was called for, resulting in the superb Lockheed C-130 Hercules.

Above: Towed by a drogue parachute, a palleted US truck falls out of the rear door of a C-119 of the 314th Troop Carrier Group, part of the 315th Air Division.

Right: Checked by its pilot parachute, the pallet swings up just before the two main parachutes open and lower the load to the forces waiting below.

Fairchild C-82 and C-119

Type: troop and supply transport.
Engines: two 3,500hp Pratt & Whitney
R-4360-20 radials. Span: 109ft 3in
(33.3m). Length: 86ft 6in (26.4m).
Height: 26ft 6in (8.1m). Speed: 281mph
(452kph) at 18,000ft (5,486m). Range:
1,770 miles (2,848km). Service ceiling:
23,900ft (7,285m). Payload: 62 troops or
equivalent weight of cargo. Weight

empty: 39,800lb (18,053kg). Weight
loaded: 74,000lb (33,566kg).
The C-82 first flew in 1944, and had a
capacity of 42 troops. Power was
provided by a pair of Pratt & Whitney
R-2800 radials of 2,100hp each. The
improved C-119 was introduced in 1947,
with an improved nose contour,
stronger wings, wider fuselage, and

improved performance and payload,
thanks to increased engine power.

Airborne Operations in French Indo-China

A considerable number of early successes with airborne forces in Indo-China had persuaded the French by 1953 that the Viet Minh could be brought to battle by the location of an airborne 'honeypot' in an area useful to them, and then destroyed in a set-piece battle of attrition. On the contrary, the Battle of Dien Bien Phu marked the end of France's colonial ambitions.

If military history were to be taught by word association the first name to follow 'French Indo-China' would be 'Dien Bien Phu', and the first thought to follow Dien Phu', and the first thought to follow Dien Bien Phu would be 'disastrous defeat'. Happily we are not subjected to this style of teaching, but many people still believe that French operations in Indo-China, and particularly her paratroop actions, were a series of blunders.

The first Indo-Chinese war began in August 1946 when, after a year of negotiations between the Nationalist Vietnamese leader Ho Chi Minh and the French, a French convoy was ambushed and destroyed at Bac Ninh. At that time Ho's military expert Vo Nguyen Giap had about 50,000 men under his command. They were armed with a mixture of weapons, some Japanese, some American and some French. Ho had not at that time been able

to enlist assistance from the Communist *bloc*, and China was still embroiled with her civil war. The Viet Minh, as the politico-military movement was known, had been in action as guerrillas against the Japanese occupation forces since 1941 and it is perhaps ironic that during the war they received assistance from the United States.

Small-scale successes

The French had kept a presence in Indo-China during the war, but in 1945 the Japanese turned on the remaining European and military population and killed or imprisoned them. With the end of the war the Nationalist Chinese and the British moved in to take control of the country, the Chinese occupying the north and the British the south. The French General Jean Leclerc arrived in 1945 with a mere 40,000 troops, but these men were veterans of the European war. When the French forces were deemed to be sufficiently strong to keep the peace the British withdrew and eventually the Chinese, too, were persuaded to go.

Now, in the words of Bernard B. Fall 'the French forces sent to Indo-China were too strong for France to resist the temptation of using them; yet not strong enough to keep the Viet Minh from trying to solve the whole political problem by throwing the French into the sea . . . The outbreak of the Indo-Chinese war can be traced back to that single, tragic erroneous estimate.'

Lack of resources was to dog all the French operations. Small unit actions against identified targets were generally a success, but there were simply not enough men available for the classic anti-guerrilla tactics of *quadrillage* (isolation of areas in a grid pattern) and *ratissage* ('raking' through an isolated grid) or for the long-term strategy of the oil slick.

The oil slick strategy was based on France's nineteenth-century experience in north Africa. Faced with a hostile country, the technique was to find a secure base and then, like a blob of oil as it spreads and coalesces with other blobs, work outwards into the country dominating the areas between the secure bases. It worked

satisfactorily in Africa where the land between the French forts was inhospitable, but in Indo-China the hills and jungles provided cover and the villages shelter and food – this was the 'water' for the guerrilla 'fish' to swim in.

These hills and jungles were broken up by *quadrillage* (gridding), and each sector was then combed out by *ratissage*. These were tactics originally employed by Nationalist Chinese who had developed *ratissage* into a sophisticated version of the cordon and search tactic. An area suspected of harbouring Viet Minh would be surrounded and then the cordon would slowly close in to the centre. When they met at the middle the troops would then turn about and work outwards again to the edges of the grid. In this way they attempted to 'purify' the area. In practice the local Viet Minh units could go to

Cradling a Châtellerault Model 1924 M29 light machine-gun in his arms, a French NCO leads a counterattack on the Viet Minh positions south of Dien Bien Phu.

ground and conceal themselves in the most ingenious ways, and larger 'regular' units would slip away as soon as the cordon began to move into position.

It was an attempt to speed up the positioning of the cordon that prompted the French to use paratroops in much the way that the Americans were to use helicopter-borne troops in the second Indo-Chinese war. It is a truism that parachuting soldiers into battle does not make them any better as troops, but rather it is the training and selection that ensures the quality. A parachute is a means to an end and the French were to use it in 150 major operations.

Considerable build-up

In the early days of the war the main troop transports and liaison aircraft used by the French were German leftovers from World War II. The Junkers Ju 52 and the Fieseler *Storch* struggled through the mists of northern Viet Nam or landed on baked mud strips in the delta, but they were subsequently replaced by American types, including 100 Douglas C-47s in 1952 and 25 Fairchild C-119s in 1954.

The French paratroop units in Indo-China were initially formed into the 25th Airborne Division, but this proved to be unsatisfactory since many paratroop units were up country or operating in remote areas of the colonies. Reorganization produced one military command for paratroops, including metropolitan French forces, the Foreign Legion paratroops and the colonial battalions of Vietnamese paratroops under training in Saigon.

The first commanding officer was Colonel Chavette, who was succeeded by Colonel de Bollardière and finally by General Gilles, who remained in command until the end of the war in Indo-China during 1954.

Between 1947 and 1953 the 1st and 2nd

Parachute Battalions of the Foreign Legion and the 1st, 2nd, 3rd, 5th, 6th and 8th Battalions of the Colonial Paratroops, an airborne armoured force, support elements, in the form of the 35th Airborne Artillery Group and engineers, were either sent out from France or assembled and trained in the Far East. There was also an SAS-type force created and commanded by Colonel Langlais.

At the end of 1953 the French could deploy 16 paratroop battalions, which with support units made a total of 25,000 men.

The first operation of the war was a jump in September 1946 near Luang Prabang in Laos, which was then part of the French colonial empire. This was followed by a drop near Haiphong to attack Viet Minh forces north of the port.

In 1947 there were major operations between Bok Khan and Cao Bang; in 1948 at Viet Tri; in 1950 around Nam Dinh while a year later there were two major drops at Nghialo and Hoa Binh, with two more in 1952 at Dong Hoi and Phu Doan on the Red River. The climax came in 1953 with drops at Lang Son, Nasan, Than Hoa, and Dien Bien Phu – there were two more drops at Dien Bien Phu between March and May 1954.

Text-book operations

These operations were the headline catchers, but for real value for money two lesser actions are worth closer examination.

By the early 1950s the northern border between Viet Nam and China had become secure Viet Minh territory. China had fought her civil war and now as the newest Communist state she was supplying the Viet Minh with arms and equipment manufactured in Russia or Eastern Europe. By 1952 the Viet Minh were strong enough to operate on semi-regular

lines and set themselves yearly strategic tasks. In 1952 they aimed to capture a jumping-off base against Laos, establish a link with Thailand and seize the valuable opium crop. For these operations they deployed 300,000 local volunteers and 120,000 provincial guerrillas, as well as a regular army of six infantry divisions and one artillery division – a total of 100,000 regular troops, well armed and trained.

The French knew of these plans but lacked the men to cover the Laotian border in a frontal defence. The best solution was to capture and destroy the enemy supply dumps in the area of Phu Doan between Tuyen Doan and Yen Bai.

Negligible losses

Ideally the French would have liked to capture Yen Bai, but once again there were insufficient troops and aircraft available. The objective became Phu Doan and the code name for the attack 'Lorraine'.

In October a ground attack by infantry and armour had put the French within 19 miles (30km) of Phu Doan, and the paratroop action would allow for the destruction of the dumps either side of the Sông Chay (*sông* is the Annamese word for 'river').

The paratroops were to jump on the morning of 9 November, seize the bridge over the river and then destroy the dumps. A tank and infantry relief column would set off on the night of the 8th and when they had made contact the joint forces would mop up the area for several days before withdrawing towards Viet Tri.

The Viet Minh had the base elements of their 308th and 312th Divisions in the area (about 400 men) with two battalions of the 316th Division with a number of 120mm 120mm mortars and 105mm howitzers.

The airborne group under the command of Colonel Ducourneau consisted of a staff and three battalions, the 1st and 2nd

Above left: Immediately after arriving at the improvised airstrip at Dien Bien Phu, a French paratrooper finds the nearest cover as a Viet Minh shell explodes.

Above: Watched by a command group and a soldier digging himself a foxhole, a French mortar team unleashes at a nearby Viet Minh concentration point.

Foreign Legion Battalions and the 3rd Colonial Parachute Battalion, two sections each with three recoilless 75mm guns, an engineer section with assault boats, and a demolition team. They were to be carried by 53 C-47s, which would make two round trips a day from two airfields near Hanoi.

Two battalions were to jump at 0930, one with the staff on a dropping zone north of the river. The planners were not entirely happy with the DZ: it was 1,530 yards (1,400m) long and 220 yards (200m) wide, covered with bushes and very tall reeds concealing some rough and very uneven terrain. The southern DZ was 1,095 yards (1,000m) by 440 yards (400m) and consisted of rice paddies. Fighters were to neutralize the neighbouring villages and Martin B-26 bombers would fly over the area throughout the operation. At 1430 a battalion would drop from 656ft (200m) on the northern DZ. The two DZs were to be marked by smoke bombs dropped by a light aircraft about three minutes before the arrival of the C-47s.

The operation was a success. The 'airhead' was secured by 2,354 paratroops whose only casualties were 7 dead and 16 wounded, evacuated by helicopter on the 10th. Strafing by the fighters caught a few groups of Viet Minh on the southern DZ. At about 1700 contact was made with the ground forces, who then assumed command of all the forces for the mopping

up and demolition operations.

The French captured 34 mortars, 30 anti-tank rockets, 40 machine-guns, 40 sub-machine guns, 250 rifles and two 57mm recoilless rifles. There was considerable interest in a truck that was captured, for unlike the other Viet Minh vehicles this was not a French import requisitioned by the Viet Minh, but a Russian-built 'Molotova' truck.

Viet Minh response

In the mopping up that followed the French discovered and destroyed more arms factories and food dumps. On 16 November, after a week of marching and fighting, the paratroops were evacuated to Hanoi by truck. However, the Viet Minh were not slow to react and a two-regiment ambush caught elements of the rearguard, destroying trucks and tanks and

Above: French troops, their weapons held high, move forward across a field bridge extemporised from the wreckage of the original structure at Dien Bien Phu.

causing some casualties. The lesson, which was to be proved valid for both Indo-Chinese wars, was that while it was relatively easy to penetrate the enemy base areas, it was essential that the raiding forces did not stay long enough for the Viet Minh to react, regroup and counter-attack.

By the following spring the Viet Minh drive on Laos had failed, and a rough parity between the two sides prompted the French to try another raid against the enemy supply lines. They chose as objective the town of Lang Son, an assembly and distribution base near the Chinese border, deep in enemy territory.

Air interdiction of the supply roads out of Lang Son had produced a bottleneck in the supply chain and the accumulation of stores and ammunition had been collected in bombproof caves north of the town.

This raid was going to be far more challenging than the earlier one, since not only must the caves and town be captured, but between the objective and the nearest friendly positions were 45 miles (72km) of wooded, mountainous terrain with few roads or paths.

Enemy forces consisted of a local battalion and two provincial companies in Lang Son, while on the Chinese border (only 6 miles/10km away) were some light anti-aircraft units. Elements of the 308th Infantry Division were 48 hours away at Thaï Nguyen. Worse still, in the 45 miles (72km) of enemy territory between Lang Son and Tien Yen, the nearest French post, a total of eight provincial companies could be deployed in the first day and between four and six after the second day.

The operation, codenamed *'Hirondelle'*, under the command of General Gilles, was in three phases: first, the drop on 17 July, which would destroy the Lang Son dumps; second, the capture of a crossing point over the Sông Ky near Loc Binh to cover the withdrawal; and third, a ground operation beginning on the 17th at Tien Yen and pushing north-westwards on an axis Tien Yen–Dinh Lap. This reduced the gap between the paratroops and friendly forces.

Total secrecy

The airborne group, under Colonel Ducourneau (the veteran of Phu Doan) consisted of a staff, the 6th and 8th Colonial Battalions and the 2nd Foreign Legion Battalion. In addition there was a section of pioneers with 14 inflatable assault craft. The ground force comprised three battalions and two commandos, a troop of tanks and an engineer company with three bulldozers. In reserve on the airfields at Gia Lam and Bach Mai at Hanoi were a battalion of paratroops with a battery of 75mm recoilless guns.

Secrecy was so vital that General Gilles did all the planning in person, assisted only by a signals officer. Orders were drafted a mere two days before the operation and units were alerted at 1400 on 16 July, from when they were then confined to their barracks. Briefing of battalion commanders was held at 1500 and they in turn spoke to their company commanders at 1600.

Light weapons only

The paratroops would only carry personal weapons, so the air support was carefully prepared. From H−15 minutes until H-hour, fighters would strafe all the enemy posts that had been located on aerial photographs of the DZs. From H to H+1 hour the parachute drops and regrouping operations would be supported by attacks on all Viet Minh who revealed themselves and from H+1 hour a cab rank of fighters would attack targets beyond a fixed support line at the request of unit commanders within the line. After dark the area would be illuminated by C-47 flare ships.

The drops over the Lang Son DZs would be made by aircraft with full sticks (28 men) since the zone consisted of large rice paddies, but over Loc Binh half sticks would be dropped. At Loc Binh the DZ was narrow and limited in length, running as it did between a river and two villages.

At about 0810 the staff and two battalions jumped near Lang Son from 56 C-47s, while four hours later the engineers with the third battalion jumped from 29 C-47s near Loc Binh.

Surprise pays off

Once again surprise paid off. It was a very hot day and the Viet Minh units were caught off guard. The militia and provincial companies fled and only the detachment guarding the dumps put up a fight until ground support from fighter-bombers was called in. There were five prisoners and 21 confirmed dead in the fighting around the caves.

With the fighting over the French had time to count the stores they had captured. The dumps contained 250 cases each holding four new Czech-made self-loading rifles, four American GMC and two Russian 'Molotova' trucks, 3,960 gallons (18,000 litres) of petrol, 771 cubic yards (588m) of engine parts and spares, 250 tyres, 1,757 lbs (797kg) of ammunition, 250 rifles and 50 sub-machine guns, 15 electric motors, 8 large machine-tools, 60·8 cubic yards (46·5m) of military cloth, 12,302 lbs (5,580kg) of tea, telephones, typewriters, 20,000 pairs of boots, documents and 500 boxes of Russian cigarettes.

The counting over, the demolition teams moved in with 1,764 lbs (800kg) of explosives and by about 1600 the caves and dumps as well as the parachutes had been destroyed by fire and explosives. The roads leading south and west were sealed off with mines, and the two Lang Son battalions moved off to contact the Loc Binh

battalions. A crossing had been prepared and the whole operation covered on the flank facing the Chinese border. The forced march was a severe trial: the problems posed by the intense heat and fatigue were aggravated by the presence of more than 300 civilians, men, women and children, who had decided to return to the French. They marched with the paratroops for 48 hours nonstop and endured all the hardships of this journey.

Around 2300 on the 18th the point scouts made contact with the ground forces near Dinh Lap. The pioneers quickly put the road back into commission and as the paratroops boarded their trucks the first Viet Minh companies caught up with the French. The Vietnamese opened fire with machine-guns, but the range was too great. The paratroopers were taken by sea from Tien Yen to Haiphong and thence to Hanoi. Of the 2,001 men who had taken part in the raid one had been killed, one

Above: A North African trooper at Dien Bien Phu brings a seriously wounded comrade in for attention at a first-aid post on 20 November 1953, D-day for Operation 'Castor'.

Left: A French paratrooper, armed with an M1A1 folding-butt carbine, searches a wounded Viet Minh before taking him in for treatment and internment on 20 November.

was missing and three had died of exhaustion in the march; 21 wounded had been evacuated by helicopter.

Phu Doan and Lang Son Loc Binh illustrated what could be done with well-trained, flexible airborne forces. The French developed a flair for this type of raid into enemy territory: it was a high-risk low-cost operation which produced very good returns. In routine patrols and minor actions the paratroop battalions had lost 5,000 men dead, missing and wounded – or more than 20 per cent of their strength – by 1953. Earlier in the war General Jean de Lattre de Tassigny had stopped the Viet Minh attacks on the Red River delta by deploying the enormous firepower available to the French and colonial forces – the Viet Minh had elected to fight a conventional war and they had lost back in 1951. To General René Cogny, commander-in-chief Tonkin, and General Henri Navarre, the C-in-C Indo-China, the lesson seemed clear: they would stop the Viet Minh offensive on Laos by laying a trap with their airborne forces. A base would be established in the rear of the Viet Minh, astride their communications, and they would be forced to attack it. Once they had concentrated their forces and ceased to operate in small mobile units, they could be hammered by the French firepower. Any Viet Minh reinforcements and supplies could be attacked *en route* by the air force, while the French artillery

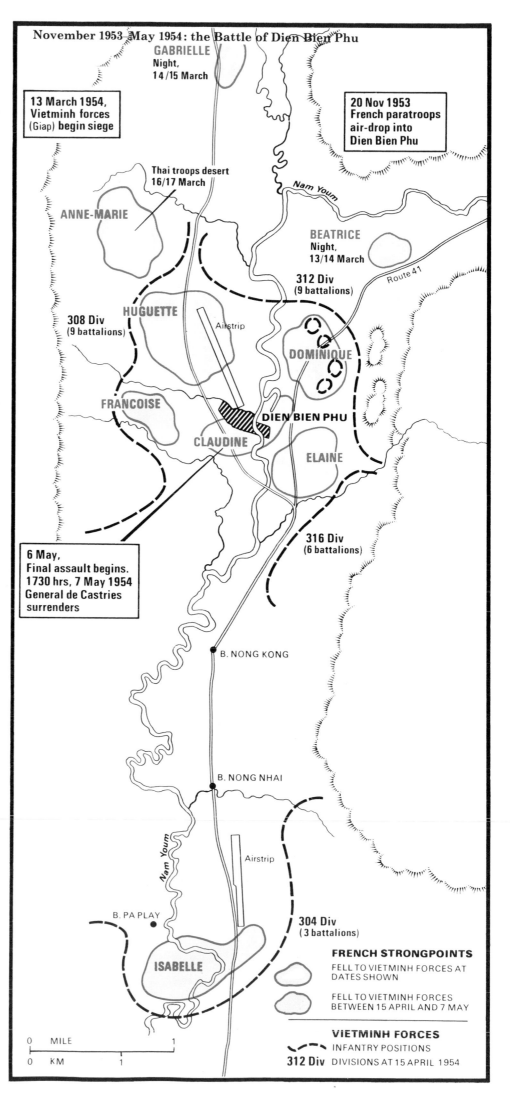

November 1953–May 1954: the Battle of Dien Bien Phu

GABRIELLE
Night, 14/15 March

13 March 1954, Vietminh forces (Giap) begin siege

20 Nov 1953 French paratroops air-drop into Dien Bien Phu

Thai troops desert 16/17 March

ANNE-MARIE

Nam Youm

BEATRICE
Night, 13/14 March

312 Div (9 battalions)

Route 41

HUGUETTE

Airstrip

308 Div (9 battalions)

DOMINIQUE

FRANCOISE

DIEN BIEN PHU

CLAUDINE

ELAINE

316 Div (6 battalions)

6 May, Final assault begins. 1730 hrs, 7 May 1954 General de Castries surrenders

B. NONG KONG

B. NONG NHAI

Nam Youm

Airstrip

B. PA PLAY

304 Div (3 battalions)

ISABELLE

FRENCH STRONGPOINTS

FELL TO VIETMINH FORCES AT DATES SHOWN

FELL TO VIETMINH FORCES BETWEEN 15 APRIL AND 7 MAY

0   MILE   1

0   KM   1

VIETMINH FORCES
- - - INFANTRY POSITIONS

312 Div DIVISIONS AT 15 APRIL 1954

would destroy attacks in the vicinity of the base. In World War II, Major-General Orde Wingate had shown during the second Chindit operation into Burma that his 'strongholds' could not only survive Japanese attacks, but also dislocate their supply routes and severely affect their offensive at Kohima and Imphal. The strongholds depended entirely on air supply, but despite this they were able to tie up large enemy forces and destroy them. It was this type of thinking that lay behind the French decision to set up a 'land/air' base at Dien Bien Phu.

Dien Bien Phu was a small village on a crossing point over the river Nam Yum. It had the remains of an airfield built by the Japanese during World War II and the bottom of the valley had a number of small hills considered suitable for defensive positions. It was, however, 140 miles (225km) from the French airfields at Hanoi and only 80 miles (130km) from the Chinese border. The valley is 10 miles (16km) long and 4 miles (6·5km) wide, flanked by hills which rise between 1,400 and 1,800 feet (425 and 550m). There were some oversights made by the planners which were to have drastic effects – the valley was prone to flooding in the monsoon season and heavy mist and rain could make flying very difficult – and the planners had not considered that there might also be ground fire from Viet Minh AA guns.

Operation 'Castor'

Operation 'Castor' began on 20 November 1953, when the 1st, 2nd and 6th Colonial Battalions dropped on the old airfield. With their reinforcements of two battalions with 75mm recoilless guns and a platoon of 81mm mortars they went into action against the two Viet Minh companies that were in the area under training. In addition to their 'tooth' elements the first drop included a company of engineers and a medical team who had flown in the 64 C-47s from Bac Mai and Gia Lam.

The valley was under French control and from the 24th aircraft began to land at the recommissioned airfield. By March there were 10,133 men in the garrison. Four battalions of the Foreign Legion, the 3rd Battalion of Moroccan *Tirailleurs*, the 2nd Battalion Vietnamese Infantry and the 3rd Battalion Thai Infantry, four 155mm guns, 24 105mm guns, as well as 20mm and 40mm anti-aircraft guns for anti-personnel work or for use against the Chinese should they send aircraft over the border. There was a small transport company with 127 vehicles including trucks, jeeps and ambulances, a battalion of sappers, two field hospitals, three catering units and a small air force with reconnaissance aircraft and five Curtiss SB2C Helldiver and Vought F4U Corsair fighter-bombers, four C-47s and a Sikorsky S-51 helicopter for casualty evacuation. It was a very impressive example of aerial supply, the climax of which was the flying in of 10 M24 Chaffee tanks – each tank needed five C-47s and two Bristol Freighters to lift it. But the French had not decided whether they were setting up a defensive position or a base for patrolling. In the end they set up neither – though extensive belts of barbed-wire were erected, the

The Indo-Chinese Theatre of War

BOUNDARY OF FRENCH INDO-CHINA TO JULY 1954

1867 DATES OF FRENCH COLONISATION

COMMUNIST CONTROLLED AREAS BETWEEN 1946-54

bunkers and trenches were inadequate and the patrols found that they could not penetrate far beyond their perimeter – General Giap had taken up the challenge and his forces were tightening up an infantry, artillery and anti-aircraft cordon which would strangle the garrison.

Between December 1953 and March 1954 Giap moved in the 304th, 308th, 312th and 316th Infantry Divisions and the 351st Artillery Division and a regiment of engineers – a total of 70,000 men. In addition 60,000 auxiliary forces of both sexes were deployed to build roads and move ammunition and supplies. They also moved 144 field guns (105mm and 75mm), 48 120mm mortars, 30 75mm recoilless guns, and later 12 six-barrel 'Katyusha' rocket-launchers. These were dug into reinforced positions with narrow embrasures, an almost impossible target for the French counter-battery fire. On the hills the Viet Minh also deployed over 180 anti-aircraft guns of between 12·7mm and 37mm calibres which could put up a flak barrage which was more severe than the fire experienced over the Ruhr during World War II.

D-day had been fixed by Giap for 12 March, by which date he had a superiority of 8 to 1. Artillery fire began to fall on Dien Bien Phu on the 12th and a day later

two C-47s and a fighter were destroyed on the airstrip. At 1715 the Viet Minh launched a heavy attack on *Béatrice*, a strongpoint held by the 3rd Battalion of the 13th Demi-Brigade of the Foreign Legion. By 2100 only one position was holding out, and after midnight there was an ominous silence: *Béatrice* had been swamped and the garrison had lost 75 per cent casualties – only 200 men regaining the main French lines.

Disaster looms

The loss in only six hours of a position held by the Foreign Legion galvanized the French staff in Hanoi. On the 14th the 5th Vietnamese Parachute Battalion was dropped to reinforce the garrison. At 1800 that evening the Viet Minh began shelling strongpoint *Gabrielle* held by Algerian *tirailleurs* and eight Foreign Legion 120mm mortars. In a night of desperate fighting eight Viet Minh battalions assaulted the one defending battalion. By dawn one position was still in French hands and a counterattack by two companies of the Foreign Legion and a battalion of Vietnamese paratroops supported by six tanks enabled the 150 remaining men in *Gabrielle* to escape.

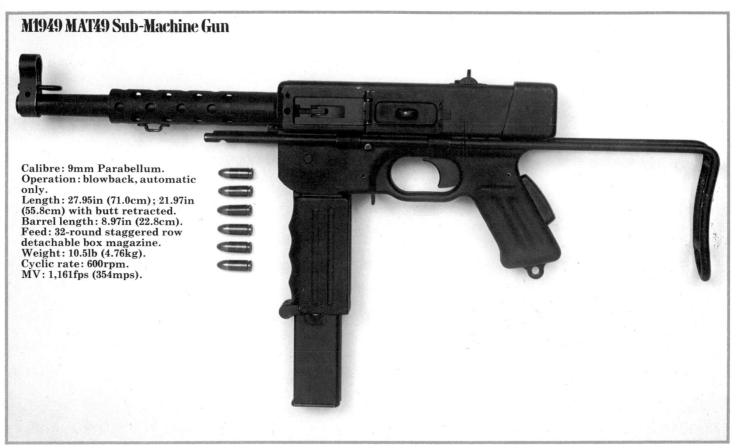

M1949 MAT49 Sub-Machine Gun

Calibre: 9mm Parabellum.
Operation: blowback, automatic only.
Length: 27.95in (71.0cm); 21.97in (55.8cm) with butt retracted.
Barrel length: 8.97in (22.8cm).
Feed: 32-round staggered row detachable box magazine.
Weight: 10.5lb (4.76kg).
Cyclic rate: 600rpm.
MV: 1,161fps (354mps).

There was now a break in the attacks as each side regrouped and dug new trenches – the French to take cover, the Viet Minh to sap nearer the strongpoints. On the 16th the men of the 3rd Thai Battalion deserted their position at *Anne Marie* and at the same time several hundred North Africans and Vietnamese went to ground as 'internal deserters' and hid in dug-outs on the banks of the Nam Yum.

However, though there were losses through enemy action and desertion there were also reinforcements. Between 16 and 27 March the 6th Battalion of Colonial Paratroops under the legendary Lieutenant-Colonel Marcel Bigeard, a field hospital and its staff, an artillery detachment and 400 volunteers making their first jump, were parachuted into Dien Bien Phu. At the beginning of April they were followed by two companies of the 2nd Battalion of the Foreign Legion under Lieutenant-Colonel Brechignac, then the 8th Battalion of Colonial Paratroops under Lieutenant-Colonel Guiraud and the 5th Battalion of Colonial Paratroops: there were now seven paratroop battalions in the valley. Command had devolved on to a paratroop mafia headed by Lieutenant-Colonel Langlais. His relations with the nominal commander, Colonel de Castries, were always good, but the hard-bitten Breton paratrooper was better suited to the strain of this siege war than the elegant cavalryman.

Constant fighting

On the night of 30 March, after exploding a mine beneath *Eliane* and firing a heavy preliminary bombardment, men of the 312th and 316th Divisions assaulted the five hills that made up the positions of *Dominique* and *Eliane*. The fighting that followed lasted for four days, with constant attacks and counterattacks. On 2 April the 308th Division attacked *Huguette* and

Bigeard scraped together a counterattack that drove the Viet Minh off for the loss of 800 dead. Another attack recaptured a strongpoint at *Eliane*, and though the morale of the garrison remained high, the position had not greatly improved.

Giap had suffered very heavy casualties, but he had a definite political aim in launching his near suicidal attacks on the French positions. Dien Bien Phu had become the object of worldwide interest and in Geneva the conference on Korea and Indo-China was scheduled to discuss Indo-China on 8 May. If Giap could crush Dien Bien Phu before the 8th the Viet Minh representatives would be in an extremely powerful negotiating position.

The end approaches

On 1 May the Viet Minh began a general offensive at 2200. The French had rations for only three days and a mere 275 rounds of 155mm ammunition, 14,000 of 105mm ammunition and 5,000 of 120mm mortar ammunition. Assaults hit the remains of *Claudine*, *Dominique* and the twin hills of *Eliane*. On 6 May Giap brought his multi-barrelled rocket-launchers into action – for a moment the French thought that the noise of the vehicle-mounted launchers was the arrival of a relief column. By dawn on 7 May the base had been reduced to a rectangle half a mile square. In these last hours Bigeard managed to mount a counterattack using the last remaining tank, commanded by Captain Hervouët who had had the plaster casts removed from his arms so that he could crew the tank.

After 55 days of siege Dien Bien Phu went under fighting – it never surrendered. Only 3,000 men survived from the total of 16,544. Over 3,000 died in the battle and a further 10,000 in the march to the prison camps and the period of 're-education' in the camps. The Viet Minh lost 8,000 dead and 15,000 wounded.

Above: Lieutenant-Colonel Langlais (wearing the beret), one of the architects of French airborne tactics in Indo-China, talks to a couple of his men.

Above: One of the German crew of a Foreign Legion heavy mortar makes his final sighting adjustments before the weapon is fired. Note the heavy base-plate.

The Suez Crisis

Though the Anglo-French landings to retake the Suez Canal from the Egyptians in 1956 may have been politically misguided, there can be no denying that the airborne aspects of the brief campaign, especially the French part, were well planned and executed, setting the pattern for the modern concept of long-range airborne operations.

For the *aficionado* of crisis diplomacy, the Suez Crisis of 1956 offers a rich diet of international plotting, unilateral nationalization of a major waterway, armed intervention by three nations against a fourth – which survived these attacks and emerged the political victor, and over all the threat of a nuclear war.

For the military historian the crisis shows the problems of setting up an alliance and sustaining a major military operation in time of peace. It also marks possibly the last time that British paratroops will jump into action – cuts in defence spending and the increased use of the helicopter have put large-scale paratroop operations beyond British means and intentions.

The jump was made on Monday 5 November 1956 by men of the British 3rd Parachute Battalion and the French 2nd *Régiment de Parachutistes Coloniaux* – the former under Colonel Paul Crook and the latter under Colonel Pierre Château-Jobert (Conan to the French, who had a way of adopting signals codenames). But what brought this Anglo-French airborne force to Egypt?

In the second half of the nineteenth century Anglo-French investment had financed the digging of a canal between the Mediterranean and the Gulf of Suez. The Suez Canal saved European shipping from a long and at times dangerous route round Africa's southern cape on its way to India and the Far East. The canal operated under French and British patronage until the overthrow of Egypt's King Farouk after World War II. The leadership of the new republic was taken up by a young army officer, Gamel Abdel Nasser, a man who emerged as an anti-Zionist and anti-colonialist. He took up the cause of the rebels in French Algeria and began to make threatening noises against Israel.

On 26 July 1956 he announced to a cheer-

Below: While other men are still descending, paratroopers of A Company, 3rd Parachute Battalion, move in to take the airport centre of El Gamil airfield at 0520

ing crowd of 50,000 that Egypt would nationalize the Suez Canal. Formal complaints were lodged a day later by Britain and France. In August planning began for French and British military intervention in Egypt. Nasser, it emerged, did not believe that the mobilization of reserves in Britain and the movement of troops to Cyprus was more than a military and diplomatic gesture. He refused to join the London Conference on the canal held on 16 August.

In September French troops began to arrive in Cyprus and on 4 September the 6th Battalion, Royal Tank Regiment sailed for Malta – a staging point on the journey to Suez.

In October the Israelis, who had been denied access by the Egyptians to Eilat, their port on the Gulf of Aqaba, mobilized on the 26th. Three days later they crossed the border and began to push into Sinai. The Israelis had been fighting for three days when the Anglo-French HQ received the go-ahead for Operation 'Musketeer', the air and sea attack and occupation of the Suez Canal. As the men of Nos 40 and 42 Commandos and the 6th Royal Tanks sailed from Malta, the RAF launched the first of a series of attacks against airfields in Egypt to initiate the 'air phase' of the operation.

Counter-productive tactics

At this juncture it is significant to note that the French regard the air phase as one of the most counter-productive parts of 'Musketeer'. Not only had many Egyptian aircraft been withdrawn out of the combat area, but the airfields had been eliminated in the first 24 hours of operations – after these attacks the RAF and French began to attack secondary targets like transport and armour. By the time the first Allied paratroops were in action world opinion had shifted in favour of the Egyptians, who were seen as the victims of an unprovoked onslaught.

By 1 November the Israeli reconnaissance units were within 10 miles (16km) of the canal. In the Red Sea the cruiser HMS *Newfoundland*, on patrol at night, sank the Egyptian frigate *Domiat*, which had ignored the British signal 'Stop or I Fire'.

By 3 November, after the Israelis had captured Sharm-el-Sheik at the entrance of the Gulf of Aqaba and lifted the blockade of Eilat, the date for the paratroop attack was advanced by 24 hours. A day later the Allied naval and amphibious force set sail from Cyprus.

The airborne forces who boarded their transports in the small hours of 5 November had been training in Cyprus since early September. Christopher Hogg of the 3rd Battalion, The Parachute Regiment had travelled with his battalion to England for a crash two-week refresher course on parachuting. Back in Cyprus in September 'We must have used a battalion's yearly quota of ammunition many times over. All day the field firing ranges echoed with small arms fire and exploding grenades... Reservists were absorbed into the platoons and were a great asset both in numbers and morale. It was a period of all-out training, each day of which might have been the last.'

Pierre Leulliette of the French Colonial Paratroops was among the first to arrive

November 1956: the Suez Operation

from Algeria. The French had been in action in Algeria against the *FLN* nationalists for two years, and behind them was the experience of Indo-China. Compared with them the British paratroopers felt comparative novices. The French had come with the working minimum of equipment and their stay at 'Camp X' was not pleasant. 'We had to stay there for a fortnight, parked on a few acres of sand, and surrounded by high barbed-wire fences. All contact with the outside world was strictly prohibited. No letters, even to our parents: we were secret. The days were torrid and the nights freezing.' The British had tried to foresee all the problems of working with the French and had posted signs on the roads reading *'Tenez la gauche'*, but to German-speaking *légionnaires* this meant little and they drove their huge trucks at breakneck speeds around the island on the right. The *EOKA* also took an interest in the foreigners, but after their experiences in Indo-China and Algeria the French had definite views about terrorists and had no intention of being a free source of arms and ammunition.

Anglo-French effort

By 1 November, the day that Brigadier Butler was authorized to brief the commander of the British parachute force, the French, who had now been cooped up for nearly two months, were seething with restlessness.

On 3 November Captain M. P. de Klef of the Guards Parachute Company was told that he had been picked to command a party of eight Guardsmen and six sappers, and would be jumping with the French. He was briefed by the commanding officer of the 2nd Parachute Battalion, part of the

amphibious force, had a brief look at the air photographs, talked to the intelligence officer and then on Sunday joined the French at Camp X.

The orders group given by Colonel Château Jobert took 30 minutes and 'was one of the briefest and clearest I have ever attended. He gave the general plan, the time of the drop, the DZ, the four company objectives, the position of his HQ and the RAP [Regimental Aid Post], probable enemy strengths and dispositions and the probable future tasks of his force... During the "O" Group the Colonel gave a very strong feeling of "This is my plan, and woe betide those who fail".'

French planning

The plan, including the British phase, was of French origin. General André Beaufre, commanding the French land forces, and deputy commander of the Allied land forces, proposed a British drop on Gamil airfield and two French drops, one to secure bridges south of Port Fuad and the other to capture Port Fuad itself. This would secure the northern entrance of the Suez Canal, and then subsequent drops could be made at El Kantara, Ismailia and Suez to capture the full length of the canal.

The DZs for the first two assaults were not ideal, but in the circumstances they were all that could be used. El Gamil airfield was about 1.5 miles (2.4km) long and 0.5 miles (0.8km) wide and bounded on the north and south by sea. This meant that the run in for the aircraft had to be either from the north-west or south-east. On the former course the pilots would be flying into the dawn sun, while the latter took them through the flak of Port Said. The airfield had been obstructed with hundreds of oil drums and appeared to be defended.

Above: The scene from the El Gamil airfield headquarters just after its capture, with the last men of the 1st Lift still coming down to join their comrades on the ground.

Right: Men of the 2è Régiment de Parachutistes Colonial break out from the DZ near Port Said. The soldier in the foreground is carrying a MAS36 CR39 rifle.

The French, with the twin Raswa bridges crossing the interior basin waterway as their objective, had a DZ only 150 yards (135m) across and bounded by sea, roads, the canal and trees. Fortunately French jumping techniques were better suited to a small area.

The areas were not to be marked by pathfinders since not only was this a daylight drop but in all probability an opposed one. A small group of pathfinders attempting to mark out a DZ or survive the night prior to the dawn assault was impractical, so an English Electric Canberra bomber was detailed to drop a flare 5 miles (8km) from the DZs to mark the run in. For Gamil a prominent sea wall marked the start of the dropping zone and was an effective release point. The French found that the beach immediately west of their DZ served as a suitable release point.

The British were to fly in Vickers Valettas, while their heavy equipment and vehicles would be slung in containers or packed on pallets and carried by Handley Page Hastings. The French would be

Right: Colonel P. E. Crook of the 3rd Parachute Battalion (left) and his tactical headquarters, including a radio operator and the liaison officer/bodyguard (hands on head).

flying in Nord Noratlas aircraft, which had the advantage of doors which permitted the less turbulent rear exit which made for a faster drop. The Valetta had an added disadvantage for the last eight men to jump, who would have to climb over the main spar which runs across the fuselage connecting the two wings. Loaded with 150 lbs (68kg) of kit this could mean a delay in exiting and consequently an increased risk of landing on the Egyptian positions.

The flight from Cyprus to Egypt took two hours. It was two hours for the soldiers sitting opposite one another to prepare themselves for the coming action.

The landings

On his French aircraft, Captain de Klef slept. He remarked afterwards that the French parachutes were more comfortable than British ones. Christopher Hogg said that by the time they took off he and his men were past worrying: 'We had nothing to do except think and drink orange juice . . . All those to whom I talked afterwards said they were calmer than they had ever been before on a jump, with a complete absence of feeling. Some read comics, some talked, some just stared into space.'

Pierre Leulliette had more vivid memories of the flight: 'My fear had already returned, like some household pet. Oh, not only me. The man opposite, looking through me, his eyes bulging, was thinking of nothing except how scared he was. Wasn't he me, that man I was staring through, my eyes bulging? . . . Close by me, the company *adjutant* looked like a sick old toad. It was touching. Now that his mask had fallen, during the night, I saw that, deep down, this ferocious warrant-officer was just an old man, an old man who probably didn't care for the army all that much, especially just then, however much he coveted the Legion of Honour.

'The dawn came. Several had preserved impassive masks. But little signs, here and there, gave them away: the tension in a crow's foot, for instance, or two lines between the eyes, a bitter twist of lips or a jutting chin. An L.M.G. gunner gave a disturbing laugh, harsh as a trumpet solo in a mortuary crypt. It made such an impression that several of us felt obliged to say a few words if only to fill the silence which followed that terrible, blasphemous laugh.'

Beneath the transports as they started their run in, the Egyptian Army had begun to react with small arms and AA fire. The intelligence reports on the Egyptian Army stated that the total mobilized strength was about 100,000 men deployed in 18 brigades: ten infantry, one medium machine-gun, three armoured, a coastal defence and three anti-aircraft. Armament was a mixture of British World War II cast-offs and Soviet armour with modern small arms. The chief worry were the tanks, Shermans, T-34s, Centurion Mk 3s and IS-3s; another problem were the anti-aircraft brigades armed with 30mm Hispano Suiza and 40mm Bofors light AA guns. Unlike the infantry, the anti-aircraft troops were well trained and motivated, and once the fighting started they put up a spirited defence.

Besides the regular units there was the part-time National Guard numbering 100,000. Though training was on a platoon and section basis, it could fight a guerrilla or sniping war in the streets of Port Said and Port Fuad. Finally there were the 3,000 men of the Frontier Force and the police force (in the opinion of some, the latter deserved almost as much military consideration as the Regular Army). The police were armed, loyal, well disciplined and it was known that they had received anti-paratroop training.

While large numbers of Egyptian soldiers had been captured or killed by the Israelis in Sinai, many had retreated on the canal area, and of these intelligence reports were rather imprecise. Captain de Klef was told that there were believed to be anti-tank guns spaced out on the east bank of the canal with section positions every 50 yards (46m) down the Treaty Road. When he saw the brigade intelligence officer he was told that the section posts were 500 yards (460m) apart: 'I secretly wondered if I went higher still whether they would become 5,000 yards apart.' In the end it emerged that there were none at all, but 'the thought of a section attack every quarter of a mile for four miles was not encouraging even though there was a strong impression on both sides (French and British) that the landing would be unopposed'.

Initial chaos

Captain P. H. Brazier of the Royal Engineers, with a group of sappers from the 3rd Troop, 9th Independent Parachute Field Squadron, had been ordered to prepare a bridge 1 mile (1·6km) to the west of Gamil for demolition and clear the airfield of obstructions. As he jumped he 'could see there was a fair amount of firing

across the DZ both from LMGs and mortars. Also a fuel store near the control tower was burning furiously, emitting a great sheet of flame and thick black smoke.'

Christopher Hogg remembers 'watching the thin sandy strip that was the coastline of Egypt slipping by beneath us. Suddenly all was action. The scream of "Red on! Stand in the door!", a glimpse of the airfield itself through the porthole, and then with the "Green on, GO!!" a mad twelve seconds crossing the spar, stamping down the plane and flinging myself through the door with the other nineteen already gone . . . The next few seconds I shall remember always: a terrific rush of air, the tug, the billowing, tearing sound and then the silence – a silence broken by the crackle of small arms fire spasmodic at first and then all over the sky.'

Ineffective AA fire

Captain de Klef, jumping with the French, recalls the informal aircraft drill, the klaxon 'a second of buffeting and blankness and then the gentle swaying accompanied by a sigh of relief, slow twists and my helmet as usual jammed down over my eyes. Twists cleared, container away and helmet pushed back. The sun was still shining, but something had gone wrong with the "practice" jump. The air was full of the sound of small arms fire. Anti-aircraft shells were bursting above us, the Noratlas aircraft were weaving and jinking all over the sky to the north, and the Frenchmen drifting down around me were firing from their parachute harness.'

Pierre Leulliette watched the first man in the two sticks to jump from the Noratlas, then 'two lumps of flesh were simultaneously catapulted, with extreme violence, into the vast silent void. Linked by an

Left: The US M2 60.5mm (2.38in) mortar. Barrel length: 28.6in (72.6cm). Weight: 42lb (19.1kg). Elevation: 40°–85°. Traverse: 14°. Range: 100–1,985 yards (91–1,816m). Bomb weight (HE): 31lb (1.36kg). Muzzle velocity: 518fps (158mps).

French Paratrooper, Suez 1956

A French *para* 'kills' his billowing parachute after jumping into the restricted DZ at Suez. He is wearing the striped camouflaged uniform which was a trade mark of the *paras* with its numerous pockets with press studs and zips. His helmet is attached to his harness by a piece of nylon cord—to prevent him losing it during his exit from the aircraft. Behind him is the rucksack that was slung beneath his reserve 'chute and which he has dumped on landing. It holds ammunition and personal effects and strapped on the outside are a pair of canvas and rubber boots— lighter and cooler than his jump boots. His helmet is similar to the US pattern but underneath the net he has secured additional camouflage.

invisible chain, we were already following them, at a speed the despatchers could no longer control. Each of us, with a single impulse, as though appalled at the sight of the huge back of the man in front of him, toppled over, was sucked out by the void, and passed through the door in turn, holding his breath.'

With his parachute deployed Leulliette felt the exhilaration that follows a successful jump: 'A new kind of joy, one of those feelings you can't admit, which you feel ashamed of later, flooded through me: war, this was war! The real thing at last!'

Despite the flak no aircraft were shot down, though nine were damaged. At Gamil the men began to collect at their RVs (rendezvous points). A Company then moved off to secure the north-west corner of the airfield while B sealed off the Port Said 'exit. The battalion HQ and elements of the brigade HQ had landed in the middle of the DZ and covered by the third company.

A Company cleared a number of Egyptian positions as it advanced along the airfield. At the far end Captain Brazier found that the bridge he had been ordered to demolish had already been destroyed by the Egyptians. His men set to work building breastworks with oil drums and equipment containers.

Hectic activity

Christopher Hogg, with C Company, set off to clear the area around the sewage farm. They cleared the farm but came under fire as they emerged from the buildings. He was about to put in a platoon attack when a French fighter swooped down and did a strafing run. The paratroops promptly took cover in the very solid, but very filthy sewage troughs.

B Company landed in a 'bloody good reception committee', but soon sorted out friend and foe, and after clearing the coast-guard buildings silenced an Egyptian anti-tank gun with a shot from a 120mm recoilless rifle.

Throughout the action the Fleet Air Arm Hawker Sea Hawks from HMS *Bulwark* were on call for a 'belly dance' or ground attack. The RAF had transported the paratroops and attacked targets deep inland, while the Royal Navy not only provided a radio relay and ground support but also, after Gamil had been secured, lifted off casualties by helicopter and flew in a medical team to assist the paratroops.

The French at their DZ at Raswa were having a busy time. Not only was the DZ occupied by Egyptian infantry, but machine-gun and Bofors fire from guns covering the bridge was being directed at the paratroops and aircraft. Vought Corsairs from the *Lafayette* and Cyprus-based Republic Thunderstreaks suppressed these positions. They were directed by General Gilles who, as the *Commandant de l'Opération Aéroportée*, was circling the area in a Noratlas equipped as an airborne command post. This technique had been first used in Indo-China and was later used by the Israelis in their operation at Entebbe. If there is no danger from enemy fighters or anti-aircraft weapons it allows good radio communications with excellent

long-range relay facilities. At Suez General Gilles communicated with the French HQ in Cyprus, the naval forces, and ground attack aircraft as well as the men on the ground.

The French captured one of their two bridges, but the other had already been demolished. There were 10 French casualties, while the Egyptians lost 60 dead.

Pierre Leulliette was part of the force that attacked the class-60 swing bridge. With excellent close support from their fighters they were able to storm the bridge, but some Egyptians still lurked among the girders which protected them from the air. 'While his comrades withdrew, covering each other, one Egyptian remained more than quarter of an hour by himself at the entrance to the bridge, defending it with his gun against our entire company, furiously and hopelessly. He was a real death commando. Then a bullet struck him. He slumped back grotesquely, like all heroes.'

Inferior resistance

Having secured the bridge, the French paratroopers watched as more of their comrades jumped to capture Port Fuad. This task had originally been assigned to the Royal Marine Commandos, who were to be lifted in by Westland Whirlwind and Bristol Sycamore helicopters, but it was thought that helicopters were too vulnerable.

The Egyptian performance, once the Allied paratroops had landed, was generally poor. There were, however, exceptions. The French encountered a sniper while they were clearing some barracks north of the swing bridge. 'We tried to neutralize him with a grenade: the furniture flew to the ceiling and the walls cracked. He kept on firing... He was waiting down below behind a pile of furniture and mattresses, which acted as a barricade. He wasn't the sort that gave up.' In the end the paratroopers fired a recoilless rifle at the house, which caught fire. 'Black with soot and blood-smeared, the man at last came stumbling out. He was yelling

Above: Colonel Pierre Château-Jobert, codenamed Conan, presents an emotive picture of a professional airborne soldier with his bare head and beard.

but still firing. Four or five bursts mowed him down. It was all over. Heroism is a lonely game. We saluted the fellow. Enemy or not, we admired him. He died alone. The more alone because everywhere else the Egyptian Army was on the run and in Sinai, in full flight'.

Many of the Egyptian soldiers changed into civilian clothes. The small British group attached to the French covered the Treaty Road. A motorcycle with two 'civilian' passengers was halted and the sharp eyes of a Guardsman noticed a bulge under a shirt: both passengers had revolvers, and crammed in the tool box and the seat were 164 rounds of ammunition, bits of uniform and identity cards. One passenger was a commando, the other an air force cadet – both thought that they would be shot. As it was one became a cook and the other a grave digger for the next 24 hours.

Now fully alerted, the Guards group signalled a car to stop: it slowed down, stopped and then tried to reverse away. A burst of fire from a Bren gun sent the car into the Sweet Water Canal, where it completely disappeared. 'A pause, bubbles and eight heads appeared on the surface and screaming for mercy, they were pulled out.'

Quick success

As darkness fell, the various airborne groups settled in for the night. Some of the French had captured a barracks and they pulled mattresses out on to the roofs to sleep. They had a dramatic night when a truck load of Egyptian soldiers arrived thinking the buildings were still in their hands.

Christopher Hogg had a quiet night. Patrols were sent out to check on Egyptian movements, but there was little military activity. He suffered other attentions: the sewage farm had attracted flies during

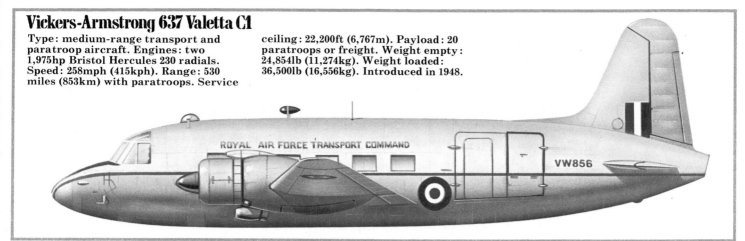

Vickers-Armstrong 637 Valetta C1

Type: medium-range transport and paratroop aircraft. **Engines:** two 1,975hp Bristol Hercules 230 radials. **Speed:** 258mph (415kph). **Range:** 530 miles (853km) with paratroops. Service ceiling: 22,200ft (6,767m). Payload: 20 paratroops or freight. Weight empty: 24,854lb (11,274kg). Weight loaded: 36,500lb (16,556kg). Introduced in 1948.

the day, but at night mosquitoes took over. They seemed to think that they had a duty to remind the paratroops that they were on duty that night. 'How well they succeeded we saw in the morning: faces were swollen and arms, hands and necks bitten so that there was hardly a piece of untouched skin visible. For weeks afterwards I carried the marks of that awful night.'

Dawn on 6 November was D-day for the amphibious forces. At 0500 men of Nos 40 and 42 Commandos landed on the beaches astride the Cassino pier. By 0530 'C' Squadron of the 6th Royal Tanks had linked up with the Marines, and by about 1000 the first of the tanks had reached the golf course south of the town. At 0615 the first wave of No 45 Commando had landed from helicopters near De Lesseps's statue and 75 minutes later the complete Commando was in position.

In the afternoon French and British paratroops disembarked at Port Said and Fuad. The British contingent consisting of the 16th Brigade less the 3rd Battalion while the French included three naval commandos, a squadron of AMX light tanks and men of the 1st Foreign Legion Parachute Regiment.

Paratroops move on

While these forces were landing, the Anglo-French paratroops were extending their perimeters. C Company, 3rd Parachute Battalion moved off towards Port Said. Suddenly the quiet of the morning was shattered as a solitary MiG fighter screamed over and raked the British troops with cannon fire. B and C Companies leapfrogged forward until they reached the edge of the shanty or 'wog' town. This was a collection of gaudy, filthy wooden shacks on the south-western edge of Port Said. A patrol which attempted to advance into this area came under heavy fire and every man was wounded. Since the air offensive had been called off by this time, an anti-tank gun was brought up and it began to blast the area. After a few shots the shacks caught fire. Another fire had also started when a destroyer had shelled an *SU-100* dug in near the town. The two fires joined and the town was soon blazing.

In the French sector there were fires of equal ferocity. Four Egyptian tanks moved into the area of the Anglo-American Oil Company tank farms and began to shell the French. The paratroopers, who had had plenty of experience fighting rebels armed with small arms, were rather surprised at coming under shell fire. They dug in and wondered if politics would prevent the air force from attacking the tanks as they lurked near the Anglo-American installations.

Pierre Leulliette watched as French fighter-bombers went into a shallow dive. They raked the tanks with machine-gun fire. 'But almost immediately there was a series of tremendous explosions. Instantaneously, massive sheets of huge crimson flame reared up, like ramparts in the blue sky. The tanks burst and caught fire. Tons of inky-black smoke enveloped the countryside in a black pall . . . Next day, entering Port Fuad, we looked like colliers! Meanwhile, the tanks had stopped firing. Their crews had probably been burnt alive inside their vehicles.'

The threat from Egyptian armour was diminishing as the AMX and Centurian tanks of the Allied amphibious force began to penetrate inland. This was an important moment for Captain de Klef, since the 6th Royal Tanks would be coming down the road into the French positions. At about 1630 they heard the rumble of tanks and the leading troops of the 6th Royal Tanks appeared. 'Though we tried to stop them they went straight past us without even a wave. Out of each steel hull protruded a steel helmet, looking neither right nor left. I was unable to give the little information I had nor find out any news of the Company, when 2 Para were due to arrive and many other things besides, so I got our motor-bike and gave chase, but it was wasted effort, for however much I waved or shouted they would not stop and all I achieved was to amuse some French paratroops who were sitting on the back of the rear tanks.'

Futile battle

After this frustration there was some perverse satisfaction for the Guardsmen when the tanks fought a futile battle with an empty pillbox further down the road.

Meanwhile the men of the 3rd Parachute Battalion had settled into some flats in the modern quarter of Port Said. The following day, like their French comrades, they set about collecting and burying the dead. In the course of this grisly but essential work they picked up small arms from Russia, Germany, Czechoslovakia, Italy, Britain and the United States as well as mortars, tanks, and numerous military vehicles.

The halt order and cease-fire of 7 November, which preceded the arrival of United Nations forces, appears to have been taken more philosophically by the British than the French, the latter feeling that they had been betrayed in Indo-China, but that this was a greater betrayal. They were a mile from El Kantara and making excellent progress down the canal.

The British pull out

The British withdrew their airborne forces soon after the 7th, but the French kept theirs in reserve on Egyptian soil in the hope that they might be able to push farther down the canal. The evacuation of the British paratroops was not entirely the result of a collapse of political will that the French suspected, but rather that they could be redeployed again if the need arose, and moreover the regiments that had already been allocated to replace them were waiting in transports off the Egyptian coast.

In Port Fuad the men of the 1st Foreign Legion Parachute Regiment were employed on internal security duties and their tough methods soon silenced any sniping or resistance. The feeling that they had been betrayed by the British and their own politicians, plus the thought that they could have rolled up the whole of the canal and removed the chief source of support and supply for the *FLN* left a very bitter taste with the paratroopers. They were to purge it in their ruthless prosecution of the urban battle in Algiers which met them when they returned from Egypt.

The attitude to the UN police troops is best summed up in the now famous novel about the 'paras' by Jean Lartèguy. In *The Centurions* the *paras* see the arrival of 90 Danish soldiers in blue caps. 'They had skin and hair the colour of butter, weapons which had never been used except on exercises, and complexions as clear as their consciences.'

That Suez was a political disaster has now become an accepted fact – the British and French withdrew with considerable loss of prestige and Nasser became the champion of the Arab world. Israel too withdrew to her borders and had to fight two more wars before she achieved a small measure of security and recognition.

Yet out of this *débâcle* it is worth remembering that a lightly armed airborne force of about 1,000 men compelled a well armed and equipped garrison to sue for peace within 12 hours of landing. A well balanced and properly supported airborne assault can achieve results far out of proportion to its size.

Airborne and Airmobile in Vietnam

The long war in Vietnam saw widespread use of airborne forces in their conventional role, and also as ground troops, but in addition there was evolved to working pitch the new concept of airmobile troops: more-or-less conventional infantry who were trained to use the mobility offered by the helicopter for fast-moving war without the usual encumbrances of a heavy 'tail'.

The major lesson of the Korean War for the US Army was the need to overcome the frustrations imposed by terrain. Only airborne troops and aircraft could do it. The famous airborne divisions emerged from Korea with their reputations intact and the Airborne School at Fort Benning, Georgia continued to train generations of a junior leadership elite. The army was not as fortunate with its aircraft and in 1952 expansively resolved to raise 12 battalions of helicopters to carry forward

Right: American infantry vault from a hovering Bell Iroquois helicopter and move straight off into the attack, a good example of the new tactics pioneered in Vietnam.

observers, some supplies, and the wounded. The primitive state of helicopter technology limited a more expansive role. As the US was locked in the Cold War, the Pentagon planners concentrated on the nuclear battlefield of the future, and here they discovered that the army badly needed a light reconnaissance aircraft organic to combat divisions. The faithful Cessna O-1 (L-19) Bird Dog was unsatisfactory and to make matters worse, the US Air Force, then less than a decade old,

feared the emergence of another Army Air Corps. Serried ranks of cost-conscious congressmen agreed.

By the mid-1950s, two eminent paratroopers, Major-General (later Lieutenant-General) James M. Gavin and Colonel (later Lieutenant-General) John J. Tolson looked to the helicopter to answer the air force's sensitivity about the army's use of fixed-wing aircraft while still giving the army its much-needed reconnaissance capability. Gavin and his staff thereupon proposed the rebirth of the US Cavalry, carrying out its time-honoured role on flying horses. The authorities frowned but Gavin sent Tolson to Fort Benning as head of the Airborne School to work out a doctrine for the efficient use of helicopters. Meanwhile, Brigadier-General Carl I. Hutton and Colonel Jay D. Vanderpool were working along the same lines at the Army Aviation School at nearby Fort Rucker, Alabama. Vanderpool 'scrounged' some helicopters, armed them with homemade weapons systems, and by 1957 was testing his 'Sky-Cavalry' platoon, thinking all the while in terms of whole divisions of the radical development.

Airborne controversy

The various aviation research projects principally centred around the Ordnance, Transportation, and Signal Corps were co-ordinated to some extent at Fort Rucker, and in 1959 the army gave the US aviation industry guidelines to develop a 'light observation, manned surveillance, and tactical transport aircraft'. Fortunately for the army, the Bell company was already well advanced in developing a turbine-powered utility helicopter, the forerunner of the workhorse of Vietnam, the UH-1 Iroquois (Huey). By now many army officers looked on army aviation development in messianic terms and the Rogers Board urged that helicopters be given to each division, helicopters that could fly at least as far as the farthest range of that division's artillery. Nevertheless, the programme was ponderously slow, bogged down in peacetime staff studies, until early in 1962 President John Kennedy's visionary Secretary of Defense, Robert McNamara labelled the whole effort to date as 'dangerously conservative'. The army's aviators leapt at the challenge and in just 90 days from its establishment the Howze Board, under the army's first Director of Aviation, laid before McNamara a 3,500 page report which recommended five new divisions, each having 459 helicopters. The Hueys would carry the troops, the new cargo-carrying double-rotor Boeing CH-47 Chinooks would carry the divisions' artillery of Honest John rockets and 105mm howitzers, the intelligence would have some fixed-wing aircraft with cameras or radar, and a new, and then undeveloped, attack helicopter gunship would complete the requirements for the 'air assault division'.

Despite severe opposition from all breeds of bureaucratic dinosaur, McNamara blessed the concept and the 11th Air Assault Division was formed at Fort Benning in January 1963. For those involved it was an exhilarating time of innovation in tactics, logistics, maintenance systems, and all manner of opera-

tions. By late 1964 it became common to see tight flights of Hueys dashing at a determined 115mph (185km/h) a few feet over the Georgia pines to a distant corner of the reservation. Arriving first, the five Huey gunships would break over a selected clearing and rake it and the surrounding trees with sustained rocket and machine-gun fire. Covering each other, the Hueys would bank and make another deadly pass, then climb and circle like hawks whilst seven other Hueys, flying in a stacked line like descending stairsteps, dropped into the clearing, disgorged the troops they were carrying and rapidly lifted off, the troops rushing to predetermined rallying points off the landing zone (LZ). As the first troopships rose in a swirl of dust, more arrived until an infantry company or more was effortlessly on the ground, fresh, and moving vigorously towards its objective. The commander overhead in his CandC (command and control) ship had brought a substantial force from miles away to inject intact deep in 'enemy' territory with total surprise, all in less than 15 minutes. This airmobile idea worked, and would prove as necessary a development for Vietnam as airborne doctrine had been for the Europe of World War II.

New theories

By the spring of 1965 Lieutenant-General Charles Rich had finished his tests for the Howze Board and was so impressed with the teamwork of the 11th Air Assault Division that he wished to keep it together. The Pentagon agreed, and with the blessing of the Vice Chief of Staff, General Creighton Abrams, the 11th AAD was fittingly reconstituted as a whole division of cavalry, the 1st Cavalry Division (Airmobile) and Vietnam was the reason for its birth.

Above: Dead and wounded of the initial 69-man reconnaissance force in the Ia Drang valley are brought in for evacuation by men of the 1st Air Cavalry Division.

The US had been propping up the Saigon regime since President Harry Truman's day despite British misgivings and the French defeat. After the partition of Vietnam, US Army advisers arrived in the south to help the Army of the Republic of Vietnam (ARVN) thwart North Vietnam's attempts to insinuate a Communist government in the south. Schooled on the conventional battlefields of Europe and Korea, the advisers found themselves in the strange position of being with ARVN units which controlled little more of the countryside than where they stood. Like the French, the ARVN was tied to fortified compounds outside which the populace lived and farmed, suffering from the demands on manpower and foodstuffs from both the local Communist guerrillas, the Viet Cong (VC), and the South Vietnamese government. The Americans urged a number of reforms upon the South Vietnamese to sway the people over to the government. They instituted programmes to place American advisers in each province and district to help fortify the hamlets and to train the villagers to hold what little they had. They checked what abuses they could see, gave the local authorities some backbone, and requested American aid and firepower as it became available. At a national level the US took many problems more or less under their wing to control corruption and try to interest the French-educated sophisticates in Saigon to look after the 'hearts and minds' of the people in the VC-dominated countryside. The US pushed forward the *Chieu Hoi* scheme to rehabilitate co-operative VC and North Vietnamese

Above: A trooper of the 173rd Airborne Brigade receives final orders and a last check before emplaning for a mission over South Vietnam.

Right: The waist gunner of a Bell helicopter searches the ground under him for signs of the Viet Cong, to be engaged with his General Electric Minigun.

Army (NVA) deserters, and moved to create a prosperous *bourgeoisie* which would identify its new-found prosperity with the Saigon government and thereupon support it. There was always, however, a trace of cancer coursing through the whole regime which no amount of American enthusiasm could cauterize. To the South Vietnamese people it was a case of knowing on which side one's bread was buttered, and in many cases people buttered both sides. Nevertheless, throughout the early and mid-1960s the US worked to give the South Vietnamese that extra boost to put them on the road to stability. Many of the US programmes were still in their infancy and despite massive aid the VC were still powerful in the rural areas. Endless ARVN patrols and operations failed to halt the VC and they and the NVA continued to run their long-established shadow governments. They enjoyed an excellent intelligence apparatus so well developed that most government operations were known, at least in part. Unless luck went with them, most ARVN units returned to their compounds empty-handed, bloodied from ambush, or with a 'suspect' or two picked up sometimes in frustration (and thereby further alienating the peasantry) as the only proof of an otherwise unproductive sweep. It was a long war.

As part of the American assistance

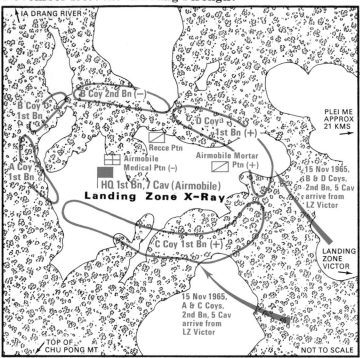

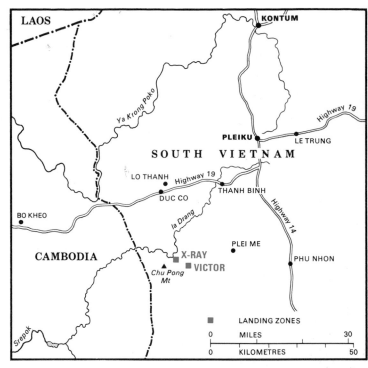

scheme, General Maxwell D. Taylor had recommended as early as 1961 the use of more US air assets. Advisers soon saw the arriving helicopters (the old H-21 Shawnee) as a chance to get ahead of the VC, to gain the element of surprise. US training and equipment had given some heart to the ARVN and the advisers wished to capitalize upon this by springing on the enemy unsuspected and forcing him to fight. On Christmas Eve 1961 1,000 ARVN troops were 'heli-lifted' into a suspected VC stronghold near Saigon and at the end of the day they had routed some VC and captured a radio transmitter.

Vietnamese imbroglio

In retrospect the seizing of a radio seems insignificant but upon such a thing hangs the course of war. For the American advisers it was a positive step forward, gained by using helicopters. But there were few helicopters available and the old pattern of walking along the mine-laden paddy dykes and through booby-trapped treelines continued. By 1965 the Republic of South Vietnam had yet to come to decisive grips with the enemy and the US decided to commit its airborne forces to tip the scale. In May 1965 the 173rd Airborne Brigade from Okinawa landed in Vietnam. The commanding general, Ellis W. Williamson, knew of Rich's experiments at Fort Benning and using what helicopters he had, taught his troops the new airmobile tactics. At first the paratroopers were leery of the ideas, especially as the new gunships flew so low and close that their spent cartridges fell around the advancing infantrymen like rain; but trust and co-ordination improved, and when the 173rd was joined by the 1st Battalion, Royal Australian Regiment and a battery of gunners from the Royal New Zealand Artillery plus two more airborne battalions from Tolson's parent regiment, the 503rd Parachute Infantry, they began to mount successful airmobile operations. One of the first, near the Dong Nai river, netted some fifty-six enemy killed, twenty-eight prisoners, and hundreds of tons of

stolen rice and documents.

At the same time the NVA was preparing to cut Vietnam permanently in half. The general officer commanding the Western Highlands Field Front (NVA), Chu Nuy Man, planned a bold thrust from Cambodia and the traditional hideouts in west central Vietnam along the Ia Drang river straight through four provinces to the sea. Such intelligence as there was predicted this move in the summer or autumn of 1965, just after Rich had finished testing his air assault division. The 1st Cavalry was a godsend to the Pentagon and the 1,600 vehicles, 400-odd aircraft and 16,000 men were sent by sea to the middle of Vietnam. The division's move in record time of eight weeks presupposed an administrative landing and it came as a shock to the troopers when they were warned that they might have to fight their way ashore, leaving their mothballed helicopters on deck. Fortunately elements of the famous 101st Airborne Division (Screaming Eagles) had also been alerted for Vietnam and they arrived in time to secure the landing place for the 'First Team'. Already US airborne units had led the way into Vietnam and had proved the worth of the new airmobile tactics in cordon and search operations. Now the 1st Cavalry Division was to head west from An Khe to test airmobility in action against a large sophisticated force.

The pace hots up

On 19 October 1965 General Chu began the Tau Nguyen campaign by hitting the Plei Me Special Forces camp about 19 miles (30km) south of the provincial capital, Pleiku. The commanding general of the US Military Assistance Command – Vietnam, General William Westmoreland, directed Major-General H. W. O. Kinnard to take his 1st Cavalry Division to help the ARVN relieve the camp and pursue its attackers, but when the division's 1st Brigade arrived in the area the enemy simply disappeared. Kinnard and his intelligence staff surmised that they had retreated back to their hideout and he sent

the division's Air Cavalry Squadron out to find them. Darting amongst the trees and ravines the light observation helicopters sparked off a contact 6 miles (10km) west of the camp, and this resulted in the capture of an NVA field hospital. In the fight for the hospital and in their sweeps the relatively inexperienced Americans learned that the NVA were well equipped, determined and skilled. When the Americans established a perimeter, the NVA would crawl so close as to make defending fires ineffective. They then sniped and closed on the startled cavalrymen at distances of 10 yards or less. The 1st Cavalry, however, learned quickly and in the hospital fight killed 78 NVA and took 57 prisoners for the loss of 5 US killed and 17 wounded.

Ambush planned

ARVN and US intelligence was now convinced that Chu's main body was repairing west through the Ia Drang valley towards the Chu Pong mountains on the Vietnamese side of the border. This area had been a Viet Minh staging area and friendly forces rarely ventured there. On 2 November 1965 the 1st Squadron, 9th Cavalry flew into a small clearing called LZ MARY and set up an ambush on the side of the hills running down from the Chu Pong massif towards the flowing Ia Drang. This was the division's first attempt at a night airmobile ambush which was exploited by a company of infantry also brought in through the dark. Here they accounted for 150 NVA killed to US losses of 4 killed and 25 wounded. Chu's forces were definitely in the area and the air cavalry, having developed the fight, made way for the infantry of the First Team to finish it.

By 9 November Chu's men were arranged in two major staging areas: the 32nd NVA Regiment was on the northern bank of the Ia Drang and somewhat near Cambodia while the 66th NVA Regiment, Chu's mainstay, and the 33rd NVA Regiment were between the river and the eastern slope of the Chu Pong massif. The 66th was in fine fettle but the 33rd had lost a third of its original 2,200 men in the battle for Plei

US Airbourne Soldier, Vietnam

This American paratrooper wears the standard tropical uniform and boots issued for Vietnam. He has two bandoliers of M16 magazines and smoke fragmentation grenades are attached to the ammunition pouches on his belt. His M16 has had the sling adjusted for ease of carrying and he has attached the bayonet scabbard to his leg by its nylon cord. In his helmet band are odd items like a bottle of insect repellant, while the pouch on his left shoulder contains a 7½ by 8 inch first aid bandage. The frame of his rucksack is just visible over his shoulders—he would be carrying his own personal kit as well as ammunition and digging equipment for the platoon.

Me. The 33rd was now consolidated into a composite battalion, but a battalion of almost regimental size. Chu's 120mm mortars and twin-barrelled 14·5mm anteaircraft machine-guns were still on the Ho Chi Minh trail in Cambodia. Secure on the rocky and wooded slopes, Chu regrouped in preparation for another attack on Plei Me.

Chu's hideout was being sought by the men of the 1st Cavalry's 3rd Brigade, commanded by Colonel T. W. Brown. The 3rd Brigade included among its manoeuvre battalions two from the famous 7th US Cavalry. In lieu of a regimental headquarters, the brigade had adopted the 7th's motto 'Garry Owen' and its *esprit*. Much of the unit had trained together during the 11th AAD experiments and they were keen to enter the fray. The brigade began to search the vast stretches of the valley by setting down squads and platoons in 'saturation patrolling' but as the search area near the massif looked so promising, Lieutenant-Colonel H. G. Moore, commanding officer of the 1st Battalion, 7th Cavalry, decided to look for an LZ where he could set down his battalion *en masse*.

'Casual' reconnaissance

On the morning of 14 November Moore and his principal officers made a seemingly casual reconnaissance flight. They were actually checking three proposed LZs, selecting the largest which could take eight to ten 'choppers' at once. From the air the terrain looked moderately open with tall brown elephant grass under scrub trees up to 100 feet (30m) tall. On the ground, however, the terrain undulated and was dotted with ant hills about 8 feet (2·4m) high. The woods grew denser towards Chu Pong and a dry creek bed ran along the western edge of what would become LZ X-RAY.

Moore returned to his base camp and sent a light cavalry observation helicopter to check the area once again. When

the helicopter reported seeing communications wire in the area of X-RAY, Moore told his battalion to mount up. At 1017 two 105mm howitzer batteries of the 1st Battalion, 21st Artillery, 5·6 miles (9km) to the east of LZ X-RAY, lashed out with 20 minutes' preparatory fire on X-RAY, as well as on two other sites for deception. The aerial rocket artillery of the 2nd Battalion, 20th Artillery, lifted off and the second the last tube round exploded, the artillery's ships rolled in and in 30 seconds expended half their load on X-RAY. They climbed and held near the LZ on call while escorting gunships from A Company, 229th Aviation Battalion, raked the areas before Moore and his B Company landed. By 1048 the ships were returning for A Company, and Moore's operations officer, his artillery liaison officer, and his air force forward air controller came on station overhead to bring in artillery and tactical air strikes by jet fighters and to relay radio messages if necessary.

Once on the ground B Company's commander sent small parties off to reconnoitre the treeline, while holding the bulk of his company in a thicket on the LZ as a reaction force. At 1120 an NVA deserter was brought in and he told Colonel Moore that the US company was faced by at least three battalions of NVA who were anxious to fight the Americans. In fact, Chu had begun his march towards Plei Me when the landings were spotted. He thereupon positioned the 33rd and 66th Regiments to the west of Chu Pong and along its base by a manoeuvre accomplished silently in just under an hour. B Company, which had found the deserter, continued searching away from the LZ north-west along a finger coming down from the mountain, two platoons abreast with the reserve platoon behind the left-hand platoon. As the left-hand platoon came off the finger and crossed a dry stream bed it moved slightly ahead of the right-hand platoon and suddenly came under heavy and accurate small-arms

fire from an estimated platoon-size NVA force hidden in the grass. Both of the platoon's flanks were exposed. The B Company commander responded by ordering the reserve to press forward and sent the right-hand platoon over to the right flank of the stricken unit.

As soon as the right-hand platoon received the order over its radio it formed a skirmish line with an M60 machine-gun on each flank and began to work its way towards the sound of the firing. *En route* its reserve squad, bringing up the rear, saw about 20 NVA disappear behind ant hills on their left flank between themselves and where they hoped to find the left-hand platoon. Immediately the reserve squad's grenadier pumped grenade after grenade from his M79 launcher into the ant hills with effect when suddenly a burst of fire from his right cut him down. The burst signalled a massive eruption of fire and the right-hand platoon now found itself in difficulty. The platoon leader despatched his two machine gun crews to cover the reserve squad and the rest of the platoon formed a tight perimeter which shook under NVA mortar and rocket fire. Soon the reserve squad and one of the machine gun crews ran into the comparative safety of the perimeter carrying the dead grenadier's launcher. The other four-man machine gun team did not make it and the enemy brought the newly captured gun to bear on the platoon.

As the firing increased in intensity the B Company commander tried to report to Colonel Moore the situation to his front as he understood it, but because of the trees, tall grass, and smoke he could not see. As he reported, he and his radio operator came under attack themselves and one NVA got to within 15 yards before the

M60 Machine-Gun

Calibre: 7.62mm NATO.
Operation: recoil with gas assistance, automatic.
Length: 43.3in (1.1m).
Barrel length: 22in (56.0cm).
Feed: disintegrating link belt.
Weight: 23.1lb (10.48kg).
Cyclic rate: 600rpm.
MV: 2,821fps (860mps).

captain of cavalry stopped him with grenade and rifle fire. He was certain that his left-hand platoon, the original object of rescue, had now to be the rescuer when the reserve platoon linked up with it. Meanwhile Colonel Moore established a command post at the LZ and was bringing in A Company to the left to protect B Company's flank, as he envisaged the two left-hand platoons of B Company being exposed as they turned to assist the isolated platoon. It was now about 1330 and the first of C Company was landing. Moore sent them to cover A Company by taking positions just off the LZ to the south and south-west. The rear of Moore's position was not covered and mortar fire was falling on the LZ but he could do little else. The rest of C Company had not landed, nor had D Company.

Exposed positions

Second Lieutenant Walter J. Marm of A Company landed and quickly moved his platoon off the LZ in a skirmish line towards the action. Almost immediately he took two prisoners and soon linked up with B Company's reserve platoon. With it Marm planned to head for the entrapped platoon, but then his command and that of the reserve platoon came under heavy fire. The same NVA unit that had tried to cut off the right-hand B Company platoon was now apparently moving to surround all of B Company and, by now, Marm's A Company platoon. As they returned fire, Marm tried to evacuate his wounded but the sergeant detailed for the mission reported that he could not get through. Then the NVA force broke off and went down into the dry stream bed to get behind Marm and in doing so ran into the rest of A Company coming up from the LZ. Savage fighting erupted in the stream and on the banks. An A Company platoon and squad leader were among the first killed.

As A and B Companies lay in several exposed positions, Colonel Moore and the circling artillery and air force officers tried to assist. The company's mortars had long since expended their basic load and the area was awash in dust and smoke. The pinned-down troopers had no prominent landmarks to guide by and could not call in effective fire. The heliborne officers could do little but guess at the friendly positions and brought fire and airstrikes in as close as they dared. The 33rd and 66th NVA Regiments were in firm control of the situation and firing became so heavy that they managed to shoot down a Douglas

Above: Men of the 4th Battalion, 173rd Airborne Brigade, are pinned down by hostile mortar fire on the side of Hill 875 during Operation 'MacArthur' in November 1967.

A-1E Skyraider, killing its pilot. Despite the fact that the LZ was 'hot', especially the north-west portion nearest the finger, the 1st Battalion surgeon was able to fly in at 1400. The doctor made it to the command post and with four medical aidmen began to treat the mounting number of wounded who made it back. Knowing the risks, the division's helicopters came in on the fifth airlift with the rest of C Company and the initial part of D. As they landed the worst wounded were hustled aboard but before they could take off a pilot and door gunner were wounded. The D Company commander was creased by a bullet and his radio operator was killed before he could unfasten his seatbelt. In the face of such fire, Colonel Moore forbade the rest of D Company to land. The D Company commander wrested the radio from his operator's body and ran off the LZ with four men who would brave the fire. They soon found themselves to the right of A Company's two platoons which were now engaging the foe that Marm had

discovered was trying to encircle B Company to his front. The D Company commander called to the rest of his men on the LZ and as they came into position around him, the B Company commander joined him to warn that there were already enemy to the rear where he and his men had been a minute before. Suddenly, the small command group had to fight where they lay. The NVA fire was vicious, men around them were dying and both the D Company commander and his mortar platoon leader were severely wounded.

It was now about 1500 and Moore had put C Company (the rest of which had come in with the fifth airlift) along A Company's right flank as a blocking force. They scrambled into position and they too received a heavy NVA attack. It looked as if the 7th Cavalry at Ia Drang would suffer the same fate as its predecessor at the Little Big Horn.

Reinforcements called in

Brown, the brigade commander, came on station above the action and Moore told him that he was being hit by approximately 600 NVA who would, no doubt, soon be reinforced. He requested another rifle company, which Brown anticipated, and B Company, 2nd Battalion, 7th Cavalry was ready for insertion as soon as the LZ cooled down. Two ships in the last flight had been so damaged that they could not fly and lay off to the side of the LZ, their crews having been picked up by the

other choppers. Brown's main contribution at this time was to land his 2nd Battalion, 5th Cavalry at LZ VICTOR southeast of X-RAY, 1·9 miles (3km) away. They were to dig in for the night and strike out for Moore's command the next morning.

Chain of command

At mid-afternoon Moore noticed that the employment of C and D companies was reducing the amount of hostile fire sweeping the LZ and as fast as possible he personally guided in the last three loads of C Company, the Scout (recce) platoon, a Pathfinder team, and the executive officer and first sergeant of D Company. Up on the line A and B Companies had pulled back to co-ordinate while C and D Companies held the perimeter only by dint of aggressive fire and welcome artillery fire on trajectories perpendicular to the airstrikes. The enemy lay only yards away from the isolated platoon, so close that the men could not raise their arms to dig for cover. The platoon leader and platoon sergeant had been killed, as had six others. The next senior, Sergeant Savage, and his medic displayed great leadership in rallying the 7 effectives and 12 wounded, many of whom remained on the line. Because the 7th Cavalry was airmobile and therefore could carry more per man, it was policy for every trooper to carry over 300 rounds for his M16 rifle, at least two fragmentation grenades, two canteens of water, and one ration packet. Each grenadier carried

Above: Men of the 2nd Battalion, 173rd Airborne Brigade in action during the assault on Hill 857 in Operation 'MacArthur' on 23 November 1967.

Above right: A Boeing-Vertol CH-47 Chinook brings in supplies to the 2nd Battalion, 506th Infantry Regiment, 101st Airborne Division, at firebase 'Ripcord' in July 1970.

approximately 30 shells and each machine-gunner carried at least 800 rounds for his M60. Most men carried more. Unless they were overrun by superior numbers the isolated platoon could hold on.

Moore issued a preparatory order to A and B Companies to attack and bring in the platoon. At 1620 the two companies moved forward from the stream bed after tube and aerial artillery preparation had been brought in as close as 275 yards (250m) to B Company's front. It made little difference. The NVA had silently moved up almost to the sides of the stream bank. Hiding in ant hills and trees they were ready when the two companies moved out. The ensuing fight was terrible for the troopers. Marm's platoon was stopped by a machine-gun just 30 yards to its front somewhere in the grass. Marm exposed himself to pinpoint its location and when his sergeant's grenade fell short, Marm raced out, scooped it up and hurled it into the machine-gun nest, dispatching the remaining crew with his rifle, an

AR-15 (M16) Rifle

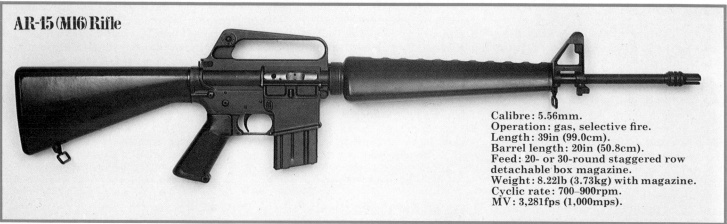

Calibre: 5.56mm.
Operation: gas, selective fire.
Length: 39in (99.0cm).
Barrel length: 20in (50.8cm).
Feed: 20- or 30-round staggered row
detachable box magazine.
Weight: 8.22lb (3.73kg) with magazine.
Cyclic rate: 700–900rpm.
MV: 3,281fps (1,000mps).

action for which he would receive the Medal of Honor. However, the loss of the enemy machine-gun did little to change the picture: American casualties mounted and as most of A Company's leaders were dead or wounded, Moore gave the company permission to fall back to the LZ. It had moved only 165 yards (150m).

B Company, too, was taking such heavy fire that it had over 30 casualties and it too had to pull back. But the hostile fire was such that neither company could retreat. A Company's forward observer was dead and as no smoke rounds were available to cover the withdrawal, Moore remembered how effective white phosphorus (WP) rounds had been in Korea and soon the 1st Battalion, 21st Artillery splashed the area with WP. The white starlike burst of burning phosphorus over the

enemy positions gave the two battered companies just enough time to crawl back with their casualties.

Perimeter tautened

Between 1700 and 1900 Moore tied up his perimeter as tightly as he could. Defensive artillery and mortar patterns were co-ordinated and Moore selected part of the LZ, enough for two helicopters, as his last stand. The 229th Pathfinders (men who are skilled at guiding in aircraft or paratroops on to improvised landing sites) cleared this final LZ of trees with engineer demolition charges and marked out the lighting panels for nightfall. They were under fire the whole time but prepared the zone without loss. Around them the exhausted and thirsty cavalrymen dug prone

positions and ate the jam from their rations for the moisture. They were heartened when B Company of the 2nd Battalion suddenly swooped in, as promised by Brown, and when at 1915 a resupply mission skidded in pushing out ammunition, water, vital medical supplies, and rations. Soon thereafter the operations officer landed with his two fire controllers but that was all for the day. The remains of the 1st Battalion, 7th Cavalry lay under a thick pall of smoke and darkness and waited for the enemy's next move.

The isolated platoon could not move from where it lay and over his radio Savage adjusted artillery to within yards of his position; the slightest error was intolerable and soon the 1st Battalion, 21st Artillery knew exactly where Savage's perimeter was. The enemy hit them three times before 0345, when the NVA sounded bugle calls from the mountain 330 yards (300m) away and they knew they were in for it again. As Savage heard the NVA speaking he sprang a 15 minute barrage with air strikes under illumination. The NVA retreated somewhat but the light played over the troopers and they repulsed another major assault in darkness an hour or so later.

The main perimeter, too, had been probed. The 66th Regiment's 8th Battalion had arrived to help. At first light on 15 November Moore called his commanders together to plan the relief of Savage's platoon. Moore also wanted a thorough check in front of the perimeter out to 220 yards (200m). They did not know it then but the NVA had crawled up during the night through the exploding artillery to their very lines. As the first troopers moved out to sweep they ran into a withering cross fire. Some men rushed out to help those who had fallen and were themselves hit and within the space of seconds the C Company CO and two of his lieutenants were seriously wounded by a machine-gun not 45 yards (40m) to their front. Moore now detailed a platoon of A Company to cross the LZ to help C Company. The A Company commander took the platoon farthest away from the contact, closed the gap with his other men, and sent the platoon off. Two men were killed and two wounded trying to cross the LZ. Their platoonmates dropped into a prone position, on line between the right flank of C Company and the left flank of their own unit. From there they provided defence in depth and protected the CP and aid station in case the perimeter was overrun.

Heavy firefight

The firing on the perimeter defence became dense as D Company, on C Company's left flank, was attacked; and at 0745 rockets, mortars, and automatic weapons fire sealed the LZ. The 7th Cavalry replied to all these new thrusts with all the firepower it had and scores of NVA were killed. A man from D Company who happened to cover a sector of C Company personally accounted for 10 to 15 enemy. At 0755 the fighting had grown so desperate that Moore had each platoon mark itself with coloured smoke. It defined their position for the NVA but more importantly it fixed it for the pilots of the striking jets which rolled in with bombs and napalm aimed so close some of it accidently fell inside the perimeter setting off the reserve ammunition and giving two men burns. The NVA had got a bead on the consolidated mortars and put some of them out of action. Moore had no choice but again to ask Brown for another company. At 0910 A Company, 2nd Battalion slid in through heavy fire and the fresh troopers went into line alongside their own B Company.

Finally, at 1000, all the tons of ordnance from the air strikes and artillery that was thrown up by the line itself began to have results and the NVA reduced their pressure to harassing fire. This gave the cavalry a breathing space to pass ammunition out to the line, to move the newly wounded back to the CP and, again, to wait. Fortunately, the 2nd Battalion, 5th

Cavalry had completed its 1·9 mile (3km) tactical march and after only light resistance entered LZ X-RAY at noon, bringing the total strength to about nine companies, four of which were badly mauled.

Moore co-ordinated with the arriving battalion commander, Lieutenant-Colonel R. B. Tully. The isolated platoon was the first consideration. As they knew the way, B Company of the 2nd Battalion, 7th Cavalry would lead Tully towards Savage at 1315 while Tully's A and C Companies provided the muscle. Probably in order to draw attention away from Tully, Moore mounted another sweep all around the perimeter and scoured the interior, too, in case any enemy had infiltrated. The troops moved through the blood-stained grass to find enemy dead stacked up behind ant hills. There were craters of churned earth, fragments of NVA uniforms, and the trails leading towards Chu Pong were soaked in blood and littered with equipment. The unsuccessful sweep of the morning left its evidence of dead US soldiers surrounded by dead NVA.

Lost platoon recovered

Tully advanced without incident up the finger and located the lost platoon which greated its rescuers with understandable emotion. In slow order and with only one serious casualty from a sniper, they retired in good order down to the LZ carrying the dead and wounded. Once in the lines the 2nd Battalion, 5th Cavalry moved to assume an equal share of the defence and everyone dug in. The Cavalry had not been forgotten by higher headquarters and that afternoon a B-52 raid was made against Chu Pong itself. Throughout the ensuing night, even though artillery ringed the perimeter in depth, the NVA still managed to probe the line, finally launching a company-sized attack against B Company of the 2nd Battalion at 0530 and again an hour later.

Intent not to fall into the same trap as

Above: Bell light transport helicopters were the backbone of the airmobile division's flexibility, flying the men and their equipment in, supporting and evacuating them.

Right: The Americans' heavy equivalent of the Bell series of helicopters was the versatile and ubiquitous Boeing-Vertol CH-47.

the day before, Moore instructed the entire perimeter to fire all its weapons at first light into the trees, ant hills, and elephant grass before it in a 'mad minute' of firing. It was a success and snipers fell from trees only a few yards from the cavalry and a platoon-sized attack was prematurely triggered. After a pause Moore decided to sweep out to 550 yards (500m), and while doing so B Company of the 2nd Battalion again took the brunt of a determined attack aided by wounded NVA who hurled grenades from where they had fallen. Firing all the way the company fell back into the perimeter and the Forward Air Controller brought in air strikes so exactly close that a 500lb (227kg) bomb was delivered on target twenty-five yards in front of the perimeter. Chu's forces had had enough and another sweep met with scant resistance. The LZ was now safe enough for the rest of the companies of the 2nd Battalion to land and Moore's weary troopers, those of B Company, 2nd Battalion, 7th Cavalry and the 3rd Platoon, A Company of the same battalion were lifted out and away from X-RAY. Moore, who would soon make full colonel, had accounted for 634 NVA known dead, another 581 estimated killed, and 6 prisoners. The NVA, who were loath to leave any equipment behind, had thrown down over 100 crew-served and individual weapons, including four Maxim machine-guns, rocket-launchers and mortars. Moore's losses were 79 killed and 121 wounded.

The lessons of Ia Drang were obvious. Moderately inexperienced troops could

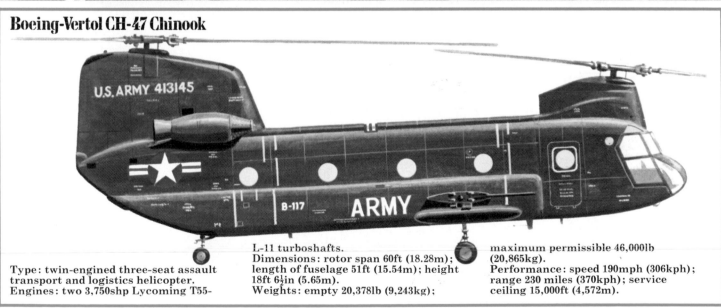

Boeing-Vertol CH-47 Chinook

Type: twin-engined three-seat assault transport and logistics helicopter.
Engines: two 3,750shp Lycoming T55-L-11 turboshafts.
Dimensions: rotor span 60ft (18.28m); length of fuselage 51ft (15.54m); height 18ft 6½in (5.65m).
Weights: empty 20,378lb (9,243kg); maximum permissible 46,000lb (20,865kg).
Performance: speed 190mph (306kph); range 230 miles (370kph); service ceiling 15,000ft (4,572m).

and did acquit themselves well in the face of a hardened enemy. They were much aided by supporting fire and reinforcements, but the helicopter was the saving grace. It made the difference between a surrounded battalion lost deep in a hostile sanctuary and an active force with an unending supply line: a force which could resupply, reinforce, evacuate its wounded, and maintain the offensive. Ia Drang also proved that the helicopter was not a fragile toy of war.

In 1967 the 173rd Airborne Brigade made a combat jump, and at other times various ARVN and Special Forces units used parachutes regularly but the elusive enemy and the vast terrain over which too few troops had to operate meant that ARVN and US commanders were keen to try airmobile operations whenever they could get the assets. Air cavalry, harkening back to Vanderpool and Tolson, was a particular success and the introduction of the Bell AH-1G HueyCobra gunship brought unequalled aerial firepower to the US and ARVN arsenal. The *esprit* of airmobile troops was tremendous and obviously the key to success in the early stages. In 1968, therefore, the 101st Airborne Division became the second US division to become airmobile (successfully resisting an attempt to erase airborne from its title) and operations became more daring, more complex. The *ad hoc* nature of the war allowed for combat-effective logistics which horrified budget-bound planners as it was an expensive way of waging war. As the US sought a way to extract itself from the morass of Vietnam, vast sums were spent on training South Vietnamese pilots and aviation staff officers to carry on, but there was not enough time. What hold on life the South Vietnamese government had, it owed primarily to airmobile operations conceived by airborne troopers.

The Arabs versus Israel

As the fighting between the Israelis and the Arab states in the Middle East has in general involved only very limited objectives, clear to both sides, the use of airborne forces has for the most part been as a means of securing tactical surprise. Nevertheless, airborne forces of both sides have played interesting parts in the last three major Arab-Israeli wars.

The most consistent trouble spot in the world since the end of World War II has been the Middle East, the main problem in the area being the continuing hostility between the Jewish state of Israel, occupying a large part of the earlier British mandated territory of Palestine, and the Arab states surrounding it, especially Egypt, Jordan and Syria. The roots of the problem are complex in the extreme, but hinge around the fact that when the United Nations sanctioned the formation of the Jewish state in 1947, many of the native population, the Palestinians, left for sur-rounding Arab countries, which since that time have been campaigning for the elimination of Israel so that the Palestinians may return 'home'.

This Israeli-Arab war has continued virtually nonstop since 1947 at political, economic and guerrilla levels, and has on four occasions developed into large-scale military operations: in 1948–49, 1956, 1967 and 1973. The issue has been further complicated by the involvement of the two superpowers, the United States in general supporting Israel, and the Union of Soviet Socialist Republics the Arab states.

The 1948–49 war, which secured at least temporary independence for Israel, was fought on 'conventional' lines by relatively small forces. But by 1956, the year in which Colonel Gamel Nasser nationalized the Suez Canal and so incurred the righteous wrath of France and Great Britain, the forces employed were larger and more sophisticated. Anglo-French operations along the Suez Canal, although abortive for political reasons, were ably supported by Israel's operations in Sinai, where armoured and airborne forces played a decisive part in the rout of Egypt's armies, and so pre-empted the offensive being

198

planned against Israel by Egypt, Jordan and Syria.

In 1956 United Nations pressure had forced Israel to hand back to Egypt the excellent buffer zone represented by the inhospitable Sinai, giving Egypt the possibility once again of invading Israel directly, and of cutting off her access to the Red Sea and thence to the Indian ocean by closing the Straits of Tiran. By 1967 all these threats were again pushing the Middle East towards war, and Israel decided to use the tactical advantage of striking first. Massive blows were to be struck principally at Egypt and Syria in an effort to destroy their offensive capability. The major prerequisite of the ambitious and daring Israeli plan was the elimination of the Arab air forces on the first day of the war, giving the Israeli ground forces the freedom to operate under undisputed friendly air cover. The Israeli air force strikes to secure this total air superiority are classic examples of the successful use of pre-emptive air operations.

In 1967 the Israeli armed forces included two parachute brigades, one regular and one reservist, with sufficient airlift capacity in their force of Nord Noratlas transports to lift one reinforced battalion at a time. The Israelis also planned to use helicopters for the movement of airborne troops, and for this they had some good machines in the Sikorsky S-58 and the Sud Aviation SA-321 Super Frelon, capable between them of lifting one battalion at a time. There were also a number of general purpose helicopters available.

No airborne operation

Various plans for the reserve parachute brigade were discussed, but eventually it was used in the conventional infantry role, acquiring an enviable reputation in the Israeli conquest of the old city of Jerusalem from the Jordanians. More ambitious plans were entertained for the regular brigade, however. Israeli forces for the Sinai campaign included three divisional-strength armoured task forces, one of them commanded by Brigadier-General Ariel Sharon, with Colonel Davidi the main force behind the establishment and training of the Israeli airborne force in the 1950s. Sharon's task force, the most southerly of the three, was to strike west towards Abu Agheila, then turn south towards Nakl before turning once again, this time west, to move through the Mitla pass towards Suez at the southern end of the Suez Canal. The main stumbling block to Sharon's advance was the Egyptian forward position at Abu Agheila, held by a brigade of infantry, six regiments of artillery and some 90 armoured vehicles. To surprise this major force Sharon decided to open his attack with an airborne novelty, a nocturnal helicopter assault landing.

At 2230 on 5 June 1967, the first day of the war, two helicopters dropped parties of paratroops behind the Egyptian artillery lines to mark out LZs for the main assault force, a complete battalion of paratroops brought in by several helicopter lifts. Despite the fact that the landings were close to their positions, the Egyptians were taken completely by surprise as the Israeli attack went in: the night had prevented the helicopters from

Below: An Israeli Sikorsky CH-53D helicopter lifts off with a load of 53 paratroops for the Sinai front during the Yom Kippur War. In the foreground is a Bell UH-1D.

UZI Sub-Machine Gun

Calibre: 9mm Parabellum.
Operation: blowback, selective fire
Length: 25.2in (64.0cm); 18.5in
(47.0cm) with butt folded.
Barrel length: 10.2in (25.9cm).
Feed: 25-, 32- or 64-round
staggered row detachable box
magazine.
Weight: 9.1lb (4.12kg) with metal
stock and 25-round magazine.
Cyclic rate: 650rpm.
MV: 1,312fps (400mps).

being spotted, and the constant fire of the artillery had drowned the noise of the helicopters' engines. The gun positions were quickly overrun, and the paratroops went on to attack the infantry positions from the rear. Although there was some sharp fighting, the infantry positions were also taken with little difficulty, the Israelis benefiting considerably from the Egyptians' lack of expertise in night fighting and their lack of initiative when taken by a surprise attack from the rear. The way was soon open for Sharon's armoured and mechanized force to pass through.

Helicopter commandos

Another airborne operation was planned for the Egyptian positions at Sharm el Sheikh commanding the Tiran straits, in conjunction with an amphibious attack by forces arriving from the Israeli port of Eilat at the head of the Gulf of Aqaba. Helicopters were to land a reconnaissance party to establish the nature of the Egyptian defences, and then at 1200 on 7 June an airborne battalion was to drop at the same moment as the amphibious attack materialized. But the amphibious force arrived early, encountered no opposition and landed its men, who found that the Egyptians had pulled out. This was confirmed by the helicopter party, which arrived shortly after the amphibious force. The parachute battalion then arrived overhead, and the paratroops were disappointed to hear of the Egyptians' disappearance, as the combat drop was now abandoned in favour of a landing. The helicopter pilots were kept busy: on the 8th they lifted a group of Sharon's men from Nakl to Ras el Sudr on the Red Sea. Then later in the day the helicopters headed off north towards the Syrian front.

Here the major Israeli objectives lay on the Golan heights, which dominate the northern end of the Jordan river valley, and where the Syrians had established powerful artillery positions. Operating by day, and flying at very low level, the Israeli helicopters delivered a battalion of paratroops on to the Golan heights on 9 and 10 June to attack the Syrian gun positions. One of the problems met by the helicopters as they tried to land was the roughness of the terrain, which in many places prevented any actual landings. Instead the

paratroops dropped down ropes to the ground before setting off to destroy the Syrian gun positions and command posts as well as severing lines of communication to the rear. Little expecting such a method of assault, the Syrians had made scant provision for the protection of their artillery, and the gunners, unused to the handling of small arms against a skilled and aggressive opponent, were quickly overrun.

The main threat to the Israeli operation, though, was not on the ground but in the air, where Syrian fighters and AA fire could have inflicted severe damage. But the approach tactics of the Israelis, with the helicopters flying very low and well

Above: Holding a bible in his left hand and an UZI sub-machine gun in his right, a young Israeli paratrooper swears a binding oath of allegiance to the Israeli nation.

grouped together, gave the fighter pilots and AA gunners little opportunity to exercise their skills, and no helicopters were lost during the operation despite the fact that they were engaged on occasion by Russian-built MiG fighters and surface-to-air missiles (SAMs).

In securing the Sinai and Golan heights the Israelis had secured their physical objectives, and in inflicting crushing defeats on the Egyptian and Syrian armies

Israeli Airborne Soldier, 1973

A young paratrooper pauses on the road to Damascus during the Yom Kippur war. His weapon, web equipment and uniform are all of Israeli origin—in the early days the IDF used both French and American weapons and uniforms. The UZI sub-machine gun (in this example with a folding stock) is an excellent compact gun which has been exported worldwide. In the opening phases of the Yom Kippur war, reservists were making their own way to their units on the front and many were still dressed in civilian clothes or a mixture, their transport too was often private.

they had eliminated, at least for the time being, the forces that most threatened their independence. Accordingly they were ready on the sixth day of the war to heed the United Nations call for a cease-fire, and the 1967 Arab-Israeli war came to an end. The underlying causes of the war were still there, though, and just over six years later open hostilities were to break out once again.

One of the first actions of the 1973 war, more popularly known as the Yom Kippur War for the Jewish holy day on which it started, was again an airborne operation. Only this time it was an airborne operation launched by the Egyptians in their massive offensive across the Suez Canal into the Sinai peninsula. The Arabs had digested thoroughly the lessons of Israel's successful tactics in the Six-Day War of 1967 Israel's main defence line in the Sinai was a series of bunkers protected by sandworks on the east bank of the Suez Canal, dignified with the name of the Bar-Lev Line. Heavy support was provided by artillery located behind the line on a specially-built north-south road for mobility. On this road were located a number of Israeli command and communications centres, at it was at one of these,

Baluza, at the northern end of the road, that Egyptian helicopter-borne commandos struck on the night of 6-7 October, causing severe dislocation in the area. Further south, similar dislocations were caused by Egyptian air forces strikes on Tasa and Bir Gifgafa.

Golan heights vital

The Syrians had also learned from the Israelis' earlier airborne successes and established their own helicopter airborne commando unit. On the first day of the war, 6 October, these commandos swarmed on to Mount Hermon, the commanding peak of the Golan heights, some 7,000 feet (2,135m) high, from their helicopters and attacked the Israeli post there. Taken by surprise both by the outbreak of hostilities and the Syrians' novel assault tactics, the Israelis quickly lost part of the command bunker. But although Syrian radio announced that the Israelis had lost this commanding position, heavy fighting was to continue on Mount Hermon right into Sunday, when the Syrians finally secured the Israeli defence complex after heavy losses on both sides. Well informed by their spy network of the layout of the Israeli

Above: Israeli paratroops exit from Nord Noratlas transports by means of side doors, an unusual method in twin-boom aircraft which normally have rear exits.

positions, the Syrians had secured an initial advantage by entering the bunkers through a secret door reserved for the hasty evacuation of the positions by the Israelis. And although the Syrians had 'secured' the position, there were still a number of Israelis holding out in isolated parts of the complex. An immediate Israeli counterattack was driven off, and it was only right at the end of the war, on 21 October, that the positions were retaken by the Israeli forces.

While the Golani Brigade launched a frontal assault up the precipitous slopes of the mountain, Israeli paratroops were landed by helicopter behind the Syrian positions to take them in rear. The Golani Brigade suffered very heavy losses in its frontal attack from the courageous and tactically proficient Syrians, and it was only on 22 October that the paratroops and Golani Brigade managed finally to raise their flags over the recaptured fort at 1100.

Mil Mi-8

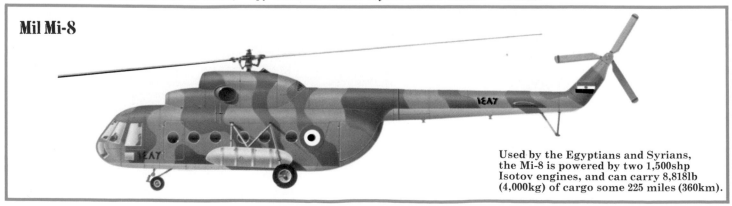

Used by the Egyptians and Syrians, the Mi-8 is powered by two 1,500shp Isotov engines, and can carry 8,818lb (4,000kg) of cargo some 225 miles (360km).

Egyptian Airborne Soldier, 1973

Armed with a folding stock AK-47, this Egyptian airborne soldier is wearing the efficient camouflaged uniform issued to airborne troops and special forces. The ordinary drafted man is content with sand-coloured drill outfit and a lesser scale of web equipment. The AK-47 and its development the AKM have a 30-round detachable box magazine and can fire automatic or semi-automatic. Egyptian forces now have a more varied range of equipment, but in the early 70s most came from the Soviet bloc.

The Rape of Czechoslovakia

Soviet Russia has made no secret of her build-up of airborne forces since World War II, but despite their size and excellent equipment, their real abilities remained obscure up to 1968. Then in the summer of that year the 'liberal' government of Czechoslovakia was ruthlessly crushed by a Russian invasion, ably spearheaded by considerable airborne forces.

Throughout late spring 1968 as the Czechoslovak crisis evolved, Soviet and Warsaw Pact armed forces were being used to an increasing extent as a major instrument in applying pressure on the Czechoslovak leadership. Warsaw Pact manoeuvres on Czech soil, after which Soviet troops remained behind, were instrumental in bringing about the temporary amelioration of the Bratislava agreement, but as it turned out the combination of propaganda campaigns, political pressure and military threat were not enough. The Soviet leadership decided that a swift and forceful *coup* was needed in order to stop Czechoslovakia's drift away from the Soviet fold into a

semi-autonomous position, a change which might encourage similar tendencies in other Warsaw Pact states. The *coup* was to be both swift and decisive: a surprise occupation of the country, an immediate change of leadership and a gradual withdrawal, all to be executed through co-operation with the conservative hard-line elements in the Czechoslovak Communist Party and State apparatus.

The crucial part was to be the occupation of the central organs of both the Party and the State while deposing the liberal leadership and replacing it with the conservative opposition loyal to the Moscow line. The military were to facilitate the political

Below: Russian paratroops relax on the grass behind the Antonov An-12 'Cub' transport aircraft that will move them, in groups of 100, into the exercise area.

RPD LMG

Calibre 7.62mm × 39mm.
Operation: gas, automatic.
Length: 40.79in (1.036m).
Barrel length: 20.5in (52.1mm).
Feed: 100-round metal link belt in a drum.
Weight: 15.65lb (7.1kg).
Cyclic rate: 650–750rpm.
MV: 2,297fps (700mps).

change and the Soviet airborne forces were chosen to produce the key to the whole operation—the seizure of the centres of Party and State in Prague, internment of all liberal leaders and eventually handing over control to the new Czech leaders and their Soviet civilian mentors.

The Soviet airborne troops were well suited for the operation. An elite force of seven divisions, each numbering 7,000 soldiers, equipped with all infantry-support weapons including mortars, AA guns, light field artillery and 45 air-portable self-propelled anti-tank guns (ASUs), the old ASU-57s as regimental support and the newer ASU-85s, of which there was a battalion of 18 to each division. Each division in full battle order to be landed or dropped into battle from An-12 transport planes which served with the airborne forces, giving them medium-range independent airlift capability.

A Trojan horse

Whereas, at the time, the Soviet mechanized infantry was already training in short-range tactical air-mobility through the use of heavy helicopters (and indeed seems to have used this tactic in the invasion, for example in the occupation of the military airbase near Hradic Kralove in north-east Bohemia), the airborne divisions were trained in medium-range operations. In action they were trained to operate a few fighting hours away from the main ground forces, thus achieving operation in depth over the whole front of advance through disruption of the enemy's troop control and logistics, capturing strategic objectives, beating off counterattacks and eventually linking up with the main advancing force. A high percentage of the airborne troops were either Party members or members of the Young Communist League and the soldiers were expected to demonstrate not only a high standard of combat training but also political consciousness and discipline.

Just before 2030 on 8 August 1968 an unscheduled *Aeroflot* (the USSR civilian air state company) An-24 landed at Prague's Ruzyme Airport, taxied to the end of the tarmac and remained parked. After a few hours another special *Aeroflot* flight came in, stating its departure airport

as Lvov in Poland. Some civilians disembarked and were cordially welcomed at the airport's customs offices, where they were met by Embassy and Czechoslovak state security officials. The plane took off half an hour later. At around midnight, an hour after the first Warsaw Pact units began crossing the Czech border, the control tower was ordered by telephone to close down the airport to all incoming and outgoing traffic. At the same time men in civilian dress began arriving, accompanied by a Soviet colonel and a representative of *Aeroflot* and took up positions around the customs offices and the foreign departures area. Then at around 0200, under air cover of MiG fighters, two unannounced military An-12s landed one after the other and taxied up to the airport building. Out streamed airborne troops, who quickly split up into combat groups and dashed off in the direction of the control tower, the hangars and the administrative building. Within minutes and without a shot being fired, the airport had been seized. While military transport planes kept pouring in at one-minute intervals, their landings and take offs controlled from the An-24 at the edge of the field, the airborne troops rounded up all those present in the airport building. While the building was being occupied by the invading troops all present, personnel, tourists, women and children were led out of the building. The women and children were separated from the men and directed into the waiting room, where the men joined them half an hour later. They were kept under guard until 0530 and then all were released to make their way back into town on foot.

Airport captured

As the planes kept landing troops and equipment, the airborne forces surrounded the field, taking up positions on all the roads leading to it. With their operation base well secured, the troops prepared to move into town, 6 miles (10km) away, for phase two of the operation.

As the Russian hold on the airport was secured and while planes kept coming in, columns began moving east into Prague. Within 90 minutes of the landing of the first An-12, the troops with their APCs and ASUs, all marked with white IFF (Identifi-

cation Friend or Foe) stripes were in the centre of the old city of Prague. On their way troops reached the presidential palace on Hradcany Hill and surrounded it, with President Svoboda inside virtually under house arrest. Positions were taken up west of the Vltava on Letza Hill with light artillery and AA guns. Roadblocks were set on the bridges of the Vltava and the old city was sealed off while troops surrounded, but still left unoccupied, the radio station on Vinohradska Street, railway stations, the post office, central crossroads and other key locations.

Party heads taken

On Tuesday nights the Party secretariat held its weekly meetings and it was during the meeting that Premier Oldrich Cernik first heard of the invasion. While the Party secretariat continued its session, chaired by Secretary Dubcek, Cernik rushed off to the government buildings in order to convene the government and it was there that the Russian troops found him. The building was surrounded by troops who then broke in, smashed the main telephone switchboard, lined all the officials present against the wall and led Cernik away. The troops remained in occupation of the building, releasing its occupants only at 1700.

At around 0400 the Soviet troops led by a black Volga sedan from their embassy reached the yellow building of the Party's headquarters. The pattern of operation was repeated. The building was first surrounded and sealed off and then the troops moved in. Breaking into the offices of the secretariat they tore the telephone out of Dubcek's hands, ripped the wire out of the wall and ordered all the officials and Party leaders present (including Smrkovsky, Kriegel, Spacek and Simon) to face the wall. All were frisked and placed under guard until further instructions.

By now, theoretically, the task of the airborne troops should have been considered completed. It seems that, according to the Russian plan, at this stage the collaborating conservatives led by Alois Indra, former chairman of the state planning commission, should have taken control. The State Security service was already co-operating to a large extent with

Contemporary Soviet Paratrooper

This post-war Russian paratrooper shows the characteristic clean lines of their uniforms. They appear to jump without leg bags or personal equipment, and while this saves them from some of the hazards of deploying a leg bag in flight it does mean that they are vulnerable on landing until they have collected their weapons from equipment containers. Though their uniforms are practical, they still favour somewhat outdated leather jackboot footwear. The wartime cloth helmet has been retained and Soviet paratroops now keep it on after landing and do not use steel helmets in action.

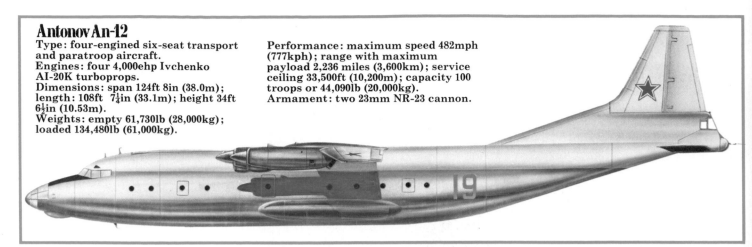

Antonov An-12

Type: four-engined six-seat transport and paratroop aircraft.
Engines: four 4,000ehp Ivchenko AI-20K turboprops.
Dimensions: span 124ft 8in (38.0m); length: 108ft 7¼in (33.1m); height 34ft 6½in (10.53m).
Weights: empty 61,730lb (28,000kg); loaded 134,480lb (61,000kg).

Performance: maximum speed 482mph (777kph); range with maximum payload 2,236 miles (3,600km); service ceiling 33,500ft (10,200m); capacity 100 troops or 44,090lb (20,000kg).
Armament: two 23mm NR-23 cannon.

the Russians, the armed forces were neutralized by orders to remain in barracks and all communications were supposed to be under the control of the pro-Soviet faction. The airborne units were to remain in position until further instructions from the Russian Embassy, from where operations were being controlled, while waiting for the ground forces, moving by road, to reach Prague.

But a new leadership had not been formed and while the pro-Soviet officials of the various communication agencies were away, the radio, newspapers and the state press agency *CTK* were operated by their strongly liberal staffs, alerting the Czech people of the occupation. The radio, switching transmitters after the main medium-wave transmitter was closed by orders from Karl Hoffman, director of the central communications administration, told the people of Czechoslovakia what could be seen from the station's windows: the Russian troops taking control of the city and surrounding the building. The city's population rushed out into the streets in an attempt to stop what was already unstoppable.

Key points seized

Sometime after 0600 the order was given to the airborne forces to occupy the centres of communication, most of which had already been surrounded. This was achieved with little difficulty except in the case of the radio station, where it proved too late for another easy walkover. A massive barricade had been set across Vinohradska Street on the way to the station. This was made up of two lorries and a red tram, and snipers began operating from rooftops and windows. While the station's staff barricaded itself in, at the same time continuously broadcasting, the streets were filling with furious crowds, who from attempts to persuade the Russians to leave their country, switched to physical attempts to prevent the troops from occupying the station.

The soldiers on top of their armoured vehicles became increasingly nervous. Whereas so far hardly a shot had been fired (except for some isolated incidents, as when two youths tried to rush into the Central Committee buildings and were shot down by a Russian soldier), there was now a danger of snipers and the crowds were becoming actively hostile, trying to set fire to the armoured vehicles and barricading the streets with anything they could lay their hands on, including two

giant steel derricks, while sparks from an armoured vehicle's antenna touching an overhead trolley-wire added to the confusion. As the troops were stopped by the barricades and the crowds' attempts to set their vehicles on fire became more daring and more successful, the troops opened fire. They tried to disperse the crowds with small-arms fire, shooting above people's heads for the most part, but occasionally lower; with machineguns they raked buildings' fronts and roofs against possible snipers; and with anti-tank guns tried to blast their way through the barricades while shooting up all other vehicles in sight in an attempt to prevent them from being added to the barricade. Soon Vinohradska Street and Wenceslas Place were in flames. An ASU was set on fire in Balbinova Street just off Vinohradska Street and two ammunition lorries caught fire and were abandoned, their exploding contents propelling splinters in all directions along the street.

Eventually the ASUs rammed the barricade, the troops stormed the station and it was soon occupied.

Above: The apparently unconcerned crew of a Russian T-54A main battle tank watch flames take a hold of their vehicle in Wenceslas Square, Prague, on 21 August 1968.

Right: Russian paratroops leave their dropping aircraft during an airborne exercise. In war it seems unlikely that more than a battalion would be dropped together.

All through the day sporadic fire was to be heard all over the city as the fighting slowly died out. The Czechs began realizing the futility of any kind of armed resistance and began channelling their resentment of their country's occupation into passive resistance.

The Soviet airborne troops remained in position, their equipment coming in by air, waiting for the ground forces who reached the city that evening.

The physical occupation of Czechoslovakia had been completed in less than 24 hours, but it would now be a long and unpleasant wait till the political objectives would be realized.

The Raids on Entebbe and Mogadishu

Although not 'airborne' raids in the conventional sense of the word, recent actions to rescue airline hostages held by terrorists, launched by special Israeli and German units, have made extensive use of airborne methods and tactics, and perhaps mark the beginning of a new type of airborne warfare, with small, highly trained units replacing larger formations.

Although many countries created their airborne forces with the intention of using them as small raiding forces for deep penetration missions into enemy territory, up to the present they have been relatively little used in this capacity. The two classic examples from World War II must remain the British raid on the German radar site at Bruneval and the German rescue of Italy's ex-dictator Benito Mussolini from his 'prison' in an hotel on the Gran Sasso.

On 27 February 1942, 119 British raiders were dropped by converted Whitley bombers near the radar site at Bruneval. In a short time, and at the cost of three men killed and seven wounded, the radar station was destroyed, its most interesting technical features being taken back to England together with a captured German radar technician. The only really hazardous part of the operation was not the air-

borne landing, but rather the evacuation from the nearby coast by a small force of six landing-craft. The success of the raid, led by Major John Frost, perhaps Britain's most brilliant airborne tactical commander of World War II, aroused great interest in British military and political circles, and also led to much heated discussion on the German side.

Mussolini the precedent

After his downfall on 9 September 1943, Mussolini had been arrested and interned in the ski resort hotel of Campo Imperatore in the Gran Sasso mountains, guarded by Italian *carabinieri*. Surrounded by mountains on three sides, the Campo Imperatore was approachable on land only by means of the funicular railway over the precipice marking the plateau's fourth side. While the Italians were consolidating their guard positions, the Germans under Hitler's direct instigation and control devised an ambitious plan to rescue the ex-dictator: under the command of Major Mors, the Parachute *Lehr* Battalion was to advance

rapidly overland to seize the bottom end of the funicular railway; meanwhile, one company of the battalion, reinforced by SS troopers and commanded by SS *Sturmbannführer* Otto Skorzeny, was to land on the Campo Imperatore in 12 DFS 230 gliders to release and protect Mussolini. Various plans had been considered for the evacuation of Mussolini, but eventually the most testing of all was adopted. The raid was launched on 12 September, and at first disaster was threatened by the appalling state of the touch-down area for the gliders on the Campo Imperatore. Although two gliders had been lost *en route* to the Gran Sasso, the rest of the force managed to get down safely. Astounded by the bravado of the feat, the Italian *carabinieri* on the plateau offered no resistance and Mussolini was rescued unharmed. The bottom end of the funicular railway was captured after a brisk fight, preventing the Italians from sending reinforcements up to the Campo Imperatore. But now came the most tricky part of the operation: the evacuation of Mussolini. Captain Gerlach of the *Luftwaffe* had been told off to land

his Fieseler Fi 156 *Storch* on the plateau to pick up Mussolini and fly him to Rome, where arrangements had been made for the latter's speedy removal to Germany. But Gerlach was horrified to learn on the Campo Imperatore that Skorzeny was also to join the party in the *Storch*. Grossly overloaded, the aircraft plunged off the edge of the precipice and dived towards the valley floor as the take-off run had been too short to allow the plane to build up flying speed. In its dive, though, the necessary speed was reached, and Gerlach was able to regain control and fly safely to Rome.

There were, of course, other such raids in the war, some of them achieving notable successes. But none can match these two as examples of what can be achieved deep behind enemy lines by small numbers of men, highly trained, full of initiative and

Below: A film reconstruction of Israeli paratroops storming through an entrance into the airport terminal buildings at Entebbe to rescue hijacked passengers.

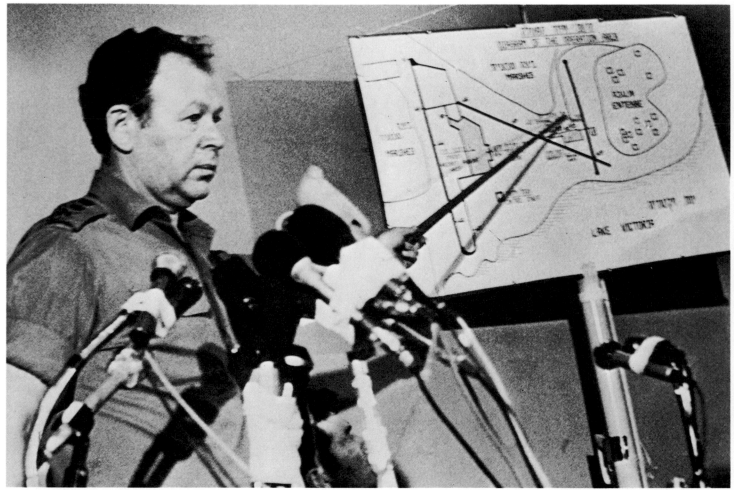

ably led, using airborne delivery techniques to ensure surprise. Since the war there have been several moments when such techniques might have been used to military advantage, but political problems, usually associated with governments' desires to avoid any risk of 'over-reaction', have almost always ruled them out. The only nation to have made full use of the possibilities of such operations has been Israel, whose politico/military situation is unique to a marked degree. This has allowed the Israelis to take the 'war', if that be the word, to the terrorists who plague them and their possessions. The most popular targets for the Arab and other terrorists working against Israel have been airliners, both Israeli and belonging to other countries who have imprisoned pro-Arab terrorists or otherwise have been thought to favour Israel. While other nations have tended to handle such situations by psychological or other 'conventional' means, sometimes involving an armed attack on the hijackers holding the airliner in question, the Israeli response has been more specifically aggressive and full of initiative, and usually carried out by airborne troops or by airborne techniques. The two classic examples of this Israeli refusal to be cowed by the demands of terrorists have been the raids on Beirut and Entebbe, in 1968 and 1976 respectively.

Terror tactics

Although a nasty military thorn in the Israelis' side, the Palestinian guerrilla movement had been more of a political than an active threat up to 1968. But with the dwindling hopes of any real chance of a negotiated peace in the Middle East,

during 1968 the Palestinians stepped up their training of para-military forces and agreed on a more aggressive policy against Israel. One of the first manifestations of this policy was an Arab raid on a Boeing 707 airliner of El Al, Israel's national airline, at Athens airport on 26 December 1968. One Israeli was killed and another wounded by the two Lebanese Palestinians, and Israel decided that something had to be done – only a short time before 12 people had been killed and a further 50 wounded in a terrorist bomb explosion in a market in Jerusalem.

The Israelis decided to meet force with force: if the Palestinians were determined to attack El Al aircraft, the Israelis would show them and the governments either supporting or condoning their actions that the Israelis could strike even harder. Commanded by Colonel Rafael Eytan, commandos were flown into Beirut airport in the Lebanon on 28 December 1968. Pouring out of their helicopters the Israelis were quickly in control of the airport, on which they destroyed 13 aircraft, eight of them belonging to the Lebanon's national carrier, Middle East Airlines. It is reported that in the midst of this destruction, Eytan calmly walked into the airport lounge and ordered black coffee from the flabbergasted barman, who also served Eytan's men with drinks. In payment Eytan offered an Israeli £10 note, signed by himself, telling the barman that he would pay for the drinks properly if the barman ever got to Israel!

A carefully planned and well executed raid in military terms, and a clear indication of the Israelis' military preparedness and abilities, the raid was nevertheless a political failure, leading to widespread condemnations that the raid was a 'pre-

Above: Lieutenant-General Mordechai Gur, the Israeli chief-of-staff, explains to the press, with the aid of a map, how Israelis carried out the daring Entebbe rescue.

meditated military action'. With what appears to be the now fashionable political hypocrisy, almost all governments ignored the Palestinian murders that had provoked the raid in the first place.

Long-range strike

More interesting and significant, though, was the Israeli airborne raid on Entebbe, which must remain a military classic for many years to come. In the early 1970s, after a spate of aircraft hijacking of all types and motives, the Israelis had formed a special force to be used in such a situation. This force, based on the airborne arm, was highly trained and motivated, and had just the right equipment for short, sharp raids some distance from Israel: Lockheed C-130 Hercules transport aircraft, jeeps for high mobility in the landing area, and a high proportion of automatic weapons for combat with local forces who might have a superiority in heavier weapons. Just as importantly, the Israeli force was selected not only on the highest of physical standards, but also on emotional maturity and intelligence. This ensured that the force was an elite within an elite, and capable of utmost flexibility and initiative on the ground, with little chance of failure caused by the dictates of the heart prevailing over those of the mind.

The problem facing Israel, and especially her prime minister, Yitzhak Rabin, at the end of June 1976 was a very complex

one: an Air France A-300 airbus, with 253 people on board, had been hijacked by a group of terrorists led by two Germans and flown to Entebbe airport in Uganda. The problem for Israel was that Entebbe is far removed from Israel (beyond the capability of her C-130 transports for a there-and-back trip without refuelling) and that only 105 of the hostages were Jewish. This latter factor made it particularly difficult for Israel to act unilaterally, for the reactions of the other hostages' mother countries had inevitably to be considered. This latter problem was further exacerbated by the fact that although Uganda's dictator, Field-Marshal Idi Amin Dada, maintained an overt posture of neutrality in the matter, covertly he was supporting the terrorists in their demands that unless Palestinian prisoners held in a number of countries were released, the hostages would be shot at 1200 on 1 July. Ugandan troops, supposedly stationed around the airport terminal where the hostages were being held by the now reinforced hijackers to help maintain the peace, were in fact helping the hijackers to guard their prisoners. Moreover, it was believed, correctly, that the Ugandans had a number of Russian-built T-54 tanks and Czech-built OT-64 armoured personnel carriers only some 20 miles (32km) away in Kampala, Uganda's capital. The arrival of these armoured forces would be a very real threat to the Israeli raiding force.

The crisis was reached early on 1 July. Although the Israelis were prepared to send in a rescue force, preparations were not really adequate, for the exact disposition of the airport and its facilities was still unknown in Israel. At the last minute the Israelis announced that they were willing

to consider the release of Palestinian prisoners. The hijackers, by now more confident of eventual success, and therefore beginning to relax their guard, responded by extending their deadline by three days, and by offering to release some of the hostages. But when released, these turned out to be all the non-Israelis. Although an emotional blow to the Israelis, this in fact eased their problem considerably. They could now act unilaterally, and the French and Israeli debriefing of the released hostages added very greatly to the amount of information available to the Israeli raiding force. While the released hostages provided excellent intelligence of the hijackers' and remaining hostages' positions within the airport terminal, black agents of the *Mossad,* the Israeli intelligence organization, had provided information on the layout of the airport and the Ugandan forces outside the terminal.

Decision time

Lieutenant-General Mordecai Gur, the Israeli chief-of-staff, now felt that an actual raid on the airport was feasible. While negotiations with the hijackers went on through a series of intermediaries, frantic behind-the-scene activity had secured Kenyan permission for the Israeli aircraft to refuel in Nairobi on their way back to Israel. The last stumbling block to the raid to rescue the Israeli hostages had been removed. At 0730 on 3 July Rabin and Gur reviewed all the facts and the former gave the latter the go-ahead for the operation.

Later that morning a full-scale dress rehearsal was held in northern Israel. The force for the raid, commanded by Brigadier-General Dan Shomron, performed very well in an attack on a dummy

Above: How it must have been at Entebbe—a MiG fighter of the Ugandan Air Force is blown up by the Israelis as a diversion and to prevent any aerial pursuit.

layout manned by Israeli troops, and all seemed to augur well for the real attack, scheduled for the next day. The force that was to enter the airport terminal and rescue the hostages was to be led by Lieutenant-Colonel Jonathan Netanyahu. Shomron, an experienced paratrooper, had led a number of penetration raids into Egypt, and in command of an infantry battalion had been the first Israeli to reach the Suez Canal in the Six-Day War of 1967. At the time he was 39 years old. Netanyahu was nine years younger, and had received a decoration for bravery in the Six-Day War. The dress-rehearsal raid lasted just 55 minutes from the time the aircraft landed to when they lifted off again.

All was ready on the afternoon of the 3rd, and at 1600, only two hours after the decision had been announced to the full Israeli cabinet, the six Israeli aircraft took off for the long flight to central east Africa. Four of the planes were C-130s carrying the airborne force, and the other two were Boeing 707s. One of these latter was to circle Entebbe airport as a flying control room and communications centre as the four C-130s landed, and the other, fitted out as an emergency hospital, made straight for Nairobi so that any wounded could receive emergency medical attention the moment they arrived there. The medical aircraft arrived in Nairobi just before midnight on the 3rd.

The route chosen for the Hercules aircraft is still uncertain. In all probability

Lockheed C-130 Hercules

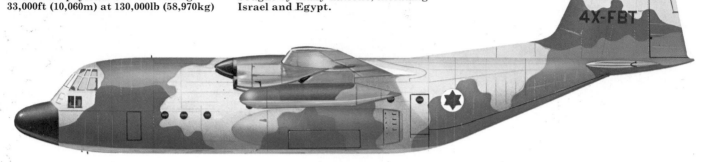

Type: medium- and long-range combat transport. Engines: four 4,508ehp Allison T56-A-15 turboprops. Span: 132ft 7in (40.41m). Length: 97ft 9in (29.78m). Height: 38ft 3in (11.66m). Maximum cruising speed: 386mph (621kph). Range: 2,487 miles (4,002km) Range: 2,487 miles (4,002km) with maximum payload. Service ceiling: 33,000ft (10,060m) at 130,000lb (58,970kg)

all-up weight. Maximum payload: 43,811lb (19,872kg). Weight empty: 75,331lb (34,169kg). Overload weight: 175,000lb (79,380kg).
Relatively conventional in basic design, the Hercules is nonetheless a high-performance turboprop transport with good STOL characteristics. It has been bought by many nations, including Israel and Egypt.

The Entebbe Raid

The Hijackers (red)
1. 0900, 27 June, 1976, an Air France A-300 Airbus with 253 people on board, takes off from Tel Aviv.
2. 1210, the aircraft is hijacked shortly after leaving Athens and is ordered to Benghazi.
3. Lands at Benghazi where it stops for $6\frac{1}{2}$ hours before taking off again.
4. The Airbus finally arrives in Entebbe c0315, 28 June, where President Amin has given the terrorists a tacit agreement of non-interference and even of help.

The Israelis (outward, blue)
1. 1600, 3 July, the Israelis send off two Boeing 707 and four Lockheed C-130 aircraft by a circuitous route.
2. The four C-130s and one 707 make for Entebbe, and the last 707 (fitted out as an emergency hospital) for Nairobi, where refuelling facilities have been arranged. C-130s land 0001-0005, 4 July. Rescue begins.
The Israelis (homeward, green).
1. 0045-0053, 4 July, the four C-130s take off for Nairobi with the freed hostages. They land between 0206 and 0239 and transfer wounded to hospital plane.
2. At Nairobi the wounded are tended and aircraft refuelled.
3. 0338-0408 the six Israeli aircraft return to Israel by another route.

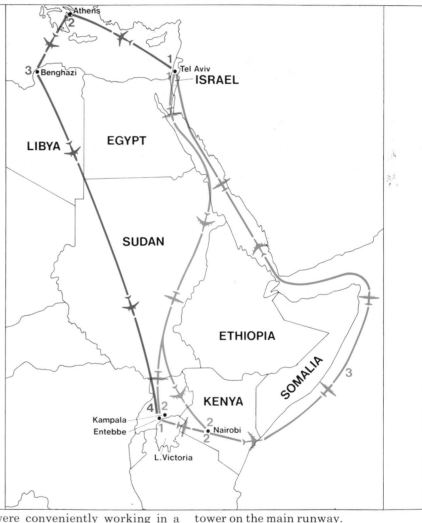

they flew down the middle of the Red Sea at high altitude, in the hope that Saudi Arabian radar might pass them off as being unworthy of investigation or as unscheduled civil flights; they then turned over Sudan, where an abortive coup the day before had led to the closing down of all but one of the country's radar stations. The communications Boeing 707, flying faster than the C-130s, had set off two hours later, and joined up with the transports during the final approach to Entebbe airport.

The three radar operators at Entebbe failed to spot the approaching aircraft (an omission for which they were subsequently shot). Arriving just one minute after midnight, the four C-130s flew quietly into the airfield, some of whose radio navigation

devices were conveniently working in a night of poor weather conditions.

The first aircraft to land did so close to the control tower. Its load of paratroops disgorged from the aircraft in their jeeps as it was still moving and made for the control tower to prevent its Ugandan controllers from turning off the landing lights. This mission was accomplished quickly and with little resistance. The hijackers and Ugandan troops round the terminal, some distance away, heard the firing, but had no idea of what it was about. Meanwhile emergency landing lights had been arranged, but these proved unnecessary as two other C-130s taxied quietly up to the terminal and sent their men straight into action at close range. The fourth C-130 joined the first aircraft near the control

tower on the main runway.

Tasks had been carefully allotted to each of several assault groups. One headed straight for the terminal to release the hostages, firing on the line of Ugandan troops guarding the terminal as they went in. Although there was some return fire, the Israelis swept the Ugandan opposition aside, killing some 20 of the African troops. Another group, meanwhile, headed off at a tangent to destroy as many as possible of the Ugandan Air Force's MiG-15, MiG-17 and MiG-21 fighters. This was to serve a double purpose: to create a diversion for the attack on the terminal, and also to eliminate the only aircraft that might pose a real threat to the slow flying C-130s as they headed for Kenya at the end of the raid. Some six of the MiGs on the airfield were destroyed by explosive devices and gunfire.

The third group of Israelis immediately headed for the airport perimeter to establish defence lines against the arrival of Ugandan reinforcements from Kampala. This might have been a very difficult and costly task, for the Israeli group had few, if any, heavy weapons with which to take on the Ugandan armour. As it turned out, however, no reinforcements, infantry or armour, arrived from the Ugandan capital during the raid, and this third group had an easy, if anxious, time of it.

Good medical support

As it had been expected that casualties would be heavy, the raiding force had 33 doctors with it. These men, trained soldiers, remained in the C-130s and provided covering fire from their good vantage points on the tail ramps of the transports.

At this point all was going according to the Israeli plan. The four transports had landed undetected, and all the initial objectives had been secured: the control tower had been taken, the Ugandan troops thrown into almost total disarray, the available Ugandan fighters decimated, and the airport perimeter secured against the arrival of reinforcements. Now, of course, there lay ahead the real object of the whole mission: the storming of the terminal and the rescue of the hostages. While Shomron controlled the operation overall from the control tower, it was now Netanyahu's turn to run things in the attack on the terminal. As the Israelis approached in their jeeps, the hostages had all thrown themselves into positions of safety on the floor. One of the German hijackers, Wilfried Boese, had loaded his gun, aimed at the hostages, but then changed his mind and left the building to engage the Israelis. After he had fired a few random bursts he turned once again towards the terminal, but was then shot by one of the Israelis. At the same time another German, Gabriele Tiedemann, was also killed outside the terminal.

Above: Israeli Defence Force/Air Force Lockheed C-130 Hercules transport aircraft. At Entebbe, the troops went straight into action from these in jeeps.

The Israelis now burst into the lounge where the hostages were being held, the whole time calling out the name of Israel and instructions for the hostages to stay flat on the floor. Those that were not already doing so dropped down again. Some of the hostages meanwhile informed the assault forces that other hijackers were upstairs. In this confused situation, three of the hostages unfortunately lost their lives: Jean-Jacques Maimoni, one of the men who had done most to keep the hostages going was accidently shot by an Israeli soldier; Pascoe Cohen was fatally wounded; and Ida Borowitz was also killed by a stray bullet. The troops had meanwhile moved upstairs where another two hijackers were killed.

Quick exit

Down below, the Israelis urged the hostages, who had been preparing for bed and were only half dressed for the most part, to make for the three C-130s designated for the task. Some ran to the waiting aircraft, while women and children were ferried out in the jeeps. So far the Israelis had lost only three men wounded, but now Netanyahu came out of the terminal to supervise the evacuation and was killed by a shot from a Ugandan soldier in the old control tower.

Despite this sad loss, the Israelis were only minutes from the successful conclusion of their mission. The defensive outposts had been pulled in, at 0045, only 44 minutes after the first plane had touched down, the initial C-130 transport carrying the freed hostages took off for Nairobi. It had been intended to refuel at least one of the aircraft at Entebbe, but only a small amount of fuel had been pumped into the tanks and Shomron decided to abandon this part of the plan. By 0054, only 53 minutes after the start of the raid, the last

C-130 had taken off for Nairobi. It almost crashed as the runway lights were finally extinguished just as it roared down the runway.

The communications plane had meanwhile been keeping the hospital plane in Nairobi well informed of the course of events, and set off with the first C-130 for the Kenyan capital. They arrived at 0206, and by 0239 all five aircraft from Entebbe had landed. The ten wounded were immediately transferred to the waiting hospital aircraft and the five aircraft were refuelled. Between 0338 and 0408 all six aircraft left for Israel, the last into the air being the hospital plane.

The raid had been a great success, marred only by the deaths of three of the hostages and Netanyahu. Once again the virtues of surprise and 'concentration in time and space' had been displayed.

Mogadishu raid

Following in the steps of the Israeli raid on Entebbe, the Germans in October 1977 also launched a daring 'airborne' rescue mission to save the passengers of a hijacked airliner.

At 1300 on 13 October 1977, a *Lufthansa* Boeing 737 airliner, flight number 181 and call-sign Charlie Echo, took off from Palma in the Balearic islands to return to Germany with holiday-makers. Only one hour later, though, Captain Jürgen Schumann reported that his aircraft had been hijacked by terrorists over the French riviera. Over the radio listeners then heard a frenzied voice shout that the aircraft was under the 'supervision and control' of 'Captain Walter Mahmoud', since identified as a notorious international terrorist.

Mahmoud then ordered the aircraft to Rome, where it was refuelled. While the airliner was on the ground, Schumann managed to drop four cigars out of the cockpit window, correctly assumed by the security forces to mean that there were four terrorists on the aircraft. Even by this stage the German authorities were having trouble keeping in contact with the *Lufthansa* jet, which had only medium-range radio equipment. The situation was eased, though, as other *Lufthansa* jets in the area could keep in contact with the hijacked aircraft and then report back to Germany. Leaving Rome, the 737 set off east, and it was another *Lufthansa* jet that was able later to report that it was about to land at Nicosia in Cyprus. Frankfurt control then instructed the other airliner to inform the 737 that Nicosia was closed down, and that it should land at Akrotiri or Larnaca instead. The 737 in fact touched down at Larnaca. Here Mahmoud demanded that the aircraft be refuelled, or he would blow it up. Pleas for the end of the hijack were made by the Cypriot foreign minister, and when the Cyprus representative of the Palestinian Liberation Movement came on the air to reinforce the plea, Mahmoud screamed that he did not wish to know.

Meanwhile, in Germany Chancellor Helmut Schmidt, had ordered an elite commando unit, *Grenzschutzgruppe* 9 (GSG 9), 30 strong, to the area. They set off in a *Lufthansa* Boeing 707, flight number 1231, but arrived in Cyprus just as the hijacked 737 took off again. Also sent to the spot was Hans-Jürgen Wischnewski, one of Germany's top trouble-shooters. Aboard the aircraft carrying Wischnewski, another 707, were an additional 31 men of GSG 9.

Meanwhile the hijacked 737 had flown on to Bahrain on the Persian Gulf, and from there to Dubai, a short hop to the south-east. The original 30 men of GSG 9 had flown from Larnaca to Ankara to await developments.

Wischnewski's aircraft, with the 31 men of GSG 9 and their commander, Ulrich Wegener, arrived in Dubai at dawn on 15 October. Also en route to Dubai were two members of the Special Air Service Regiment, an elite British unit, with a supply of 'stun grenades', which explode without scattering metal fragments, but stun all in the vicinity for about six seconds with their blast. These had been offered to the Germans by the prime minister of Great Britain, James Callaghan. During Saturday, the original 30 commandos returned to Germany, changed aircraft and flew off to Crete, to await developments.

In Dubai Wischnewski had spoken to the hijackers by radio from the control tower, but without success. It was therefore decided to attempt to rescue the airliner's passengers and crew with the men of GSG 9, although the issue was complicated by local demands that troops of the United Arab Emirates should also be used. Not trained in anti-terrorist operations, these troops would have been a distinct liability at a purely military level. Reconnaissance of the aircraft was carried out by men of GSG 9 disguised as mechanics.

Mahmoud's madness

But then on Sunday morning, the 16th, the 737 suddenly took off, only 40 minutes before Mahmoud's first deadline for blowing the aircraft up. For some time it was uncertain where the aircraft was, as Oman had refused it landing permission. Finally it arrived in Aden with fuel for only another 10 minutes' flight left. Despite a South Yemeni refusal, the 737 landed at Aden. Wischnewski's aircraft also headed for Aden, but it too was refused landing permission, despite German offers of financial aid for the country. Wischnewski was thus forced to divert to Jiddah in Saudi Arabia.

In Aden, however, Mahmoud seemed to have lost control of himself, and after allowing Schumann to examine the nosewheel of the 737, slightly damaged when the aircraft had to land on the sand, as the Aden authorities had blocked the main runway to prevent a landing, he forced the German pilot to kneel as he climbed back aboard the aircraft and then shot him in the head, killing him instantly.

The following morning, with co-pilot Jürgen Vietor at the controls, the 737 left Aden and flew to Mogadishu, the capital of Somalia. The German 707s also headed towards this spot, one from Jiddah and the other from Crete. The Germans, seeing how unbalanced Mahmoud was becoming, had decided that only force would suffice, and Chancellor Schmidt had persuaded President Siad Barre of Somalia to allow the Germans a free hand in Mogadishu.

Throughout the evening of the 17th, reports reaching the rescue headquarters

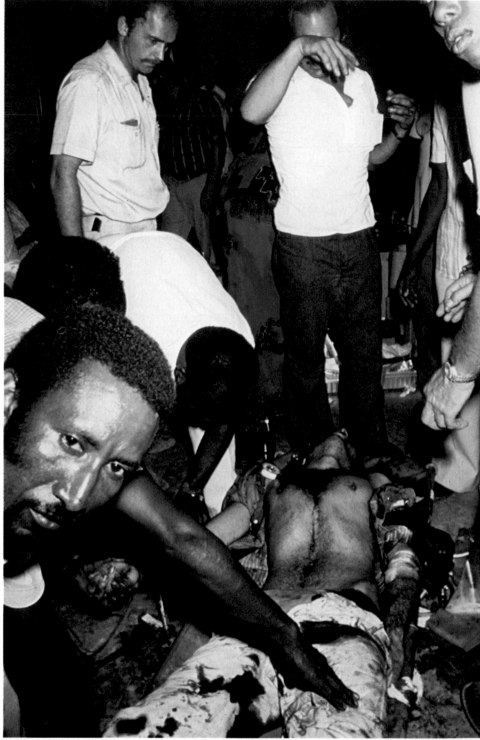

in Frankfurt indicated that the hijackers were becoming more and more erratic in their behaviour to the passengers of the hostage 737. The Germans promised to release 11 'political' prisoners held in German goals, and even to fly them to Mogadishu. This seemed to mollify Mahmoud somewhat, and he told the 737 passengers that he had put off his deadline for blowing up the aircraft until 0230 on Tuesday, by which time the prisoners from Germany should have arrived. He also warned the Germans in the control tower: 'Do not try any tricks. This will not be another Entebbe.'

By this time, however, the preparations of GSG 9 were almost complete, and only 40 minutes before Mahmoud's deadline, the rescue operation began. The two hijackers in the 737's were engaged in distracting conversation by the personnel in the airport control tower, while the two other terrorists guarded the passengers in the airliner's cabin, one at each end. Some

Above: Watched by Somali officials, one of the hijackers wounded in the successful German rescue effort lies dying of his injuries in Mogadishu airport.

Above right: The Lufthansa Boeing 737 bakes in the sun at Dubai airport as the hijackers negotiate with the authorities of the United Arab Emirates.

28 commandos, in camouflage clothing and with their faces blackened, had crept out to the 737 undetected. Then as a diversionary explosion some distance off distracted the terrorists, the main doors and emergency exits of the plane were blown open within three seconds. Then stun grenades were thrown into the aircraft, probably by the two British SAS men. The German commandos streamed aboard, shouting to the passengers to get down out of the line of any fire that might start. The two hijackers in

The Mogadishu Rescue

The Hijackers (red)
1. 1400, 13 Oct 1977—Lufthansa Boeing 737 hijacked shortly after take off.
2. Refuels at Rome. The pilot signals that 4 hijackers are aboard.
3. Refused landing permission at Nicosia—refuels at Larnaca.
4. Flies to Bahrain.
5. Flies on to Dubai. Takes off on 16 Oct just before deadline expires.
6. Lands at Aden. Pilot later killed.
7. Flies to Mogadishu—lands 17 Oct.

Boeing 707 of GSG 9 (blue)
1. Leaves Germany for Cyprus.
2. Arrives as hijacked 737 takes off.
3. 14 Oct—Commandos return to Germany via Ankara and change aircraft.
4. 15 Oct—flies to Crete.
5. Sets off for Mogadishu, held over Djibouti for 4 hours, lands in Somalia after dark on 17 Oct.
6. 0150, 18 Oct, rescue begins.

Boeing 707 of Wischnewski (green)
1. Leaves Germany with Wischnewski and 31 men of GSG 9.
2. Arrives at Dubai, dawn 15 Oct.
3. Takes off for Aden, refused landing permission, diverts to Jiddah.
4. Flies to Mogadishu to co-ordinate operation. Lands 17 Oct.

the cabin were shot, and as the passengers started to pour out of the emergency exits, Mahmoud appeared in the door from the cockpit. He was immediately shot, as was the last hijacker also.

The whole operation had lasted 11 minutes, and had been very successful: only four passengers, one stewardess and one commando had been injured, all only slightly; three of the hijackers, including Mahmoud, had been killed outright, and the fourth, a woman, had been shot in the thigh.

GSG 9 is part of the 22,000-strong West German Border Protection Force, and is a special commando unit established after the German failure against the Arab terrorists who killed many Israeli competitors at the Munich Olympic Games in 1972. The group, numbered in sequence after the eight standard border protection groups, is 178 men strong, and has special training, featuring unarmed combat, use of all the weapons likely to be used by terrorists, and added extras such as lock-picking and intimate knowledge of the airliners used by *Lufthansa*. The force is organised into six 30-man groups, four of them combat groups and the other two a command group and a logistics group.

Conclusion

So far, the history of airborne forces has been too short and perhaps too inconclusive for any reasonable predictions for the future of such forces. What must be admitted is that there have emerged from World War II and later airborne operations certain tactical lessons for both airborne and conventional land forces, lessons which are still being digested for the future.

What, then, is the future for airborne warfare? The problem of trying to see what may or may not happen in the years to come is more difficult here than in many other aspects of military affairs, principally because the lessons of the past are inconclusive. Combat airborne operations are only some 40 years old, and although much has been tried and achieved, no clear pattern has emerged.

With the exception of the Cretan adventure, Germany made no efforts in the field of strategic airborne warfare during World War II, much to the chagrin of Kurt Student and his subordinate commanders. Although the forces available to the airborne arm continued to grow throughout the war, these were rarely concentrated or used in their intended role, but rather as high-grade infantry for special purposes, usually defensive. It should be noted that with very few exceptions airborne warfare has not been used for defensive purposes, and so from the middle of 1942 Germany had little opportunity for large-scale airborne operations.

The two other major exponents of airborne warfare during World War II, the United States and Great Britain, suffered from a dichotomy in command and aims, perhaps inevitable when the air transport on which the airborne forces were dependent was controlled not by those using it, but by air force staffs whose attentions were to a major extent focused elsewhere; and perhaps inevitable in a situation where Allied efforts were often not fully coordinated even when the objective was clear and conventional. As most senior officers, therefore, were used to the problems of command in traditional ways, it was difficult for the relatively junior officers commanding the airborne formations to get their points of view heard, let alone accepted. In these circumstances, therefore, it was impossible for the Allies to emerge from the war with anything like a conclusive assessment of the value of airborne warfare. Small-scale tactical operations, such as those in Tunisia and Sicily, had enjoyed only moderate success, redeemed in part by the fighting qualities of the troops involved; as airborne operations, though, they had left much to be desired. The airborne side of the Normandy

landings, though, especially the British paratroop and air-landing operations, had gone remarkably well despite the near disaster of the actual landings, especially in the American sectors. The lesson learned in the Tunisian and Sicilian landings, that if quantity 'x' could go wrong in conventional operations, '3x' could, and usually did, go wrong in airborne operations was reinforced yet again, though much was redeemed from the apparent chaos of the airborne operations by the fighting abilities, initiative and sheer tenacity of the American and British airborne forces.

The most adventurous airborne operation attempted by the Allies in World War II was the daring effort to build an 'airborne carpet' between the forward elements of the British XXX Corps and the Zuider Zee, so that the former could push forward and ensure the seizure of the major port of Rotterdam, thus helping the Allies to maintain their eastward thrust, already hampered by the paucity of supplies, especially of fuel, arriving from the French ports to the west. Much has been written about the operation, especially the part played by the British 1st Airborne Division at the apex of the airborne salient,

and overall it must remain a classic example of what might have been achieved by the large-scale use of airborne forces. All the more remarkable, also, is the fact that the plan was both inspired and endorsed by a senior Allied ground force commander, in this case General Sir Bernard Montgomery, commanding the 21st Army Group. Very rarely indeed, during World War II, did so ambitious a plan involving 'untried' forces receive so much encouragement from the high command. Daring though it was, the whole operation failed in its major objectives, a fact often disguised behind the defence of Arnhem by the British 1st Airborne Division, and the magnificent efforts of the US 82nd and 101st Airborne Divisions farther to the south. The real lessons to be learned from the 'Market-Garden' fiasco, though, are the problems inherent in divided command: the 21st Army Group commanded in general, the 1st Allied Airborne Army

Left: Russian airborne troops in training for winter operations. Here 'tank-riding' infantry vault from a moving ASU-85 airborne self-propelled assault gun.

commanded the forces dropped and landed in front of XXX Corps, and the RAF and USAAF controlled both the transports and support aircraft needed by the airborne forces. Considering the problems faced by the airborne formation commanders, it is a great tribute to the easy collaboration of the Allies that the operation ever got off the ground, let alone got as close as it did to the success desired of it.

The Wingate philosophy

Despite its scale, the Allied landing of XVIII Airborne Corps as part of the Rhine crossing operation by the 21st Army Group was little more than a glorified tactical operation, Allied intelligence having overestimated the strength of the defending German forces. More interesting, though, would have been the strategic operations proposed by Colonel 'Phil' Cochran, a convert to the Wingate philosophy of deep penetration by light forces supported from the air, with the intention of disrupting the enemy's rear areas sufficiently to dislocate their forward defences and so facilitate the advance of the conventional ground forces. Fate, or rather the unenterprising nature of the Allied planners, prevented Cochran's plans from reaching fruition, much to the detriment of subsequent analysis of what the Allied airborne forces might have achieved in World War II.

Airlift possibilities

More indicative of the present and future trends in airborne war, however, are the operations conducted under the inspiration of Lieutenant-General George Kenney in the South-West Pacific Area, particularly in New Guinea. In this theatre, by the use of aircraft for transport purposes, Kenney pioneered the widespread use of air-mobility as a major weapon. In a position of air inferiority, the Japanese

could do little or nothing to counter this American/Australian method of advance, which gave the Allies a freedom of action hitherto only dreamed of, and thus enormous strategic and tactical flexibility with its resultant reduced casualties.

The French experience in Indo-China and the American airborne involvement in Korea added little or nothing to the science of airborne warfare, even though they did further enhance the reputation of paratroops as fighting soldiers. Fighting against negligible opposition, the British and French at Suez, and the Israelis against the Arabs in Sinai demonstrated the value of tactical airborne warfare yet again.

Airmobility the rage

More recently, however, airborne war in the widest sense of the word has once again moved forward. In Vietnam the Americans have developed to a high level of sophistication the concept of airmobility pioneered by Kenney: with the addition of helicopters as transport and flying heavy support, specially trained and conventional troops can now be moved around the battlefield as the situation demands.

In about the same period, the Russians in their invasion of Czechoslovakia, spearheaded by the 2nd Airborne Division, have shown what may be achieved in strategic terms by the bold use of airborne forces. Although the fact that there was no ground or air opposition must be taken into account, the Russian move into Czechoslovakia was nevertheless an impressive indication of the value and efficiency of the large airborne forces still maintained by the Russians. Although it may be doubted if the value of parachute-dropped airborne forces will be as great in a future war as it was in past conflicts, especially when the increased power of modern aircraft is taken into account, the USSR nevertheless holds a powerful weapon in

Above: American airborne forces in training. Here men of the 1st Battalion, 505th Infantry Regiment, 82nd Airborne Division, drop from a C-130 over Normandy.

its parachute divisions.

Perhaps the major lesson of World War II insofar as airborne forces were concerned was the need for centralized command. The Germans were in this respect in a fortunate position, for as the *Luftwaffe* controlled the airborne forces, air support and transport was no problem. Nonetheless, the army eventually became jealous of the *Luftwaffe*'s airborne prerogatives, despite the fact that it had earlier voluntarily withdrawn from its involvement in airborne matters, and liaison with conventional ground forces became strained, with notable exceptions such as the 1st Parachute Division in Italy, where excellent relations with the other divisions commanded by Field-Marshal Kesselring were enjoyed.

Command problems

The Allies found themselves in an altogether more fluid command situation, with consequent problems during airborne operations, notably Operation 'Market-Garden'. Unlike army/navy joint operations, where it is just about possible to establish a temporal or geographical command boundary, airborne operations cannot be based on a divided command. Although it is easy for non-military persons to say that control of all forces involved in airborne operations should be in the hands of the airborne commander, practical and emotional problems must inevitably raise their heads. Airborne warfare was new in World War II, and it took some time for commanders to develop the right amount of flexibility in their previously rigid command structures. Matters have improved considerably since the war, largely

as a result of the growing realization that the armed forces of any country are not three separate entities fighting their own wars, only slightly inter-related with each other, but rather three aspects of the same war, divided only by tactical and equipment factors.

The future

Almost inevitably, though, airborne forces have found themselves in a more complex situation. Matters have improved, however, as specific parts of the air force of countries with airborne forces have normally been earmarked for airborne purposes, and the growth of helicopter forces within the armies of countries such as Russia, the United States, Britain, France and Israel has meant that air-mobility has become far more effective than before.

Pioneered by the United States in the Vietnamese war, the large-scale use of air-mobility for conventional forces seems to offer an alternative to what may now be considered 'traditional' airborne forces: with helicopter transport for men and *matériel*, and air support from other helicopters armed with guns, bombs and missiles, hitherto undreamed of battlefield mobility has become the norm, and this is particularly important in these days when widespread mechanization of ground

Above: Most countries today have at least rudimentary airborne forces. In this illustration are seen a pair of Romanian paratroopers during a landing exercise.

forces has led to high battlefield speeds.

There will still remain a part for 'conventional' airborne forces, in all probability, especially as intervention forces and for special purposes such as the seizure of key areas in front of advancing ground forces. At the same time, 'friendly' airborne forces may enjoy a role in defensive warfare: perhaps the seizure of areas apparently threatened by an unexpected angle in the enemy's advance. Only the future can tell.

4.85mm Individual Weapon

Calibre: 4.85mm. Operation: gas. Length: 30.3in (77.0cm). Barrel length: 20.4in (51.85cm). Feed: 20-round box magazine. Weight: 9.11lb (4.12kg). Cyclic rate: 700–850rpm. MV: 2.953fps (900mps).

In the early 1970s it became clear that Britain needed a new assault rifle. This is the gun that was developed, and it is at present undergoing NATO trials to produce a standard cartridge.

Index

Picture Credits

The publisher would like to thank the following photographers and organizations who have supplied pictures for this book. Photographs have been credited by page number. Where more than one photograph appears on a page, credits are made in the order of the columns left to right and then from top to bottom. Some references have, for reasons of space, been abbreviated as follows:

Etablissement Cinématographique et Photographique des Armées: ECPA
Imperial War Museum, London: IWM
Ministry of Defence, London: MOD
Süddeutscher Verlag: SV

Endpapers: USAF/Bundesarchiv/IWM/ECPA/Paul Popper/US Marine Corps/Associated Press Ltd. **Half-title page:** Camera Press/MOD/Camera Press/Straits Times, Singapore. **Title page:** Bundesarchiv/Camera Press/ECPA/IWM/Keystone/MOD/Novosti/Paul Popper/USAF/US Army. **Credits page:** Camera Press/ECPA/IWM/Paul Popper/USAF/US Army. **26-27:** SV. **31:** Novosti. **32-33:** SV. **34:** Bundesarchiv/IWM. **35:** SV. **36:** Bundesarchiv. **38:** J. G. Moore collection. **39:** SV. **40-41:** SV. **42:** SV. **43:** SV. **44:** IWM. **45:** SV. **46:** SV/Bundesarchiv. **48:** SV. **49:** Bundesarchiv. **50-51:** IWM. **52:**

Bundesarchiv/SV. **54:** J. G. Moore collection. **55:** SV. **56:** Bundesarchiv. **57:** Bundesarchiv. **58:** Bundesarchiv. **59:** SV. **60:** IWM. **61:** Bundesarchiv. **62-63:** IWM. **64:** SV. **66:** IWM. **67:** Bapty. **68:** Bundesarchiv/IWM. **69:** IWM/SV. **70-71:** IWM. **72:** SV. **73:** SV/Ernst Winterstein collection. **74:** IWM. **75:** SV. **76-77:** IWM. **78:** IWM. **79:** US Army. **80:** USAF. **82-83:** Camera Press. **84-85:** USAF. **87, 90, 92-93:** USAF. **94:** Camera Press/US Army. **95:** J. G. Moore collection. **98:** US Army. **99:** J. G. Moore collection. **100:** US Army. **102:** USAF. **103:** IWM. **104, 105, 106-107:** US Army. **108:** Camera Press. **109:** IWM. **110:** USAF. **112-113:** IWM. **114:** IWM-117: David Shepherd. **118, 120, 122, 123, 124, 125:** IWM. **126:** USAF. **127:** IWM/Camera Press. **128-129:** US Army. **130:** IWM. **131:** IWM/USAF. **132:** IWM/US Army. **133:** US Army. **136-137, 139:** IWM. **140-141:** US Army. **142:** USAF. **146:** US Army. **147:** US Army. **150-151, 153, 154:** IWM. **156-157, 158:** Novosti. **160:** SV/Ernst Winterstein collection. **162:** SV. **163:** SV/Bundesarchiv. **164-165:** USAF. **167:** US Army. **168:** US Army/USAF. **169:** US Army/USAF. **170-171:** ECPA. **172:** Photo USIS. **173, 174:** ECPA. **177:** ECPA/Paul Popper. **178-179:** IWM. **181:** IWM/ECPA/USA. **184:** ECPA. **186-187:** US Army. **188:** Bill Hall Pix. **189:** US Army. **192:** USAF. **193, 194, 195, 196, 197:** US Army. **198-199, 200:** Camera Press. **202:** Photographers International. **204-205:** Novosti. **208:** Camera Press Ltd. **209:** E and TV Films Ltd. **210-211:** EMI Films Ltd. **212:** Camera Press. **213, 215:** EMI Films Ltd. **216, 217:** Frank Spooner Pictures (Catherine Leroy). **218-219:** Novosti. **220:** USAF.